T0314929

MADE IN CHINA

MADE IN CHINA

*When US-China Interests Converged
to Transform Global Trade*

ELIZABETH O'BRIEN INGLESON

HARVARD UNIVERSITY PRESS

Cambridge, Massachusetts & London, England

2024

First printing

Publication of this book has been supported through the generous
provisions of the Maurice and Lula Bradley Smith Memorial Fund.

Library of Congress Cataloging-in-Publication Data

Names: Ingleson, Elizabeth O'Brien, 1989– author.
Title: Made in China : when US-China interests converged to transform
    global trade / Elizabeth O'Brien Ingleson.
Description: Cambridge, Massachusetts ; London, England : Harvard
    University Press, 2024. | Includes bibliographical references and index.
Identifiers: LCCN 2023030809 | ISBN 9780674251830 (cloth)
Subjects: LCSH: Globalization—United States—History—20th century. |
    Deindustrialization—United States—History—20th century. |
    Globalization—China—History—20th century. | Capitalism—Social
    aspects—China—History—20th century. | United States—Commerce—
    China—History—20th century. | China—Commerce—United States—
    History—20th century. | China—Economic conditions—1949– | United
    States—Economic conditions—1945–
Classification: LCC HF3043 .I64 2024 | DDC 382.0951—
    dc23/eng/20231020
LC record available at https://lccn.loc.gov/2023030809

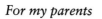

For my parents

CONTENTS

NOTE ON LANGUAGE AND DATA

This book uses the pinyin system of romanization, except in cases where English-language records from the time did not use Chinese characters and instead used Wade-Giles romanization for Chinese names.

The question of which polity represented China—the Communist People's Republic of China or the Nationalist Republic of China in Taiwan—was a deeply contentious one throughout the Cold War. I use the term "China" to refer to the People's Republic of China (PRC) for the sake of brevity and readability, but also because in July 1971 US customs law designated the name "China" to the PRC, and in October 1971 the United Nations General Assembly did the same. In North America, language usage similarly carries larger implications of political power in relation to its hemispheric neighbors. I use "United States" to refer to the nation, but when referring to people from the United States I use the term "American" interchangeably with the adjectival shorthand "US."

On trade data, I use figures collected and published during the 1970s by the US Department of Commerce and the Central Intelligence Agency (CIA), which A. Doak Barnett compiled in 1981 in *China's Economy in Global Perspective*. I do so largely to help us understand what US capitalists *thought* about trade prospects in the 1970s. It was Commerce Department and CIA data that US trade organizations, businesspeople, and journalists used in their analyses and decision-making processes.

For most of the 1970s, China did not publicly release its own trade statistics. Briefly in the mid-1970s, China published some national data.

In 1979 the State Statistical Bureau released national figures, but their starting point was the post-Mao era, beginning with 1977. In more recent times scholars have collated Chinese trade numbers for the 1970s. Dong Wang has shown in *The United States and China: A History from the Eighteenth Century to the Present* that there are discrepancies between the data from the United States and the data from the PRC. She shows that the differences between the US and Chinese statistics lay not in total trade numbers but instead in the trade balance—the difference between how much China purchased and how much it sold. The main deviations between the US and Chinese trade figures were in 1973 and 1974. The Chinese data present the trade imbalance as smaller than US figures suggested. Wang and others who have examined these figures do not speculate as to why these are the only years of the 1970s when the numbers are different. Barnett notes that the differences between Chinese and US statistics were largely a consequence of inconsistencies in how shipping and insurance were collected. Perhaps one further explanation lies in the very fact that the imbalance was so politically sensitive. Chinese leaders may have sought to downplay the imbalance at a time when self-reliance was so hotly debated.

For statistics on the United Kingdom, Japan, West Germany, and other capitalist nations, I have used data from these countries' governments that was published in Hong Kong and UK trade journals.

MADE IN CHINA

Introduction

Making "Made in China"

AT FOUR O'CLOCK in the morning on July 9, 1971, Henry Kissinger and a handful of his closest staff boarded a plane in Pakistan, bound for China. Coming after months of back-channel diplomacy, the flight was arranged in utmost secrecy. Even the US State Department was unaware of their journey. As far as they knew, Kissinger had food poisoning and was lying low in Pakistan. Kissinger was perfectly healthy, but the deception allowed the national security advisor to spend two days meeting quietly with China's premier, Zhou Enlai. Working on behalf of Chairman Mao Zedong, Zhou would determine with Kissinger whether their two nations would be able to begin the process of reestablishing diplomatic relations. Given the historic depths of animosity and the uncertainty about how successful the talks would be, both sides kept the trip strictly confidential. "There were James Bond aspects of this trip," recalled one advisor, Winston Lord, "since it was totally secret."[1]

Yet on the flight from Chaklala to Beijing, Kissinger suddenly realized that, in the excitement of the early morning subterfuge, he had forgotten to pack extra shirts. John Holdridge, another advisor, offered his. Holdridge, however, was over six feet tall and his shirts did not quite match Kissinger's shorter, fuller figure. The ill-fitting shirts were less sophisticated than the occasion demanded, but there was a further diplomatic sensitivity too—sewn onto their collars were labels reading "Made in Taiwan." At the very moment the United States and China sought to pave the way

1

for renewed political ties, Kissinger wore a shirt spelling out the single biggest hurdle to normalization. Writing later about the incident, Kissinger quipped, "I was telling the literal truth when I told our hosts that Taiwan was a matter close to me."[2]

The "saga of my shirts," as Kissinger dubbed it, has been remembered as a humorous moment of forgetfulness. Lord later joked that Kissinger "looked like a penguin" when he wore them. Holdridge mused, "The episode showed that Kissinger, too, was human." The labels simply added an ironic twist, they suggested.[3]

More than just an amusing anecdote, however, this incident reveals the material outcomes of East Asia's changing economic landscape since the start of the Cold War. In 1971 it was becoming increasingly more common for shirts sold in the United States to be made in Taiwan. Textiles were Taiwan's largest export, constituting more than 30 percent of its total exports in 1970, the bulk of which went to the United States.[4] The entry of Taiwan-made goods was a recent and rapid trend, but it followed on from Japanese exports that had entered the United States in increasing numbers since the late 1950s. And in this, Taiwan joined other nations in the region, particularly South Korea and Hong Kong, that had also recently begun increasing their exports of textiles and other consumer goods to the United States.

By the early 1970s, manufacturing processes were becoming internationalized, with East Asia emerging as a central hub. Thirty years later, as the twentieth century came to an end, it was "Made in China" that could be found on the undersides of coffee mugs or stitched on the labels at the necks of dress shirts. The labels had become the ultimate symbol of globalization. Behind them lay cheap labor, cheap goods, globalized supply chains, and, increasingly, deep historical tropes of a Chinese threat.

There was nothing natural or inevitable about the shift from "Made in Taiwan" in 1971 to "Made in China" just a few decades later. While there were noticeable continuities between the two countries—most particularly, low-paid Asian workers who made the goods—there were also crucial differences. The foremost difference was that China was a communist nation. China's communism had been the core factor driving US support for industrial development in Japan, Korea, Taiwan, and elsewhere early in the Cold War. In the 1950s and 1960s the United States actively sought to assist these countries' export-oriented development by lowering trade barriers and providing vast sums of aid. Bolstering the economies of noncommunist nations was part of the United States' wider fight against China and the Soviet Union, both of which in the early 1950s had sought to build an international socialist world economy.[5]

China was not only a communist nation; it was also extremely poor, with a weak industrial base—another key reason the emergence of "Made in China" was not inevitable. The country was still recovering from the brutal devastation and widespread starvation that Mao's agricultural reforms of the late 1950s had caused. Between 1958 and 1962, tens of millions of Chinese citizens died from starvation, exhaustion, or torture.[6] Just a few years later, in 1966, Mao launched the Cultural Revolution, a new system of terror that once again violently overhauled China's economic and social structures. Thousands of families were forcibly separated, and students were sent from cities to rural areas to work in agricultural production. When the head of China's armed forces, Lin Biao, mysteriously died in 1971, martial law was lifted yet the country remained mired in the throes of the Cultural Revolution. The extraordinary growth that China consequently experienced in the span of just one generation was, to many observers within and beyond China, inconceivable in the 1970s.

How and why, then, did China converge with global capitalism? And when did this convergence begin? A vibrant body of scholarship is starting to explore these questions, focusing on the debates between, and experiments by, Chinese policymakers and businesspeople. An earlier debate among scholars sought to understand what Kenneth Pomeranz memorably described as the "great divergence" in industrialization between Northwest Europe and East Asia since the mid-eighteenth century.[7] By the late nineteenth century Europe was transformed by the Industrial Revolution, but China's economy languished, exacerbated by Japanese, European, and American imperial competition. Another century later, however, China's place in the global economic system had changed dramatically. In distinction to the great divergence, a group of economists have put forward the notion of "convergence" as a means of understanding China's integration with global capitalism in the latter part of the twentieth century.[8]

As scholars have turned their attention to what might be labeled the "great convergence," Deng Xiaoping's reforms, announced in December 1978, loom large in many accounts. Scholars disagree, however, on the extent to which these reforms marked a new beginning in China's engagement with global capitalism. One group of scholars do see them as a starting point, tracing the origins of China's extraordinary economic growth to Deng's leadership. It was in the 1980s that China escaped the debt trap that ensnared other developing nations and that ultimately led to the Soviet Union's collapse. In these scholars' telling, the reform era of the 1980s and 1990s enabled China to develop its own unique form of political economy that converged with the global capitalist system and enabled China to lift so many of its people out of poverty.[9]

A second group of scholars, however, emphasize continuity between the Mao and Deng eras. Experiments with marketization and trade, they argue, occurred from the very founding of the People's Republic of China (PRC).[10] One scholar goes so far as to suggest an "unending capitalism" in China even at the height of communist rule. In his telling, consumerism—which persisted in small pockets of the country—was a sign that Mao's economy was, in fact, a variety of capitalism. The PRC was therefore never the socialist haven Mao strove so hard to achieve.[11]

In this book I similarly blur the "1978 divide," but unlike scholars who emphasize continuity throughout the Maoist era, I see the major turning point in China's convergence with capitalism to lie in the late 1960s and early 1970s. I join a third group of scholars who locate the sources of China's twentieth-century convergence with capitalism in the latter years of the Cultural Revolution.[12] Exploring Maoism at the grassroots as well as from above, these scholars situate the Cultural Revolution as a critical moment in China's political economy. The paradox of the Cultural Revolution, this body of literature shows, is that by causing such extreme social and political upheaval, it unintentionally opened the way for new institutions and reform policies to emerge.[13] Amid the social and political chaos of the 1970s, Chinese leaders within and beyond the elite levels of politics experimented with economic reorganization that laid the groundwork for the reform and opening that came afterward.

I add two overlooked dynamics to these conversations among scholars of China, both of which are crucial to understanding China's convergence with global capitalism. The first is China's foreign trade, which began to rapidly expand in the 1970s. Throughout the 1950s and 1960s, China had maintained small levels of trade with foreign nations, especially the Soviet Union and the Third World. From the late 1950s, China also began to trade with some capitalist nations, such as Japan, Britain, and West Germany.[14] But it was only during the 1970s that Mao began to increase China's overall levels of trade for the first time since the communists' vic-

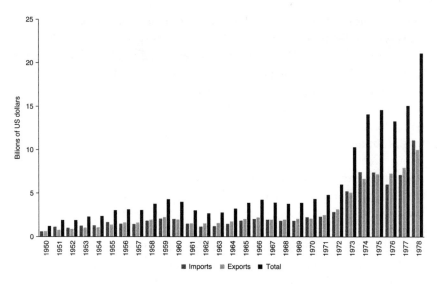

Figure I.1. China's foreign trade, 1950–1978.

tory in 1949. And it was China's engagement with advanced capitalist democracies—not members of the socialist world—that drove this growing trade. At first these changes were only slowly perceptible. In 1969 China's total trade stood at $3.8 billion, about the same as throughout the 1950s and 1960s. In 1971 this rose to $4.8 billion. By 1974 the value of trade skyrocketed to $14 billion. China's total trade remained around this level until 1978, when it jumped to $21 billion. From there it continued to rise, persisting well into the twenty-first century.

China's growing trade in the 1970s was central to its convergence with the capitalist world. It provided China with technology. It assisted China's economic development. It led China to expand its trade institutions, such as trade fairs and advertising outlets. And, most importantly, it was entwined with the second dynamic I focus on in this book, often taken for granted by scholars whose primary focus is on China: changes within US capitalism itself. In order for China to converge with global capitalism, the United States and its economy needed to accommodate China's needs.

For twenty years the US economy had been underpinned by Cold War divisions between capitalism and communism. In fact, US-China trade was the ultimate casualty of the economic Cold War, blocked by a strict embargo since the outbreak of the Korean War in 1950.[15] The small amount of trade that did flow between the United States and other communist nations was understood in binary terms—as East–West trade—not in integrated terms.[16] In the 1970s this binary remained in place, but elements of it began to soften when it came to trade with China. In 1971 the United States finally lifted its twenty-one-year trade embargo, and China began to be seen, not through the Cold War lens of communist threat, but instead through the lens of capitalist profit. This was often despite the fact that profit did not always, or readily, materialize for many businesspeople in this decade.

In most parts of the world, the Cold War ended in the late 1980s when the Soviet Union dissolved and the US-led vision of neoliberal capitalism became the key organizing principle for social development.[17] But in the case of US-China relations, the Cold War ended without systemic collapse in either nation. Instead, Cold War divisions between these two nations fizzled out during the 1970s through a gradual convergence between the Chinese state and US capitalists.

In addition to asking why China converged with global capitalism, then, I am interested in the reverse, too. Why did US capitalists start to incorporate China—the world's largest communist nation—into their visions of the future? And what did these visions look like?

THE ANSWERS TO these questions require us to look at China's convergence with global capitalism as a multidirectional process that involved decisions both within and beyond China itself. Scholars are beginning to show the importance of neighboring countries, such as Hong Kong and Singapore, to this integration. Many emphasize the role of overseas Chinese people in bringing China into the capitalist system.[18] But in order to understand these dynamics more fully, we need to look also at the largest and most powerful player in the capitalist economy at the time: the United States. The capitalist system with which China began to converge was not static but instead a shifting, dynamic arrangement that itself underwent significant transformations in the 1970s—and the changes within the United States lay at the heart of many of these developments.

By drawing together China's expansion of trade with the economic changes happening within the United States, I argue that China's convergence with global capitalism took shape in the 1970s because some US businesspeople, with the encouragement of Chinese policymakers, began to see trade with China as a means of accessing cheap labor rather than a place to absorb US goods. In the process, they reconfigured what it meant to even speak of "US-China trade."

Over the course of the 1970s, businesspeople from the United States and policymakers in China worked together to transform the very meaning of the China market: from a place to sell US goods to a site instead of cheap labor. This was a significant reimagining of how trade should operate, and it lay at the heart of China's integration with the capitalist order. It was a transformation that was profoundly shaped by the wider economic and political changes occurring in both nations during the 1970s. As the patterns of global trade shifted and US corporations increasingly outsourced their manufacturing to cheaper overseas labor, some business leaders saw China as holding the potential to not only join but also assist in this process. For their part, pragmatists within the Chinese politburo experimented with ways of increasing their exports to fund their purchases of industrial goods.[19] Both groups, as we shall see, were met with considerable opposition from within their nations, but their efforts nonetheless prevailed.

For hundreds of years US-China trade had looked very different. Since first contacts in the eighteenth century, US merchants had understood trade with China to mean expanding their exports.[20] Throughout the United States and Europe, the imagined possibilities of a vast landmass teeming with potential customers compelled businesspeople to trade with China.[21] Mid-nineteenth-century British milliners selling cotton fantacized about the profits they would make if each Chinese person would only increase the length of their coats by one inch. One economic historian later labeled these projections "a little game, which we may call 'count the customers.'"[22] In the late 1890s the United States' Open Door policy, with its exuberant rhetoric promoting economic expansion, reinforced the idea that the China market could yield huge profit by absorbing surplus American goods.

By 1937 Carl Crow, an American journalist turned adman, crystalized these ideas in his best-selling book *400 Million Customers*. The intrepid Missourian had spent twenty-five years living and working in Shanghai. A swashbuckling account of his experiences selling US goods to consumers in China's emerging metropolis, the book was wildly popular. By the end of its first year alone, *400 Million Customers* had won the National Book Award and gone through four editions. Crow's evocative title quickly saw "four hundred million customers" become a metonym for the potential profits to be made from trade with China.[23]

Yet the China market never reached its fabled heights. Around the same time that Crow published *400 Million Customers,* Japan invaded Manchuria, triggering the start of years of warfare that would escalate into the Second World War. Immediately after the war, the United States did become China's largest trading partner, although the value of trade was low.[24] And when US and Chinese troops came to battle during the Korean War in the early 1950s, trade ceased altogether as the United States imposed a complete embargo on bilateral trade.

It was in the 1970s that businesspeople from the United States and China began to trade with one another after more than twenty years of isolation. The allure of wealth that had drawn foreign businesspeople to China for hundreds of years reemerged among the new generation of American traders. Fascination, hope, excitement, frustration: emotions guided their decisions as much as hardheaded economics—often more so. They were driven by feelings similar to those of American businesspeople in the Open Door era, but US merchants in the 1970s also began to see something new in the China market. Working alongside businesspeople in China, they reframed the meaning of trade. What had once been a fantasy of 400 million customers slowly started to become one of 800 million workers instead.

This was a halting and incomplete process: many American corporations and businesspeople who turned to China still saw the old dream of new export markets. But over the course of the decade, some began to see China as a potential labor source. Importers worked with Chinese businesspeople not only to buy premade clothing and shoes but also to outsource the production of goods designed in the United States and made by Chinese workers.

Just thirty-odd years after Crow published his best-selling book, US businesspeople and Chinese pragmatists began to transform the centuries-long vision of the China market. To understand how and why this occurred, I focus on the new generation of US businesspeople who traded with China in the 1970s and the relationships they formed with Chinese traders, Chinese policymakers, and US diplomats.

For the first time since World War II, businesspeople from across the United States began to jockey for visas and insights into a trade market to which their European and Japanese rivals had had access for years.[25] Some were Chinese American, children of missionaries, or longtime students of Chinese language and history, but others were executives from large corporations who knew little about China. By the end of the twentieth century, the corporations most associated with US-China trade were large multinationals like Walmart and Apple, yet their way was paved by a motley group of businesspeople in the 1970s, including Veronica Yhap, Charles Abrams, and David Rockefeller.

Following this new generation of traders, I unpack the decisions they made, the trade organizations they created, and the consumer cultures they engendered to facilitate the entry of Chinese goods into the US market. Maverick entrepreneurs and suited executives from huge American corporations are not the usual protagonists in histories of 1970s US-China relations. Instead, President Nixon and Chairman Mao, and the elite policymaking they represent, have dominated the narratives of bilateral relations in this era. Scholars have written extensively on Kissinger's secret diplomacy of the early 1970s, but few have paid much notice to businesspeople like Veronica Yhap who rebuilt trade ties in the same period.[26] Just as Nixon and Kissinger quickly turned their gaze back to geopolitics after adjusting trade rules, so too have historians devoted only passing interest to the trade relationship that unfolded.[27]

This lack of attention to US businesspeople who traded with China in the 1970s is partly because the value of trade was tiny—only around $2 billion by the end of the decade. It is partly also because archives of US corporations and businesspeople are often closed to scholars. But I have drawn on thousands of never-before-used internal corporate papers that document the dealings of hundreds of American businesses that traded with China during this decade. Filed away in the Gerald R. Ford Library in Michigan, they reveal the significant cultural and political importance of trade, regardless of its minor economic value. When we look at trade in qualitative rather than quantitative terms and focus on businesspeople and corporations, we see a fundamental transformation in the bilateral relationship that ultimately had long-term repercussions for global capitalism and labor.

As we shall see, however, the transformation of the China market was a fraught and contested process. The newly developing trade partnerships between the United States and China were met with resistance from Taiwan traders and diplomats as well as manufacturers, labor leaders, and workers across the United States. Bringing these different groups together reveals that there was nothing natural or inevitable about the way the trade relationship unfolded: it relied, at every step, on the decisions—and shared visions—of those with more political and economic power than others.

THE TRANSFORMATION OF the China market from 400 million customers to 800 million workers was enabled by three interconnected factors: cultural, diplomatic, and economic. It relied upon a cultural change that saw the two nations move from Cold War foes to amicable trade partners; from Red China to Made in China. It was propelled by differing diplomatic approaches to how trade could be used to assist geopolitical negotiations. And it was underpinned by economic transformations in both nations. All three of these factors intersected in ways that ultimately reconfigured the very meaning and practice of US-China trade.

The first of these factors led to a cultural reimagining of China. For decades a whole generation of Americans had seen the PRC as Red China. Since the Chinese Communist Party (CCP) came to power in 1949, US policymakers from both parties galvanized the threat of "Red China" to justify an expanded military and economic presence in East Asia. When US and Chinese troops battled during the Korean War, hostilities between the two nations soared. By the mid-1960s, President Lyndon Johnson escalated the war in Vietnam in an attempt to contain communism in Asia, which he attributed to China's aid to North Vietnam. But some Americans saw in Maoism not threat but revolutionary hope. Black civil rights activists, including Huey Newton, Mabel Williams, and W. E. B. Du Bois, turned to China's communism for answers to the racial injustice they experienced at home.[28] By the mid-1960s, in the context of the ongoing devastation of the war in Vietnam, even policymakers in Washington began to reconsider just how threatening Red China was.[29]

In the 1970s, US businesspeople—hardly communist sympathizers—played a pivotal role in recasting China from Cold War foe to trade partner. Some turned China's communism into a purchasable revolutionary fashion statement. They capitalized upon the 1960s countercultural adoption of Maoist clothing and the Little Red Book by putting sky-high price tags on goods that had once symbolized anticapitalist revolution.[30] Others simply rendered China's communism unremarkable, neither radical nor threatening. Still others marketed and profited from China's ancient past, selling antiques and porcelains or goods that harkened back to Americans' eighteenth- and nineteenth-century fascination with chinoiserie.[31]

Through advertisements, department store displays, and internal advice to others within the US business community, the China traders of the 1970s diluted the politics of China's communism. In the process, they transformed the ways consumers throughout the country understood China's communism: as apolitical and unthreatening. From Fifth Avenue fashion elites to Mao-coat-wearing university students, American consumers were offered a celebratory commodification of China—one in which the Chinese origins of imported goods were a central component of their desirability.

These cultural changes helped importers sell Chinese goods of all kinds. By the middle of the decade several companies used consumer interest in an exotic China to advertise everyday imports—shirts, shoes, and gloves—whose only connections to China were labels declaring "Made in China." As US business and fashion elites exoticized their new trade partner, they helped promote a cultural acceptance of the word "China" appearing on the labels on everyday consumer goods. But this was not a linear change. In 1978 the leading US business organization for China trade still had to remind its own members that the term "Red China" was "unacceptable to the Chinese."[32] Some US consumers, moreover, protested the changes they noticed taking place in their local department stores. The transition from Red China to Made in China was uneven. Yet throughout the 1970s, US capitalists set in motion a remarkable evolution in how US consumers understood the erstwhile Cold War enemy.

The second factor that was crucial to the reworking of the China market was the difference in the two nations' visions of the relationship between trade and diplomacy. The first years of US-China trade developed in the highly charged political period of rapprochement, which was unexpectedly protracted. Kissinger's secret diplomacy was successful enough to lead to the dramatic meeting between President Nixon and Chairman Mao in Beijing in 1972, but the two nations soon became caught in diplomatic limbo. They ended more than two decades of Cold War isolation yet struggled to achieve full diplomatic relations. Throughout the 1970s, US and Chinese leaders shuffled back and forth, negotiating recognition and debating the issue that lay at the heart of their delay: the nature of America's military and political relationship with the Nationalists in Taiwan. It took until two new leaders—Jimmy Carter and Deng Xiaoping—came to power for the two countries to finally reestablish diplomatic relations, which they announced in December 1978.

Throughout the decade, American policymakers saw the immediate political benefits of trade as more important than the economic benefits, the value of which was negligible. Most policymakers were focused on the geopolitics of the bilateral relationship, especially given that the value of trade with China was so low relative to other US trading partners. Indeed, John Negroponte, a foreign service officer who accompanied Kissinger to China in 1972, argued that the US State Department did not consider trade with China economically important at all. Members of the State Department would see China's limited manufacturing facilities and ask, "What are we going to buy from these people?" Negroponte recollected in an interview decades later.[33] The subsequent Ford and Carter administrations also saw trade as providing more political than economic benefits.[34] Those policymakers who did consider trade more closely—and they were far outnumbered by those focused on geopolitical concerns—did so by drawing on a long tradition of viewing trade as a tool of statecraft, wielded in order to assist the diplomatic process.[35] They understood trade to be another form of people-to-people ties, akin to the cultural, scientific, and educational ties that were also being reestablished in this era.[36]

Chinese leaders, however, approached the relationship between trade and diplomacy differently. Their strategy was deliberate: increases in the level of trade would come only after progress had been made on geopolitical issues, especially negotiations over Taiwan.[37] Unlike the United States, China did not see increased trade ties as something that should come before diplomatic negotiations had been settled. Rather, China held out the promise of increased trade as a carrot—as something that would come only after improvements in political relations. This approach had an outsized impact on the way the trade relationship unfolded. Throughout the decade, the contours of the trade relationship were determined by whether or not China chose to purchase goods from the United States, a decision deeply connected to the state of diplomacy. When total trade was high, it was a consequence of high levels of Chinese imports of US goods. Similarly, when the value of total trade diminished in the mid-1970s, it was a result of Chinese decisions to cut back on its imports from the United States.

Both the United States and China treated trade as an incentive—but one to be offered at different points of the negotiation process. The United States used it as an incentive *prior* to full diplomatic normalization, as an indication of its commitment to the rapprochement process. China used trade as an incentive to be provided *after* improvements in geopolitical

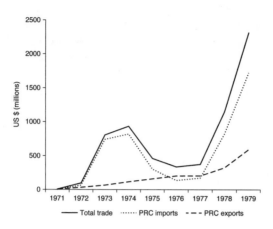

Figure I.2. US-China trade, 1971–1979.

negotiations. These diverging attitudes came to complement one another in a surprising way: Chinese exports to the United States took on diplomatic importance. One of the major economic problems that emerged in this decade was a trade imbalance in the United States' favor. The total value of China's imports was greater than its exports to the United States and, especially as diplomacy began to stall in the middle of the decade, Chinese officials wanted this redressed. In response, American diplomatic and business leaders worked to increase US purchases of Chinese goods. They did so precisely because of their own assumptions that good trade relations were important for assisting the parallel diplomatic efforts. The National Council for US-China Trade—established by the Nixon administration in 1973 but privately run by American businesspeople—led these efforts to help Chinese exports enter the United States.

Some of the titans of American business therefore found themselves purchasing rugs and tea rather than selling cars or factories. Chinese businesspeople made it clear to the new generation of China traders that they would not be able to sell China large industrial goods until after the diplomatic situation improved. By and large, then, during the era of rapprochement Chinese politics set the agenda and American businesspeople responded.[38] American diplomats and businesspeople might not always have seen it that way, but Chinese political priorities played a pivotal role in determining the trade ties that unfolded.

The third factor that enabled the transformation of the China market from 400 million customers to 800 million workers was the economic

13

transformations occurring in both countries at the time. In the United States, corporate executives increasingly turned to overseas sources of manufacturing.[39] Corporations had long been multinational in scope, but for centuries they focused on extracting resources, such as bananas, cotton, or oil, dependent on the forced labor of enslaved peoples.[40] In the nineteenth century, manufacturing-based multinational corporations became increasingly more common, especially in the United States and Europe.[41] These corporations often manufactured in a host country in order to sell to consumers within that market and thereby avoid the tariffs their exports would have otherwise faced.

But during the Cold War, a new kind of manufacturing multinational began to emerge: one that outsourced production, and therefore labor, to low-wage economies to sell to customers across the globe, including back home. They were aided by developments in technology, such as containerized shipping and aircraft that could move goods farther and faster; but they were reliant most of all upon political choices that supported their emergence.[42]

These shifts remained contested in the 1970s, including in Congress, which repeatedly introduced legislation aimed at limiting tax incentives for corporations' offshore manufacturing.[43] But ultimately Congress could not pass the legislation, and as the decade drew to a close, US imports of manufactured goods increased dramatically.[44] These imports did not complement but instead replaced domestic production. By the end of the decade the value of imports as a percentage of domestic production reached 40 percent. In 1970 the figure had been 14 percent.[45] Historian Charles Maier evocatively captured the changes of this decade, writing that the United States had pivoted from an "empire of production"—sustained by its expansion of goods to overseas markets—to an empire, instead, of consumption.[46]

Over the course of the decade, some American businesspeople began to look at China through this prism of a global search for offshore production. As American corporations expanded their manufacturing operations in other parts of the world, they began to see China as offering the potential to join—and assist—in this process.[47] For most of the decade China did not permit foreign direct investment, but it did offer cheap labor. Americans had long associated Chinese people with low-cost labor. The nineteenth-century congressional debates about Chinese immigration—and labor unions' push to exclude Chinese workers from entry into the United States—had reinforced the notion that Chinese people offered inherently cheaper labor.[48] Echoes of these ideas reemerged in the 1970s and became entangled with the changing manufacturing processes that were beginning to take shape.

These changes in US capitalism were aided by Chinese pragmatists who increasingly experimented with using exports to fund their development efforts. As they found ways to increase their sales to US businesspeople, Chinese traders encouraged the trope of hardworking Chinese laborers. They created advertisements that featured not only the goods for sale but the diligence and care the Chinese workers had applied in making the goods. Chinese traders sold their workers as much as they sold their products.

Yet China's increasing trade and engagement with capitalist nations came at a time of considerable political instability. Mao's health deteriorated in the first few years of the decade, and he suffered multiple heart attacks. His ailing condition intensified the power struggles among rival political factions. Political moderates such as Zhou Enlai and Deng Xiaoping favored a more open approach toward the capitalist world, including the United States. But radicals, led by Mao's fourth wife, Jiang Qing, vehemently opposed such deviations from the Maoist principle of self-reliance. In late 1974 and 1975 these radicals gained control of most of the levers of elite power. Under their leadership, trade, which had so recently and rapidly expanded, began to slow down. This plateau was exacerbated by a global economic recession that had been triggered by the 1973 oil crisis.

In early 1976, Zhou Enlai died and by September of the same year, Chairman Mao did too. In the political turbulence that followed, Mao's successor, Hua Guofeng, arrested Jiang Qing and the other members of the "Gang of Four." The moderates were back in charge, this time led by Hua and Deng. From October 1976 until December 1978, they and other leaders of the CCP debated how best to accelerate trade with capitalist nations. By the end of December 1978 Deng Xiaoping had emerged as China's chief leader and declared the formal start to China's Four Modernizations, the core principles of the reform and opening period.

By then, however, the foundations of the budding US-China trade relationship had been laid. The American businesspeople who traded with China in the 1970s were neither soothsayers, foreseeing and pioneering limitless trade with China, nor simply part of the inevitable integration of China into the global system. While many saw themselves as groundbreakers—particularly given that the Chinese economy was still only developing its manufacturing capacity—they faced a considerable

15

number of challenges. These very challenges help explain why the trade that developed with China was not inevitable: trade was difficult and profit was far from certain.

THE CONTINGENCIES AND uncertainties of US-China trade in the 1970s were significant, and few predicted that the relationship would boom anytime soon. Throughout the decade, most Americans interested in trade focused their attention not on China but on Japan and its impact on the United States.[49] One economist, reflecting in the early twenty-first century on the projections of his peers in the 1970s, noted, "China is remarkable by its absence in these books . . . no one took notice of China yet."[50]

But there was, in fact, one key group of Americans who loudly and consistently paid attention to China's economic potential well before economists and policymakers of the twenty-first century did. From the very reopening of trade ties in the early 1970s, organized US labor representatives and workers, especially in the textile industry, warned of the impact that trade with China would have if greater industry safeguards were not implemented. Their concerns came in a volatile context when US imports of manufactured goods were rising, manufacturing employment was decreasing, and the combined effects of skyrocketing inflation and unemployment spurred a new concept, stagflation. As workers and organized labor in the United States protested the ways the increasingly globalizing world was emerging, they saw China as holding the potential to exacerbate these dynamics.[51]

Their efforts culminated in a landmark petition launched in late 1977 calling for quotas on imported Chinese goods. This was the first time US manufacturers had attempted to limit Chinese goods since the CCP came to power in 1949. As American workers began to mobilize against Chinese imports, their efforts quickly became a diplomatic problem. US diplomats repeatedly sidelined or silenced workers' concerns out of fear that they would delay diplomatic efforts toward normalization. These diplomats not only failed to envisage a strong Chinese economy; they also could not see how US workers—especially women of color in the textile industry—mattered to the regeneration of the United States' place in the world after its retreat from the war in Vietnam. To them, the far more important issue was easing the Cold War estrangement that had separated the United States and China and leveraging the rapprochement to assist détente with the Soviet Union.

16

The 1977 petition for quotas on Chinese textiles failed, largely due to US political interference. The loss not only revealed a political prioritization of geopolitics over domestic workers. It also revealed the changing practices of US companies that were importing low-cost Chinese goods as part of their slow adjustment toward offshore manufacturing. As they altered their own production processes, domestic manufacturers themselves began to see the China market as a source of inexpensive labor.

The chapters that follow examine the intersection of trade, labor, diplomacy, and culture in these early years of US-China trade. Each explores roughly a year in the life of the trade relationship. We begin with the Nixon shocks of 1971 and conclude in February 1980, when the two nations finalized their first trade deal. Following the story in this way highlights the uncertainties, contingencies, and ebbs and flows in the newly developing trade relationship. It anchors bilateral trade itself at the center of the narrative, tracing the slow transformation of the China market from 400 million customers to 800 million workers.

The key policies and legislation that defined how the trade relationship would develop structure the narrative arc of this book: Nixon's 1971 ending of the trade embargo; China's 4-3 Program of 1973; Congress's passage of the 1974 Trade Act; Mao's Three Worlds Theory of 1974; Zhou Enlai's Four Modernizations of 1975; Hua Guofeng's 1977 industrialization program; US glove workers' petition for quotas on Chinese imports in 1977; Deng Xiaoping's reiteration in 1978 of the Four Modernizations; and, finally, the 1980 bilateral US-PRC Trade Agreement. Interspersed throughout are the stories of the many people who built or resisted the new trade relationship.

As we explore the depth and pace of change in this rapprochement moment, we see the uncertainty with which American businesspeople and the Chinese state rebuilt trade ties. This story reveals the often unintentional—but ultimately momentous—transformations they put in motion. The end result of this messy process was that American capitalists and the Chinese state worked together, with assistance from US diplomats, to alter the very meaning of the China market: from 400 million customers to 800 million workers.

CHAPTER 1

The Nixon Shocks

IN THE SUMMER OF 1971, President Nixon made two surprise announcements to the American public that would have extraordinary long-term consequences. On July 15 the former Cold Warrior declared he would soon travel to China. Just weeks before, in anticipation of his announcement, he had ended the more than twenty-year trade embargo on China. On August 15, one month later to the day, he revealed that he would bring an abrupt end to the Bretton Woods system of dollar–gold convertibility. With this, the era of fixed exchange rates would soon be over. Journalists, and indeed Nixon himself, compared the diplomatic and economic shocks of 1971.[1] Within the space of a month the president had ended two pillars of the Cold War era: isolation from China and fixed exchange rates. The Nixon shocks, as they came to be known, were paired because of their similarities in style rather than substance.

But the Nixon shocks shared more than just stylistic commonalities. When we position US businesspeople and corporations at the center of our analysis, we see that the substantive changes that underpinned the shocks—reopening to China and the end of the Bretton Woods system—had long-reaching and unintended consequences for the developing US-China trade relationship. The end of Bretton Woods, which had structured capitalist trade and finance since the Second World War, fueled a tectonic shift in the US economy that made it easier for manufacturers to invest in overseas production facilities. These changes had begun to emerge during the Cold War, in places such as Taiwan and Japan. But the end of fixed exchange rates, alongside developments in faster shipping and communications, accelerated this process at precisely the moment when détente, rapprochement, and Ostpolitik softened the Cold War divisions between capitalism and communism.

This transformation in the US economy was crucial to China's eventual convergence with global capitalism. The end of the US embargo on China, the changes in US manufacturing, and the softening Cold War binary intersected when it came to US-China trade in the 1970s. In this chapter I take us back to the moment when these dynamics began to unfold. I begin by exploring the first Nixon shock to understand what US policymakers intended to achieve in reopening ties with China and how trade complemented these aims. I then contrast this to the motivations of Chinese policymakers. Leaders in both nations understood and used trade as a tool of diplomacy, but in very different ways. The result of these differences meant that Chinese sales to the United States gained heightened diplomatic importance.

I then turn to the second Nixon shock and the crises in other aspects of the American economy it was responding to. As Nixon reopened trade ties with China, the international monetary system that linked together the capitalist world teetered on the brink of collapse; the United States faced its first trade deficit of the twentieth century; labor unions across the country protested in streets against rising imports and unemployment; Congress pursued legislation seeking to protect domestic producers from increasing imports; and Nixon's trade representatives attempted to reach agreements on textile trade with China's neighbors—Japan, Hong Kong, South Korea, and Taiwan. Labels, such as those on shirts declaring "Made in Taiwan" or others declaring "Made in Japan," were at the center of many of these anxieties. US policymakers and businesspeople did not connect the new China trade to these problems. Nor did they connect it to the second Nixon shock. Business and political leaders saw Chinese imports differently. Even as rising imports from other parts of Asia led to mounting concerns, they celebrated imports of Chinese goods as assisting the diplomatic thaw.

The fact that, at the time, the two Nixon shocks were understood as being different in substance helps us see just how unintended their long-term repercussions were for US-China trade. Many of the businesspeople we will meet throughout this book were directly affected by both changes. At the same time that corporate executives and bankers saw opportunities for trade with China, Nixon's end of dollar–gold convertibility made it easier for them to invest their capital abroad.[2] China did not permit foreign direct investment for most of the 1970s, so while corporations expanded their operations in other parts of the world, China offered trade but not investment opportunities. Even as multinational corporations faced obstacles in their trade with China, they were also changing their business practices more broadly in response to the floating of exchange rates.[3] The transformation of the China market, from a site of customers to a site of workers, became bound up with these shifts within global capitalism. As US corporations altered their practices elsewhere, they began to see China differently too.

Small American importers in the opening years of trade were crucial to these long-term repercussions. I examine a process I label "fashion diplomacy," in which US importers accelerated a cultural reconfiguration whereby China slowly began to be seen as a trade partner rather than a Cold War foe. Fashion diplomacy relied upon a celebratory commodification of China in which the Chinese origins of imported goods were a central component of their desirability. American importers bought clothing, jewelry, bags, and shoes from China and transformed them into coveted symbols of elite cosmopolitanism, circulating within highbrow fashion circles. Working alongside the department stores that stocked their goods, importers marketed a China that was exotic, ancient, and sometimes leftist; a diluted radicalism expressed via consumption.

Fashion diplomacy downplayed the political aspects of China's communism. Taking their cues from the fashion world in Paris and London, New York's Seventh Avenue and its wealthy customers were at the forefront in reconfiguring domestic US attitudes toward China: the Red China fears of the 1950s gave way to seeing China instead as an enticing and beneficial trade partner.[4]

In the early 1970s, fashion diplomacy seemed to affirm US policymakers' assumptions that trade operated like other forms of people-to-people exchanges—creating space for cultural connections and interpersonal ties. It seemed, also, to mark a return to late nineteenth-century ideas about Chinese goods as cosmopolitan symbols of middle- and upper-class sophistication.[5] But the combined effects of Chinese policymakers' approach to trade and the changes in the US economy meant that US importers and their fashion diplomacy did something else of far more consequence. They played a pivotal role in reshaping the meaning of the China market itself, which became seen not as a site for selling US goods but instead as a place from which to import.

The First Nixon Shock

In early April 1971 the US men's table tennis team visited Beijing at the invitation of Chairman Mao. The team's tour of China was celebrated around the globe as a moment of interpersonal diplomacy and a visual demonstration of thawing bilateral relations between the two nations. In China, newspapers, radio, and television stations reported on the team's ten-day travels throughout the country, helping to reconfigure the United States from Cold War enemy to potential partner.[6]

It is less remembered, in the histories of this era, that a week after the US table tennis team's visit, President Nixon announced he would remove many of the trade restrictions with China that had been in place since the Korean War.[7] On April 14 he removed the embargo on US exports to China. American oil companies could now sell fuel for use in Chinese ships and aircraft, American industrial companies could now sell products to China, American ships and aircraft could now carry Chinese goods, and Chinese traders could now use American dollars in their foreign trade negotiations with any nation.

Nixon noted in a press statement that by ending the US embargo he aimed to "create broader opportunities for contacts between the Chinese and American peoples."[8] Writing to the director of the CIA and the secretaries of State and Defense a few days later, Kissinger echoed these sentiments, explaining that the economic changes were made "with the objective of furthering the improvement of relations."[9]

Trade was not a high priority for either man, but Nixon and Kissinger nonetheless hoped it would help the process of rebuilding diplomatic and cultural ties, just as they understood increased trade ties as crucial to détente with the Soviet Union. They saw trade as part of the larger people-to-people ties that were being created through initiatives such as ping-pong diplomacy.[10] These were, initially, unidirectional changes: only granting permission for US companies to sell to China. Two months later, on June 10, Nixon removed even more restrictions on trade and allowed the PRC to sell goods to the United States.[11]

Between April 1971 and February 1972, leaders from the United States and China reopened trade ties while they laid the groundwork for a diplomatic thaw. Accounts of these months in histories of US-China relations are dominated by the high-level diplomacy of Kissinger's secret trip to China or the story of the US table tennis team. Above all, they are understood through the drama of Nixon's live television broadcast on July 13,

21

in which he announced—to the shock of audiences across the United States and the globe—that he would travel to China in 1972.

A focus on trade relations, however, reveals that even though Nixon and Kissinger understood trade as an important mechanism in the rebuilding of people-to-people ties, Chinese policymakers took a different approach. In the months immediately following Nixon's lifting of the trade embargo, China refused to import anything from the United States. By the end of 1971, US-China trade totaled a mere $5 million—and the entire $5 million came from Chinese sales to US importers. As part of a deliberate strategy, China did not purchase a single item from the United States prior to the diplomatic meeting between Nixon and Mao in February 1972, but it did sell some goods to the United States.

China's refusal to buy from the United States in these opening months reflected a different understanding of the relationship between trade and diplomacy. Mao saw trade not as a tool of goodwill to be cultivated prior to diplomatic talks—as US policymakers did—but instead as something that would come only after thorny geopolitical issues had been negotiated. Even though US policymakers assumed trade ties were another form of interpersonal ties, like cultural and educational exchanges, in practice, trade operated in very different ways to the reopening cultural and scientific exchanges of the era.

"WHAT WE HAVE DONE," Nixon announced to a room filled with media executives regarding his recent end to the trade embargo, "is simply open the door." Continuing the Open Door metaphor from America's late nineteenth-century China policy, he added, "Now the question is whether there will be other doors opened on their part."[12] Nixon spoke on June 6, just a few days before Kissinger's secret trip to China to negotiate diplomatic rapprochement. He eased trade restrictions to signal to Chinese policymakers his commitment to normalized diplomatic relations. For Nixon, the loosening of trade and travel restrictions were more than symbols of goodwill; they were part of the political process toward full diplomatic relations. Writing his memoirs years later, Nixon noted with satisfaction that Zhou had indeed been paying attention to the speech and its message.[13] Trade was, in this way, a step toward diplomatic relations.

Nixon's discussion of the end of the embargo came during a press briefing devoted to the state of the domestic US economy. Much of the briefing focused on placating rising concerns about inflation, but on China

Nixon struck a very different note. China needed to be reconceptualized, he declared, as one of "five great power centers" along with the United States, Western Europe, Japan, and the Soviet Union. "Japan, with 100 million people, produces more than Mainland China, with 800 million people," Nixon noted. China's economy was weak, "but," he continued, "that should not mislead us." Distinguishing between the state and its people, he argued: "When we see the Chinese as people . . . they are creative, they are productive, they are one of the most capable people in the world. And 800 million Chinese are going to be, inevitably, an enormous economic power."[14]

In just a few sentences, Nixon suggested that China's future economic strength would be driven by production. As he contrasted China and Japan's economies, he observed that Japan "produces more" despite having a far smaller population. The inevitable power he saw in China would be propelled by its huge population. Nixon did not connect the dots any further—he did not speak any more explicitly about China's productive potential. But from the very start of the reopening to China, he intimated that the future of the Chinese economy would be underpinned, not by the older China market of 400 million customers, but instead by a new China market teeming with 800 million workers.

Nixon was remarkably prescient about the repercussions that might come from the end of the US embargo. "The very success of our policy of ending the isolation of Mainland China will mean an immense escalation of their economic challenge not only to us but to others in the world," he warned.[15] His solution to this potential competition was not to shy away from the challenge but instead to focus on the US domestic economy. The potential for multipolar competition "can be a constructive thing," Nixon noted in his attempt to assuage US economic concerns. Opening to China was, therefore, part of Nixon's larger justification for domestic reform.

For all Nixon's talk of China's potential, there was a considerable contrast between his long-term vision hinting at China's 800 million workers and the short-term means of getting there. Even as he alluded to China's future productive capacity, the economic advisors around Nixon prepared for the short-term implications of trade with China by drawing on very different visions. They saw a China market to which they could sell. In April, Peter Flanigan, a key economic assistant to Nixon, had written to Kissinger about the "major problem" of excess capacity for the US airline industry. "One of the major potential markets for these planes could well be Communist China" he suggested.[16] Flanigan wanted to sell old jets to

China to ease the pressures on the industry at home. Pete Peterson, another of Nixon's economic advisors, saw the potential for US wheat sales to China. "Grain is one of the principle potential exports from the Free World to China," Peterson and the Under Secretaries Committee informed Nixon in early June. Opening avenues for China trade "would have very favorable political results" for domestic farmers.[17]

Nixon's talk of eventual Chinese economic power was likewise very different from the projections he was receiving privately. The CIA estimated that trade could one day total around $470 million. At best, the Under Secretaries Committee noted, drawing on the CIA data, "a modest, long-term trade potential exists." But, they warned Nixon, "it would most likely take several years for the volume of trade to reach even the lower end of the estimate range of two-way trade."[18]

Similarly, in a March 1972 report on foreign economic policy, the State Department argued that despite the "historic allure" of the China market, the prospects for trade were "poor." It nonetheless saw some potential in purchases by the PRC that "could become significant to a number of US industries, among them such key economically depressed industries as aircraft manufacturing and machine tools."[19] As with Flanigan and his old jets and Peterson and his wheat, the report reflected a long-standing vision of the China market as a place where US sales to China could assist the ailing American economy.

The State Department report concluded that US policymakers should continue to pursue trade ties, despite the poor economic prospects, because of the diplomatic benefits trade would yield. American companies would be working directly with Chinese traders, which would provide "tangible evidence of momentum in the improvement of relations between the two countries," the report noted. This "tangible evidence" would help diplomatic negotiations move toward normalization.[20] For the policymakers working on trade with China, it was trade's symbolic assistance, as part of the repertoire of people-to-people ties, that truly made the difference. And the trade opportunities were understood in terms of what the United States could sell to China.

These sober projections of China trade and the focus on US sales to China reflected the immediate expectations and priorities of US policymakers. Nixon's long-term conception of China's productive capacity and economic power had oratorical heft, but it did not inform the day-to-day projections of his advisors, who were far more concerned with the immediate realities than the future potential of China trade. Given that Nixon's

China comments were made with an eye to Kissinger's secret trip to China, it is likely that he spoke so effusively about China's economic potential in order to further appeal to Mao and Zhou.[21] Zhou had, in fact, commented to Kissinger days later that he particularly appreciated the president's projections of "China as a country of potential strength."[22]

The realities of the Chinese economy in the early 1970s made it difficult to imagine China as a major economic power—the country's economy and society had been turned upside down by the chaos of the Cultural Revolution. As a result, Nixon's long-term vision that hinted at 800 million workers went largely unnoticed by the media at the time. Throughout the decade, the short-term visions articulated by his advisors dominated how US policymakers and many business elites understood trade with China.

What was a mere hint in Nixon's speech soon became an explicit concern among a different group of Americans. As the United States reopened ties with China, labor leaders—particularly those in the textile industry—soon began to warn of the impact an economically strong China would have on the workers they represented. They too saw a potential of 800 million workers, and they worried what that would mean for them. But with commerce at such a low level, Nixon was not concerned about the impact that ending the China embargo would have on US workers; he focused instead on the immediate-term benefits that trade would bring to diplomatic negotiations. As he would soon discover, Chinese leaders understood the relationship between trade and diplomacy very differently.

ZHOU MAY HAVE noticed Nixon's comments about using trade to open diplomatic doors, but in practice he and his colleagues approached trade differently. Their strategy was a deliberate one, which the Politburo articulated in late May 1971. In preparation for Kissinger's upcoming visit, Zhou convened a meeting with the Politburo in which they outlined their priorities for a potential opening to the United States. Their report enumerated a list of eight "basic principles" to guide rapprochement. For the Politburo, trade was far less important than Taiwan, which dominated the list. In fact, points one through four all concerned the island. They spelled out the need for the United States to withdraw its troops from Taiwan; insisted that "no foreign intervention should be allowed" regarding the island's status; asserted the importance of "liberating" Taiwan through peaceful means; and expressed "resolute opposition" to "two Chinas."

The fifth basic principle outlined a willingness to open liaison offices, which would serve as unofficial embassies until full diplomatic relations could be established. Point six returned to Taiwan, reaffirming the PRC's refusal to countenance two Chinas, including at the United Nations. The seventh basic principle laid out the conditions for building a trade relationship with the United States. The eighth and final basic principle stipulated that the United States should withdraw all troops from Indochina, Korea, Japan, and indeed the whole of Southeast Asia. Taiwan dominated the report, but the war in Vietnam was also high on China's list of geostrategic considerations. With these basic principles, China sought to leverage its opening to the United States to fit its broader regional aims.[23]

The seventh basic principle, on trade, was the only one that did not focus on geopolitics. "We will not raise the question of Sino-American trade," the Politburo decided. If US negotiators brought it up, "we may discuss it with them only after the principle of an American troop withdrawal from Taiwan has been accepted." With point seven the Politburo had resolved, therefore, to withhold discussion of trade regulations until progress was made on the questions regarding Taiwan.

The seventh basic principle was deeply connected to Mao's policy of self-reliance, and all eight principles would continue to operate as core tenets of Beijing's US policy throughout the decade.[24] When it came to trade, time and again Chinese policymakers would invoke the rhetoric of self-reliance and remind their American counterparts that geopolitical issues, particularly regarding Taiwan, came first. China's approach would go on to play an important part in how the trade relationship would develop. In the middle of the decade, when diplomatic negotiations began to stall, Chinese radicals invoked self-reliance in order to justify cutting back on US trade. Toward the end of the decade, pragmatists would come to use the promise of increased trade as a lure for progress with US policymakers on other issues. In both these moments, trade was understood as something that would expand only after progress had first been made in geopolitical negotiations.[25]

LEADERS OF THE two nations adopted differing approaches toward trade, but neither side saw commerce as a central motivation for diplomatic rapprochement. Instead, geopolitics and domestic politics compelled the thaw in diplomatic, cultural, and trade ties—most particularly with regard to the two nations' relationships with the Soviet Union and the

United States' desire to use Chinese assistance to negotiate a retreat from the war in Vietnam.[26] In other words, neither country pursued engagement *because of* a desire to trade with one another. To them, trade mattered as a tool toward other political concerns.

The biggest hurdle to the reestablishment of diplomatic ties was the nature of the United States' relationship with Taiwan. When Kissinger met with Zhou in Beijing for their undercover meetings (with Kissinger wearing shirts that his aides had scrambled to find for him on the plane ride over), Zhou made the PRC's position unambiguously clear.[27] "In recognizing China the U.S. must do so unreservedly. It must recognize the PRC as the sole legitimate government of China and not make any exceptions." Kissinger hedged his response. "We are not advocating a 'two Chinas' solution," he said. "Or," he continued, "a 'one China, one Taiwan' solution." Moreover, he pledged that the United States was willing to remove two-thirds of its military forces from the island of Taiwan. This would happen "within a specified brief period of time" after US troops had left Vietnam.[28]

On the question of diplomatic recognition, Kissinger also indicated support while buying more time. He promised, "We can certainly settle the political question within the earlier part of the president's second term."[29] These two private pledges—US troop withdrawal from Taiwan and normalization by Nixon's second term—would go on to haunt American policymakers in later years, as Zhou and other Chinese leaders held them to Kissinger's promises. Kissinger dubbed his approach one of "strategic ambiguity," which worked in the short term but would create diplomatic challenges in the long run.[30] For now, however, Kissinger and Zhou reached a point acceptable enough to both sides. Zhou extended a formal invitation for Nixon to visit China with the aim of formalizing the agreement. "Eureka!," Kissinger wrote in a single-word telegram back to Washington.[31]

While rapprochement was compelled in large part by international concerns—desires to end the Vietnam War and both nations' relations with the Soviet Union—it was also driven by rising domestic constraints in both countries. In China, the domestic upheaval of the first years of the Cultural Revolution played a key role in pushing Mao toward rapprochement with the United States. Mao needed a political breakthrough that would boost his domestic credibility and reassert his control. He also needed to demonstrate strength against the Soviet Union after fighting between the Soviets and Chinese had broken out in 1969 on China's northern borders.[32] The turmoil engulfing Chinese politics meant that what had once seemed politically impossible—improved relations with the United States—now looked to be a solution.[33]

Nixon was also conscious of the domestic politics of rapprochement, not because he was embattled but because he wanted to avoid becoming so. The 1972 election was already in his sights, and he was determined that if the opening to China worked, it needed to become a diplomatic coup for him.[34] For years, policymakers and academics had debated the possibility of reopening relations with China.[35] In 1967, even before coming to office, Nixon had argued in the pages of *Foreign Affairs* that "taking the long view, we simply cannot afford to leave China forever outside the family of nations, there to nurture its fantasies, cherish its hates and threaten its neighbors."[36] The mood in academic and policy circles was changing, and congressional anticommunists were considerably weaker than they had been in the 1950s when Nixon himself was at the front of the pack.[37] But in 1971 China still remained a communist foe for many American voters.

Nixon's plan for combatting voter concerns about his opening to China was to project decisiveness, cultivate drama, and speak of peace. On July 15, just a month after his Kansas City speech, he held a press conference in Washington that was broadcast live on televisions around the world. Viewers at home, watching as the summer day mellowed into evening, may have been expecting a presidential update on the economic problems of rising inflation and deepening unemployment. Instead they were shocked, some into disbelief, as Nixon—the red-baiting anticommunist crusader of two decades earlier—announced that Kissinger had secretly flown to China and met with Zhou. Nixon too would travel to China early the following year, at a time yet to be confirmed. "I have taken this action," he announced, "because of my profound conviction that all nations will gain from a reduction of tensions and a better relationship between the United States and the People's Republic of China." He hoped that his would be "a journey for peace, peace not just for our generation but for future generations on this earth we share together."[38]

Nixon positioned his efforts toward rapprochement with China squarely within his broader foreign policy narrative of a new world order centered upon peace. He had entered office in 1969 on a promise of ending the war in Vietnam and pursuing détente with the communist superpowers. While he spoke of peace, the reality of his time in office looked very different. His and Kissinger's decision to bomb Cambodia in the spring of 1970 directly contradicted their assertions they were pursuing peace. As did Nixon's sending of the National Guard to Kent State University in Ohio and Jackson State in Mississippi, where they shot and killed unarmed students who were protesting these bombings.

As the resistance to the ongoing war in Vietnam continued to swell across the United States, Nixon privately spoke with his advisors of the need to play up the "peace line" in the media. This line, he said, would position him "as a world leader, reducing the danger of war, and so on, using China and the China trip to build the initiative and build our leadership there."[39] Nixon hoped his improving relations with China would change how the American public and media assessed his foreign policies. Kissinger commented bluntly on the phone to the president in April 1971, "We've got to have a diversion from Vietnam in this country for a while."[40]

Nixon's surprise message about his upcoming China trip was crucial to that diversion. It had been so deliberately orchestrated that even European and Asian allies were not warned about the announcement until thirty minutes prior to his going on air.[41] And it worked as he and Kissinger had intended. Their use of drama and secrecy allowed the news to reverberate with stunning effect across the globe.

In Beijing, Tang Wensheng, Mao's English-language translator, listened as Nixon's announcement was broadcast from the radios throughout the Foreign Language Institute. She had translated Zhou's conversations with Kissinger during his secret trip a few days earlier and was one of the few people in the world to know in advance what was coming.[42] As Nixon's voice rang out throughout the corridors, she began to hear exclamations of surprise and astonishment from colleagues learning of the changing dynamic between the superpowers.[43] In Japan, the Nixon shock triggered outraged cries of betrayal. The United States had made a remarkable turnaround in its China policy, and Japanese leaders were furious they had not been consulted.

Even Nixon's closest White House advisors were caught off guard. They might have been preparing the slow and steady policies needed to reopen trade, but they had no idea about Kissinger's visit or Nixon's plans to visit China himself. Union leader George Meany, president of the AFL-CIO, called it "the number one stunt by the number one stunt man."[44]

The first Nixon shock—the announcement of the upcoming diplomatic summit in China—was driven by geopolitical considerations and domestic politics, not economic imperatives. Neither Nixon nor Mao pursued rapprochement *for* economic reasons. Instead, trade mattered as a tool—although leaders in both countries used that tool in different ways. China's seventh basic principle positioned trade as something that would come only after diplomatic progress had been made, not as an incentive to be used beforehand. As a consequence, the Chinese were willing to sell small amounts to US importers, but they refused to buy the planes or wheat US policymakers and businesspeople were hoping to sell them. China did not make a single purchase from the United States until after Nixon and Mao signed the Shanghai communiqué in February 1972. Instead, US imports of Chinese goods dominated the early months of the trade relationship. And precisely because US policymakers saw trade as a sign of wider progress, they saw these imports as assisting the bilateral thaw.

The Second Nixon Shock

Amid these changes in trade and diplomacy with China, the United States headed toward its first trade deficit in nearly eighty years. Not since the 1893 depression had the United States imported more than it sold abroad. The costs of military spending for the Vietnam War had become a huge drain on the United States' balance of payments, but trade in US goods and services was not the only thing in flux. The US financial system was also under enormous pressure and beginning to crack. It was dependent upon an international arrangement—known as the Bretton Woods system—that had been in place since 1944.

The Bretton Woods system was named after the area in northern New Hampshire where, toward the end of the Second World War, representatives of forty-four Allied countries, led by the United States and Britain, met for the United Nations Monetary and Financial Conference. Over twenty-two days the assembled delegates agreed to a number of conditions that would structure the new international monetary and financial order.[45] China was at the conference, represented by the Nationalist Party.[46]

The conference established the parameters of international finance after the war. One of the measures introduced was a new method for valuing national currencies. The delegates agreed that national governments would adjust the value of their currencies in relation to the US dollar. In turn, the value of the US dollar would be linked to the value of gold: one ounce of gold would be worth $35. They created the International Monetary Fund (IMF) to oversee these changes. Dollar–gold convertibility was crucial to the deepening postwar US hegemony. A few years later, in 1947, President Harry Truman declared, "We are the giant of the economic world."[47]

The postwar American Century was funded and sustained by the Bretton Woods system, but by the spring of 1971 this economic lifeline was unraveling.[48] Investors and corporations began to worry that the dollar was depreciating too rapidly, which was partly a result of the deteriorating US trade balance and partly a result of investors' collective decisions to move their capital out of the United States in the first place. The end result was that there were too many US dollars in the international financial system. Those who held US dollars turned increasingly to European banks, which gave them higher interest rates.

By the summer of 1971 this short-term movement of capital sparked a crisis in the value of the dollar that affected monetary systems around the world.[49] The problem was that the dollar was undervalued in relation to gold; one ounce of gold was no longer worth $35 but instead considerably more. It was in the middle of the dollar crisis that Nixon lifted the trade restrictions with China, including restrictions on China's use of dollars in its transactions with foreign trade partners. The international monetary system was collapsing, but Nixon still used trade as what he thought was a positive means of assisting diplomacy with China.

On August 15, just one month after his shock announcement that he would be traveling to China, Nixon addressed the nation with another live television broadcast in which he announced his New Economic Policy. In an attempt to protect American jobs, he imposed a 10 percent tariff on all imports; in an attempt to curb inflation, he imposed a freeze on all wages and consumer prices—for ninety days, there would be no pay raises and no increases in the price of goods; finally, in an attempt to stabilize the dollar and ensure that the prices of goods valued in dollars were internationally competitive, he announced he would end dollar-gold convertibility and fixed exchange rates. These measures would be "brutal and effective," he declared.

Nixon linked these economic changes to his vision for a new world order—what he described as a "new prosperity without war"—and to his broader theme of peace. "This Sunday evening is an appropriate time for us to turn our attention to the challenges of peace," he declared. "Prosperity without war requires action on three fronts: We must create more and better jobs; we must stop the rise in the cost of living; we must protect the dollar from the attacks of international money speculators." His measures would ensure that "the unfair edge that some of our foreign competition has will be removed." American labor and manufacturing would become more competitive, he asserted.[50]

Nixon's ending of dollar–gold convertibility was intended to be temporary. For the rest of 1971 Nixon, Treasury Secretary John Connally, and others worked to find ways to restore fixed exchange rates and dollar convertibility once more.[51] Yet the unilateralism underpinning the Nixon shock ultimately undermined his ability to later work multilaterally with other countries to revive an international order based on fixed exchange rates.[52] As a result, free-floating international exchange rates became a fixture of the international system, accelerating the process of globalized international finance. By the 1980s free capital markets had crystalized into a neoliberal ideology, but in the early 1970s free-floating financial markets were the unintended result of a muddied scramble to temporarily prop up the US economy.[53]

The end of the gold standard would not prove helpful to American workers as Nixon had promised. Instead it directly aided business and finance leaders throughout the United States, some of whom went on to play pivotal roles in the unfolding China trade. It dramatically eased the process of moving capital abroad and helped multinational corporations invest in manufacturing facilities wherever labor was cheapest. This would spur a global race to the bottom in how labor was valued in manufacturing industries.

David Rockefeller, head of Chase Manhattan Bank, was delighted by the freeing up of capital that Nixon and Connally had instigated. Speaking late one evening to Kissinger, Nixon noted that his announcement "has people like Rockefeller walking on the clouds." Rockefeller had called Nixon, thanking the president for his actions and reportedly claiming "it was the greatest thing since MBFR"—a reference to Nixon's announcement of non-nuclear force reduction negotiations with the Soviet Union.[54]

Capitalists like Rockefeller understood the significant benefits that would come their way as a consequence of Nixon's delinking of gold and the dollar. He did not, however, connect China to these developments. This was largely because China did not offer investment opportunities to Rockefeller or others until the very end of the decade. But these changes in global capitalism brought about by the end of the Bretton Woods system altered how US businesspeople approached questions of trade and finance. As we shall see, these developments also encouraged Chinese pragmatists to adapt to the opportunities that would come from opening up to investment from capitalist nations.

In the 1980s these changes in global capitalism would enable China's own manufacturing capacity to grow exponentially, as it took advantage of corporate America's pursuit of cheap labor. But in 1971, at the early stages of US-China relations, US policymakers and corporate leaders did not think to connect the end of the Bretton Woods system with the faltering economy of Mao's China.

AS THE NIXON administration began to create new avenues for trade with China, it was a different story for clothing and textiles entering the United States from the other side of the Taiwan Strait. Since the 1950s, Taiwan had sold textiles to the United States in increasing quantities. In early May 1971, David Kennedy, recently retired treasury secretary and ambassador-at-large, traveled to Taipei to negotiate curbs on Taiwan's textile exports. As part of his Asia trip, he also visited Hong Kong, Japan, and South Korea to negotiate similar bilateral textile restrictions.[55] By June, just days after Nixon loosened the restrictions on China trade, Taiwan agreed to impose voluntary restrictions on some of the textile goods it sold to the United States.

The restrictions on Taiwan goods came as American workers increasingly fought against rising textile imports. By the end of the summer, the International Ladies' Garment Workers Union (ILGWU) and other AFL-CIO affiliates organized a third wave of Buy American campaigns. They rallied in support of the Foreign Trade Investment Act, introduced to the House of Representatives in September 1971, which became known as the Burke-Hartke bill after Democratic senator Vance Hartke and representative James Burke.

The Burke-Hartke bill would have implemented some of the toughest protectionist measures in the twentieth century. It proposed quotas—not just tariffs—on over 7,000 import items.[56] This would have capped the number of textiles coming into the US market, unlike tariffs that would have imposed a cost but not a limit on volume. Under the terms of the bill, US-based multinational corporations would be forced to pay stringent new taxation on their foreign earnings. Organized labor was furious at the rising levels of imports and the displaced jobs they brought. George Meany saw the bill as a way to "stop the growing export of American jobs, capital, technology, production by multinational corporations based in the United States."[57]

The Burke-Hartke bill came in the wake of a similar bill that would have protected the American textile industry but had been recently defeated: the Mills bill.[58] Named after its congressional sponsor, Wilbur Mills, the Mills bill passed the House in November 1970 but was later blocked in the Senate. Paul McCracken, chairman of Nixon's Council of Economic Advisers, warned that if the Mills bill were passed, "we may be on the verge of a trade war with Europe and Japan."[59] Big-business lobby groups and internationalists within the Nixon administration fought hard throughout 1970 and 1971 to kill the Mills bill.[60] Seeing the efforts of American labor groups, they organized their own lobby groups, including the Emergency Committee on American Trade, founded in 1967 by David Rockefeller.[61] By October 1972 they had formed the Business Roundtable, a group of 150 of the largest US corporations that would go on to hold extraordinary influence in Congress.[62]

Corporate interests and liberal internationalists won their battles in the early 1970s: Congress did not pass the protection measures. In fact, unlike the Mills bill, the House did not even come to a vote on Burke-Hartke.[63] Nonetheless, organized labor continued its efforts to protect American-manufactured goods and halt the corporate move toward shifting manufacturing abroad. In its advertisements and picket lines, the ILGWU linked the buying of American-made union products with the protection of American jobs. Taiwan, which sold high volumes of textiles to the United States, was one of the main targets of the Buy American movement.[64]

Another major target in the textile union's sights was Japan. Nixon had used the opening to China and later his slamming shut of dollar–gold convertibility to leverage his negotiations with Japan on voluntary textile restraints. In August 1971 he noted to his advisors that he hoped his dual shocks—his television announcements that he would travel to China and the end of dollar–gold convertibility—would "jolt" Japan into agreement on textile restrictions.[65]

Yet Japanese textiles continued to enter the United States. In particular, Japan increased its exports of goods made with synthetic materials: the disco decade's signature Lycra, for example. Unlike cotton goods, products using man-made fibers were not subject to the restrictions that had been in place since 1962 aimed at protecting the American textile industry.[66] It was cheaper, therefore, for Japan to export Lycra than cotton.

The increase in Japanese textile exports was also encouraged by the decreasing costs of shipping as a consequence of containerization.[67]

In early August 1971, at their quarterly meeting in San Francisco, the AFL-CIO executive council condemned the "gross mismanagement by the Nixon administration" that had led to the "economic mess" facing the United States. The union leaders moreover urged Nixon to "consider anew the question of Chinese communist membership in the United Nations." They took an anticommunist position, arguing that China's policies had not changed enough to warrant such a shift in US strategy. "Why does the Nixon administration believe that peace in our time and for future generations would be served by according the Mao Tse-tung regime membership in the UN?" They pointed instead to the injustice of "the expulsion of the Republic of China, a founding member of the United Nations."[68]

Even as they fought Taiwan on economic matters, then, the AFL-CIO's anticommunism propelled their geopolitical support for the island. Not all council members agreed—four dissented and one abstained from the executive council's statement condemning Taiwan's removal from "the China seat." But Meany and the vast majority of the labor leadership pushed their anticommunist line hard.

Speaking at a press conference afterward, Meany denounced "Red China" as "a dictator nation which denies freedom to its people and is not eligible for United Nations membership." When asked about trade, he replied, "I don't think we could sell them anything unless we give them the money to pay for it." In these early stages of the trade relationship, Meany, the longtime Cold Warrior, saw China through an anticommunist lens: emphasizing the political threat rather than the economic threat China posed.[69]

Many rank-and-file members agreed. "Your anti-communist stand has the approval of the great majority of Americans who believe our great American heritage is in jeopardy," Earl Rees from California wrote to Meany. "We certainly back your stand against this newest 'friendship' with Red China," Paul and Aurora Jones wrote from their home in Oregon.[70]

In the wake of Nixon's new China policy and the changing landscape at the United Nations, many involved with the AFL-CIO were concerned first and foremost with anticommunism. A husband and wife from Minnesota, who signed off as "Mr. and Mrs. Andrea Tobler," wrote to Meany thanking him for the "courage and strength of conviction . . . in the face of so much mistaken opinion to the contrary." "We truly believe," they continued, "that the so-called 'silent majority' is with you on this issue and not with the man who gave them the name." Meany, not Nixon, was their voice, the Toblers wrote.[71]

One supporter of the AFL-CIO who did connect the opening to China with US labor at the early stages of reopening was evangelical radio personality Carl McIntire. "God bless you man!" McIntire wrote to Meany, supporting the union leader's stance against China. "We are going to be flooded with slave labor goods out of Red China," McIntire predicted. "President Nixon wants a half slave world to work with him for his miserable peace."[72] McIntire's language of slave labor would go on to become a central component of labor leaders' fights against Chinese imports, particularly in 1977 when the first group of US workers launched a petition for import restrictions on China. Like McIntire, the leaders behind the petition drew on language of slave labor when discussing China, echoing the late nineteenth-century debates about the "coolie" trade.[73] Fighting slavery meant imposing restrictions on China—its people in the nineteenth century, and its goods in the twentieth.

As policymakers in Washington and Beijing began to reopen trade ties, labor leaders were already focused on fighting foreign imports, particularly those from Asia. It was "Made in Japan" and "Made in Taiwan" that evoked their concerns, but China would soon be added to that list. Yet in the early stages of US-China trade, it was retailers and importers who focused most on China's potential. To them, China—and its workers—were not a cause for concern but instead powerful advertising tools representing cosmopolitan sophistication.

The Fashion Diplomacy of Dragon Lady Traders

From her Fifth Avenue apartment in Manhattan, Veronica Yhap, an architect in her early thirties, had been following the nightly bulletins and newspapers as they filled with news of ping-pong diplomacy and easing trade and travel restrictions with China. Born in Shanghai to a wealthy family, Yhap and her parents fled to Hong Kong on the eve of the CCP's victory in 1949.[74] After she finished school, she flew to the United States to study architecture at Mills College in Oakland, California, before moving again to New York City, where she completed graduate studies at Columbia University. She remained in New York, where she worked as an architect and met her husband, Ernesto Yhap, an engineer at IBM.[75]

As Nixon lifted the barriers to trade with China, Veronica Yhap imagined a role for herself in the newly opening trade relationship. She had a wardrobe filled with Chinese jackets and dresses that she had bought years ago when visiting family in Hong Kong. In recent months she had received several compliments when she wore them.

While some Americans remained wary of Red China, the high-end fashion world coveted Chinese clothing. The appeal was compounded by the fact that this latest trend came to Fifth Avenue via France. Gray and blue workers' uniforms were bestsellers at Paris's Galeries Lafayette, the *New York Times* reported in its fashion pages in August. Parisian crowds were particularly eager to buy workers' suits that had been made in China, which they felt had a "special cachet" of authenticity.[76]

Seeking to capitalize on the excitement for Chinese fashion, Yhap spoke with executives at Bloomingdale's and Abraham & Straus to gauge their interest in stocking Chinese clothing in their department stores. She brought with her the clothes she had in her own wardrobe. Would they be interested, she inquired, in selling such goods in their stores? The executives jumped at the opportunity. Soon after, Yhap telegrammed a friend in Hong Kong, Winnie Yeung, whom she had met in California as a student at Mills College. The department stores were interested and wanted samples as soon as Yeung could send them.

Yhap and Yeung, along with two other friends, soon set up a company, Dragon Lady Traders. Yhap had decided on the name in haste—Dragon Lady had been her nickname in college. Dragon Lady was a character in a popular adventure comic of the late 1930s, *Terry and the Pirates*. Coming in a context of growing Japanese aggression, the Chinese heroine blended danger, strength, and erotic allure. She could be a damsel in distress while also bravely fighting Japanese fascism. These contradictions worked together to reinforce the trope of a tough yet delicate Asian woman in American popular culture.

Dragon Lady was a Chinese comic character, but this did nothing to stop American journalists of the early 1960s from frequently likening her to the de facto first lady of South Vietnam, Trần Lệ Xuân.[77] They simply saw an Oriental other. Coming at the time of Yhap's college days in California, the journalistic coverage of South Vietnam's leaders likely also inspired her dorm-room nickname.

The racial and gendered dynamics underpinning Dragon Lady Traders also echoed those of the Japanese geisha, who in the 1950s came to epitomize the mix of strong yet demure and highly erotic Asian womanhood. In the years after the Second World War, American importers of Japanese goods profited off the image of the geisha as a desirable form of exotic Asian femininity.[78] These deeper ideas operated close to the surface for Dragon Lady Traders. By the mid-1970s, a few years after establishing Dragon Lady Traders, Yhap thought about changing its name "to something," she reflected, "a little more dignified." Yet her lawyers and business partners resisted, feeling this would undermine the name recognition they had built. Yhap had reworked the trope into a profitable brand. One of the key benefits of this approach, Yhap acknowledged, was that Dragon Lady Traders brought an additional significance. "It's also meaning it's a company run by a woman," she added after some consideration "and we like that."[79]

The company offered American consumers a familiar, and therefore unthreatening, way of conceptualizing China. By connecting goods from communist China to these larger associations of Asian femininity, Yhap's Dragon Lady Traders helped instigate a cultural reconfiguration of China from red threat to a source of familiar racialized gender norms.

In the early autumn of 1971, Veronica Yhap's new job as an importer was already taking off. Among the retailers that Yhap worked with were two Manhattan-based stores: Design Research, which specialized in Scandinavian fabrics, and Betsey, Bunky and Nini, a store that fashion columnist Bernadine Morris described as "the citadel of way-out fashions."[80] A definition of "way-out fashions" was never given, but China implicitly fit the mold. In the first few days, Design Research sold almost all its padded gray cotton jackets, retailing for $33 each. It also stocked long printed coats that Morris described as "mandarin-looking." These coats were more expensive, setting customers back $120. For $70 shoppers could also buy blue or brown pants made of a silk and cotton blend. At these prices, the clothing was "not in the working-class category," the *Washington Post* noted, adding that the prices were "expected to drop as mass production increases."[81]

References to class were a subtle reminder that prospective shoppers were buying from a communist country. Far from being a source of concern, however, this was an idea that, ironically, promised elitist luxury. But the mention of mass production also suggested that the promise of the China market extended much further: one day Chinese clothing might be accessible on a wider scale. For the time being, wealthy shoppers in New York could buy workers' jackets for themselves and their children. Children between the ages of one and six could wear jackets for a price anywhere between $26 and $35.[82] *Time* magazine described "the new Nixon

Figure 1.1. Veronica Yhap poses for the *New York Times* wearing a Mao jacket that her newly formed company, Dragon Lady Traders, sold to customers for $130.

look in American foreign policy" as leading to a "Chicom chic" in fashion.[83] What was so integral to this ChiCom chic phenomenon was the overt connections to China's communism and the appeal this brought. Young New Yorker children could wear Chinese workers' coats in the ultimate reflection of their parents' cosmopolitanism.

American consumers' changing relationship with China built on fertile ground that had been tilled since the 1950s height of the Red China scare. Throughout the 1960s, white liberals and some Chinese American community leaders positioned Chinese people in the United States—immigrants, refugees, and citizens—not as threats but instead as model minorities, a designation that was cultivated in distinction to Black Americans.[84] As Cold War liberals reframed how Chinese *people* were understood in the United States, many leftists saw the Chinese *state* as a site of radical possibility too. Some civil rights leaders saw in Maoism revolutionary hope for ending white supremacy and racial violence at home.[85]

By the 1970s, US importers began to put dollar signs on these changing attitudes about Chinese people and the Chinese state. Their fashion diplomacy packaged and sold China to a new wealthy and culturally influential segment of American society. Veronica Yhap explained to journalists that her company was "trying to introduce Americans to the real China of today." By selling "the people's suits worn by Chinese workers and peasants," she saw herself as bringing authentic Chinese goods to American consumers. They often came with a steep price tag. The Mao suits Yhap sold retailed at $130, which, she noted, were "popular in colleges."[86]

By advertising Chinese jackets and workers' uniforms as exotic Maoist commodities, Yhap and other US importers helped reconfigure larger public ideas about China's communism. For university students, the appeal lay in purchasing signifiers of radical politics—the "commodification of dissent," as historian Thomas Frank has put it.[87] But the real impact of these items was not radical at all. On the contrary, the imported Maoist goods helped remove the political aspects of how liberal Americans thought about China's communism. At a time when Andy Warhol began producing his iconic portraits of Mao Zedong, this was an era of the kitchification of China's revolution.[88] No longer a threat, China's communism could be a mere fashion statement. US importers and the goods they sold were essential to changing public perceptions of the United States' former Cold War foe.

VERONICA YHAP HAD been working with her childhood friend Winnie Yeung in Hong Kong to import clothing from China, and by October she traveled to China herself. Getting a visa had been difficult. Communication channels were starting to open more widely, but the United States and the PRC did not have embassies or consulates to approve visas. Some Americans therefore used the Chinese embassy in Ottawa, Canada. Others, including Yhap, went to the PRC's Hong Kong–based agency,

China Travel Service. She and her husband flew to Hong Kong, where they went straight to the China Travel Service. They filed a visa application upon arrival and, after a nerve-wracking wait, were eventually able to obtain a Chinese visa.

From Hong Kong, the couple took a train to Guangzhou in China's south—which at the time English speakers called Canton. There Yhap attended the Canton Trade Fair. These twice-yearly fairs—the largest and most important trade events in China's calendar—were managed by the China Foreign Trade Center. From April 15 until May 15 and again from October 15 until November 15, the massive halls of a giant trade complex were filled with all kinds of Chinese-made items for sale—machinery, antiques, and textiles.

Yhap was one of three American businesspeople who traveled to China for the 1971 fair. Alongside her were Van Lung, who had established a new company, Sino-American Export-Import Corporation, and Georg Hansen, who headed up East Asiatic Company.[89] Van Lung was born in Yunnan Province but moved to the United States as a young man. In 1955 he had established a restaurant in Washington, DC, Yenching Palace, which soon became a hot spot for the DC political elite. It was rumored to be the location where secret negotiations between US and Kremlin representatives unfolded during the Cuban missile crisis.[90] Henry Kissinger often frequented the restaurant, and Lung reportedly taught the statesman about Chinese cooking in the lead-up to Kissinger's secret trip to China in 1971.[91] The East Asiatic Company, which Georg Hansen represented, was one of Denmark's largest corporations. Hansen traveled to the Canton Fair on behalf of the company's New York offices. Mere months after trade and travel restrictions had been lifted, Yhap, Van Lung, and Hansen together became the first representatives of US-based businesses to attend the fairs.

During her negotiations at the Canton Fair, Yhap placed orders for her Dragon Lady Traders company, including canvas bags that featured Chinese characters on their front. "To serve the people," the characters read.[92] She also traveled to Shanghai and revisited the house where she once lived. It was so big that eleven families now lived in it. She recalled later, "On the grounds there are about three apartment buildings." Seeing the changes, she reflected, "I do remember the house is really enormous. I must say that that was the only point during my entire trip that I could not help but feel a little sad and nostalgic."[93]

When she returned to the United States, Yhap's goods instantly sold out. She told the *New York Times* that American customers were so excited that they would buy clothing even if it did not fit. "If we run out of large, they'll take medium, and if we run out of medium, they'll take small. It's incredible," she gasped. Bloomingdales stocked Chinese workers' blue uniforms that Yhap had imported, which she noted excitedly had "vanished into the closets of New York fashionables."[94] By January 1972 Dragon Lady Traders had already made over $25,000.[95] A few years later, they were trading millions of dollars of clothing each quarter.[96]

Yhap used Chinese workers' clothing to appeal to working American women. "Most American designers have a specific concept of Chinese styles, and it's always that of the clothes worn during dynasty when ladies of the court wore beautiful brocade gowns with sashed waists and flowing sleeves," she told the *Washington Post*. "It was all right in its day, but it doesn't fit in today's way of life," she continued. The chongsan (a tight-fitting dress with side slits) was also "really dated," she declared. "How can anyone wear it comfortably during a busy workday?"[97] In promoting Chinese clothing, Yhap promised American women both Chinese authenticity and the modern woman's practical professionalism.

"Their bestseller is the classic Mao jacket, padded slightly for warmth, with a removable (and washable) white inner collar and buttons concealing snap closings," *Time* magazine enthused.[98] Dragon Lady Traders also imported pantsuits targeted at both men and women. "But I've adapted them slightly," Yhap told the *Washington Post*. "Instead of the same, solid colors seen everywhere on adults, I've asked the government factory to make them up for me in bright colors and patterns used in upholstery and mattress covers. Also, I've added sashes for the American woman, though Chinese women prefer the comfort of the loose jacket." She recounted the Chinese traders as being "incredulous" at her request of colors. "Americans must be really crazy," they had conveyed to her. "Do they want to wear that (bright colors and patterns such as peacocks and flowers) on the streets?"

The factory managers Yhap dealt with were willing to meet her design specifications despite their protests, and she came home with more than simply premade clothing. Businesspeople from other capitalist nations, particularly in Europe, similarly had limited success in obtaining clothing that was adapted to their needs. As Yhap joined them, she became part of a slowly emerging new era in which Chinese factories increasingly exported foreign-designed goods that their workers had made in China.

Other icons of the US fashion scene joined the China craze. Oscar de la Renta, one of the fashion world's biggest names, reflected on the recent news that Kissinger had flown to China. "When he made that trip to Peking in July, I knew China was in," he explained. American designer Donald Brooks felt similarly. "I'd been fascinated by the Far East since I was a child, and there have always been traces of the Orient in my collections—floral interpretations, coromandel screen details—but when it became likely that China would be admitted to the United Nations, I knew that this was it. I was dealing from instinct."[99]

Giorgio di Sant'angelo, one of the leaders in avant-garde fashion, had been "into Indian costumes a couple of years ago." Readers of Bernadine Morris's *New York Times* fashion column were not offered an explanation as to what Indian costumes entailed—perhaps they did not need one—but, they read, di Sant'angelo "had no trouble switching to Chinese culture" for his spring collection. "Of course," readers were informed, "he interpreted the clothes in his own way, such as clingy leotards with loose mandarin sleeves worn under panel-front skirts." Illie Wacs, from fashion house Originala, had purchased Chinese silk from Italian importer, Emil Sormani. "The silk worms are superior," Sormani explained. China was "the biggest fashion news since mini skirts," Morris proclaimed.[100]

Time magazine felt that Nixon's own diplomatic theatrics fueled the consumer excitement. "The new Nixon look in American foreign policy" was responsible for the China craze, the magazine explained to its readers in December 1971. "Chairman Mao's favorite jacket in particular—and just about anything else Chinese—is selling in Manhattan boutiques this fall like rice cakes at the Spring Festival."[101] Readers were invited to associate China with high fashion and rice cakes, not communism. Nixon's efforts may have provided an impetus for consumer interest in China by ending the embargo, but it was the fashion diplomacy of Dragon Lady Traders and the New York fashion world that enabled it.[102]

In the lead-up to Nixon's February trip to China, *Ingenue*, a magazine targeted at teenage girls, featured advice on how to capture the "essence of Chinese beauty." It contained makeup techniques for achieving "smooth, round hairstyles; smooth, round face; almost oval eyes; outlined rose lips."[103] American women were encouraged to appropriate an imagined Chinese "look" through playacting—dressing up in clothing and wearing makeup that might help them to imagine themselves as Chinese.

Perhaps the most visible sign of this appropriation occurred in February 1972 when the *Ladies' Home Journal* featured on its cover a photograph of the US first lady, Pat Nixon. In anticipation of her trip with President Nixon to China at the end of the month, she was photographed smiling at the camera and wearing a dress that the journal described as "opulent Chinoiserie . . . for grand evenings." Her floor-length red and green dress was the work of Donald Brooks. With "brilliant jade accents," "long draping sleeves," and "obi-like sashed waist," the dress channeled what Brooks felt was a Chinese aesthetic.[104] It was part of Brooks's recent collection of designer dresses inspired by China that he had released the previous fall.[105]

By the summer of 1972, fashion diplomacy extended to panda diplomacy. Washington Zoo unveiled two eighteen-month-old giant pandas, which the United States had received from China in exchange for two musk oxen sent to the Peking Zoo. Thousands of Americans queued for hours each day to see the panda pair, Ling-Ling and Hsing-Hsing.[106] Toymakers seized on the enthusiasm. The *New York Times* reported that toy companies were "rushing to meet" what was forecast to be a "panda-based boom" in plush toys.[107]

Fashion diplomacy bridged the divisions between US and Chinese approaches toward trade, but it also relied upon appropriating Chinese clothing and "styles" as their own. As the US fashion world adopted China, the excitement for Chinese imports it generated helped create a cultural shift in the US view of China, from Red China to trade partner.

FOR MANY IN 1971, the US economy seemed to be in turmoil. Imports were causing diplomatic tensions; US workers took to the streets to demand better conditions; and by late summer Nixon had frozen prices and wages and ended dollar–gold convertibility. But as the opportunities for trade with China slowly emerged, they struck a very different note. China trade was exciting, opulent, exotic. It did not fit the larger dynamics of decline and disarray. Precisely because of its communist state structures, policymakers in Washington did not connect China to the economic troubles that other capitalist nations seemed to pose. But the cultural reconfiguration of China's communism from Red China threat to amicable trade partner was not universal. Many, particularly those in the labor movement, continued to see China through an anticommunist lens.

Amid these changing cultural dynamics in the United States, Chinese policymakers and their interests played an outsized role in determining whether any goods would flow between the two nations. China refused to buy goods from the United States in this early period, prioritizing its exports instead. As the trade relationship developed, US importers

44

Figure 1.2. In February 1972, *Ladies Home Journal* featured First Lady Pat Nixon on its cover to coincide with her upcoming trip to China with President Nixon. She wore a China-inspired dress by American designer Donald Brooks, and in a seven-page spread inside the magazine modeled more such clothing by some of the leading figures in American fashion.

increasingly aligned with China's trading preferences because they and the fashion diplomacy they promoted were essential to Chinese interests too.

Dragon Lady Traders and other small US importers who came after Veronica Yhap led the way in rebuilding trade ties, and a growing group of Americans were certainly buying what they were selling. While the United States faced its first trade deficit in the twentieth century, the $5 million deficit it shared with China was barely perceptible. By the end of 1971, for the first time in the twentieth century, the United States imported more than it exported. This was a shift that would become chronic to US trade for the remainder of the twentieth century and into the twenty-first. China did not cause this change, but its trade with the United States would go on to be shaped by the economic and diplomatic developments that began to unfold in 1971 as a consequence of the two Nixon shocks.

Leaders in Beijing and Washington did not connect the two Nixon shocks beyond their superficial similarities and were instead focused on diplomacy. It would not be long before their diverging views on how trade figured into the diplomatic negotiations would start to cause challenges in the relationship. For the time being, however, more and more US businesspeople began to trade with China. As Veronica Yhap had learned in the fall of 1971, an integral part of that process took place at the Canton Trade Fair in Guangzhou. In the wake of Nixon and Mao's summit in February 1972, China started to invite more American businesspeople to its fairs. Just down the road from the trade fair grounds, Guangzhou Zoo furthered the panda diplomacy by displaying a literal sign of friendship: it erected a banner above its entrance gate reading "All the People of the World, including the American People, Are Our Friends."[108] It came just in time to greet American businesspeople who arrived in Guangzhou for the Canton Trade Fair.

CHAPTER 2

The Canton Trade Fair

O N   A   M I D - A P R I L   E V E N I N G   in 1972, thousands of businesspeople from across the globe crowded shoulder to shoulder in the open-air reception hall of the Dongfang Hotel, a towering Soviet-built concrete structure at the heart of Guangzhou. They had gathered to mark the official start of the Chinese Export Commodities Fair, referred to in English as the Canton Trade Fair. Held twice a year since 1957, these were the biggest events in China's foreign trade calendar. Chen Yu, the seventy-one-year-old director of the fairs, welcomed the traders. "Withstanding all kinds of foreign pressures, we have already built a poor and backwards Old China into a prosperous socialist country," Chen proclaimed. Repeating the official line from Beijing, he noted that China's socialism had "always adhered to the policy of independence and self-reliance." "But," he added, "this does not exclude the development of trade with other countries in the world." China's trade was based upon the key principle of "equality and mutual benefit," he explained.[1]

Chen was a savvy political navigator, having been one of the few Guangdong provincial leaders to survive the Red Guard purges in 1967, at the height of the Cultural Revolution.[2] During that period, China adhered to an interpretation of the Maoist concept of self-reliance—*zili gengsheng*—that saw little need for foreign trade at all. By April 1972 the tides in Beijing were turning once more and a newly reinstated group of leaders with more moderate economic views promoted a different understanding of

Figure 2.1. Foreign businesspeople listen to Chen Yu's speech at the official reception opening the Spring 1972 Canton Trade Fair.

self-reliance. Collectively referred to as "pragmatists," this group within the politburo pushed for increased trade—especially with the capitalist world—through a more flexible approach toward import substitution. They advocated for China to import large-scale infrastructure items like fertilizer factories using cash generated by increased sales of exports. This could still be a form of self-reliance, they argued.[3]

One of the architects of this new approach, Li Xiannian, stood beside Chen as he spoke in Guangzhou. Voicing these changes, Chen added that the long-standing principle of equality and mutual benefit could be achieved through "mutual exchange" and an "increase in trade."[4] Chen announced to the world that things were changing. In fact, mutual exchange and expanded trade were decisions made "in order to enhance China's ability to be self-reliant," he proclaimed. Excerpts of Chen's speech were published in *Renmin Ribao* (*People's Daily*), China's national newspaper. It was directed not just at foreign traders gathered in the tropical heat of Guangzhou but also at those in Beijing who opposed the pragmatists' new approach to trade.[5]

As pragmatists experimented with new ways of approaching development, China's foreign trade indeed expanded. By the end of 1972 it reached around $5.9 billion, the highest point since the PRC's founding. Japan was China's biggest trading partner by far, accounting for $1.1 billion in total trade.[6] The two nations had been trading since 1957, and their leaders spent 1972 negotiating full diplomatic relations, which they achieved in September. It was in this year that China also increased its trade with the United States. State-owned export companies had sold small amounts to US importers like Veronica Yhap in 1971; in 1972 China began to buy from the United States as well.

This timing was important. It was only after Nixon and Mao's high-profile meeting in February 1972—only after improvements in diplomacy—that China began to purchase goods from the United States. As the Politburo had outlined in its seventh basic principle in May 1971, trade would be developed following improvements in geopolitical negotiations. The increasing US-China trade was deeply tied to, and limited by, diplomacy.[7]

American businesspeople who traveled to the Canton Trade Fair came up against these limits. But they saw, too, a whole new world of opportunities. Surrounded by seasoned global traders, the Americans were made immediately aware of the scale of competition they faced. It was business as usual for the 21,000 other foreigners who walked the halls of the exhibitions, but this did nothing to dampen the sense of discovery many of the newcomers felt toward their own trip to Guangzhou.

Upon returning to the United States, some businesspeople brought their experiences and purchases back home not only through advertisements and department store displays but also through their writing. Directed to other American businesspeople, they dispensed advice in corporate magazines, academic journals, books, pamphlets, and newspaper columns. The advice produced by US businesspeople of the 1970s spurred a new generation of self-declared experts on China, often collectively described as "China hands."[8] Even though a number of women and Chinese American businesspeople traded with China, white men were the overwhelming majority of the new China hands producing the advice.

Remarkably, most of the English-language writing about the Canton Trade Fair comes from these China hands of the 1970s. The fairs are not part of the wider scholarship on international trade fairs and have received only limited attention in histories of China.[9] In this chapter I explore the history of the fairs and provide one of the first sustained analyses of them. I use the advice literature produced by the new China hands in two ways: drawing on it for what it reveals about life at the Canton Trade Fairs and historicizing it for what it tells us about American businesspeople's own understanding of China trade in the 1970s.

In doing this, I draw together two dynamics: China's changing trade practices in the early 1970s, and the proliferating advice literature written by US businesspeople who traded with China.[10] Analyzing these two dynamics side by side reveals a fundamental friction. On the one hand, a dominant subsection of US businesspeople produced a form of travel writing—imperial eyes—that relied upon what literature scholar Mary Louise Pratt deems an "anti-conquest." These authors distanced themselves from conquest by writing of the challenges and limits of China trade. But as they did so, they simultaneously asserted a claim to expertise, often underpinned by racial and gendered logics of hierarchy.[11] In their descriptions (and in many cases prescriptions) of modes of behavior, many positioned themselves, and the United States, at the center of a new frontier of trade expansion.[12]

On the other hand, Beijing's expanding trade remained deeply bound by the Politburo's decision that trade with the United States would only come after improvements in diplomacy. As we have seen, with the seventh basic principle in May 1971, the Politburo resolved to link trade with diplomatic progress.[13] Regardless of the Americans' own sense of discovery, Chinese merchants placed hard limits on the unfolding trade with the United States.

A crucial cultural transformation emerged from this friction. The China hands' advice literature and the Chinese limits on trade worked together to enable a recasting of the two nations from Cold War foes to amicable trade partners—from Red China to Made in China. This was seen most clearly when US businesspeople wrote of the challenges they faced in China trade. Many framed the very challenges themselves as part of the appeal of trading with China, and they did so in ways that downplayed China's communism. One of the most striking aspects of the literature was that its authors rarely, if ever, used the term "communism." Even though attending the trade fairs in Guangzhou meant entering a hall with a towering portrait of Mao, flanked on either side by portraits of Stalin and Lenin, these US capitalists often explained the difficulties they experienced and the trading process they encountered as a consequence of China's exotic difference rather than its communist state structure.

Circulating among the high-rise buildings of corporate America and the offices of small importing firms, the advice literature did not simply help normalize the wider diplomatic changes unfolding between Beijing and Washington, it also capitalized—literally—upon the idea of an enticing, rediscovered, China. The US business community reframed their own understandings of China, producing a cultural transformation with far-reaching and ultimately lasting consequences. Nonetheless, as the composition and volume of China's 1972 trade figures reveal, the expansion of commerce had necessitated diplomatic progress first. American businesspeople might have extolled a new frontier of China trade, but it was Chinese interests that determined whether or not that trade potential would be realized.

Controlling Trade

It was no accident that China's trade fairs were held in Guangzhou. The city had long been one of the most important sites for China's international trade. For close to one hundred years, starting in the mid-eighteenth century, the Qing Empire limited its trade to the port city. From 1757 until the first Opium War, in the late 1830s, foreigners who wanted to trade with China could do so only from Guangzhou. They were housed in tightly controlled quarters and were only permitted to visit select parts of the wider city. Women were banned from Canton altogether.[14]

The Canton Trade Fairs of the mid-twentieth century echoed these earlier arrangements. The inaugural fair opened on April 25, 1957: symbolically timed to coincide with the two-hundred-year anniversary of the establishment of China's old Canton trade system. They were held along the Pearl River at the site of the factories of the Canton system—a reminder of Mao's desire to once more control China's trade relationships.[15] Visiting businesspeople were likewise only permitted to travel to certain areas beyond the fair, and always in the company of Chinese chaperones.

Around a thousand businesspeople from nineteen countries traveled to Guangzhou for the 1957 launch of the Canton Trade Fairs. The overwhelming majority of attendees, nearly 70 percent, came from Hong Kong alone.[16] Since the mid-1950s, the economic ties between Hong Kong and China had become linked in an important yet brittle system whereby food, textiles, and migrant labor flowed from China in exchange for access to international markets, insurance, shipping, and banking services in Hong Kong.[17] Between 1952 and 1963, Hong Kong received around 9 percent of all Chinese exports, a percentage that would increase substantially in the years that followed as China moved its trade relations farther away from the Soviet Union.[18]

While Mao harkened back to the old Canton system, the fairs also reflected the Cold War context in which they operated. With the Canton Trade Fair, China joined the circuit of international trade fairs. Throughout the Cold War, capitalist and communist nations had opened pavilions for commercial transactions while competitively showcasing sanitized depictions of social life in their countries. For example, in 1956 the United States sent a traveling exhibition called "People's Capitalism" to trade fairs in Colombia, Guatemala, Chile, and Bolivia, touting the benefits of mass consumption.[19] A year later, the United States showcased its "Supermarket USA" exhibition at the Zagreb International Trade Fair, demonstrating the variety of choices available at American supermarkets.[20] Perhaps the most notorious of the Cold War fairs were reciprocal 1959 expositions held first in Moscow and then in New York. It was at the Moscow exposition that Nixon and Khrushchev fiercely debated the merits of American- and Soviet-style kitchens, fast becoming a metaphor for the superpowers' Cold War battle for hearts and minds.[21]

Blending commerce with displays of technological progress, trade fairs have long been an integral part of international relations. Throughout the nineteenth and twentieth centuries, trade fairs—especially World's Fairs—became platforms for cultural expansion and displays of nation building across the globe, displaying what historian Robert Rydell describes as "visions of empire."[22] Veritable cornucopias, World's Fairs blended scientific and technological displays of modernization with entertainment, mass consumption, and racial hierarchy.[23]

The Canton Trade Fairs were an opportunity for Mao to demonstrate China's industrial progress to the world, but they also revealed Cold War geopolitical dynamics. The fairs were housed in the Sino-Soviet Friendship Building, a reflection of the significant reliance China had on the Soviet Union for its economic development in the early Cold War.[24] Between 1950 and 1959, Moscow accounted for 47.8 percent of China's foreign trade.[25] Over that decade, thousands of Soviet advisors moved to China to train Chinese people in skills needed to build a socialist society. Together they established infrastructure like hydroelectric plants, roads, and bridges. As the Soviet Union expanded its economic ties with China and assisted the development of Mao's new socialist state, it provided, as historian Odd Arne Westad has put it, "the Soviet Union's Marshall Plan." Even larger than the United States' economic assistance to war-torn Europe, the huge influx of Soviet advisors and money helped China rebuild its economy after decades of war.[26]

But the relationship between the two communist powers had been riddled with fractures from the start. By the time Mao established the trade fairs, the fault lines were beginning to crack at the surface.[27] Stalin's death in 1953 had pushed Mao to consider anew his own position within the international communist movement. By the mid-1950s Mao began to see himself as more qualified than the new Soviet leadership under Nikita Khrushchev to prescribe the principles of communist revolution.[28]

The Canton Trade Fairs were therefore an important part of Mao's efforts to broaden China's economic and political relationships beyond the Soviet Union. From the late 1950s, Mao advocated a change in China's trade and development policies that was more outward-facing. In the spring of 1956 he declared, "We must study the advanced experiences of all nations." China needed to "send people to capitalist countries to study technology, no matter if it is England, France, Switzerland, or Norway."[29] In the second half of the 1950s, Chinese economic planners, including Chen Yun, Zhou Enlai, and Bo Yibo, worked to implement this pivot, which included establishing the Canton Fairs.[30] Yet the fact that the fairs were held in the Sino-Soviet Friendship Building reflected the considerable structural limitations to China's expansion efforts; Beijing continued to rely on Soviet aid until the early 1960s.[31]

At first the Canton Trade Fairs seemed to indicate a new era in China's foreign trade. Just two weeks after the inaugural fair came to a close, on May 30, 1957, the United Kingdom ended the embargo that it had imposed, jointly with the United States and other capitalist nations, during the Korean War. Britain's about-turn was due in part to pressure on Downing Street from the British business community in Hong Kong, who saw expanding opportunities in the China market. Soon thereafter Belgium, Denmark, France, Japan, and the Netherlands similarly ended their embargo. By September, China and West Germany had signed a one-year trade agreement in Beijing. The United States would soon be the sole nation upholding economic isolation of China.[32]

Despite the optimistic start, however, the value of trade conducted at the Canton Trade Fairs—as with China's foreign trade more broadly—remained low in the first decade since their establishment. In early 1958, not quite a year since the inaugural fair, Mao moved away from gradualist integration with international trade and instead focused on accelerating China's domestic economic development.[33] Workers' uprisings in Poland and Hungary in late 1956 had confirmed Mao's view that he needed to expedite China's own revolution lest he too faced domestic unrest.[34] As 1958 began, Mao launched the Great Leap Forward, a radical reorganization of China's industrial output. Mao boasted that the changes would see China's agricultural and industrial production "exceed Britain in seven years and overtake the U.S. in ten years."[35] The result, however, was disastrous. Mao's restructuring of the countryside wiped out China's agriculture, causing the deadliest famine in modern history.[36] The Chinese Ministry of Foreign Trade and Guangdong Provincial Government continued to stage the Canton Trade Fairs even amid the social and economic devastation of the Great Leap Forward, although the value of its foreign trade remained steady—and low.

The Canton Trade Fairs established a structural mechanism for contact with merchants across the communist and noncommunist world alike. As China increased its efforts to win influence in the newly emerging Third World, the fairs became another tool in China's cultural diplomacy arsenal.[37] They also became a means for expressing antiforeign lectures and propaganda. In September 1958, at the height of the Second Taiwan Strait crisis, the British Foreign Office reported that visiting German and Japanese businesspeople had been on the receiving end of considerable antiforeign sentiment.[38] Even though the crisis played out between the United States, Taiwan, and China, the Germans and Japanese were some of the few representatives from capitalist nations invited to the fair and therefore bore the brunt of Chinese posturing.[39]

While international politics made its way into the fairs, for the most part Chinese officials kept major domestic issues hidden from view and used the events to instead showcase China's industrial achievements. They placed tight controls on the movements of their international visitors, buffering them from the harsh realities of Mao's revolution just outside the fair's complex. In 1959, Guangdong—the province in which the Canton Trade Fairs were held—experienced a 35.6 percent decline in grain output as a consequence of the Great Leap Forward.[40] With such a depleted harvest, people living in the city of Guangzhou and other parts of the province began to starve: a situation that was most acute in China's nearby southwest provinces but was spreading throughout the country.[41]

Local hosts of the fairs hid these conditions from their foreign visitors. Instead, directors of the fair emphasized the international ties it forged. During the closing banquet of the 1959 spring fair, for example, Sun Leyi, deputy director of the fair, declared, "The achievements of this fair show that people from all trade circles in the world are very eager for peaceful trade; it also shows that China is committed to developing normal international trade."[42]

For the most part, Chinese hosts were successful at shielding their foreign guests from the horrors of Mao's Great Leap Forward. Writer and activist Shirley Graham Du Bois attended the 1959 spring fair during an eight-week tour of China with her husband, W. E. B. Du Bois.[43] She recalled afterward the wonderment she had felt at the fair: "Any American would have been amazed at what we saw on the five floors of that building . . . beautiful fabrics, rugs, fine china, silks and jade ornaments might have been expected, but not the shining precision tools, hospital and dental equipment, musical instruments, including pianos, optical instruments, televisions, radios, cameras of all sizes, electrical equipment, and on and on."[44]

As Graham Du Bois saw it, China offered not just finery but an alternative model of development. China was a place for technology and equipment, not just porcelain. With hindsight we see the profound chasm between her observations and the lived reality of Maoism. Yet in 1959 Maoism offered Graham Du Bois concrete—and hopeful—alternatives to a context of racial violence and oppression at home.[45] Just months before the Du Boises' visit, President Eisenhower had been forced to send the National Guard to Little Rock, Arkansas, to protect nine black students from white mobs at the newly desegregated Central High School. For the Du Boises, communism and especially Maoism offered solutions to the racism and violence they witnessed and experienced. Throughout the 1960s Mao's revolutionary promise extended across the globe as people in Asia, the Americas, and Africa overthrew colonial rule and drew new lines on the map.[46]

The only time the fair looked like it might be forced to close was in the fall of 1967, at the height of the Cultural Revolution. The military, civilians, and workers clashed violently throughout the year in Guangzhou, killing thousands of people.[47] It was a situation repeated in cities throughout China. Chen Yu, who would go on to lead the Canton Fairs and give the opening address to a packed crowd in April 1972, was governor of Guangdong Province at the time. Chen was one of the few leaders to retain a political position during the Cultural Revolution, although no longer as governor. Calling the chaos "extremely detrimental" to the international prestige the fairs brought China, Zhou Enlai directly intervened to prevent the Red Guards from interrupting the fair.[48]

The 1967 fall fair did open but was postponed by a month. Red Guards did not, in the end, smash antiques and burn wall hangings as they had threatened to do in the name of Mao's call to destroy old ideas, culture, customs, and habits.[49] They did, however, succeed in banning British businesspeople based in Hong Kong from attending, in the wake of the 1967

Hong Kong riots.[50] Moreover, they insisted that foreign businesspeople recite excerpts from Mao's Little Red Book.

Coverage of the fair in China's *Renmin Ribao* played into the propaganda, emphasizing the global support for Mao Zedong Thought.[51] One article published in November featured nine photographs spread over a full page depicting the "foreign friends" who had come to the fair. The photographs were accompanied with captions such as "Vietnamese comrades from the frontline of the anti-American struggle visited textiles and light industrial products" or "Chairman Mao tied our hearts together. The staff of the fair presented Chairman Mao badges to Congolese friends."[52] Behind the propaganda, however, the 1967 fall fair was heavily patrolled by troops, and foreign visitors were confined to an even smaller section of the city than usual.[53]

Chinese and foreign businesspeople nonetheless continued to conclude transactions at around roughly the same rate as for previous fairs, reaching deals of $406 million.[54] Despite the political maelstrom outside its gates, the fair continued with its heady mix of nationalism, cultural diplomacy, and commerce. Even as the Cultural Revolution tore through the nation, the Canton Trade Fairs remained both a staged performance of national progress and a crucial site of economic activity. This combination, like China's trade in the mid-eighteenth century, enabled Mao to control China's dealings with foreign merchants. Throughout the 1950s and 1960s, China's level of foreign trade remained about the same. It was not until the early 1970s that China began to significantly increase its levels of foreign trade—and it was capitalist nations that soon became its largest partners.

CHINA'S CHANGING APPROACH to trade in the early 1970s was accelerated by the death of military leader Lin Biao, who died in a suspicious plane crash in September 1971. Mao framed Lin as a Soviet sympathizer and ardent critic of rapprochement with the United States. With his death, Zhou and other pragmatists not only gained traction in their efforts to rebuild ties with the United States but they also gained impetus to radically restructure the approach underpinning China's development. For twenty years China's industrialization had been tied to its militarization. Building a railway, for example, was connected to militarized fight against the United States and, later, the Soviet Union. The death of Lin Biao gave pragmatists an excuse to unravel this military-industrialization nexus.[55]

As historian Covell Meyskens has shown, after Lin Biao's death the CCP began to "demilitarize their approach to national development" and focus instead on importing industrial technology.[56] In January 1972 Zhou and other pragmatists, including Vice Premier Li Xiannian, Hua Guofeng, and Yu Qiuli, produced a report on a new technology import program. They focused on "clothing supplies for the whole nation" and they saw importing chemical fiber technology as crucial to this project. This new technology, worth around $400 million, would also help China increase its exports of textiles, the report added.[57] In March 1972 Zhou received Mao's permission to rehabilitate more than 400 bureaucrats who had been purged during the Cultural Revolution and who would now work toward closer trade relations with capitalist nations.[58] By 1973 these pragmatists unveiled a full-blown program, known as the *sisan fang'an,* or 4-3 Program—a reference to the $4.3 billion price tag attached to China's new industrial imports.

The 4-3 Program would be a key mechanism for China's expanding trade with capitalist nations in the 1970s.[59] In earlier stages of the Maoist era, many pragmatists had floated some of the ideas underpinning the program, but it was only after the death of Lin Biao—and with it the end of the radical years of the Cultural Revolution—that a vision of industrialization linked to trade with capitalist nations was able to take root. Historian Jason Kelly has explored the earlier attempts by Chinese policymakers to increase foreign trade, arguing that China's trade in the 1970s, and the 4-3 Program in particular, built on "established ideas" that had developed in the 1950s and 1960s.[60] But just as the Canton Trade Fairs facilitated only limited trade due to the turbulence of the Great Leap Forward and Cultural Revolution, so too were pre-1970s ideas for an expanded trade program nascent and interrupted rather than established. The 1970s therefore marked a period of change rather than continuity in China's political economy. It provided, for the first time, the capacity for Chinese pragmatists to *implement* their ideas and use the Canton Trade Fairs to expand China's trade with capitalist nations.

IT WAS IN this context that the China Council for the Promotion of International Trade (CCPIT) invited fifty-six Americans to the spring Canton Trade Fair. Some of the attendees were executives from large multinational corporations, such as Boeing, Monsanto, and RCA. Others were representatives from department stores, including Bloomingdales, Neiman-Marcus, and Macy's. But most of the Americans came from smaller importing companies such as Far East Importers, Young's Food Brokerage, and Seabrook Foods. About half of the invited US companies had head-quarters in New York, but representatives came from all over the country, including San Francisco, Minneapolis, and Florence, Alabama. Six of the invited businesspeople were women, and about the same number were Chinese American.[61]

To get to the fair, many of the invitees traveled together with assistance from China Travel Service, China's Hong Kong–based agency that facili-tated foreign travel. Gathering on the platform of the Hong Kong train station, they met one another and their Chinese guides for the half-day journey to Guangzhou. Once the group of Americans boarded their train, it was an hour and a half ride to Lo Wu at the PRC border. Some of the Americans were unable to get seats so they stood in the aisles for the du-ration of the journey. They sped around the edges of Hong Kong, catching glimpses of Hong Kong University, Faring Golf Course, expan-sive garden spaces, and a number of small towns and markets.[62] When they disembarked at the border, Red Guards checked their passports and then directed them to walk across the Lo Wu footbridge. With the Sham Chun River beneath them, the passengers crossed to the mainland.[63]

The Americans had arrived in Bao'an county, an area that would one day become the sprawling metropolis of Shenzhen but was, in 1972, a poor border town prone to political volatility.[64] They had to wait for an hour in a holding center alongside hundreds of other passengers before continuing on to Guangzhou. One American described the waiting room as "huge and bare, with overstuffed furniture and an assortment of mag-azines about agricultural triumphs."[65] Servers provided the waiting pas-sengers with lunch, which was "excellent" recalled Bernard Rocca Jr., who was attending the fair on behalf of the Greater San Francisco Chamber of Commerce. As they ate, CCP operas blared out of speaker systems. The second train was packed with businesspeople from all over the world; but Rocca Jr. noted with relief, "We all had comfortable seats in an air-conditioned car."[66] Even in April the humidity would have been trying.

Some of the other travelers in the carriage had different issues on their minds. "Ah, the bloody enemy," one European businessman muttered under his breath. Coming with too much money and no experience, the Americans were likely to bid up the prices, he and his continental compa-triots grumbled to one another. They snickered as they watched the new-comers furiously reading Mao's Little Red Book in the hope of remembering a quote or two for use in negotiations. "Such falsities don't impress the Chinese," the veteran traders believed.[67]

When they finally arrived at the train station in Guangzhou, the Americans filed onto a bus for the last leg of their journey. It was a short drive to their hotel, just a few blocks away. The Dongfang Hotel, where the fair's opening ceremony was held, was easily the largest hotel in Guangzhou, standing eight stories high with over 1,400 rooms. Its stark concrete exterior and minimalist interiors reflected the influence of Soviet architecture. On one side was Liu Huahu Park, with its palm-tree-lined trails and a huge lake in the middle. Nearby were all kinds of amenities, including a laundry, hair salon, bookstore, and cinema.[68]

The spring Canton Trade Fair came as China continued to expand its foreign trade, as the fair director, Chen Yu, made clear in his speech at the opening ceremony. Since the death of Lin Biao in 1971, foreign trade was no longer as politically suspicious as it had been at the height of the Cultural Revolution. Two of the most senior Chinese officials attended parts of the event. Li Xiannian, the vice premier and finance minister, came down from Beijing to attend the opening ceremony alongside Chen Yu. Li was a close advisor to Zhou Enlai and one of the key economic supporters of the turn toward trade with capitalist nations and the importation of foreign technology. A few weeks later, on May 1—International Workers' Day—Mao's wife, Jiang Qing, visited the fair. She met with a number of businesspeople, especially those from Eastern Europe.[69] As a leader of China's ultra-leftist radical group, Jiang's choice to arrive on May Day and meet with East European communist traders was an important reminder that her loyalties still remained with communist nations. Li and Jiang represented two bitterly divided political factions and held deeply opposing ideas on how to define *zili gengsheng,* or self-reliance. Yet their attendance at the fair was a rare recognition of the importance China gave to foreign trade in 1972.[70] A few years later they would clash, but in the aftermath of Lin's death these tensions were muted.

The fairgrounds were huge. Three buildings housed the fair stalls, two of which were five stories high with domed, cavernous halls in the middle.[71] Machinery and technical tools were displayed in one building; carpets, live birds, and rattan furniture in another; and consumer goods, including porcelain, foodstuffs, apparel, jewelry, and antiques, were in the third.[72] It was not uncommon to see businesspeople rushing from one building to another in order to get to their different meetings on time.[73]

While there was a festival feel to the fairs, the trade experience itself was a grueling process. Most negotiations took place in the open halls of the imposing gray stone buildings. The Chinese corporations set up tables covered in white tablecloths and topped with glass. Businesspeople had tight windows for negotiations: from 8:30 a.m. until 12:30 p.m., and again from 2:30 p.m. until 5:30 p.m. They waited their turn to speak with their Chinese counterparts, sometimes watching (and listening to) their competitors ahead of them. One Englishman who had been to more than twenty fairs commented in 1972, "They play one off the other." The competition was fierce. A Dutch trader told a US journalist, "Everybody beats everybody over the head like mad because everybody wants a piece of the cake." He explained, "We want to get on the record—so we buy at ridiculous prices." As this Dutchman saw it, the fact that China privileged those who had an ongoing trade relationship with China could be a strong motivation for concluding deals that were not economically sound.[74]

With very few exceptions, most companies wishing to trade with China were required to at least begin their negotiations at the Canton Trade Fair. For many, it was the only interpersonal contact they had with Chinese traders. Some major economic deals would require American businesspeople to travel later to Beijing. But even large companies, such as Boeing, were first required to initiate negotiations at the trade fair before continuing to the Chinese capital.

Nonetheless, the total value of deals US businesspeople concluded at the spring fair was low. Most estimates placed it at around $5 million. This was all the more stark given China's overall emphasis on increasing trade. By the time the fair ended on May 15, China had brokered more deals and exchanged more goods than at any previous fair. The Japan Association for the Promotion of International Trade reported that it had sold around $60 million worth of goods and imported an even larger $100 million. Machinery topped Japan's list of exports, totaling around $32 million. China was expanding its trade, but it was in no rush to conclude deals with US companies.[75]

Not only was the total value of US deals considerably lower than those made by China's other trade partners, but each of those deals involved only US imports of Chinese goods. China did not conclude a single purchasing deal with any American company at the spring 1972 Canton Trade Fair. This was partly because China used the fairs as a key way to acquire the foreign currency needed to finance its technology imports. Even as Chinese merchants purchased large sums of goods from Japan,

Figure 2.2. Foreign traders sit at tables out in the open with white tablecloths, cups of tea, and cigarettes.

for example, they still sold more. But politics also played a role in their decisions with the Americans.

Chinese traders had invited US representatives from Boeing and RCA to discuss purchases from the American traders, but they did not conclude their negotiations. Ernest "Tex" Boullioun, a gregarious businessman from Arkansas who headed up Boeing's Commercial division, spent hours in meetings with representatives from the Civil Aviation Administration of China (CAAC). But the CAAC did little more than indicate its interest in the Boeing planes.

Following closely from Washington, the National Security Council noted the absence of US sales at the fair. One staffer observed consolingly to National Security Advisor Henry Kissinger that conversations were well underway. "Peking has reportedly made a firm offer to buy several Boeing 707 aircraft," he relayed. China was also "negotiating other purchases from Lockheed, and has asked Hughes Aircraft Corporation to submit a proposal for a domestic communications satellite system," he added hopefully.[76] No contracts, however, had been signed. American corporations may have looked to China as a source of sales, but Chinese traders were not yet willing to buy.

The Chinese reluctance to purchase was driven by geopolitical concerns.[77] In the spring the United States had escalated its bombing of North Vietnam following the North Vietnamese and Soviet offensive in Easter. Even as the United States and Soviet Union continued to fight a proxy war in Vietnam, they also reached a major breakthrough in the Strategic Arms Limitation Treaty (SALT) negotiations for nuclear arms controls.[78] Together in Moscow, Nixon and Brezhnev signed SALT I on June 18, 1972. In these contexts of both détente and the war in Vietnam, Mao had remained cautious about rapprochement with the United States.[79]

It took another high-level meeting between Henry Kissinger and Zhou Enlai in Beijing, just one day after that between Nixon and Brezhnev, to help solidify the progress in US-China relations. After these geopolitical developments China began to buy from the United States.

In September and October, China's state-owned agricultural corporation—China National Cereals, Oils and Foodstuffs Import Export Corporation (Ceroilfood)—purchased $43 million of wheat and corn from American suppliers. These purchases came in the wake of a devastating drought that had destroyed much of China's harvest.[80] They were far smaller than the grain deals Nixon had signed with the Soviet Union, which were worth around $1 billion, but these were the largest purchases China made from the United States in 1972. Nixon celebrated them, saying they "only scratch the surface of an immense trade potential between our two countries." In the lead-up to the election and his attempt to win the vote of American farmers, Nixon used a long-standing trope of the lucrative China market, framing it in terms of US sales.[81]

But even with this major grain deal, China had to use foreign subsidiaries of the US companies to coordinate the imports. The grain came from farmers in the United States but it was the French company Louis Dreyfus and Co. that handled both transactions.[82] Without correspondent banking relations, it was far easier for a sale of this scale to be handled by subsidiary companies that already had financial ties to China. This would soon become a familiar dynamic in a whole range of Chinese imports from the United States. American policymakers and businesspeople celebrated trade as a tool for peace and friendship, but the structural limitations between the two economies meant that the beneficiaries would be the US subsidiaries.

Televising Diplomacy

There was one exception to China's reluctance in early 1972 to buy directly from American businesspeople. But it was an exception that proved the larger pattern. On January 22, just one month before Nixon was due to arrive in China for his summit with Mao, China purchased technological equipment to assist with Nixon's trip. Executives from RCA Global Communications Inc. (Globcom) had traveled to Shanghai to meet with representatives from China's state-owned National Machinery Corporation (Machimpex) and together they signed a deal worth $2.9 million. RCA Globcom sold two earth station satellites, microwave terminal equipment, and its latest technology: Videovoice, which allowed for simultaneous live streaming of image and sound.

With this technology deal, audiences across the United States would be able watch Nixon's travels to China on live television. "A trip to China is like going to the moon," Nixon had gushed to reporters as he prepared for his upcoming visit. "If there is a postscript that I hope might be written with regard to this trip," he said at his farewell ceremony, "it would be the words on the plaque which was left on the moon by our first astronauts when they landed here: 'We came in peace for all mankind.'"[83] As the first American president to travel to China, Nixon was determined to dramatize the event to his advantage. It was an election year, and with the war in Vietnam dominating the headlines, he was worried. Journalists were all too willing to go along with his theatrics. All three networks interrupted their regular programming to broadcast Nixon's farewell live from the South Lawn of the White House. Over sixty camera crew and reporters followed him to China, including leading conservative commentator William F. Buckley Jr. They sent back hours of footage and hundreds of columns documenting the trip.

Behind Nixon's hyperbole there was, in fact, a concrete connection between the moon landing and his trip to China. Both were live-streamed to audiences throughout the world using the Intersat: an international satellite communications system, jointly operated by eighty nations.[84] Apollo 11 astronauts had beamed down signals from the moon to satellites orbiting the planet, transmitting stunning new images of them walking on the moon's surface. A few years later the RCA earth stations in Beijing and Shanghai sent up signals to satellites over the Pacific Ocean. An earth station in Jamesburg, California, received the satellite's signals, and the president's visit was broadcast live onto living room screens throughout the United States, including full four-hour coverage of the official banquet dinner in Shanghai.[85]

This was a staging that China was willing to indulge because Mao, too, wanted to capitalize on the publicity generated by the president's visit. He had been promoting his new opening to the United States for months, encouraging newspapers to publish articles and photos of visiting Americans, including extensive public coverage of Kissinger's trip to China in October 1971.[86] But this equipment was the only purchase China made from the United States before the June 1972 talks between Kissinger and Zhou. And the purchase itself was tied to diplomatic negotiations.

The satellites served political functions, but they were also crucial to China's developmental needs. They were used not just for television but also for telephones, telex, and data communications around the world. The satellite RCA set up in Beijing had direct communications with Asia, Africa, and Europe. The satellite in Shanghai directly linked China to the United States and Latin America.[87]

The RCA sales, then, were a prime example of the pragmatists' new focus on technology imports.[88] After the June Kissinger-Zhou talks, on August 17, RCA signed off on a further deal with China worth $5.7 million. RCA's executives had attended the spring 1972 Canton Trade Fair but, as with all US exporters, not completed any sales. The August deal required RCA to install another earth station in Beijing and add extensions to the one in Shanghai.[89] But the United States was not the only, or even the most important, supplier of technology at that time. China also purchased Japanese satellites when Japanese prime minister Tanaka Kakuei flew to Beijing in 1972 for a historic visit celebrating full diplomatic relations. Indeed, China bought even larger quantities of satellites from Japan than it did from the United States.

Realizing the limits of their efforts, perhaps, neither RCA nor the White House celebrated the satellite sales as examples of US modernizing efforts or a victory for American "financial missionaries."[90] A generation earlier, US engineers and merchants saw themselves as bringing change to China.[91] And throughout the first two decades of the Cold War, American policymakers, community workers, engineers, and corporations had worked throughout Asia and Latin America in attempts to foster economic changes in their own image under the auspices of modernization theory.[92] The RCA sale was certainly celebrated as a breakthrough, but it was understood in very different terms than these earlier contexts of US technology transfer. It was celebrated for its diplomatic importance as well as the ex-

THE ORDER OF NEW CHINA HANDS

In appreciation of your outstanding
personal and professional efforts expended
in contributing to the successful
completion of RCA Glöbcom's project to install, within
record time, the first satellite
communications earth station for
the People's Republic of China, you are
hereby awarded the
Order of New China Hands.

RCA Global Communications, Inc.

Awarded To:

Figure 2.3. In 1972 RCA created certificates for 134 employees, declaring them
members of a newly invented "Order of New China Hands."

ample it provided for other US companies—not for US-led changes it might bring China.

In November 1972, for example, RCA celebrated the efforts of the 134 employees who had worked on setting up the Chinese satellites. At a ceremony in New York City, company executives awarded the engineers with plaques deeming them part of the "Order of New China Hands." The honorific created a fictional club that made instant China experts of the RCA workers. The engineers had worked quickly, but they had hardly done work that was any different from what they had done in other nations.

Nonetheless, RCA's chairman, Howard Hawkins, declared the China project "one of the greatest achievements in the company's history." He added, "Since my recent visit to China I can tell you that the Chinese have great respect for the RCA people."[93] Hawkins equated trade with friendship. As the company's own magazine promoted, "We hope that our actions will contribute in some small way not only to development of China trade but also to peace and understanding."[94] RCA's declaration of its Order of New China Hands may have been ceremonial, but it revealed just how quickly Americans began to assert their expertise and connect their actions to peace and friendship.

As Hawkins sat down to reflect on his experiences and provide advice to businesspeople aspiring to trade with China, he presented his experiences with China in dry, technical terms. He explained how initial contact was established and how they negotiated contracts. He not only addressed the limits of trade that he encountered, but framed them in positive terms. "We will provide no more equipment and services than the Chinese want," he wrote in his advice article, "and are happy to agree to such cooperative arrangements." Hawkins celebrated RCA's success with the Order of New China Hands, but he also understood the restrictions imposed by Chinese interests. He felt that these decisions were not only "consistent with China's posture of self-reliance" but "also good business methods for trade with China" that other US companies should follow.[95] In his depiction, to be a China hand was to accept, and work within, the confines China imposed upon its trade.

Hawkins did not use the term "communism" in his written advice to other businesspeople, but he did include a reminder: "Keep in mind that the Chinese are excellent businessmen and that they have a different political system." He concluded with another reference to China's state structure, this time in more veiled terms. "Modern communications are and should remain above ideological differences, as the means to transcend political, social, and cultural barriers that separate people and nations."[96] His upbeat and complimentary description of "the Chinese" depicted China as no longer the Red China threat of the 1950s and 1960s but instead as an amicable, indeed talented, trade partner.

IN SEPTEMBER 1972 China made a third major purchase, after its purchases of RCA equipment and US wheat. The CAAC signed a deal with Boeing airlines to buy ten 707 aircraft. After months of negotiations and multiple setbacks, the company finally struck a deal.[97] In May the CAAC had hosted Boeing representatives in Beijing, after the Americans had first met with representatives at the spring Canton Trade Fair in Guangzhou but not completed any sale. They were led by Tex Boullioun, described by one company history as "the world's greatest airplane salesman."[98] A committed poker player with a taste for adventure, Boullioun excelled in his globetrotting job, which involved high-stakes sales. In the late 1930s he rode his Harley-Davidson from his hometown of Little Rock, Arkansas, to the Pacific Northwest, where eventually he began a career with Boeing. By 1967 he had become vice president of the company, and soon after the China deal, in late 1972, he was promoted to president.

But the Boeing deal was not China's only airline purchase in 1972, nor was it the largest. Just as with RCA, China turned to other capitalist nations for technology; the United States was one of many. By the summer CAAC had signed contracts with airline companies from the United Kingdom and France—not yet Boeing. Their message was clear: the CAAC could very easily turn elsewhere.[99] Eight months after the Boeing contract was signed, the CAAC purchased twenty Hawker Siddeley Tridents from the United Kingdom—double the number of planes purchased from Boeing. China's airline industry was still in its infancy, but the CAAC made sure to let the Boeing executives know that it had many other options. The Boeing planes did, however, have a particular appeal: they could carry more passengers for a longer distance than any other type of aircraft.

China also expanded its international flight routes with other nations. In January 1973 Pakistan International Airlines expanded its operations from Shanghai by opening additional flights between Islamabad and Beijing. In February Ethiopia Airlines flew an inaugural path from Addis Ababa to Shanghai. These airlines joined Aeroflot, Air France, and North Korean Airlines in offering direct flights to China. But even as China expanded its international aviation agreements, it still had limited flight facilities. In 1973 the nation had only a hundred civil airports, most with runways less than 7,000 feet long. Shanghai, Guangzhou, and Beijing were the sole centers equipped to handle large, long-range planes.[100]

By September 1974, on the second anniversary of the establishment of Sino-Japanese diplomatic relations, China announced its first air route connecting Tokyo to Beijing. Japanese Airlines (JAL) and the CAAC struck the deal after twenty months of negotiations; as with so many issues at this time, the sticking point had been JAL's ties with Taiwan.[101] For American businesspeople, this new flight path became the fastest way to reach Beijing. One could fly from the United States on JAL, Northwest, or Pan American and arrive in Tokyo before connecting to Beijing along the new route. In all, the trip would take less than twenty-four hours. This was a considerable improvement over the previous route, in which business-people would fly from the United States to Hong Kong, take a train to Guangzhou, and only from there travel to Beijing.[102] China was turning toward the capitalist world and using foreign trade to do so.

Even with all the international competition, the September 1972 con-tract between the CAAC and Boeing was widely celebrated in the United States. A key component of the success, much of the reporting empha-sized, was the Americans' capacity to navigate the negotiation process itself.[103] Byron Miller, head of Boeing's international commercial sales, told the *New York Times,* "It was by far the most rigorous negotiation I've ever been involved in." The proceedings had extended for five months, during which time "the Chinese went over every technical and financial detail with the meticulousness of the highest-paid corporation lawyers." Miller reported that the chief Chinese negotiator was "one of the best lawyers I've ever seen."[104] Miller emphasized the practical side of trade with China, rather than its state structure.

Absent from the reporting on the deal was a sense that the planes pro-jected US power. In 1958, when Pan American Airlines flew the first Boeing jetliners across the Atlantic Ocean, the planes were celebrated for their symbolism of American superiority. They were unveiled just a year after the Soviet Union had sent the world's first satellite into orbit and were admired for providing the fastest means of commercial air travel. As the Cold War competition extended to technological dominance, the Boeing planes became an expression of American strength, ingenuity, and technical knowhow.[105] Pan American declared the jetliners "a witness to the American tradition" and a realization of "Yankee traits of resource-fulness and perseverance."[106] But during the 1970s economic crises, and China's readiness to turn to other countries, Boeing's sale to China held a different resonance. The Americans saw their sales as an object lesson in how to trade rather than a patriotic triumph.

Nonetheless, the sales did exceed most outsiders' expectations. It was the largest single payment China had made to a foreign nation.[107] In May 1972 Sir John Keswick, chairman of the Sino-British Trade Council and of Jardine, Matheson & Co., one of the biggest British companies trading with China, predicted that Boeing would not sell more than one or two planes because national security concerns would come in the way. "I can't believe that confidence between the United States and China has been sufficiently established that the Chinese are likely to commit their aircraft industry to the United States at this stage," he had argued.[108] The sale required the Nixon administration to specially approve an export license, given the continued restrictions the United States imposed on sales of strategic goods to China.[109] Some bureaucrats within the Pentagon had also raised concerns that China could use the Boeing planes to fly supplies to Hanoi.[110]

A further surprise to the British and other foreign traders was the way in which the PRC paid for the planes: cash. Even hardened Japanese and European businesspeople were shocked to hear China paid such a considerable sum up front rather than through deferred payments. It was the largest single payment China had made to a foreign nation.[111] The Hong Kong–based *China Trade Report* speculated hopefully that the astonishment among the foreign trading community might lead the PRC to consider using foreign credit.[112] Chinese officials "had not realized" that deferred payments were not an indication of financial or economic weakness, the *Report* noted.[113]

In June, Foreign Minister Bai Xiangguo said in London that China was willing to explore possibilities for making purchases using deferred payments. Hong Kong–based reporters speculated that China had already done so with Japan.[114] Sun Fang, deputy secretary-general of the fairs, similarly noted in May, "It is not our policy to have foreign credit but we think that in trade, to make payments on a long-term basis, is acceptable and not abnormal." But Sun affirmed there was a difference between long-term payments and credit, the latter of which he was not advocating.[115] China's opening to the United States was part of its wider turn to the capitalist world—but it turned haltingly and with caution. Even though Beijing toyed with ideas of credit as it experimented with import substitution, the Chinese would not begin to use credit until the end of the decade.

Boeing's success soon became used as a prime example within the US advice literature of how to trade with China. The first lesson that many of the China hands pointed to was the importance of beginning at the Canton Trade Fairs, even if just for the personal relationships it provided.[116] But perhaps the bigger lesson was just how tightly China wanted to control its trade with the United States. As the Boeing sales were celebrated in the United States, they were only one part of China's much larger aviation expansion in the early years of the decade.

A "Mating Dance"

Large industrialists attempting to sell to China came up against the limits of the China market. But importing companies and smaller American exporters emphasized the exoticism of their experiences or they framed the challenges they faced in terms resonant of a hardened frontier masculinity. After attending the 1973 spring fair, for example, businessman Wallace Chavkin wrote an article, published in the *Columbia Journal of World Business,* describing trade with China as "an unfulfilled promise."[117] Chavkin depicted the protracted pace of negotiations as frustrating. American businesspeople needed to show strength when concluding negotiations, he suggested. "Even when, eventually, a deal is about to be closed there is always the possibility that at the last minute a competitor will be given the nod," Chavkin wrote. "That is when the experienced China-trader shows his mettle—it is a bitter pill, but he accepts it without losing heart and prepares to begin again."[118]

In Chavkin's account, US businesspeople needed to be hardened to the experiences of trade, yet he also encouraged them to persist nonetheless. He used his account to bolster a self-image of stoic, resilient masculinity, able to accept the "bitter pill" that might come their way. Even though Chinese corporations chose to work with Chavkin's foreign competitors, this did not dampen his attempts to enter the China market. The China market might be an unfulfilled promise but the truly committed will make it through regardless.

Chavkin found the trade experience challenging, but he extolled the virtues of the people he encountered. "Underlying all thinking about the broader picture of Sino-American trade relations must be a clear understanding of certain basic characteristics of the Chinese people," he wrote. "They are self-reliant and they believe in the old-fashioned virtues of courtesy, respect and forthrightness."[119] In his depiction was only a hint at China's political system: Mao's emphasis on self-reliance.

Martin Klingenberg similarly emphasized the challenges of trade with China. He wrote his first contribution to the advice literature just months after returning from the 1972 spring Canton Trade Fair. A young lawyer from Oklahoma, in 1971 he established his own trade consultancy, the China Trade Association.[120] Given how new the trade with China was for American businesspeople, Klingenberg cultivated an expertise in his writing that aimed not only to assist other businesspeople but also to present himself as an expert and promote his company's services. Writing in the pages of the *Virginia Journal of International Law,* he sought to provide "an analysis and description of what actually happens at the Fair." He hoped, therefore, "to introduce the United States businessman to the Chinese way of doing business."[121]

From the outset, Klingenberg emphasized just how different he felt the China trade was, and he presented the experience as challenging. "The American businessman must understand that the procedures and techniques of doing business with China differ greatly from those familiar to him," he declared. He did not make any mention of China's communism other than to note at the very beginning of his article that the CCP came to power in 1949. The impression he left his readers with was that China was an intriguing nation, worthy of other businesspeople's interests—assuming, he entreated, they were up for the challenge.

Discussing the processes of trade negotiations at the fair, Klingenberg noted that the procedure always began with offers of tea and cigarettes. China's Peony brand cigarettes were especially common. Klingenberg instructed his readers, "If cigarettes are desired they may be smoked; in any case the tea should be accepted." Of this first meeting, Klingenberg explained, "the United States businessman should [have] a totally relaxed attitude since little of significance occurs before the second discussion." It was not until the follow-up meetings that negotiations turned to price. "However," he warned, "the foreign trader should not push the discussion towards price." Even though his trade experience with China had only extended over a few months, Klingenberg commented on what he felt were the characteristics of "the Chinese." They were "extremely skilled negotiators," and American businesspeople needed to be careful not to "force the pace of negotiations." Klingenberg concluded that the process was "fascinating" and "over the long run potentially rewarding."[122] He emphasized long-term profits over short-term ones, making it clear that the excitement trumped immediate economic returns.

Klingenberg's final observations were, however, particularly striking. He ended his article by writing, "Business with the Chinese is a sensuous, slow, formal, highly courteous advance-and-retreat mating dance. When the negotiations are over, the Western businessman knows that he has been up against highly skilled and very shrewd negotiators."[123]

Between the pages of the venerable *Virginia Journal of International Law,* Klingenberg depicted a formal business meeting in lascivious terms—a mating dance no less. That China was no easy conquest increased the thrill. Klingenberg's comments were an entreaty; a salacious hint of what might come from trade with China. As with Howard Hawkins of RCA, Klingenberg presented his Chinese negotiators as talented business-people. They were not, in his depiction, in need of American tutelage.

The rest of Klingenberg's article was written in a noticeably matter-of-fact tone, so this comment stood out. But in some respects, his conclusion was an extension of his argument about the challenges involved in the trading process. The very fact that he presented business with China as difficult allowed Klingenberg to assert his own prowess in conquering the obstacle. The process of writing about what he had learned from that challenge and containing that experience through advice was in itself a means of asserting dominance. The difficulty of the China trade was a central component of its appeal. In his depiction, China was not a communist enemy but a partner—a mating partner in fact—worthy of the challenge.

Marcus Polo at the Trade Fair

The business community's transformation of China into an enticing trading partner worked in tandem with the efforts by US importers and retailers to sell China through references to its ancient past. The fashion diplomacy explored in Chapter 1 positioned the Chinese origins of imported items as a crucial component of their desirability. The advice literature both extended and amplified these ideas. We see this in the example of Stanley Marcus, head of the Dallas-based Neiman-Marcus department stores, who published an article in the *New York Times* after attending the 1972 spring fair. The piece recounted his experiences and served as a veiled advertisement for his company. "Marcus Polo at China Trade Fair: Adventures of a Dallas Executive," the headline trumpeted.[124] Through a punning connection to Marco Polo's thirteenth-century voyages, the title left no doubt of the adventure and discovery Marcus had embarked upon.

Marcus himself opened his article not with Marco Polo but with a different European explorer: Christopher Columbus. The Genovese, who "returned from his first trip to America and expounded on the glories of the New World," stood as a warning against "the temptation to become a China expert after a few days' visit." Marcus was aware of the pitfalls of the overnight expert, but he was less shy about his sense of discovery. "Although the People's Republic of China has done some consumer goods business with Western countries in the past few years, I imagine Neiman-Marcus was the first customer for top-quality merchandise." Of course, European and Japanese merchants had been trading with China for two decades prior to his arrival, but precisely because Marcus operated under a fiction of discovery his excitement and sense of the exotic were rendered more visible.

Marcus wrote of the "ancient Chinese" and noted that "in the majority of instances a price was calculated on the abacus."[125] It was the ancient China he played up in his advertising to US customers too. He spent over $20,000 on antiques during his time at the Canton Trade Fair, buying jade carvings; silk wall hangings in rich reds, purples, and blues; porcelain; jewelry; and an entire collection of robes, some over 200 years old.[126]

Upon returning to Dallas, he hosted a cocktail party at his home for the Texas elite on a balmy September evening. Waiters in coattails circulated trays of champagne as guests admired Marcus's recent purchases. He placed the antiques on display throughout the many rooms of his home. Lloyd Stewart, columnist for the local *Fort Worth Star-Telegram* reported on the evening, breathlessly noting that there had been "necklaces of twisted silver filigree, so fine that the beads looked as if they were made of spun sugar."[127] In a similar vein, the *Dallas Morning News* described the party as invoking "picture book visions of the Imperial Court in Peking 100 years and more ago."[128]

One of the centerpieces of the event was a large, embroidered bedspread. It was spun using threads in an imperial yellow that only the emperor had been permitted to use, Dallas readers were told. The bedspread was lined with gold silk thread and it featured a circular moon gate pattern in its center.[129] Bracelets made of agate, jade, ivory, or gold were sold hours before the party ended. The following month, Marcus hosted similar parties in Houston and Atlanta. When the unsold antiques were finally placed on the shelves of the Neiman-Marcus department store in Dallas, they came close to selling out within five hours of opening.[130] Texas consumers scrambled to be among the first to buy the unique items. Recalling this frenzy three years later, Marcus described how it had confirmed his initial hunch that, even in the South, Americans in the early 1970s were "hungry for anything that was Chinese."[131]

While Marcus was able to cultivate an excitement among his wealthy Texan and Georgian customers, not all his clients shared the same enthusiasm. In May he received a handwritten note from Richard Smythe, one of his Dallas customers. Enclosed in the letter was Smythe's wife's credit card to the Neiman-Marcus department store. Smythe's note was short and to the point. He instructed Marcus, "Please cancel our account effective the same date that you start selling communist merchandise in your stores."[132] Despite the fanfare following Nixon's February visit, China was still Red in the eyes of many Americans. In his memoir, Marcus later described himself as a "pro-United Nations liberal" thriving in "rigidly conservative" Dallas.[133]

Marcus bought from China in order to capitalize on consumer excitement, but he himself also felt the excitement. Captivated CEOs expressing the excitement they tried to cultivate in their consumers was, in fact, commonplace among the newly minted China hands. During his trip back to Guangzhou for the Canton Trade Fair in November, Marcus was so excited about his recent purchases that he tried on one of the robes he had bought, posing for a photograph in his hotel room. His Polaroid picture captured an earnest thrill amid the flurry of the fair, recalling an earlier portrait of the nineteenth-century artist James McNeill Whistler. Whistler too had donned a robe for his portrait.[134] Separated by more than a century, the two men posed in their robes upon an impulse that had long been part of Americans' pull toward Chinese culture: to appropriate it as their own.[135]

Yet Marcus also expressed considerable frustration at his experience of trading with China. Chinese traders were "unaware of the characteristics of the free market," Marcus claimed. Compounding the problems was "the Westerner's lack of understanding of how the Chinese do busi-

Figure 2.4. Stanley Marcus snapped a quick Polaroid photograph of himself wearing a two-thousand-year-old robe in his Guangzhou hotel room, November 1972.

ness."[136] After Marcus attended the fall trade fair, his enthusiasm continued to wear off. By May 1973 he wrote a letter to his supplier complaining about a recent arrival of antiques, "We've just received a shipment of antiques . . . it's interesting to note that the 'honest' Chinese delivered several carved pieces with mismatched tops." Some of the vases had lids that were of the wrong color, and a large jade object arrived with cracks through it. Marcus concluded, "Of course there's nothing that can be done except to be more careful with the Chinese next time."[137]

But Marcus was soon to discover further limits on the China trade. He declined the Chinese invitation to attend the 1973 fall Canton Trade Fair after his disappointing shipments, and he did not receive subsequent invitations. To refuse an invitation once was to find that they would be far harder to come by again. Even with these challenges, Marcus continued to stock Chinese antiques in his stores throughout the decade, employing a third-party trader based in Hong Kong to help him purchase the goods. Selling an enticing and ancient China to Texan customers, Stanley Marcus shaped the much larger cultural process in which China was transformed from the Red China threat some of his customers still continued to fear, to instead an amicable trade partner. It would not be long before another cultural shift began to emerge alongside this: one in which an exotic China helped sell everyday items made in China.

The New China Hands

The new generation of US China hands helped create a culture and community through the very act of writing their advice. Throughout the decade "doing business with China" became a ubiquitous phrase, reflecting the practical yet prescriptive approach many of the authors adopted.[138] The authority claimed by American China hands and the trading culture that developed among them was underpinned by gendered and racial notions of who was deemed an expert. Businesswomen and Chinese Americans were less likely than their white male counterparts to compose books or articles lecturing on the trading process.[139] Nonetheless, businesswomen were highly visible in newspapers and magazines. Many were importers of goods such as clothing and tea, which newspapers used to present an exotic appeal to readers. In the main, Chinese Americans were less visible in printed media despite being some of the most successful US businesspeople throughout the decade.

Eleanor Lambert, who worked as a fashion consultant, was one of six women who traveled to Guangzhou for the spring 1972 fair, where she purchased fabrics to sell to designers back in the United States. She returned with linen and embroidered silks. Some of the linen came in gold, grape, and emerald. "They would make marvellous gowns for the couture," she told the *New York Times*. "Even their everyday china and linens are absolutely lovely."[140] A decade earlier, Lambert had worked with the ILGWU to encourage female consumers to buy union-made clothing, creating a series of advertisements associating union products with high-end fashion.[141] Her purchases in 1972, rather than touting goods produced by American workers, promoted the highbrow Chinese gowns and household porcelain, encouraging American consumers to adopt a more positive view of China. But she continued to do the cultural work of associating China with quality.

Francine Farkas, vice president of Alexander's department store, also attended the 1972 fair and spoke to a number of journalists about her experiences. She explained that over the course of her ten days at the fair she had been taken aback by both the quality of the items on display and their prices. She had been expecting to order low-priced goods, "but I shopped two price levels higher because of the superior quality of the goods available." She bought kimonos and silk shirts as well as jewelry, porcelain vases, and carved jade, all of which were soon to be displayed in the department store's New York branches.[142]

Farkas saw her buying mission as carrying more than just economic benefit. To the *New York Times,* she observed, "I feel that through trade we can open other doors." She understood her own actions and those of the other Americans at the fair as creating the people-to-people ties Nixon so lauded. "Every business conversation is at least 50 percent talk of friendship," she recounted. Certainly many of the Chinese references to friendship and connections—or *guanxi*—would have reflected an emphasis on seeing trade as a long-term development. The idea that China preferred to trade with "old friends" circulated in the stories foreigners shared at the fair and would soon make its way into the advice literature some businesspeople began to write.

Veronica Yhap, owner of Dragon Lady Traders, was one of the few women who contributed to the business advice literature, doing so in audio form. In 1976 she participated in an interview with Julian Sobin, president of Sobin Chemicals. Sobin interviewed twenty-four business-people in 1976 and 1977, and he recorded and collated the interviews into a twelve-hour audiocassette package, *The China Trader.* The cassettes hit the market in January 1978. For a hefty $300, listeners could hear first-hand accounts of trade with China. Advertisements touted the interviews as revealing "the context and practicalities of doing business with the People's Republic of China."[143] The interviews were conversational, providing extraordinary and candid insight into the experiences of the chosen businesspeople and their companies. Of all the interviews Sobin conducted, only one person was Chinese American and only one a woman. Both exceptions pertained to Veronica Yhap.

Sobin began by asking Yhap a number of personal questions, none of which he posed to the businessmen he interviewed. "May I ask if you are married," he inquired at one stage. When she answered in the affirmative, he added, "How do you think a husband should feel about a wife going to the fair alone with all those men?" To this Yhap responded, "That's a very chauvinistic comment to begin with, right? Nobody would ever ask you that question, nobody would ever think about asking the wife that question, right? How do you feel about it that your husband travels so much?" Part of Yhap's exasperation was that these questions came after nearly fifteen minutes of interview that had not touched on the topic of trade. "Do you feel really Chinese," he probed at one point. "No, I don't," she responded. After a pause, she continued:

YHAP: I feel completely American. In fact, I really feel that I am a New Yorker more than anything else.

SOBIN: But I can't really believe this. I have the feeling that the Chinese have Chinese blood and that they have a Chinese cultural frame of reference for ten generations starting before you and after you.

YHAP: But that's all gone.

SOBIN: Isn't it reasonable for me to think that you have a different, much closer perspicacity, and sensitivity to the subtleties of the Chinese behavior with each other than I do, for example?

YHAP: In terms of language, yes.

SOBIN: No, even if you spoke in English.

YHAP: No. First of all I can't really imagine what it would be like speaking English to the Chinese in China. I think the language really helped me a lot . . . but basically the culture is completely different. Our values are completely different. I mean, I left so young . . . and then having gone to college in this country, my whole background, my cultural background is completely different with the exception of my language.

SOBIN: It's easy for me to see you're a capitalist. You look very distinguished and you look very chic, very debonair.

Yhap was one of the most successful American businesspeople to trade with China. As we explored in Chapter 1, she was one of the first Americans to travel to the Canton Trade Fair in the fall of 1971, alongside only two other US traders. Sobin opened the interview acknowledging Yhap's experiences and considerable understanding of the China market. "You've probably done more than any other individual to establish premade Chinese fashion goods in the United States," he began. But before even allowing time for her to respond, he added, "You're an American citizen aren't you?" Sobin dwelled on Yhap's heritage and marital status for nearly half the interview. He eventually turned to the pragmatics of trade but spent significantly less time discussing them with her than he did with the twenty-three businessmen he interviewed.[144]

Two years earlier Yhap had participated in an interview with Arleen Posner from the National Council for US-China Relations. The contrast between the two interviews was stark. Yhap spoke with Posner for an educational program Posner ran called China Conversations. The series focused on a range of topics aimed at introducing American listeners to aspects of contemporary Chinese life. The Broadcasting Foundation of America distributed her tapes to libraries, schools, and radio stations.

"I think to the average importer looking at the China market, it's quite a puzzle," Posner observed to Yhap. "Perhaps you could tell us what the first thing an American importer should do if he wishes to buy from the People's Republic of China." Posner gave Yhap the time and space to explain the processes of trade to listeners—the majority of whom might well have fit the pronoun Posner used. Yhap made clear the importance of beginning by writing to Chinese representatives to initiate the relationship. In the letter, the American businessperson should introduce their company and details about what they wished to buy. "Be as concise as possible," Yhap counseled. "It's always better to have the letter translated into Chinese," she added. This was not just a matter of courtesy; otherwise, Yhap explained, the letter would "sit on the translators' desk for a long time before it gets passed down to the concerned department."[145]

In her advice, Veronica Yhap did not emphasize the exotic nature of trade with China. She instead focused on the pragmatics of the process. Of the new China hands that emerged during the 1970s, Yhap would go on to become one of the most innovative and successful, even if her white male counterparts did not readily listen to her advice. While she did not frame her advice in terms of a rediscovered China, she and her business partners at Dragon Lady Traders certainly sold items from China by advertising them as ancient. They would soon use this consumer interest to additionally sell everyday clothing items, where the only exotic connection to China were labels declaring "Dragon Lady Traders, Made in China."

AS TRADE BETWEEN the United States and China reopened and goods started to flow in both directions across the Pacific Ocean, American businesspeople found themselves competing with foreign businesspeople who had been trading with China for years. At the Canton Trade Fairs, Americans were confronted with both the scale of competition and the limits Chinese businesspeople placed on their foreign trade. Even as Chinese leaders expanded their overall foreign trade, they only reluctantly turned to American companies to fulfill their needs. And the major sales that US companies did complete—airplanes from Boeing, satellites from RCA, and wheat from US farmers—were only one component of a much larger buying spree China conducted. Chinese pragmatists were pushing through an agenda of expanded overall foreign trade—what would become the 4-3 Program by 1973—but the United States remained only a small part of these efforts.

Many US businesspeople interpreted the challenges they faced as part of a larger adventure that China trade offered them. In the advice they wrote for one another, they fueled a fiction of discovery that placed the United States at the center of a new trade frontier. They did not speculate that trade would spur social or political change in China. Earlier generations of American traders had hoped that trade might lead to social or political change in China, but the new generation of the 1970s did not understand their efforts in this way. Their writing instead assisted a cultural shift within the United States. They built upon cultural trends within the United States that were reconceptualizing China as no longer a Cold War foe but instead an amicable trade partner. The striking absence of the term "communism" within the literature both reflected and assisted this much larger conceptual transformation. These new China hands asserted expertise, yet the practice of trade was largely *out* of their hands. It was Chinese traders—and Chinese leaders in Beijing—who determined whether or not trade deals were made.

CHAPTER 3

The Changing Meanings
of the China Market

"SURGING TRADE WITH CHINA," a *New York Times* headline declared in December 1973.[1] After little more than two years, China trade had surpassed even the most optimistic expectations of observers in the United States. In February China purchased $78 million of cotton from the Texas-based Plains Cotton Cooperative Association; in July it purchased $500,000 worth of US tobacco; in August, China received $150 million worth of Boeing 707 airplanes, in a deal signed the previous year.[2] By the end of 1973, sales of American goods to China were nearly twelve times higher than in 1972. Just a year earlier, the House majority and minority leaders, Thomas Boggs (D, LA) and Gerald Ford (R, MI), had recently returned from a tour of China, and they reported that trade would develop "slowly."[3] In March 1973, Assistant Secretary of State Marshall Green predicted that the year's trade might reach around $200 million.[4] But by late 1973, their estimates had fallen way short. Total trade jumped to $805 million, up from $95 million a year earlier.[5]

These unexpectedly high figures engendered an excitement among many US businesspeople who saw potential fortunes to be made in China. The high-profile sales of aircraft and agricultural goods made the prospects of trade with China alluring and journalists jumped on this message. The *Washington Post* promised its readers that the aircraft sale was only the beginning: "other deals would follow Boeing-China deal."[6] The *Chicago Tribune* announced of the cotton sales, "Big Chinese Order for

U.S. Cotton Spurs Trade Prospects."[7] Of the tobacco sales, the Department of Agriculture shared in the zeal. "This may represent a breakthrough in tobacco trade," a report declared.[8] Reading such accounts from his home in Louisiana, Democrat John Rarick, known for his staunch anti-communism, later complained in Congress, "Many American businesses are currently looking toward Communist China with dollar signs twinkling in their eyes, dreaming of making a buck from the Chinese."[9] In his estimation, China still had the communist qualifier.

After only two and a half years, trade with China appeared to be thriving, even if it constituted just a tiny fraction of the United States' overall trade figures. But it unfolded just as the wider economic landscape in the United States became increasingly fraught. The two shocks of 1971 might have given Nixon the boost to beat George McGovern in the 1972 presidential election, but it was a short-lived reprieve. Throughout the year, organized labor groups continued their fights against rising unemployment and imports. As 1973 came to a close, the United States experienced its third consecutive trade deficit for the twentieth century. Moreover, the OPEC oil embargo sent the price of oil sky high, quadrupling it by early 1974.

The news coming out on US-China trade seemed to buck the wider trend toward decline in the United States. Yet it was too new and uncertain to offer any substantive respite to the ailing economy. The China market of the late nineteenth century had promised to absorb American overproduction and alleviate economic crisis, but in the early 1970s China trade—and what it represented to US businesspeople—was less straightforward than the media reporting suggested.[10]

While the excited headlines extolled the China market as one that received US goods, they belied the tensions among and between US businesspeople and labor leaders. What, exactly, did this newly reopened China market mean for the US economy? Answers varied. Many large American corporations saw opportunities to sell to China, but not all businesspeople shared this vision. Smaller importers turned to China as a source of consumer products and, eventually, cheap labor. Union leaders, too, debated the implications of the newly opening trade with China. Manufacturing industries, especially textiles, saw China as a new threat joining an already rising tide of imports. But dockworkers, especially on the West Coast, saw potential wealth to be made from the arrival of Chinese goods shipped across the Pacific Ocean.

In these opening years, the meanings of the China market were uncertain. One thing, however, was becoming clear to US businesspeople whether they were exporting grain or importing chemicals: the United States needed to buy more Chinese goods. Between 1972 and 1974 the United States sold far more to China than it bought. American exporters may have celebrated the unexpected windfall that came from their agricultural and technology sales, but China sent a number of signals—both explicit and suggestive—that this could not last unless American purchases of Chinese goods also increased. In these early contestations over what trade would look like, the interests of Chinese traders and US importers began to converge. American businesspeople needed to see the China market, both argued, as a place not just to sell goods but also to buy them.

The Kellogg Sale and the 4-3 Program

On the surface, Carl Crow's articulation of the China market as one of 400 million customers started to reemerge in the early 1970s. Boeing's 1972 sale of ten 707s heralded this message, and by September 1973 a sale of eight fertilizer factories reinforced it. The M. W. Kellogg Company, a Houston-based engineering firm, signed $290 million in contracts to sell eight ammonia fertilizer plants to the China National Technical Import Corporation (Techimport), one of the PRC's eight state-owned corporations.[11] Kellogg's deal with Techimport included knowledge transfer too.[12] Under the agreement, Kellogg engineers from the United States would travel to China to help set up the fertilizer factories at the eight locations in China. In addition to these big-ticket items, in 1973 China purchased US wheat, corn, soybeans, and cotton in unprecedented amounts—wheat was the single largest commodity the United States sold to China in this year. Together these deals suggested that the China market was not only reemerging but also starting to fulfill its promise of wealth.

Kellogg executives celebrated the deal as much for the diplomatic breakthrough they saw it representing as for the economic boon. In late November 1973 they hosted ten technicians from Techimport who flew from Beijing to Houston to celebrate the deal. At the reception held in the upmarket Hotel Warick, Clark P. Latten Jr., Kellogg's president, toasted their success. "We as individuals are participants in a very important and historical event," he contended. The deal "may be remembered far longer

Figure 3.1. The front-page photo of W. M. Kellogg's magazine celebrated delegates from Techimport who visited Kellogg's Houston headquarters in November 1973.

than the eight ammonia plants." To his mind, their arrangement was "the beginning of a new era of friendship between the United States and the People's Republic of China." And more importantly, he continued, it was "evidence" of the "basic agreements reached between the leaders of our two great nations."[13] Latten saw his company as enacting US political aims of building people-to-people ties. The Chinese delegation's visit was featured on the front page of Kellogg's corporate newspaper, accompanied by a large photo of the delegates and Kellogg executives.

Carl Chang and Chester Wang, engineers at Kellogg, would have received the company newsletter like the hundreds of other workers at the company. They would have seen the photograph announcing the deal and celebrating the Techimport delegation's arrival. They would have had to turn to the back page, though, to see any acknowledgment of their own involvement in the sale. Tucked into one of the final paragraphs, the newsletter listed their names among over a dozen others. "Carl Chang of process engineering, and Chester Wang of heat transfer, served as translators at home office and at site visits," the newsletter read.[14] As Chang and Wang accompanied the Chinese engineers, they used not only their language skills but also their expertise in chemical engineering, because part of their job was to explain to their Chinese visitors how the equipment worked. They were what historian Mae Ngai describes as "cultural brokers," mediating between Chinese engineers and Kellogg bosses.[15]

Chang and Wang would have spent more time with the Chinese visitors than almost any other Kellogg employee, although no one would have known this from reading the corporate newsletter.

Despite the corporation's fanfare, the Kellogg fertilizer plants made up only eight of more than a hundred turnkey plants that China had purchased from foreign suppliers since 1971. Since Lin Biao's death in September 1971, China had increasingly turned to capitalist nations for technology imports. By January 2, 1973, Mao approved a technology import plan that consolidated these efforts, which the State Council passed in March 22. Yu Qiuli, director of the State Planning Commission, submitted a report to the Politburo outlining plans for purchasing complete industrial factories and equipment in the chemical, steel, fertilizer, and fiber industries. The "Report and Request for Increasing Equipment Imports and Expanding Economic Exchange" was dubbed the "4-3 Program" for its total cost of $4.3 billion. The massive initiative involved imports of 43 coal mine facilities and huge industrial projects, including a $600 million steel plant for the Wuhan Steel Works.[16]

Lin Hujia, vice director of the State Planning Commission, described the logic of the 4-3 Program to the Politburo. "Should we eat two million metric tons of imported wheat or buy ten chemical fertilizer plants?" Lin asked. "I believe that we all agree to buy the ten fertilizer plants."[17] The aim was to accelerate China's industrialization through imports that would help meet its development needs. In addition to Kellogg, China turned to foreign companies across the globe, especially those in Japan, France, the United Kingdom, and Sweden. By the end of 1974, Machimpex and Techimport had signed some forty-five contracts with companies from advanced capitalist nations; Kellogg was one of only a few US-based companies included in the deals.[18]

With the 4-3 Program, then, Chinese pragmatists seemed to reinforce the idea that the newly reopened China market would provide US capitalists with opportunities for sales. But a crucial component of the 4-3 Program was to find ways to pay for the imports without incurring foreign debt. Here Chinese exports were particularly important. They would provide much of the cash needed to fund the import program. In November 1972, Vice Premier Li Xiannian called for China to "increase the number of exported material," especially arts and handicrafts, which could be used to increase foreign exchange.[19] Li would go on to play an important role in China's reform and opening in the 1980s. Following Li's statement, by April 1973 the State Council sent an order to both the

Ministry of Foreign Trade and the Ministry of Light Industry demanding that they expand factory and workshop outputs in order to fund foreign imports.[20]

Chen Yun similarly pushed for new ways to fund China's industrialization efforts. In October 1973 he suggested to the Ministry of Foreign Trade that China use its "abundant domestic workers to produce goods for export." Cotton textiles were a particularly good source of exports, Chen argued. "We have labor and can generate foreign exchange earnings for the country. This is, in the final analysis, to speed up the country's industrial construction."[21] Chen had been a key figure in China's economic development programs of the 1950s but had been ousted during the Cultural Revolution. Like many of China's economic planners, Chen was rehabilitated to the Politburo in the early 1970s. He would eventually go on to play a leading role in the early stages of China's reform and opening of the 1980s.[22]

Chen positioned Chinese labor at the heart of China's development. "There are many Chinese people," he reminded those gathered from the Ministry of Foreign Trade. Using this labor force to accumulate foreign trade earnings "is easy to understand." As far as he saw it, none of what he proposed contravened Mao's principle of *zili gengsheng,* or self-reliance. "We have to insist on self-reliance," he asserted, but foreign trade could contribute to this.

Even as pragmatists like Chen and Li promoted the importation of technology to further China's development, the China market they envisaged was not only a place for foreign countries to sell to. Instead, the China market, in Chen and Li's estimation, was driven by Chinese exports, too. For Chen in particular, China's development would rely upon a China market that was underpinned by its 800 million workers.

"WHAT CAN YOU Expect in China?" the cover story of *Industry Week*'s July 1973 magazine asked. Readers were faced with a man in suit and tie sitting in a Chinese restaurant. His mouth was agape and he was holding a single chopstick in each hand, balancing a piece of apple pie precariously between them. Using his chopsticks incorrectly while consuming apple pie and drinking tea from porcelain cups, the jocular businessman was enjoying himself; expect to do so too, the magazine suggested.

The accompanying article, written by William Miller, reported on the Canton Trade Fair, China's major trade event held twice a year in Guang-

Figure 3.2. "What can you expect in China?" A white, middle-aged corporate executive demonstrates to *Industry Week* readers the exotic appeal of trade with the PRC—an appeal that promised the symbolic and literal familiarity of apple pie.

zhou. "If your company receives one of the coveted invitations from the People's Republic of China to attend the Canton Trade Fair . . . you may or may not find it worthwhile from a business standpoint," Miller wrote by way of introduction. "But you'll like the apple pie they serve you in Canton. It could be the best you've ever eaten." Miller did not explain why profitability would be unpredictable. His article did not deal with the practicalities of business itself. Rather, he emphasized the adventure of the fair: the apple pies and the hotel facilities. "The only certainty is that your business trip there will be different from any you've made before," he assured.[23] The image of Miller eating apple pie suggested Americans would still find the comfort of familiarity alongside the novelty of chopsticks. Miller's China market had more to do with tourism than profit.

Miller wrote of "swarms of bicycles and pushcarts . . . parting occa-
sionally for a rare automobile"; of "teams of women" who "busily sweep
the pavement"; of "uniformed children [who] march in cadence behind a
teacher who seems to double as a drill sergeant." Miller also described
Chinese domestic life. "Inside the small homes and apartments, beneath
portraits of Chairman Mao, families also seem to be constantly eating,
belying the popular notion that the 800 million citizens of the world's
most populous nation are hungry."[24] The China that Miller described was
the one that the CCP cultivated for their foreign visitors.

Miller referenced the Mao portraits inside homes, but he was less interested in China's political system than in presenting a world in which
an American businessperson would have an enjoyable time. "If nothing
else," he concluded, "a visit to China provides a respite from the cares of
home." The Watergate scandal exploded during his week in China: four
of the president's closest aides resigned, which Nixon announced in a dramatic televised address to the nation. Miller did not know about these
events until he arrived in Hong Kong and bought an English-language
newspaper. Leaving Guangzhou meant going "back to reality," Miller
wrote.[25] Life at the trade fairs was otherworldly, he suggested. There were
hints of China's communism in his descriptions of the marching students
and Mao portraits, but they were rendered unthreatening and simply part
of the welcome reprieve China trade provided from the capitalist "reality."

The trade-tourism that Miller advertised was precisely the problem for
Chinese officials. By the 1973 fall Canton Trade Fair—the fourth since
the Shanghai communiqué—the number of American businesspeople invited to China was determined much more directly by the extent to which
they were willing to buy. Some companies that had previously been invited did not receive invitations this time around because of the small
amount of goods they purchased at earlier fairs.[26] Still, many Chinese
traders complained that numerous US businesspeople at the 1973 fairs
had continued to be more interested in "sightseeing" than commerce.[27]
For their part, American importers complained that the prices of antiques
at the spring fair had doubled and in some cases tripled.[28] Some businesspeople told the New York Times that "the shock" of these price increases
had prompted them to declare they were "finished with the Canton Fair."[29]

Hollywood actress Shirley McLean reported having had similar sentiments when she visited the 1973 spring trade fair during a tour of China
she led in April. "I watched the Chinese deal with the Arab, French, Italian,
and American merchants," she recalled later in a best-selling book. The

foreigners seemed "continuously impatient over deals that had gone wrong, took too much time, or had become too expensive." For their part, "the Chinese looked on blandly as their interpreters explained the objections, and then leaned back, almost patronizingly, to smoke their cigarettes."[30]

Other US importers fared much better at the 1973 fall fair. They detected hints of change from their Chinese counterparts—a direct result of the 4-3 Program Mao had approved. Chinese textile company Chinatex discussed with a number of foreign businesspeople the possibilities of manufacturing goods according to foreign companies' designs and specifications. "China is now seriously considering manufacturing for export, to specification," the National Council for US-China Trade advised US business leaders.[31] Around this time Bob Boulonge and Robert Gill, executives from J. C. Penney, reached a $2.5 million deal with Chinatex for towels. The Chinese corporation would brand the towels with a single label that read "J. C. Penney, Made in China." Usually, Chinatex stitched in two labels—the Chinese brand and the foreign brand. Penney's other apparel purchases from China, including shirts, would still have the double labeling system, but the changes to the towels augured well for the retailer's future inventories.[32]

These changes came at a time when senior Chinese economists debated the role of manufactured cotton goods in China's foreign trade. In 1973, Chen Yun seized on the fact that the international price of raw cotton was much lower than the price of manufactured cotton goods. Even though China's cotton yields were severely depleted, they could still import cotton and maintain self-reliance by exporting the more lucrative manufactured cotton goods.[33]

The towels that Bob Boulogne and Robert Gill purchased were produced as part of the wider changes Chen and other pragmatists were experimenting with. By agreeing to sew single labels onto the towels, Chinatex was responding to Beijing's interest in increasing sales of domestically produced cotton goods using imported cotton. Chinatex was also responding to Penney's requirements—the single labels made it easier to sell the towels to American consumers. Penney executives hoped that Chinatex might start to put single labels on other textiles too, making the China market even more appealing.

JUST OVER A year after signing the Shanghai communiqué, a number of key institutional changes emerged to assist the unfolding trade relationship.

First, the Nixon administration established a new institution in Washington to support the China trade: the National Council for US-China Trade. On March 22, 1973, twenty men from some of the nation's largest corporations met with officials from the State and Commerce Departments in Washington, DC, for the National Council's first meeting. Bureaucrats from the State and Commerce Departments had handpicked the businessmen, who hailed from such corporate giants as Boeing, Hewlett-Packard, Cargill, and Chase Manhattan Bank.[34] Donald Burnham, chairman of Westinghouse Electric Corporation, served as the National Council's first chairman. David Rockefeller, president of Chase Manhattan Bank, and William Hewitt, president of Deere and Co., joined Burnham as vice chairmen. The National Council was to serve as a nongovernmental counterpart to China's CCPIT.[35] Even though the National Council had close ties to government, it did not receive federal funding; instead, its operations were financed through membership fees.

A few months later, the National Council's executive committee chose Christopher Phillips as its president. Phillips was a career diplomat and had been working as deputy ambassador to George Bush at the United Nations during the time when the China seat was switched from Taiwan to the PRC. Phillips was the only diplomat in the National Council's leadership team; his colleagues were all corporate executives. With Phillips at the helm, the State and Commerce departments hoped the National Council would traverse both the diplomatic and corporate realms. In fact, its headquarters were in Washington rather than New York, the trade and financial heart of the nation. But other than Phillips, the leaders in the National Council were titans of American industrial capitalism.

Of the twenty men on the founding executive committee, two (David Rockefeller from Chase Manhattan Bank and Richard Wheeler from First National City Bank) were heads of financial firms, and one (Walter Surrey from Surrey, Karasik and Morse) came from a law firm. The remaining seventeen executives were heads of industrial manufacturing corporations. These businessmen saw the China market as a site for exports. Only one member of the National Council's initial board came from a company with importing interests: Kurt Reinsberg from the New York–based firm Associated Metals and Minerals Corporation. This export-focused outlook soon became a source of tension among the members of the newly inaugurated National Council.

Around the time the National Council was established, the United States and China established new diplomatic institutions as well. In July the two countries opened liaison offices in Beijing and Washington, a sign that ties were strengthening. These offices were not embassies, but they did provide a means of diplomatic communication between the two governments: the early stages of institutionalized political contact. The relationship with China was gaining momentum, yet Nixon was preoccupied with the unfolding Watergate scandal. He was facing increasing pressure to release the tapes of secret White House conversations, which the media had disclosed around the same time as the liaison offices and the National Council were established.

As the United States and China celebrated the opening of the liaison offices, the US Commerce Department also announced it would be opening a trade center in Taiwan. Commerce Secretary Frederick Dent described the new center as "a symbol of our commitment to strong economic ties with the Republic of China and a concrete action for facilitating the sale of American goods on a continuing basis."[36] Some Taiwan officials, however, were concerned that the trade center would one day replace the US embassy in Taiwan. They worried that trade would replace diplomatic recognition as the main glue joining the two societies.[37]

Compounding Taiwan's concerns was the fact that Secretary of State William Rodgers did not accompany Commerce Secretary Dent to Taipei. The two men had visited Japan and South Korea together, but when Dent visited Taiwan, Rodgers returned home to the United States. The island's English-language newspaper, *China News,* was outraged at Secretary Rodgers's absence. "How is it that the United States has political matters to discuss with the Japanese and Koreans but not with us?" the newspaper's editorial asked. Now that the United States was developing its political relationship with the PRC, it asked, "are we to be classed as apolitical?"[38] Their fears were confirmed when, by the end of the year, the State Department had imposed an informal ban on any meetings between the president or secretary of state and Taiwan's leaders.[39]

By the middle of 1973, then, the United States and China had established new economic and diplomatic institutions, both providing formal avenues for expanding the trade relationship. In Taipei, however, the new American trade center raised concerns that their diplomatic ties would be replaced with a relationship based more singularly on trade.

The third key institutional change in US-China trade occurred in June 1973. As Eugene Theroux and Christopher Phillips began to set up the National Council, the organization's new vice chairman, David Rockefeller, flew to Beijing in the hope of expanding financial ties with

China. Rockefeller, head of Chase Manhattan Bank and brother to New York governor Nelson Rockefeller, arrived in China on June 22 for a ten-day trip with five other Chase executives.[40] Traveling on behalf of Chase and the National Council, Rockefeller flew to China as both banker and diplomat. In fact, he additionally represented the Council on Foreign Relations, Rockefeller University, and the Museum of Modern Art, in which he held leadership roles.[41]

Rockefeller's ties to China had long familial roots. His father, John D. Rockefeller, had traded with China in the late nineteenth century. In the 1920s Chase National Bank had been the official supplier of private finance for Soviet trade too.[42] Since 1971 Chase Manhattan had handled the finances of the China mission to the United Nations.[43]

Over the course of his stay, Rockefeller met with Chen Xiyu, the newly appointed head of the Bank of China. After years of instability during the Cultural Revolution, the Bank of China was beginning to strengthen its relations with foreign nations. Just one month before Rockefeller's arrival, for example, Bank of China representatives led by Ken Tao-ming, General manager of the People's Insurance Company, left China for a six-week tour of Albania, Algeria, Lebanon, and the United Kingdom. During their tour of the Middle East and the United Kingdom, the Chinese bankers met with financial leaders and businesspeople and toured banking facilities.[44]

When Chen and Rockefeller met in June, Chen indicated that the Bank of China was interested in establishing a relationship with Chase. He suggested that Chase Manhattan Bank and the Bank of China could create the first correspondent financial relations between the United States and China. This would allow for reciprocal, yet limited, financial transactions to occur between the two countries. "I lost no time in accepting the proposal," Rockefeller recalled later in his memoirs.[45] In addition to handling the finances of the Chinese UN mission, Chase Manhattan was now also the first US bank to establish correspondent banking relations with China.[46] This meant that Chase could now work with the Bank of China to assist US companies buying and selling with China.

However, the correspondent banking relations were hindered by legal technicalities. Financial transactions between the United States and China needed to be facilitated by a bank in a third country. If an American company or citizen wanted to send money to the Bank of China, Chase would need to turn to one of its branches in another nation, such as the UK, Japan, or Germany. That nation's branch would then send the money it had received from Chase onward to the Bank of China. Some US businesspeople also turned directly to the third-country bank themselves. For example, Italy's Banca Nazionale del Lavaro handled transactions for US importers and exporters in its New York branch and dealt directly with the Bank of China.[47]

The need for third-country banking was compelled by a problem referred to as the claims/assets dispute. The dispute began during the Korean War. On December 16, 1950, in response to China's entry into the war, President Harry Truman imposed a complete embargo on trade with China, cutting off all commerce entirely. Truman additionally directed the Treasury Department to block and freeze the financial assets of Chinese citizens that were held in US banks, meaning they could not be withdrawn and they also stopped accumulating interest. Less than two weeks later, Chinese premier Zhou Enlai responded with a directive for local authorities to seize all property held by US citizens in China. Schools, churches, hospitals, and homes owned by Americans living in China thus became the property of the Chinese Communist Party.[48]

For over twenty years, Chinese investments in the United States did not accrue interest, leading to millions of dollars of losses. The American citizens who owned private property in China likewise faced huge losses. Legally, the claims/assets dispute raised problems for the flow of both capital and goods. If goods came directly to either country, they would be seized and used as retribution for the unresolved dispute.[49] Thus, for example, a shipment of cotton pants could not enter American waters directly from the PRC and instead needed to be carried on third-country ships. Similar limitations applied to financial transactions—they could not be directly handled by US or Chinese banks.

The dispute remained unresolved at the start of the 1970s, but Rockefeller was unfazed by the legal hurdles they raised. Indeed, he speculated that his success augured well for a quick resolution of the claims/assets dispute. Speaking to journalists in Hong Kong after his meetings with Chen Xiyu, he stated, "The expectation on both sides is that the problem will be resolved within a matter of weeks." After that resolution, he noted that "we expect to handle a full range of services in the U.S. for the Bank of China."[50] His hopes were ambitious, but by November it did seem to US policymakers that the claims/assets dispute might finally be close to resolution. Kissinger had flown to Beijing to further discuss movements toward normalization, and by the end of the year he and Zhou reached an in-principle agreement to settle the dispute.[51]

Upon his return to the United States, David Rockefeller put pen to paper and published his reflections on the trip in the *New York Times*. "Whatever the price of the Chinese Revolution," he wrote, "it has obviously succeeded not only in producing more efficient and dedicated administration, but also in fostering high morale and community of purpose."[52]

Rockefeller's musings came at a time when he himself was concerned about the impact that new leftist movements in the United States were having on the corporate world. In 1971 he had dismissed these movements. "Since the early writings of Karl Marx," he wrote, "critics have been predicting the demise of the corporation and the downfall of the American business system."[53] Just a few months before he left for China, he brooded that "capitalism today, as frequently in the past, is the object of strident criticism." But in the end, he concluded, capitalism would be saved by its "inherent strength and flexibility."[54] As far as Rockefeller was concerned, the solution to the anticapitalist movements was to develop corporate social responsibility. Corporations, not governments, should provide the answers to the demands social reformers were calling for—a viewpoint that was central to the emerging neoliberal order.[55] Rockefeller fought to defend capitalism in the United States, but he turned also to China as a source of profit. As far as he was concerned, it was not communist China that threatened the capitalist system, it was the American left.

Taiwan's Trade Imbalance and "Buy American"

As Taiwan watched with concern the development of trade and diplomatic ties between the United States and China, its leaders implemented programs that emphasized the long-standing friendship it shared with the United States. In the early 1970s Taiwan held a significant trade imbalance with the United States. Unlike America's trade with China, however, the imbalance was in Taiwan's favor. In 1973 the United States imported $724 million more than it sold to Taiwan.[56] In a signal of goodwill, Taipei began to lessen the trade imbalance by increasing its purchases from the United States. Unaware of the secret discussions in which Kissinger had indicated to Zhou that the US would reject a two-China solution, Taiwan's leaders remained hopeful that some form of two-China solution could be reached.[57] At the same time that Taipei worried its relationship with the

United States would be reduced to one centered on trade rather than diplomacy, its leaders hoped that positive trade relations could be a way of encouraging the United States to maintain diplomatic ties with the island.

Thus, in early 1973 Taiwan launched a "Buy American" campaign. The policy encouraged Taiwan trade groups to increase their purchases of US goods. Just over eighteen months later, by October 1974, six different Taiwan delegations had traveled to the United States on purchasing missions.[58] The Nationalists were intent on presenting Taiwan as a loyal US customer, thereby cementing the importance of the two countries' bilateral ties.

In April 1973, Y. T. Wong, director general of Taiwan's Board of Foreign Trade, led one such purchasing mission to the United States.[59] The members of the mission collectively signed $750 million worth of purchasing deals, including an agreement to buy 5.5 million metric tonnes of grain over five years.[60] Over the next three years, American grain companies sold $800 million of wheat, corn, and soybeans to Taiwan.[61]

In February 1974 a delegation of seventeen executives from Taiwan department stores visited the United States. Leading the group was S. J. Par, head of the Far Eastern Department Stores—a chain with stores across the island. The group spent twenty days in the United States, visiting American and trade exhibits. They met with leaders from Dallas-based Sanger-Harris and Marshall Field in Chicago. In New York they met with executives from Macy's and visited the New York Gift Show at the Coliseum conference center.

Speaking at a press conference, Par told reporters that the color televisions from American brand RCA were the most popular televisions among affluent Taiwan consumers, more than Japanese sets. This was despite the fact that Japanese sets were considerably less expensive. "The quality of the RCA product is better," he noted by way of explanation. And, another delegate interjected, "the remote control satisfies the Taiwanese curiosity," a feature that was not included with Japanese models. Another member of the delegation told American reporters that his store had recently imported $1 billion worth of American goods, which had entirely sold out in three months.[62]

A few years earlier, RCA had sold satellites to China to promote Nixon's trip. Now Taiwan purchased its televisions to assist trade with the United States. Soon after their return to Taiwan, the delegates from the Far Eastern Department Stores held special exhibits of American goods—including the RCA televisions—in three of Taiwan's largest cities. As the three governments sought to use trade in varying ways to their own advantage, RCA became a willing beneficiary of their efforts.[63]

In addition to sending trade delegations to the United States, Taiwan's leaders sponsored exhibits of American goods throughout the island. In March 1974 the Taiwan Board of Foreign Trade sponsored an exhibition showcasing American industrial equipment. The cost of the "Ampro 74" exhibition stood at around $75,000, and was paid for by Taiwan's Board of Foreign Trade.[64] American companies sold over $50 million worth of industrial equipment in the first week alone.[65] Ampro 74 opened the same month as the United States Trade Center in Taipei.[66] While the center had raised concerns among some Taiwan government ministers that the United States was limiting its relations to economic matters, for five years the Nationalists paid the annual $50,000 cost of renting the center's space.[67] Trade therefore played a complicated role in the relationship between the United States and the Republic of China (ROC). Taiwan's leaders might have protested economic ties as a potential symbol of their diplomatic demotion, but they also readily sought to promote these ties in an attempt to demonstrate they were indispensable to the United States both politically and economically.[68]

Taiwan's New York–based propaganda office, Chinese Information Service, publicized the Buy American campaign in some of the largest American newspapers, positioning Taipei as assisting its friend. An advertisement in the *New York Times* explained, "The declared aim of the program is to help the United States ease its balance-of-payments problem."[69] Another, which appeared in both the *Los Angeles Times* and the *New York Times,* declared that Buy American was "not a mere slogan" but an example of putting its ideas into action.[70] Taiwan was the United States's twelfth-largest trading partner but with its Buy American policy the island was "shooting for seventh" by mid-decade.[71] Taiwan's Board of Foreign Trade even encouraged Taiwan importers to purchase from American firms even if goods from other nations were cheaper.

Taiwan's Buy American policy adopted the language of the US labor movement, but the reality of its purchasing efforts was more complex. While its advertisements and trade exhibits promoted their purchases of RCA televisions and other American goods, the vast majority of Taiwan's actual Buy American purchases were agricultural goods, not manufactured ones. Taiwan was buying American grain far more than it was buying consumer goods. The publicity and the trade shows presented Taiwan as aligned with American workers who had been fighting a "Buy American" movement of their own. But Taiwan's campaigns did not mitigate the problem American workers faced in the US-ROC relationship: the increasingly high level of imports entering the United States from Taiwan.

Selling Mao's China

Unless they were following the pages of specialized corporate magazines, American consumers would not have known that the emerging trade relationship with China was so heavily imbalanced or that Chinese traders were pushing their US counterparts to purchase more Chinese goods. Walking into department stores around the country, from Dallas to New York City, they would have seen special exhibitions showcasing Chinese products. Cordoning off whole floors, department stores in many of the largest cities in the United States erected extravagant displays of Chinese wares for sale.[72] It was not just pricey antiques on offer; many department stores also catered to a clientele wanting inexpensive everyday items. Macy's in New York stocked Chinese bamboo baskets and gifts. At Alexander's in Chicago, bamboo baskets sold for 90 cents and conical bamboo hats retailed at $9.95.[73] The vice president of Bloomingdale's, Carl Levine, went to the Canton Trade Fair in 1973 and brought back bamboo baskets, ceramics, jade, and semiprecious jewelry.

China also came to American homes by way of television. In January 1973 two networks devoted prime-time slots to films about China.[74] ABC screened *Chung Kuo*, a highly anticipated documentary that Italian director, Michelangelo Antonioni, had filmed in 1972 with Mao's permission. Beijing later condemned the film during heightened fighting between the political factions.[75] On January 30, 1974, *Renmin Ribao* published a full-page attack denouncing Antonioni's purpose as "not to understand China" but to "humiliate it." Antonioni presented an idealized vision of China as rural and underdeveloped. As far as Beijing saw it, "the film endeavors to deny the significant improvement in the living conditions of our people, saying, 'Beijing people are poor, but not miserable.'" "Thanks to the director's mercy," the *Renmin Ribao* continued, "he also said that we are not tragic; but his real intention is to laugh at our 'poor.'"[76]

In Europe and the United States, however, the film won widespread acclaim for its striking cinematography and rare footage of an unfamiliar world. By the late 1980s *Chung Kuo* was revived in China as a nostalgic depiction of a simpler life. Nonetheless, in the waning years of the Cultural Revolution, it was political collateral in Beijing even as it was celebrated across Europe and the United States.

In the winter of 1973, American television viewers were also privy to an NBC documentary featuring veteran reporter Lucy Jarvis. In contrast to Antonioni's film, *The Forbidden City* explicitly depicted an upbeat story of progress. Chinese people were better off under the Maoist regime than at any other point in history, according to the documentary. Around half the focus was on ancient China and the history of Beijing's Forbidden City. "The sundial was ancient in China when it was new in Europe," said the narrator. "The Chinese were using the compass when Christ was crossing the sea." Interspersed with this narrative was footage of China that Jarvis and her team shot in 1972.

Linking contemporary China with its ancient past, *The Forbidden City* emphasized the egalitarian nature of Maoism. Peasants were now permitted to enter the Forbidden City, viewers were told, and their children could attend university. In reality, the education system in China remained in tatters, but the cultural transformation of China from red threat to ancient exotic was well under way in the American imaginary. Jarvis's documentary, screened alongside Antonioni's film, assisted that process.

These cultural engagements with China helped generate consumer interest in Chinese items. One American couple traveling from Long Island to California added a detour to Dallas in order to purchase two nineteenth-century robes from Neiman-Marcus. A man in California ordered a robe for his daughter over the telephone, the *New York Times* reported.[77] New Jersey chain Einstein Moomjy sold carpets from the Chinese city of Tianjin ranging from $1,750 to $2,600.[78] The company advertised its rugs as coming "from Peking to Paramus"—the New Jersey borough of Paramus was one of the biggest shopping destinations in the country.[79] The alliterative connection between the two cities traced the rugs' movement and lent them an air of global cosmopolitanism. Ted Einstein, the company's chairman, reported that in 1972, when the rugs were first stocked, some people had visited the Paramus store "just to see them."[80] But despite this curiosity, Einstein felt that the consumer purchasing response to the rugs was tepid. "I don't think there's a craze about Chinese things," he told the *New York Times*.

**FROM THE PEOPLES'
REPUBLIC OF CHINA**
Work Jackets for Men
and Women. Sturdy blue
cotton outer jackets,
worn by Chinese
workers and peasants,
Quilt lined $25 PPD
Unlined $14.95 PPD
Matching peaked cap
$2.95 PPD
strap shoe black canvas
$5.95 PPD
canvas work shoe,
step-in $5.95 PPD
Please state
size when
ordering

Sizes 5 to 8
Sizes 6 to 10

Check or Money order, no C. O. D.

PEOPLES' WARE INC.
2210 DELANCEY PLACE
PHILA., PA. 19103

Figure 3.3. An advertisement for jackets promotes
them as "worn by Chinese workers and peasants."

For some corporate marketing strategies, China's communism was a selling point. In 1973, Foreign Cargo, a store in Kent, Connecticut, stocked Mao caps and Chinese soldiers' shirts retailing for $2.50 and $5.95, respectively. Kathy Kennedy, the manager at Foreign Cargo, discussed her company's bottom line, telling the *New York Times* that "the Nixon trip last year made a difference, and it was favorable."[81]

Consumers could also buy work jackets from a Philadelphia-based company, People's Ware. The jackets were available for $25 if quilt-lined,

99

or $14.95 if unlined. For only $2.95 more, consumers could buy a matching Mao-style cap. These items were advertised as "worn by Chinese workers and peasants."[82] A crucial component of their desirability was the capacity for American consumers to feel a sense of ownership over seemingly authentic Chinese clothing and objects. Similar to Pat Nixon's dress or Stanley Marcus's antique robe, a major part of the appeal was that these jackets offered a way of connecting to China via possessing authenticity.

US Dockworkers and the China Market

The excitement for the new trade with China extended to dockworkers from the International Longshoremen's and Warehousemen's Union (ILWU) and port authorities along the Pacific Coast. Unlike other dockworker unions, the ILWU was not a member of the AFL-CIO and did not share its anticommunist views, dating back to the early 1950s. Instead, the dockworkers saw the unfolding trade as offering new economic opportunities. The early 1970s were a tumultuous time for US dockworkers, who were hit hard by the economic recession and slowing shipments of goods. Indeed, just days before Nixon landed in China in February 1972, the longest dock strike in US history had come to an end. The ILWU had been striking for 130 days at twenty-four ports all along the West Coast calling for better pay and working conditions.[83]

Amid the economic downturn and decreased trade shipments, the ILWU saw the PRC as a potential reprieve. Harry Bridges, the ILWU's longtime president, had both a personal and a professional interest in the unfolding trade opportunities with China. Bridges was an Australian-born union leader who spoke publicly in support of communism and in the 1950s was called before the House Un-American Activities Committee on multiple occasions. He was incarcerated several times but always denied charges that he was a member of the US Communist Party. Bridges had been president of the ILWU since 1937. Now, at seventy, Bridges turned his attention to the PRC.[84]

In June 1973 Bridges hosted a delegation of twenty-two Chinese journalists who traveled throughout the United States. During their San Francisco stop, Bridges provided the journalists with an elaborate banquet at his local union chapter. They were met by about a thousand ILWU workers in a hall festooned with a sign proclaiming "The friendship of our peoples will continue to grow." Bridges later escorted them to visit some of the longshoremen's homes.[85] Following the Chinese journalists' visit, Bridges personally wrote to Huang Chen, the head of the newly established PRC Liaison Office in Washington, DC, seeking to establish a relationship between the San Francisco port and China. "Comrade Chen," he opened, the longshoremen have "traditionally been in the forefront of improving both political and economic relations with the People's Republic of China and in years gone by in support of the revolutionary movement in China."[86]

Bridges explained that the employment opportunities for longshoremen were limited and saw the developing trade with China as an opportunity for increased employment. "I am most anxious to see if something can be done so that vessels going to and from the United States use the port of San Francisco where possible."[87]

Huang agreed for the *Caspian Sea* to transport 15,000 bales of cotton from San Francisco Port to Shanghai. This was, however, a Pyrrhic victory. The deal was only reached after the San Francisco Port Authority offered to store the cotton on the dock free of charge and to waive the normal charges for use of the port.[88] China's huge purchase of US cotton, which had spurred excitement in other sectors of the agricultural industry, came at a short-term cost for the San Francisco port.[89] San Francisco port authorities nonetheless hoped the CCPIT would reward them by directing future shipments their way. On the day the *Caspian Sea* was loaded with the cotton, the ILWU held a ceremony to mark the occasion. Large red banners carried words of welcome in both English and Chinese and, as with so many of these ceremonies, toasts were drunk—with Chinese beer, the ILWU's newsletter noted.[90]

Bridges's solidarity with Chinese workers went further than he was perhaps aware. At the same time as he was leading strikes along the Californian coast, dockworkers in China were themselves protesting their labor conditions. The two largest docks, Shanghai and Guangzhou, became hotbeds of protest, encouraged by radical leaders who incited divisions among the dockworkers.[91] One of the major points of contention was the managerial cadres' intention to reinstate a system of flexible work shifts.[92]

Dockworkers in Shanghai were additionally concerned about state shipping companies' new purchases of technology that improved the methods for moving cargo. They feared that the new technology threatened their jobs.[93] In 1974 they protested that "the leadership had looked upon the workers not as the masters of the wharf but as the slaves of tonnage."[94] These were a part of efforts, led by the radicals within the Politburo, to critique the China's pragmatists' 4-3 Program for the impact it would have on Chinese workers. The radicals' major concern was the expanding trade with capitalist nations, but they successfully harnessed dockworker agitation to suit their purposes.

In the United States, other ports along California's coast were eager to ensure that San Francisco would not retain the advantage. Sensing this, the CCPIT fueled the competition among the West Coast ports. In 1970 the ports of Los Angeles and Long Beach had merged. Albert Perrish, former president of the Los Angeles Harbor Commission, spoke to the Los Angeles Times about the potential of reopened trade with the PRC. The possibilities would be "astronomical" if trade with "red China" did open.[95] The three ports of Los Angeles/Long Beach, San Francisco, and Oakland all vied for support from the Chinese authorities in attempts to strike agreements for the use of their port facilities. All three contacted the National Council for US-China Trade on various occasions in attempts to secure Chinese trade exhibitions or to attract visiting Chinese trade delegations to their ports. The interest was so high that in mid-1974 the National Council changed its membership criteria to include port authorities. The port authorities of Seattle and New Orleans were the first to join the National Council, and the ports of New York/New Jersey, Los Angeles/Long Beach, San Francisco, and Oakland followed soon after.[96]

Not all dockworkers, however, shared Harry Bridges's enthusiasm for China trade. The International Longshoremen's Association (ILA), based on the Atlantic and Gulf Coasts, saw things differently. In 1972, in the wake of Nixon's January trip to Beijing, John Bowers, vice president of the ILA, called on dockworkers to block goods coming in from the PRC. Before his workers would handle Chinese goods, he demanded, China's leaders must pressure Hanoi to release US prisoners of war.[97] Unlike the West Coast–based ILWU, the ILA was a member of the AFL-CIO.[98] The two unions had a long history of antagonism, going back to the personal animosity between Harry Bridges and longtime ILA leader Teddy Gleason.[99] In the 1970s the ILA aligned with the majority of leaders in the AFL-CIO, tapping into their long history of anticommunism. Practicalities likely played a role too. To the ILA, based on coasts farther away from the PRC, the promises of the China markets were far dimmer.

102

The Diplomacy of the China Market

By October 1973, diplomatic progress toward normalization began to stall. A State Department briefing paper argued that trade could be used to "contribute to the development of a degree of interdependence and stability in our bilateral relations." The paper warned, however, that "means must be found to facilitate Chinese exports to the U.S."[100] As the briefing paper circulated in the corridors of the State Department, American importers expressed their own frustrations at what they felt was an unwillingness on the part of the National Council for US-China Trade to promote this aim. In their eyes, the National Council was not doing enough to assist Chinese sales.

US importers' frustration came to a head just as the National Council leadership was about to leave for its first visit to China. On the eve of their departure, a group of the council's importing members called for an emergency meeting. The National Council's entire organizational structure was too export-oriented, they cried. This was even seen in the composition of the National Council's inaugural trip to China. William Batten, chairman of J. C. Penney, was the only importer in the delegation. He was also the only importer on the National Council's board, they complained.[101] With 1,600 stores across the United States, J. C. Penney was one of the largest retailers in the world. In 1977 the company sold around $750 million of imported goods alone, constituting about 10 percent of the company's entire sales.[102]

J. C. Penney was thus not only unrepresentative of smaller US importers, but a direct competitor to the medium and small importing companies, the importers argued. Nicholas Ludlow, a staff member at the National Council who attended the meeting, reported back to the National Council leadership that "the term 'outrageous' was actually used by at least one participant."[103] As one importer put it in a letter of complaint to Phillips, the National Council was perceived as "primarily geared to servicing the large export-oriented industrial and trading firms."[104] In fact, the National Council's leadership did not initially even include J. C. Penney in its list of representatives who would travel to China. Batten's inclusion was an afterthought, when they realized there was not a single importer in their entourage.[105]

Despite the problems with its importer members, the National Council's leadership saw their organization as playing an important political role. This was the first time an official delegation of US businessmen had

103

traveled to China since 1949. "This is an historic mission," Phillips underscored to the delegates. It was a trip, he reminded them, that was fulfilling the Shanghai communiqué's aims of progressively developing trade ties. "It is important that nothing be allowed to tarnish the credibility of this mission," Phillips warned. This meant that delegation members needed to see themselves as representatives of the National Council rather than as individual businessmen and they should therefore abstain from "initiating discussion of their own companies."[106] Counseled to avoid revealing themselves as self-interested capitalists, the businessmen were also warned not to raise the issue of claims/assets, which at that stage seemed close to resolution. Discussion of prospects for foreign direct investment—not permitted in Mao's China—was also off-limits.[107]

The National Council met with representatives from its organizational counterpart, the CCPIT. The CCPIT's president, Wang Yaoting, explained to his guests that his council placed great importance on a balanced trade relationship. "China adheres to the policy of balancing imports and exports," he noted. He added that "China does not insist on an absolute balance" but "the imbalance cannot be too big." The National Council's records from the meeting noted that "Mr. Wang emphasized that this is one of the questions to be considered in the development of trade relations between the two countries." Wang's warning to the National Council was that the trade imbalance needed to be less lopsided.[108] The problem was not only that US-China trade was too imbalanced, but that it was also heavily weighted in the United States' favor. A balanced trade relationship was important to China for ideological reasons—its emphasis on self-reliance—but it was also important because its export sales would provide China with the foreign currency it needed to purchase advanced technology.[109]

Wang also raised China's lack of Most Favored Nation (MFN) trading status. He noted to the National Council's leadership that the tariff would "certainly have an adverse influence on the development of Sino-American trade" if it continued. "We hope . . . that in accordance with the Shanghai communiqué, you will take this matter into consideration."[110] The National Council did indeed push for Congress to grant MFN status to China, but they would soon be inhibited by congressional action linking MFN to human rights. The congressmen pushing this link had the Soviet Union in mind, but as we will see, their actions affected China trade too.

Upon their return, the National Council's leadership promoted their trip across the country. Speaking to the World Affairs Council of Pittsburgh, for example, Charles Weaver, head of Westinghouse, said China had "superb food; no crime or security problems . . . happy well-fed and well-clothed people; and an inescapable feeling that Chairman Mao's revolutionary party line has been good for the 800 million Chinese people."[111] It was the leaders of US capitalism who worked hardest to reframe China from Cold War foe to amicable trade partner.

Heeding the warnings Wang had expressed in Beijing about the trade imbalance, the National Council also changed its membership structure. In December 1973 it created tiered membership categories, knowing full well that most US importers of Chinese goods were smaller companies and could not afford the high membership fees. A company earning a gross income of $20 million or less only had to pay $500 instead of the $2,500 fee that only companies like Philip Morris, General Motors, and J. C. Penney with billion-dollar budgets could afford.

The National Council also established an importers committee soon after, which its leaders hoped would act as a "collective voice" for US importers of Chinese goods. The committee aimed to "persuade" Chinese traders to "adapt to the peculiarities of the American market" as well as to advise Congress on trade matters.[112] Kurt Reinsberg, vice president of Associated Metals and Minerals Corporation, a company that imported raw materials from China, became the head of the importers committee. In June 1974 Reinsberg wrote to the board of directors expressing the hope that the newly established committee "will help substantially to increase Chinese exports to the United States."[113] Politically, this would help redress the trade imbalance, but it was also in Reinsberg's and other importing firm's direct interests. To them, the China market offered an untapped potential for imports.

IN THE OPENING years of US-China trade, the China market—long a site of fascination and intrigue—once again emerged as an idea, as much as a place, for American businesspeople. With lucrative trade deals and new diplomatic and economic organizations, China trade seemed to be off to a better start than many in the United States first expected. The boom was driven by Chinese purchases of US goods, which far outweighed the value of goods its state-owned companies sold to the United States.

This imbalance of trade would soon begin to cause problems in US-China trade, as negotiations toward normalization stalled and as radicals wrenched more control of China's economic policymaking from pragmatists in the Politburo. One of the key ways to redress the trade imbalance was for US businesspeople to increase their purchases from China. Some groups within the United States did indeed begin to reconceptualize the China market as a place not just for customers but for purchases too. Westcoast dockworkers, department store marketers, and US consumers reconsidered the China market as an emerging place from which to import goods. As they did so, their own interests began to converge with those of Chinese traders who wanted US businesspeople to see the China market as a place to buy from, not just sell to.

CHAPTER 4

The Limits of the China Market

I N E A R L Y A P R I L 1 9 7 4 the UN General Assembly convened a special session to discuss the relationship between raw materials and economic development. Since the 1950s the world trade system, organized through the General Agreement on Tariffs and Trade (GATT), set low prices for raw materials and high prices for manufactured products—often made using those same raw materials. With commodities bringing in considerably less profit than manufactured goods, newly decolonized nations in the Global South—many of whom relied upon exporting raw materials—were unable to garner meaningful funds for their development projects. By 1974 a group of 77 nations from the Global South used the UN special session to try and end this lopsided trading regime. As they saw it, international trade lay at the heart of the inequality they experienced. Energized by the strength of the OPEC oil embargo, they called for "economic decolonization" and proposed a revolutionary new vision for the international system: a New International Economic Order (NIEO).[1]

After joining the United Nations in 1971, Chinese diplomats had worked with leaders from the group of 77 nations, who first united in 1964 and soon dubbed themselves the G-77. China had participated in the meetings and planning in the years leading up to the declaration of the NIEO.[2] Mao used the occasion of the special session to unveil a new foreign policy vision in which he firmly aligned China with the developing nations of the G-77. He sent Deng Xiaoping to speak on his behalf. "China is a socialist country, and a developing country as well. China belongs to the Third World," Deng claimed.[3] In a profoundly important recalibration, Mao centered development—not revolution—at the heart of China's foreign policy.[4]

This was the first time a PRC official had addressed the UN General Assembly since obtaining the China seat from Taiwan in 1971. Mao turned what was already a historic moment into an opportunity to announce ideas that became known as his "Three Worlds Theory."[5] The three worlds that Mao envisaged were divided by stages of development and imperialism. The United States and Soviet Union constituted the First World, Deng explained to the General Assembly, and both "attempt to dominate around the world." The Second World consisted of developed nations in Europe as well as Japan. The Third World, with which China associated itself, consisted of developing nations in Asia, Africa, and Latin America. Mao not only positioned development at the center of international politics; he also indicated a foreign policy shift: from an alliance with the United States against the Soviet Union, to a position that instead opposed both superpowers.[6]

The Three Worlds Theory marked a crucial moment in the history of China's political economy. By centering development, Mao weakened the political divisions between communism and capitalism. As Chen Jian argues, "it further reduced the influence and power of the profoundly divided international Communist movement."[7] For China, the Cold War had begun to end with its turn toward capitalist trade in the early 1970s, and by 1974 Mao solidified this shift.

Scholars who have examined the Three Worlds Theory have understood its significance in political terms: as part of Mao's larger turn away from socialist allegiances toward a solidarity based upon a shared stage of economic development.[8] China's decision, in the early 1970s, to support the United States and South Africa in defeating the Marxist MPLA in Angola had been the ultimate sign of its declining status as revolutionary leader.[9] The Three Worlds Theory was the political articulation of this shift away from world revolution.

The histories of these developments treat as incidental the fact that Deng announced Mao's Three Worlds Theory at the special session for the NIEO. In this chapter, however, I interpret the context of the NIEO as crucial to the Three Worlds, revealing it to be an articulation of economic ideas as much as political ones. The NIEO's focus on raw materials and development was fundamental to the vision Mao articulated.

As China's leaders experimented with economic reforms in the 1970s, the NIEO legitimized their efforts of using international trade to support development without accruing foreign debt. Higher prices for raw materials would enable China and other Third World nations to fund their development projects. "What was done in the oil battle should and can be done in the case of other raw materials," Deng declared.[10]

For all its posturing, the speech Deng delivered belied the deep chasm within the Politburo about how best to fund China's development efforts. Since China's turn to foreign trade in the early 1970s, and particularly since the 4-3 Program of 1973, pragmatists had pointed to raw materials and other exports, such as antiques, handicrafts, and textiles, as keys to funding China's technology import program. Mao's Three Worlds tapped into their focus on raw materials, but it also voiced radicals' warnings: Deng cautioned about "preventing capitalist restoration and ensuring that socialist China will never change her colour." As radicals at home become increasingly louder in their opposition to China's import program, Mao used the special session to legitimize his vision of development, tempering it with assurances that trade with capitalist nations did not mean China would become capitalist itself.

Ultimately the NIEO would be undone by its own weapon. The oil crisis ended up crippling the non-oil-exporting Third World nations, whose development in fact relied upon importing oil. In Latin America in particular, national leaders took on considerable debt in order to finance their development projects. This would eventually lead to the debt crisis of the 1980s, triggered first by Mexico and extending quickly to other parts of the region.[11] China was spared the worst of this because it did not rely upon oil imports in the way some members of the G-77 did. But Mao's focus on raw material exports did not, in the end, provide the solution to China's development. It would be manufactured goods that provided the key: an export-oriented development.

Even though raw materials did not remain at the center of China's growth, the Three Worlds Theory institutionalized a vision of Chinese development that was tied to international trade. It centered exports, in general, as a key component of China's development. In the mid-1970s this structural focus on exports went on to shape the US-China trade for two reasons: the diplomatic impasse between the two nations, during which Chinese sales to the United States gained heightened importance; and a fundamental transformation of American manufacturing and trade. The Trade Act of 1974, passed around the same time as the NIEO, provided its own institutional vision of global trade—one that fought against the NIEO but complemented China's growing focus on using exports to fund its development.

The Three Worlds: Chinese Development and Exports

The UN special session on raw materials and development took place at the height of the OPEC oil embargo. Between October 1973 and March 1974, Arab leaders cut off their supply of oil to the United States and its allies in retaliation for US support for Israel in the 1973 Arab-Israeli War. OPEC leaders, many of whom had been part of the Arab oil embargo, additionally collaborated to increase the price of oil. American customers were forced to pay skyrocketing prices for gasoline. The oil price surges sent shockwaves throughout the industrialized world. In the United States, they triggered widespread debate about American middle-class ideals themselves. Refrigerators, cars, and—during the bitter cold winter—heaters became the center of introspection about just how energy-dependent American lifestyles had become.[12]

Speaking in the UN chamber, Deng declared that the oil crisis revealed the importance of the Maoist principle of self-reliance, or *zili gengsheng*. Self-reliance required nations to "take in their own hands the production, use, sale, storage and transport of raw materials," Deng explained in the UN chamber. If Third World nations could sell the raw materials "at reasonable prices on the basis of equitable trade relations," they would be able to develop their industrial and agricultural production "and pave the way for an early emergence from poverty and backwardness."

Pragmatists in Beijing had been pushing this particular interpretation of outward-facing self-reliance since their turn to foreign trade in the early 1970s. Trade could still be a component of self-reliance, they argued. Raw materials had been a key export for financing the large-scale import program Zhou and other pragmatists had implemented in 1973 with their 4-3 Program. Commodities such as chemicals, hog bristles, textiles, handicrafts, and petroleum all became central to the pragmatists' focus on increasing exports to pay for industrial imports.

During the oil crisis, Zhou directed the State Planning Commission to increase its oil exports in order to capitalize on the sky-high prices. In 1974 he increased China's quota on unrefined petroleum exports from 4 million tons to 6 million tons. China's refined petroleum exports increased too, from 1.5 million tons to 1.6 million tons.[13] These were new records for the PRC. Spurred on by the oil crisis, Beijing worked to position itself as a new international source of energy. The vast majority of China's sales went to Japan, but portions also went to North Vietnam and North Korea. Oil constituted around 8 percent of China's total export earnings, making it one of China's key exports in 1974.[14]

In order to increase its oil exports, however, China cut back on its domestic consumption of oil. In 1974 Beijing reduced oil quotas to the industrial sectors by 2.3 million tons; the oil quotas for fuel and chemical industries were cut by 1.4 million tons; and the quotas for small-scale industries were cut by 600,000 tons.[15] The pragmatists' interpretation of self-reliance meant that they used exports to pay for their industrialization efforts instead of accruing foreign debt. But this came at a domestic cost.

The question of how to pay for imports of industrial equipment and how to balance domestic energy needs with industrialization sparked bitter disputes within the Politburo. Li Xiannian, one of the supporters of the 4-3 Program, insisted that coal should be used more often at home, ensuring that enough oil could be exported abroad. But radicals began to insist that Li and others were claiming that "it is forbidden to burn our oil so that we can give it to foreigners"—a line they voiced repeatedly in their challenges to the industrial program.[16] In March 1974, *Renmin Ribao* similarly expressed caution that China needed to continue to "adhere to the policy of independence and self-reliance." Foreign technology should be used only as a step toward development without contravening China's independence.[17]

These limitations spurred Chinese leaders to find ways of increasing China's own oil production. Soon after Deng spoke at the United Nations, Chinese engineers made a breakthrough by successfully drilling the first deep-sea oil rig in the East China Sea. The Shanghai Municipal Revolutionary Committee, which organized the expedition, praised the engineers as "assuming great political responsibility for opposing U.S. and Soviet maritime hegemonies."[18] They positioned the oil discovery squarely within the Three Worlds vision: opposing both superpowers, strengthening China's self-reliance, and providing raw materials that could be used for foreign trade.

Between 1968 and 1978 China's crude oil production grew from around 16 million metric tonnes to 1 billion metric tonnes. In the space of just ten years, China transformed itself from an oil importer to an oil exporter.[19] This was all the more remarkable given that the country had only three main oil reserves and these produced more than 70 percent of its output between 1949 and 1976.[20] Oil played an important part in paying for China's technology import program, but even with the new discoveries China's pragmatists knew that it would not be enough on its own to ensure they maintained self-reliance.

Despite the push to sell more oil, China's imports—including petroleum, steel, chemicals, and textile plants—cost far more than the cash it took in from exports. Double-digit inflation sparked by the oil crisis forced global export prices to skyrocket, leading companies that usually purchased from China to hold back. This in turn meant that China was not able to generate the same levels of cash that it had earlier in the decade. China's textile exports were hit particularly hard. Adjusted for price increases, China's sales of textiles to Hong Kong were 22 percent lower than they had been in 1973. Its non-oil exports to Japan also decreased, sinking to only three-quarters of the previous year's exports.[21] By the end of 1974 China experienced its biggest trade deficit since the communist takeover in 1949.

This record-breaking trade deficit further divided an already volatile Politburo. It fueled the radicals' opposition to trading with advanced capitalist democracies. Jiang Qing and Zhang Chunqiao, leaders of the radical faction in the Politburo, blamed the 4-3 Program for "transferring the energy crisis in the capitalist world to China."[22] They pushed instead for a barter system of trade: acquiring goods via direct exchange rather than purchasing them using cash. The more the Chinese economy felt the impact of the external crisis, the more momentum the radicals gained in their calls for a return to a stricter interpretation of self-reliance.

OBSERVING FROM THE OUTSIDE, American businesspeople hoped that China's focus on oil might ease the global shortage. Many sought to sell equipment and technology to assist the oil discovery process. But they faced considerable limitations in their ability to sell their oil equipment to China, driven in large part by the stalling diplomatic negotiations in Beijing and Washington. Nicholas Ludlow, editor of the *U.S. China Business Review,* felt that "US oil firms could well be a key bond linking the two economies." Writing in January 1974, he projected that "within five years the People's Republic of China could be earning $1 billion annually in hard currency from its exports of high-grade oil." "Ten years from now," he continued, "those earnings could be $2 billion yearly." US oil companies were "critical to the speed of development of China's oil resources," he declared.[23]

Ludlow's eagerness came in the wake of W. M. Kellogg's successful deal in September 1973 in which the company sold eight ammonia factories to China. Along with many others in the business community, Ludlow hoped that a similar degree of success might open up for oil technology. In late April 1974, for example, *Industry Week* editor William Miller wrote of the uncertainty many businesspeople felt about China trade, pointing to oil as a potential solution. "The US's trading future with China is enigmatic—almost as enigmatic as China itself," he began, drawing on a well-worn orientalist trope of incomprehensibility. Nonetheless, China did offer some hope for American businesspeople. "The most intriguing possibility is oil equipment," Miller noted. If China continued to develop its oil capacity, he speculated, a "natural swap" could arise: "Chinese oil for US oil technology."[24]

As Miller saw it, the China market was first and foremost a place of potential customers. It presented American industrial leaders with opportunities to sell their oil equipment to Chinese engineers. China seemed poised to offer another form of economic assistance, too: a new source of imported oil. Chinese oil would alleviate US dependence on Middle East suppliers, provide relief to US consumers, and give China the foreign exchange it needed to buy US industrial products. Many other American businesspeople shared Miller's vision of China's oil potential. Harned Hoose, a businessman who ran his trade company from his Los Angeles mansion, proclaimed that China had "oil reserves rivalling those of the Mideast."[25] Selig Harrison, a researcher who interviewed "more than 200 oilmen," predicted that "Peking appears likely to reach the current production level of Saudi Arabia by 1988 or soon thereafter."[26] It would later turn out that China did not have oil reserves to rival Middle East suppliers, but in 1974 many American businesspeople saw great potential in China for oil.

Despite these hopes, the success that Kellogg experienced in 1973 with its sale of fertilizer factories did not extend to oil equipment. Exxon, Gulf Oil, Baker Trading Corp., and Phillips Petroleum clamored for ways to sell their oil production and refinement technology to China, but only one smaller US company was successful. In November 1974, Michigan-based WABCO Corporation signed a $7 million deal to supply mining trucks to the PRC. This was, however, only a tiny fraction of China's total petroleum equipment imports for the year.[27]

For the most part, China was not interested in buying petroleum equipment from American companies. Throughout the oil crisis, *Renmin Ribao* slammed US oil corporations for their increased profits during the crisis. Oil companies' expanded pockets had revealed, *Renmin Ribao* declared in February 1974, the "greedy face of oil monopoly capital yelling energy 'crisis' to drive up market prices and make huge profits!"[28]

Instead, China turned to companies in Japan, France, West Germany, and the United Kingdom as part of its 4-3 Program. Between December 1973 and October 1974 alone, China signed six contracts with Japanese industrial oil corporations worth just over US$98 million. Since mid-1972, China had signed twenty-one contracts for petroleum equipment with Japanese corporations, worth over US$592 million. WABCO might have provided some mining trucks, but Japanese and Europeans firms supplied China with offshore drilling platforms, oil supply boats, ethylene plants, and polyethylene plants.[29]

The promise of Chinese oil was hampered by rising problems in US-China trade more broadly. Throughout 1974, Chinese businesspeople and diplomats canceled agricultural trade deals, pulled out of diplomatic negotiations on the claims/assets dispute, and postponed a visit by Chinese business leaders to the United States. The Watergate scandal in the United States and rising factional politics in China meant that leaders in both nations were considerably constrained in their diplomatic efforts toward normalization.

Nixon had pledged to reach full normalization with China in his second term, but by 1974 his attention was focused elsewhere as he became increasingly mired in public revelations of his involvement in the illegal hotel break-in.[30] In August, for the first time in US history, the sitting US president resigned. Observing the changing dynamics, Mao worried that Washington was using China as a pawn to assist its détente with the Soviet Union. American diplomats were "standing on China's shoulders" to cooperate with the Soviets.[31] Trade with the United States was strengthening as diplomacy stalled, and China therefore cut back on its business with the United States.

None of these problems were visible, however, in the trade ledgers. Taken by the numbers, 1974 was a record-breaking year for US-China trade. By the summer of 1974 the United States was trading more with China than with the Soviet Union. Many American commentators predicted that China trade might even reach $1 billion by the end of the year.[32] Total trade came close to that, at $933 million. The vast majority of US exports to China—which drove the record-breaking numbers—were not oil technology but agricultural products: wheat, cotton, soybeans, and corn.[33] The composition of US exports reflected the severe food shortage caused by drought in China. It also meant that after just three and a half years, the United States had become one of China's biggest trade partners, second only to Japan.

Agricultural products pushed bilateral trade figures up during the oil crisis but they were also the first products to be canceled as diplomacy began to stall. Miller's observations in *Industry Week* captured the confusion many businesspeople felt. "Where is U.S.-China trade headed?" he had asked. The answer Miller pointed to—increased sales of US industrial equipment—unintentionally perpetuated the very problem Chinese businesspeople wanted their American counterparts to redress. The United States needed to increase its imports in the immediate term, China insisted, not wait for the mid- or long-term when China's oil capacity might eventually develop.

Selling China's Workers

To combat China's deepening trade deficit, the CCPIT sharpened its focus on exports. In June 1974, the Ministry of Foreign Trade unveiled a new magazine promoting China's wares. *China's Foreign Trade* was published in Chinese and English and from 1976, in Spanish and French too.[34] Its pages were filled with advertisements for Chinese goods, from Seagull brand wristwatches to Tsingtao beer. Interspersed were articles reporting on all manner of goods for sale. In the inaugural edition, Minister of Foreign Trade Li Qiang penned an article outlining the "big new developments" that had happened in China's foreign trade in recent years. He singled out 1971, when China began to expand its national economy, as the key turning point in these initiatives. Since then, "China has established trade relations with over 150 countries and regions and has signed governmental trade agreements or protocols with more than 50 of them," Li recounted.[35]

Coming amid the political turmoil between the radicals and the pragmatists in Beijing, Li's article—and, indeed, the magazine itself—aimed to assuage foreign traders' fears of China's faltering interest in trade. "Without doubt, the prospect is that our trade with other countries of the world will continue to broaden." In fact, he added, "China welcomes technical interchange with other countries . . . on a planned and selective basis." Li emphasized China's exports, assuring foreign importers that "there will be a steady increase in the quantity of industrial and agricultural products . . . with a wider range of variety and designs." China would ensure that "packaging and presentation will continue to be improved." The country would "gradually" export more, and its purchases would be "increased accordingly."[36] The Ministry of Foreign Trade might have been affirming its commitment to trade, but it did so with exports at its center.

The advertisements accompanying the articles did not simply focus on the products China had for sale. Instead, China also sold its workers. Photographs of workers making the products featured prominently throughout the magazines. As with visual culture throughout the Maoist era, Chinese workers were presented as smiling participants in the construction of an industrial socialist nation.[37] These advertisements, however, were targeted at foreign businesspeople in capitalist economies. They often included not only images but also descriptions of the people who made the products. An advertisement for Tsingtao beer, for example, noted the "great care" that workers took in the fermentation process. "In the spacious germinating room, workers can be seen hard at work—carefully turning over and over sprouting barley." Moutai was made by "the local working people," another advertisement boasted.

In advertisements for watches, silk, porcelains, radios, bicycles, and more, the people making the goods were integral to the sale itself. They were depicted as careful and skillful craftspeople, producing high-quality goods for foreign consumers. As Chinese leaders increased their trade in the 1970s, *China's Foreign Trade* was central to the reconfiguration of the China market as a site of workers, not customers.

As China pushed American and foreign traders to see its market as a site of workers, it also expanded the Canton Trade Fairs, where so many of its export deals were made. In the spring of 1974 the Ministry of Foreign Trade unveiled a new exhibition center to house its fairs. China's increasing international trade since 1971 meant more and more foreign businesspeople traveled to the fairs, and the country now needed an even larger complex. The timing could not have been worse—in the middle of the global recession, the oil crisis, rising animosity toward foreign trade from the radicals within the Politburo, and a record-breaking total trade deficit. The building of larger trade fair halls was nonetheless an infrastructural

Figure 4.1. Chinese advertisements often included images of workers making the products and accompanying descriptions of their hard work and high-quality goods, such as this advertisement for Seagull wristwatches.

change that made it much easier for the long-term expansion of China's foreign trade.

At the opening ceremony celebrating the new grounds of the 35th Canton Trade Fair, technicians lit fireworks and sent red balloons high into the sky. Tied to the ends of the balloons were streamers carrying quotations from Mao's speeches and writings.[38] "The recently completed Chinese Export Commodities Fair building stands magnificently on the banks of the picturesque Liuhua Lake in Guangzhou," *Renmin Ribao* exulted. Atop the roof of the building were giant red banners proclaiming "Victory along Chairman Mao's Revolutionary Line" and "Long Live the Unity of People All Over the World." The banners were "dazzling under the sun."[39]

Wang Yaoting, the CCPIT's director, doubled down on China's prioritization of exports during the grand opening. Throughout the month he did not send a single representative from China's import corporations to meet with foreign businesspeople. Chinese buyers were always in the minority at the fairs, but this was the first time they were not present at all.[40] Wang's message was clear: China wanted to end its trade deficit by expanding its exports.

Figure 4.2. A postcard produced by the Chinese Ministry of Foreign Trade celebrating the newly opened Canton Trade Fair in April 1974. The red balloons feature streamers with quotations from Mao.

Yet Wang's efforts and the celebrations for the new fairgrounds were overshadowed by the deepening global recession. China's total earnings at the spring fair were lower than in previous years. Chinese officials were focused on increasing their sales, but the global recession made this much more difficult. Inflation had hit the global economy so hard that, converted into foreign currencies, Chinese prices had skyrocketed. One American businessman commented bitterly that he and his colleagues were "fighting over peanuts." Another noted exasperatedly that essential oils "rocketed in price from US$2 per pound to US$30 per pound."[41]

Coming just a few weeks after Deng's speech in the UN General Assembly, in which he announced Mao's Three Worlds Theory, Canton Fair officials highlighted their ties with Third World traders. Lin Liming, the fair's new director, declared to the 4,000 guests gathered for the closing reception, "China is a developing socialist country and belongs to the Third World." Reporting on the new exhibition halls, *Renmin Ribao* promoted the fair's ability to "actively support friends from the trade circles of countries and regions of the Third World to meet their requirements

118

as much as possible."[42] In this depiction China's provision of goods to the Third World was a benevolent form of friendship. No mention was made, of course, of the fact that selling these items was in China's own interests—particularly at the time of the PRC's largest-ever trade deficit.

China's prioritization of Third World trade raised the consternation of some American importers. The *Chicago Tribune* reported that "drunken Arab traders pulled the pigtails of Chinese school girls while their Chinese hosts politely proffered them bargain basement deals."[43] China gave preference to its "third world comrades," one businessman complained to the newspaper. This perceived special treatment came irrespective of the Arab traders' "intolerable conduct." "These guys are robbing them blind" he bemoaned, "and laying hands on the virgins of China as well."

In telling this account, the businessman drew a sharp distinction between the exploitative Third World traders and his American colleagues. He felt that "it was pretty tough on the morale" for many American traders. Some were so discouraged by China's lack of interest, they left the Canton Trade Fair early.[44] His depiction of Arab traders as extortionist villains held heightened potency for the *Tribune*'s readers, many of whom would have spent the winter lining up in their cars to purchase gas. In his view, China was simultaneously economically discriminatory and vulnerable to the wily Arab traders. Meanwhile, he watched on with dampened spirits, eventually returning home sooner than planned. In this businessman's eyes, he and his colleagues were merely honest capitalists.

Another American businessman interviewed by the *Chicago Tribune* saw things differently. He expressed frustration at his colleagues' annoyance at China's preferential treatment for some foreigners over others. "Americans are new friends, not old friends," he remarked. "If you're an old friend the price is better and you know what you're in for." This was why these traders from the Middle East received preferential treatment, the businessman argued. China regularly asserted the importance of *guanxi* (connections) in its trading processes. The trouble was that American businesspeople "move too quickly and haven't learned about the mysteries of Oriental ways." While seeking to promote understanding, he too used language that reinforced an orientalist exoticism. China trade, in his eyes, was opaque.[45]

The oil crisis and subsequent global recession made it more difficult for China to sell at the rate its leaders had hoped for. This frustrated American businesspeople looking to profit from the China market. While the Ministry of Foreign Trade sold China's workers through its advertisements, it was less reliable at selling its goods at the Canton Trade Fair. These troubles mid-decade made pragmatists in the Politburo more vulnerable to attacks from the radical faction. But the longer-term structural changes that were occurring—the unveiling of larger exhibition halls and the creation of an international trade magazine—were crucial tools in recasting the meaning of the China market: as a place from which to buy.

AMERICAN IMPORTERS, WHOSE own interests lay in seeing China as a place to buy from, nonetheless faced structural problems in their attempts to purchase from China, in addition to the short-term problems caused by the recession. Most pressingly, China was not subject to Most Favored Nation (MFN) trade status, the reciprocal trading arrangement among all nations in the GATT. MFN could also be extended to countries that were not part of the GATT—including China—but only through bilateral trade agreements. Without MFN status, Chinese goods entering the United States were subject to higher tariffs. Chinese businesspeople mostly got around these impediments by selling their goods well below market price. Even with this maneuvering they were forced to sell some imports—such as canned foods—at greater prices than their competitors because of the high duties.

Behind the scenes, American businesspeople lobbied Congress to provide China with MFN status. They focused on a bill before the House—the Trade Reform Act—that would make it easier to provide China with MFN status. As it stood, Romania was the only communist nation to have such trade benefits with the United States.[46] The Trade Reform Act would allow the president to negotiate bilateral trade deals, including with communist nations. Businesses trading with China saw great promise in a bilateral trade deal that would include the provision of reciprocal MFN status. The Board of Governors of the American Chamber of Commerce (AmCham) in Hong Kong argued that "if Congress approves the Trade Reform Act, both the American consumer and the American businessman will benefit." Consumers would have greater access to a "wide range of low cost products" and "the businessman" would profit from "the continued favourable reception his exports will receive in China."[47] AmCham's Hong Kong branch defined "businessman" in terms of US exports, but behind the cheap consumer products they touted lay the interests of US importers. The organization's leaders were well aware that US exporters' capacity to succeed in China relied upon the success of US importers.

The Trade Act was therefore a crucial mechanism for ensuring an increase in US purchases of Chinese goods. By providing MFN status to China, it would bring the tariffs on Chinese items entering the United States into line with imports from other parts of the world. The problem, as far as supporters of MFN status for China were concerned, was an amendment to the Trade Reform Act co-sponsored by Henry Jackson and Charles Vanik. The Jackson-Vanik amendment linked the provision of MFN trading status to human rights. It prohibited the United States from providing MFN status to communist nations that restricted the movement of its people. "When we're talking about free trade, let's talk about free people too," Jackson insisted.[48] Their amendment was targeted at the Soviet Union. Jackson and Vanik were concerned about Jewish citizens attempting to flee the Soviet Union and the persecution they faced there.

While unintended, the Jackson-Vanik amendment affected China too, which also restricted the movements of its citizens. Debate over the amendment had slowed down the passage of the Trade Act, which was first introduced in April 1973 and would remain in limbo until December 1974. When Congress did finally approve the bill, it was with the Jackson-Vanik amendment in place: an inadvertent blow to US-China trade.[49]

In an age of rising congressional support for human rights, the Jackson-Vanik amendment sought to make the provision of trade privileges conditional. But it also limited how human rights were defined in relation to trade: as an issue of immigration. As we shall see in Chapter 8, when Congress debated the US-China trade deal in 1979, this narrow conception of human rights would ultimately limit how trade could be used to leverage human rights concerns in China. If the core problem tied to trade was China's immigration policies, then its leaders could find ways of fixing this without addressing other human rights concerns.

The capacity for US importers to purchase goods from China were further impeded by the ongoing claims/assets dispute. Until the problem was resolved, neither country could hold trade exhibitions of the other's products, goods could not be shipped directly between the two nations, and financial transactions had to be channeled through third-party banks. These were not insurmountable challenges, but they did make trade both more cumbersome and more costly.

When Kissinger met with Zhou in November 1973, they came close to resolving the claims/assets issue. But in the months that followed—as diplomatic ties faltered and Mao sidelined Zhou—China had yet to approve the in-principle agreements Kissinger and Zhou had reached. Washington was still waiting to hear from Beijing in April 1974 when the issue arose again. As Deng Xiaoping prepared to travel to the United States to speak at the United Nations in New York, legal concerns arose about what kind of plane he should fly on. If he flew in a Chinese-owned plane, it would be legally open to seizure the moment it landed on US soil. Because both sides had outstanding financial claims, any goods arriving directly from the other country were liable to requisition.

When the State Department warned China's Liaison Office in Washington about the problem, Deputy Chief Han Xu accused the Americans of "blackmail." The Americans were using this to compel Chinese leaders to approve the in-principle agreements. In the end, however, Deng did not fly using Chinese aircraft.[50] Two months later, Beijing put an end to US hopes of resolving the dispute anytime soon. On June 14, Lin Ping, from China's Foreign Ministry, rejected the claim/assets compromises that Kissinger and Zhou had reached the previous November.[51]

American importers faced other problems too. Shipping was often delayed due to China's limited port facilities; goods sometimes arrived in the United States broken due to poor packaging; and American importers had little influence on the items' designs. The challenges they faced diminished the prospects of making lucrative profit from the China trade.

AS CHINESE BUSINESSPEOPLE emphasized the importance of increasing their exports in general—and to the United States in particular—they turned away from the National Council for US-China Trade, which they felt was too export-oriented. The National Council's leadership included executives from some of the largest industrial corporations in the world: International Harvester, Westinghouse, and General Electric. These corporations were interested in selling goods to China—oil equipment, for example. Even though the National Council had established an importers' committee in late 1973, its leaders saw imports merely as a means of providing China with the foreign exchange it needed to buy American technology.

China instead strengthened its relationships with rival trade organizations that more clearly met their economic interests. Throughout 1974, the CCPIT invited a range of American trade organizations to China. The San Francisco Chamber of Commerce, the American Arbitration Association, the Electronic Industries Association, and the American Importers Association all received such invitations. The National Council did not.[52]

Of the invitations that the CCPIT extended, none stung the National Council more than the invitation extended to the American Importers Association (AIA). Some within the National Council began to fear that the CCPIT was starting to think of the AIA as the representative body for American importers, relegating the National Council to serving US exporters only. The National Council's importers committee, formed in December 1973, was not enough to assuage Chinese concerns over the trade imbalance.

Throughout the mid-1970s, leaders from the National Council and the AIA squabbled among themselves about who was best placed to assist American importers in buying from China. In the spring of 1974 the CCPIT had extended Canton Trade Fair invitations to both the AIA and the National Council. Both organizations were given space to set up information desks at the fair to assist US businesspeople. At the previous fairs, the National Council had been the sole American organization with this privilege. In its magazine the National Council presented the inclusion of the AIA as a sign that China's emphasis "was clearly on selling."[53] Privately, however, Nicholas Ludlow, the magazine's editor, was concerned. Writing to Christopher Phillips, president of the National Council, he noted, "This invitation is an explicit signal from the Chinese that the National Council is ineffective in this area [imports] and has done nothing visible in over a year of its existence on a practical level." If the CCPIT's displeasure were to become public, he warned, "it could be very embarrassing for us, especially among importer members."[54] Ludlow was worried about diminishing membership.

Ludlow was born in the United Kingdom in 1942 and spent time after university living in Hong Kong and visiting China—a journey US citizens had been unable to make until Nixon lifted the travel embargo in 1971. By age thirty-two he was living in Washington, DC, leading the National Council's publications department and coordinating a range of administrative projects within the organization. Ludlow speculated on the reasons for the AIA's invitation to the Canton Trade Fair. He wondered whether the CCPIT was acting "in the spirit of wanting to play them off against us." He suggested it was "a rebuff more in the spirit of US policy toward China." Given the perceived closeness between the National Council and the US government, the CCPIT might be using the National Council to send a broader message, he suggested. Ludlow was not wrong, but Christopher Phillips did not see it this way, scribbling an angry "NO" in the margin as he read this. As far as Phillips was concerned, this was not an issue of punishment for Washington's policies but instead merely a sign of the importance China placed on increasing its sales of goods. Ludlow nonetheless urged Phillips to see that the National Council needed to create a program that would "promote Chinese products at ground level."[55]

The blows kept coming. On April 4—just a few days before Deng's Three Worlds speech before the United Nations—the CCPIT canceled a trip to the United States that the National Council had been due to host. Chang Tsien-hua, head of commerce at the Chinese Liaison Office in Washington, and his assistant, Tung Chi Kuang, walked the short distance to the National Council's offices to inform Christopher Phillips and his team that the CCPIT would not visit the United States in 1974 as had been previously planned. When the National Council visited China in November 1973, the two organizations had reached an in-principle agreement for a reciprocal visit from the CCPIT to occur at some point in 1974. Regardless of these previous pledges, Chang explained, the trip would now be, Chang said, "substantially delayed."[56]

The National Council had been eagerly anticipating the CCPIT's arrival. In February, Phillips had promoted the expected Chinese visit among the National Council's members. The Chinese tour would be one of "the major events this year," Phillips had promised.[57] The delegation was "expected before this summer," the National Council's magazine predicted in February.[58] With the news in April of the CCPIT's canceled visit, the National Council began to debate what was going wrong.[59]

To make matters worse, in late August the CCPIT did send an agricultural delegation to the United States. Rather than coordinating with the National Council to assist with the planning, the CCPIT turned instead to the New York–based Committee for Scholarly Exchange with the PRC. The National Council did not even find out about the agricultural visit until three days before the Chinese arrived. Without prior knowledge of the trip, it was too late for many of the National Council's members to prepare any meetings with the Chinese visitors. When news of the Chinese visit reached John Hanley's office in St. Louis, for example, the Monsanto president was furious. The Chinese were due to arrive in mere days, "much too late to plan an effective meeting," he complained to the National Council. If there had been time for "appropriate preparation," Hanley rebuked, "there could have been much mutual value in having them meet with selected portions of Monsanto's research management."[60] The CCPIT's sidelining of the National Council and the rising frustrations of its members—around 250 corporations by mid-1974—threatened its major source of funding.

These actions pushed the National Council to heed Ludlow's advice and increase its focus on assisting Chinese exports to the United States. In December 1973 it had changed its fee structures to make it easier for smaller importers to join the National Council. It also established an importers committee that aimed to coordinate issues and concerns of American importers. In January 1974 the National Council moreover created its own magazine aimed at promoting trade with China. Nicholas Ludlow became the magazine's editor.

The inaugural issue of *U.S. China Business Review* revealed that the National Council's leadership—recently back in Washington from its official visit to China in November 1973—was well aware of China's desire to increase its sales to the United States. It featured a range of articles dedicated to Chinese goods. One article provided details about "how to start imports from China."[61] A few pages later, readers could turn to a feature article: "An Importers Introduction to the Canton Fair."[62] They could also learn about the National Council's importers committee or the CCPIT's export corporations.[63] The issue included two articles about American technology sales to China, but there were no articles providing advice tailored directly to exporters. It was not until four issues later, in July, that the magazine published an article directly addressing American exporters: "How to Start Exports to China."[64] In the very selection of topics, Ludlow ensured that the National Council's public image focused on increasing American purchases of Chinese goods—with an eye to potential readers within the CCPIT.

These actions, however, did little to assuage Chinese concerns that the National Council was more interested in selling than in buying. In September, Chang Tsien-hua, the commercial counselor at the Chinese Liaison Office, complained to Christopher Phillips of the export-orientation of the National Council's leadership. "To my knowledge, most NCUSCT members are exporters," he commented. "Those importing from China are few in number." Phillips replied that the National Council was the "only organization devoted exclusively to promoting imports from the PRC." The AIA, by contrast, had interests in countries across the globe.

Chang downplayed Phillips's concerns about the AIA. It was common practice for the CCPIT to deal with many trade organizations within a single country, he explained. In the UK, for instance, the CCPIT worked with the Sino British Trade Council (an organization similar to the National Council although with direct links to the government), but it also engaged with other British trade groups. The CCPIT's invitation to the AIA was a "friendly exchange" and did not "preclude any NCUSCT efforts to promote trade," Chang continued.

The biggest problem, Chang noted, was the trade imbalance, for which he placed responsibility on the National Council and its heavy focus on exporters. "There is much for you to do," Chang warned Phillips. Pushing back, Phillips commented there was "much for both to do." Chang agreed the PRC needed to work on improving its delivery times and packing. Many US importers who did want to trade with China were still being met with delays or broken goods. But Chang's central message was clear: If the National Council wanted the CCPIT to treat it as the key organization for US-China trade, it needed to find a way to increase US imports from China.[65]

On October 6, less than a month after Phillips and Chang met, the CCPIT's vice chairman, Li Yung-ting, hosted a three-man delegation from the AIA. This was the third trip of AIA members to China in 1974 alone. By contrast, the CCPIT hosted the National Council only once, in November 1973, and canceled its 1974 reciprocal visit. In a span of ten days, Li hosted Gerald O'Brien, AIA's executive vice president; Charles Rostov chairman of the AIA's China Committee and president of Transocean Import Company; and Simon Katz, president of New York Merchandise Company.[66] The men boarded a plane in Tokyo bound for Beijing. The flight, the first direct connection between Japan and China, was a new route that had opened just a few weeks earlier.[67] As the US importers flew to China, they did so not as leaders of China's opening to the capitalist world but as beneficiaries of a wider set of changes China was pursuing with Japan and other capitalist nations.

Li had explained to the American businessmen that they were there to discuss "promotion of Chinese exports to USA and introducing in detail [the] U.S. market." Writing to the AIA's members upon their return, O'Brien noted, "We feel that we have established the position and reputation of AIA as the spokesman for American importers."[68]

Following these events closely from Washington, Nicholas Ludlow was furious. He wrote to the National Council's leadership again in November, this time exclaiming that he was "sickened" by what he saw as the National Council's slow efforts to increase Chinese imports. Ludlow warned: "We are heading for a very serious confrontation with the AIA's promotion." This was all the more urgent because members of the AIA's China Division were potential paying members of the National Council. "While I think in the long run the Council has by far the best potential in this area because we are specifically concerned with China," Ludlow wrote, "it is not going to do much good in the minds of our constituents who are coming up for [membership] renewal."[69]

Ludlow called for the National Council to embark upon a range of actions to support the increase of Chinese exports to the United States. He pointed to exhibitions of Chinese goods, employing a full-time staff member dedicated to imports, holding seminars and symposiums, and coordination of off-the-record lunches for US importers.

Chang Tsien-hua, head of commerce at the Chinese Liaison Office, agreed. He met Phillips again in January 1975 and suggested that National Council "could be more active" in promoting bilateral trade. "You need not limit activities to your own members—go outside the membership," he instructed Phillips. "If you do this, membership will be enlarged simultaneously." Chang knew exactly how to hit on the National Council's fears. Noting the small membership of the newly formed importers committee, he explained, "If the committee remains as it is, it may not be able to play a major role in promoting trade." The problem, Chang noted, was that many of the American companies importing from China were small and their purchases "have little value on enlarging trade." He indicated that "large department stores should be interested in importer committee activities," and if they were to join, then "the committee would be very successful indeed."[70]

Agricultural Cancellations

As China centered exports as a key component of its development in general and its trade with the United States in particular, it began to cancel imports of US agricultural goods. In the first few years of reopened trade, China's state-owned agricultural corporation, Ceroilfood, had purchased considerable quantities of US agricultural goods. Its agricultural imports were driven in part by a severe drought that swept through China and across the globe, including Argentina, Australia, India, the Soviet Union, and Peru.[71] But in 1974 Ceroilfood canceled many of its contracts with the United States. In June it revoked an order for 48 million bushels of US corn worth $700 million.[72] Toward the end of the year, it retracted a large wheat purchase that had been due to arrive in 1975 and 1976.[73] Contracts that US sellers had once celebrated were now being canceled.

Representatives from Ceroilfood claimed the United States' previous sales had been of poor quality. They had found bugs in some of the grain, and in some instances the United States sent chaff rather than wheat. Shanghai dockworkers protested against the incoming grain from the United States, which they complained had been infected with TCK smut—a fungus that causes diseases in crops.[74] Vice Premier Li Xiannian encouraged the protests, imploring the dockworkers in February 1974 to "conscientiously do a good job in quarantining imported grains."[75] By October 1974, Li and Hua Guofeng issued a report resolving, "Let us make up our mind not to depend on grain imports. [We] must be independent and self-reliant."[76]

The US State Department interpreted China's withdrawal from previously signed agricultural contracts as motivated primarily by stalled diplomacy. In November, George Bush, who had become chief liaison officer to the PRC just a few weeks earlier, assessed the developing trade situation. In a telegram to the State Department he suggested that the cancellations were a sign the PRC was "disappointed at the slow pace of political normalization and irked by American self-satisfaction at the phenomenal growth of trade." He concluded that the trade imbalance was "a difficult pill to swallow, a contradiction to their tenets of self-reliance and of opposition to both the superpowers."[77] He followed up in January 1975, noting that the trade imbalance was "undoubtedly a factor" in the "apparent Chinese desire to look, when possible, to other sources of supply [for their grain]."[78]

The cancellations were indeed a product of the slowing diplomatic process, but they were also a result of internal divisions in Chinese politics. They reflected the radicals' increasing ability to resist the pragmatist's trade agenda. As it became clear that China would experience its first-ever deficit in foreign trade, Jiang Qing and Zhang Chunqiao increased their critique of the 4-3 Program. They pushed for a cutback in China's imports to alleviate the trade deficit. As early as March 1974 the Ministry of Foreign Trade produced a report instructing China to "restrict our imports and strive to expand our exports." The PRC should "avoid imports from the United States when it is unnecessary and . . . when there are alternative supplies."[79] Canceling US grain purchases was therefore a quick way to lessen the impact of the looming trade deficit and depletion of foreign exchange.[80]

Even with the cancellations, however, grain and other agricultural commodities continued to flow from the United States to China throughout 1974. They were the product of deals signed in earlier years that China did not cancel. In fact, the shipments of grain were so large they became the major reason for the year's record-breaking total trade figures. The combined value of US wheat, soybean, corn, and cotton exports constituted 70 percent of *total* US-China trade in 1974.[81]

On the surface these figures suggested that US-China trade was gaining momentum. The *New York Times* reported in June that "trade with China surges ahead of U.S.-Soviet level."[82] But the high figures for 1974 were buttressed by US goods that were *shipped* to China in 1974. The canceled contracts portended a far bleaker future for bilateral trade. The disjunction between China's unwillingness to sign contracts and the soaring total trade figures sent conflicting messages to American businesspeople about just what might come from the China trade.

As the Politburo radicals and pragmatists fought bitterly over the direction of China's economic development and the role that foreign trade would play within it, American businesspeople were forced to navigate the conflicting messages coming out of China. The first four years of trade saw record-breaking sales of US goods, but these were accompanied by ever-increasing Chinese cancelations of its purchases. On March 7, 1975, the US Department of Agriculture announced that China had again canceled an order of US goods. This time it was 233,000 bales of cotton. The department suggested the cancellations were "due to a combination of an improved supply situation in China and a possible shortage of foreign exchange."

Not wishing to deter American farmers, a few weeks after publicly announcing the cancellation, the department's magazine, *Foreign Agriculture,* published a speech given by Richard Goodman, a senior administrator at the department's Foreign Agricultural Service. Speaking at a Seattle Conference on China Trade, Goodman had reassured his audience that China "continues to represent an enormous potential market—as westerners have recognized ever since Marco Polo." He felt there was "little doubt" that China would continue to search for grain and cotton. The problem, Goodman noted, was that "the United States, at least up to now, seems to have been viewed by the Chinese as a residual supplier." He remained hopeful that this would eventually change. "With China having the largest population in the world—a population that continues to expand and seek better living and improved food security—there is every reason to hope that American farm products might continue to find a growing market there."[83] Goodman and the Department of Agriculture encouraged American businesspeople to see China as a source of customers. The China market in his estimation was one of Marco Polo–like adventure—and sales.

The impact of China's cancellations was compounded by the fact that, by 1975, it had not made a single new purchase of wheat, corn, or soybeans from the United States. Ceroilfood, China's trade corporation responsible for such purchases, continued to buy grain from its other major sources—especially Canada, Australia, and Argentina. By May 1975 alone, Ceroilfood had signed contracts with Canadian suppliers to purchase 3.1 million metric tons of wheat. This was a huge coup for the United States' northern neighbor, whose supply of grain to China had decreased in 1972 and 1973 when the United States entered China's wheat market. The United States had temporarily supplied grain that had once come from Canada but by 1975 Canada was back selling grain to China at its previous levels.[84]

"Why these drastic fluctuations?" Alexander Eckstein, an economist, asked in the pages of *Foreign Affairs* in October. Were the swings in bilateral trade a result of "renewed impact of political factors, especially on the Chinese side"? Or were there more "serious disabilities" that were "partly political and partly economic"? How should American businesspeople interpret the fact that the United States was "only a residual supplier of grain" and "only a minor source for the industrial plants," he asked.[85] The answer, Eckstein felt, was the slowing diplomatic process toward normalized relations.

Even Pullman's successful deal to sell eight ammonia plants two years earlier started to seem uncertain. In 1975 Jiang Qing attempted to stop the Pullman employees from building one of the fertilizer plants in the northern city of Daqing. The city was the site of China's biggest and most important oil field. Mao had pointed to the oil refinery as a symbol of self-reliance since its creation in 1960.[86] Jiang argued that building a Kellogg factory in the area was "comprador philosophy" that would compromise the ideal of self-reliance. As the pragmatists and radicals battled over the future of China's development, the prospect of building an American fertilizer factory at one of the most symbolic demonstrations of self-reliance was a step too far for Jiang. Her resistance waned only when she saw Mao's signature approving the location of the factory.[87]

During an especially contentious meeting in the summer of 1975, the Gang of Four contended that the policy of importing chemical fertilizers and exporting oil was "selling out the country." Jiang and Zhang were particularly sharp in their denunciations. They spoke of Zhou, Deng, and the pragmatists as "Han traitors" and "slaves of foreigners." The problem, Zhang contended, was "not just the Ministry of Foreign Trade" but also "in our Party, and first of all in the Politburo."[88]

These debates over technology imports and foreign trade affected China's other trade partners too. By 1975, CCPIT trade officials began to scale back their purchases of foreign goods across the board. Despite Zhou and Deng's calls for modernization through technology imports, China's purchases of turnkey plants noticeably decreased from previous years, hitting its two major suppliers—Japan and West Germany—particularly hard. By December, total Chinese turnkey purchases stood at $142.6 million. Two years earlier the figure was $800 million.[89]

Despite the setbacks, the US Liaison Office remained optimistic about the long-term prospects for American industrial corporations. "Over the long term," they cabled Washington, "there is very large potential for U.S. sales of plant, machinery and technology to China." The diplomatic impasse would, though, need to be resolved. "While we would not advocate political concessions to secure a greater share of PRC foreign trade, we believe the Chinese are serious when they say that full trade relationship cannot develop until political relations are normalized."[90] In other words, the prospects of trade were not enough of an incentive to *drive* engagement policy with China, but US diplomats did have a sense that the China market would eventually become a lucrative one. In the Liaison Office's estimation, this was, however, a China market conceived primary through sales to China. Even as the office cabled Washington with concerns about the lack of US purchases of Chinese goods, its long-term vision of the China market was much more in line with Carl Crow's 400 million customers.

The Trade Act of 1974

These fluctuations in US-China trade and Mao's Three Worlds Theory, institutionalizing Chinese development through trade, occurred against the backdrop of the shifting landscape of corporate, labor, and state power in the United States. Between 1965 and 1973, US manufacturing corporations experienced a 40 percent decline in profitability. The oil crisis added a further 25 percent decline in profits in 1974 alone.[91] As the business world reckoned with these changes, it was their workers who felt the costs of the corporate slump. Labor groups had spent the early years of the 1970s lobbying hard for congressional legislation that would protect manufacturing jobs, particularly through the Mills Bill of 1971 and the Burke-Hardt act of 1972. By 1974, big business—including executives from beleaguered manufacturing firms—fought back with the Trade Act of 1974, a major new trade legislation passed by the Senate on December 13, 1974.[92]

The Trade Act of 1974 was approved in the shadow of one of the most consequential series of events in twentieth-century American politics: the Watergate scandal, impeachment process, and subsequent resignation of the sitting president. Nixon's corruption and deception shattered public faith in the office of the presidency and initiated an era of a vastly more empowered Congress.[93] Yet, through the Trade Act, Congress chose to decrease its own trade powers and expand the scope of the executive branch at precisely the moment public faith in the president had eroded. Internationalists within Congress feared their protectionist colleagues far more than they did a president with expanded trade powers. From their vantage point in 1974, there was no question that the president would uphold a globalist outlook. The Trade Act, sociologist Nitsan Chorev argues, was a deliberate and concerted effort by internationalists in business and politics to curb protectionist demands.[94] It diluted Congress's ability to protect American workers.[95]

The new legislation moreover encouraged American corporations to outsource their labor abroad.[96] It buttressed a process that had already been developing by encouraging the leaders of industrial capitalism—"dinosaurs of the Fordist economy," as business historian Benjamin Waterhouse describes them—to adapt their structures of production and outsource their labor abroad.[97] As America's industrial giants reevaluated how they understood production, management, and trade, they deepened the process of deindustrialization by dividing their manufacturing along international chains of supply.

These changes within American capitalism came at the very moment when China made clear its desire for US businesspeople to see the China market as a site of workers, not customers. The idea of what US-China trade meant was shifting in tandem with the changes in US capitalism. American businesspeople and legislators did not know it at the time, but at the height of the oil crisis, with the passing of the Trade Act of 1974, the two nations came one step closer to the making of Made in China.

IN THE SAME period that China began to promote its market as offering workers rather than customers, American corporations experimented with their own manufacturing processes. Aided by newly containerized shipping, they increasingly turned to overseas sources of production and expanded their imports.

In 1973, for example, J. C. Penney imported only around 10 percent of its goods. The vast majority of items in its 1,700 stores were manufactured in the United States. Its confidential five-year plan aimed to change this. Named simply "The Company Plan," it aimed to have imports make up 14 percent of Penney's total merchandise by 1978. Penney's was not alone in this: its competitors, as company executives knew all too well, were making similar changes.

The Company Plan, which Penney executives circulated among themselves, listed China as a key source of increased imports in its five-year outlook.[98] And it explicitly tied its decisions to the ending of Bretton Woods: "The recent two successive devaluations of the dollar have fragmented our normal trading patterns." The changes to the US dollar had "disrupted some of our current activities," but it had also "opened up new import opportunities in various parts of the world." In fact, it noted, "a major effort will be exerted in developing these new markets including such areas as South America, Eastern Europe, China, Russia, and India." Ending Bretton Woods had encouraged companies like Penney's to turn to overseas production.

As J. C. Penney engaged with these markets over the next five years, the Company Plan noted, their efforts would "eventually result in the addition of many important sources of supply for our future growing needs."[99] J. C. Penney's executives outlined a method of adapting to fluid exchange rates by turning their attention to foreign suppliers with cheaper labor, including China. The company made no efforts to hide its interest in low-cost workers. As the company's magazine publicly celebrated: "Penny representatives seem convinced that Chinese export prices [have] little relation to production cost."[100] In other words, Chinese goods were as cheap as they came—because price did not reflect workers' wages.

As part of this plan, in May 1974 Bob Boulogne, director of J. C. Penney's International Buying department, traveled once more to China on a buying mission with four of his colleagues. Shepherded through itineraries that included visits to the Great Wall, the Ming Tombs, and the Summer Palace, the executives traveled for more than just business.[101] Bob Boulogne explained that he saw the China market as "fascinating," with "immense potential."

Boulogne and his team purchased flannel shirts, cotton flannelette fabric, girls' jeans, denim jackets, men's and boys' jeans, corduroy woven jeans, woolen fisherman-knit sweaters, and men's cashmere sweaters. The items would be stocked in stores across the United States.[102] J. C. Penney was the largest retailer of clothing in the United States, and early in the trade negotiations Boulogne decided to focus his efforts on clothing rather than other items such as shoes or toys.[103] His focus on textiles, he said, felt like a "very logical step for us."[104]

"Foreign markets are important sources of merchandise for Penney," Boulogne commented in the company's magazine. "They are important . . . for merchandise that offers good standards of quality at lower prices than domestic merchandise."[105] China offered, he explained, cheap labor at high quality. In the company's magazine, Boulogne articulated a vision of global trade based upon a race to the bottom.[106]

J. C. Penney soon found this initial excitement about China overshadowed by the realities of trade. In 1977 businessman Julian Sobin interviewed Boulogne on his trading experience as part of a twelve-part cassette series offering business advice. Over the five years of trade, Chinese imports had presented J. C. Penney with a number of challenges, including delays in shipping, incorrect labeling, and inconsistent supply. Boulogne admitted to Sobin, "Julian, I have talked to a lot of people who have said that they were interested in going into China to trade and to set up business and I've always discouraged every one of them that I could." Sobin, who imported chemicals from China, agreed: "Me too, Bob." Boulogne continued, "unless you have the resources, and the money, and the patience, and the time, it could be a disaster." The difficulty of the trade relationship meant that "we are operating in total darkness and that's the biggest problem," Boulogne said. "It's uncertain," Sobin reiterated.[107]

Boulogne reflected, "The fair is more superficial. . . . But I think when you visit Peking and spend time, which you just never have at the fair, and you can meet with them without the pressures of the fair . . . you begin to understand how different their ways of doing business are and really it is a very tough market and a very difficult enterprise." Sobin asked whether Boulogne saw export potential for China to sell more apparel to

Figure 4.3. Bob Boulogne, head of international buying at J. C. Penney, traveled to Guangzhou to negotiate imports with Chinese officials at the Canton Trade Fair. He is pictured posing with Chinese vases, but it was textiles that the retailer was most interested in purchasing.

the United States. "In consumer goods I don't think there is any question in my mind, that's where it is." Boulogne explained that he focused his purchases on cotton goods because the US tariffs were lower than those on Chinese synthetic goods. In synthetics, "the Chinese are penalized very, very heavily," he clarified. "So we are skirting the problem somewhat by concentrating on the cotton field."

Nonetheless, Boulogne told Sobin, "all this investment you've made in time and effort . . . may be out the window" if some unforeseen political change occurred or "some radical element takes over." He admitted, "In other markets we would say, well, we'll come back when it's ready." If they were facing similar problems in other foreign markets, he said, "we just probably at this point would decide to get out." But, he continued, "we don't dare."[108]

In 1977, when the interview took place, J. C. Penney was not profiting from its Chinese imports. "Actually up to now we've lost money on Chinese goods," Boulogne explained. "We certainly don't count on it for our own profits at this point." The company had made a deliberate choice to continue importing from China despite the economic loss. This was because of what Boulogne described as a "feeling" of the China market: "It's got to develop; it's got to be important." China trade was different from trade with other nations, he contended. "With this market, there's no other market like it; it's too big. We cannot take that chance [of leaving]."

J. C. Penney was willing to accept these risks, based upon the potential of a future lucrative China market. Given the company's size, these losses barely made a dent in its coffers. "In view of all the purchasing we do around the world," Boulogne explained, imports from China were "very minute." Unlike smaller American importing firms, J. C. Penney could afford to absorb the economic loss, at least in the short term.[109]

The limits of the China market were significant, even for a large importing company like J. C. Penney. But as Penney implemented its changes in retailing and manufacturing, it incorporated China's own experiments with increasing its foreign trade into its vision. Penney's Company Plan revealed how the developments occurring in the two nations worked together to create a new idea of the "China market": one not for US exports but for imports.

CHINA'S INSISTENCE ON increasing its exports also forced American industrial firms to rethink their understanding of the China market. Not only did China show little interest in US oil technology; it insisted that if industrial firms did want to do trade, then they would need to buy from China instead. Throughout the decade, corporate leviathans from Ford Motors to Coca-Cola did not sell to China but instead bought tea, carpets, and even trees. These changes were part of the broader changes in the US view of the China market: as a site not only of customers but of workers too.

John Banning, executive director for Ford Motor's overseas initiatives, discovered China's approach toward exporting companies in late 1973, shortly after he paid the $2,500 membership fee to join the National Council.[110] Banning wished to establish ties with China and, by joining the National Council, he hoped to gain assistance in doing so. He initially worried that the car company's ties with Taiwan might inhibit its trade with China. Ford had recently completed a major investment in Taiwan, purchasing a local car-manufacturing plant for $36 million. This was the single largest investment by a foreign company in Taiwan's history and a reflection of the larger changes happening in globalized manufacturing processes.[111]

Ford's ties to Taiwan did not hamper its relationship with China in these initial stages. As we shall see, this changed in 1975 and 1976 when China did start refusing to work with companies that traded with Taiwan. But in late 1973, the motor company faced an entirely different set of hurdles, as Banning soon discovered. If Ford wanted to one day sell cars or components to China, the National Council advised the company, it should first demonstrate its commitment to the relationship. Speaking on the telephone to the National Council's president, Christopher Phillips, Banning learned that if Ford wanted to sell to China, the company should begin by *purchasing* goods from China.[112]

Many US corporations that complied with these requirements hoped that eventually, after establishing a rapport with the CCPIT, their goods would be more attractive to Chinese buyers. Thus it was that General Motors also developed purchasing relationships with China. In September 1974 Richard Kerwath from General Motors Overseas Operations wrote out a shopping list of items the motor company wished to buy.[113] He sent the list and an accompanying letter to Huang Wenchun, first secretary of the commercial section of the PRC Liaison Office, explaining that General Motors wanted to buy steel "such as hot rolled and cold rolled sheets, hot rolled bars and billets," as well as aluminum ingots, copper, zinc, and pig iron.[114] Even though General Motors purchased small amounts of goods from China, their efforts did little to bring about the sales General Motors executives hoped would eventually come. The company did not break into the China market until the late 1990s.[115]

It was a similar situation for Du Pont Chemicals, which sent its head of purchasing, John Brentlinger, to the 1974 spring Canton Trade Fair. This was "the single most significant gesture Du Pont can offer of its sincere desire to explore purchasing of products from China," the chemical company's marketing manager privately declared.[116]

Coca-Cola similarly bought tea and arts and crafts from China throughout the decade. The company moreover sponsored cultural and sporting exchanges between the two nations, as an indication of its commitment to the relationship.[117] Coca-Cola's chairman, J. Paul Austin, regularly raised with his Chinese counterparts the prospect of their buying his beverage. By December 13, 1978, just as diplomatic normalization was coming to a head, the company did reach a deal to sell its drinks to China, although the two sides were unable to finalize the deal until 1983.[118]

Commodities Required For Direct Use
in General Motors Production Facilities

1. Steel products such as hot rolled and cold rolled
   sheets, hot rolled bars and billets

2. Aluminum ingots

3. Copper

4. Zinc or zinc ore concentrates

5. Ferro-silicon, ferro-chrome and ferro-manganese

6. Silicon metal

7. Pig Iron

8. Plastic resins such as polyethylene, polypropylene and
   poly-vinyl-chloride

Commodities General Motors Is Interested
In Purchasing For Use by Allied Companies

1. Antimony

2. Manganese

3. Molybdenum

4. Tin

5. Tungsten

Figure 4.4. General Motors, as with most US companies at the time, learned the importance of purchasing from China before any chance of sales might eventuate. In September 1974, executives drew up a shopping list of items the company sought to import.

Throughout the 1970s, Coca-Cola's executives had no way of knowing that its efforts would eventually succeed a decade later. But like J. C. Penney, Coca-Cola could afford to absorb the financial cost of purchasing Chinese tea rather than selling its sugary soft drink. The company's leaders operated on the hope that one day they could sell to the fabled China market's immense number of customers.

Even RCA purchased goods from China despite its early successes in January 1972. In October 1973 Nicholas DiOrio, director of RCA's consumer electronics, wrote up what he deemed a "small shopping list of electronic components" as well as a list of food items RCA's subsidiary, Banquet Foods, wished to purchase at the Canton Trade Fair. The company was particularly interested in importing bamboo shoots and water chestnuts from China.

The National Council's Eugene Theroux, who worked with DiOrio on his shopping list, noted that the two Chinese corporations he was working with were "very favorably impressed indeed that RCA was making an effort to make purchases from China." Even though RCA wanted to sell to China, it was demonstrating its seriousness by making purchases at the Canton Trade Fair first. Theroux had explained to the Chinese businesspeople that RCA was "genuinely interested in two-way trade, and mindful of the fact that the trade balance currently tips markedly in favor of the U.S." RCA's efforts, he emphasized, were also aimed at helping China redress the trade imbalance.[119] By 1975 another of RCA's subsidiaries, St. Louis–based Banquet Foods, imported a range of foodstuffs from the PRC, including shrimp and water chestnuts.[120]

Things did not always end well for the exporting firms. One New York–based conglomerate, ICD, lost $35 million when an order for cassia trees from China came off the ship with broken branches.[121] ICD did not receive compensation for the loss, but this was not enough to dampen the company's interest in China. In the years after receiving the cassia trees, ICD continued to import a wide range of goods from China, including pianos, guitars, canned foods, and other kinds of trees.

Speaking with Julian Sobin in 1976, David Cookson, an ICD executive, remarked on the emotional pull that trade with China brought. He and Sobin discussed the challenges of financial profit in their trade with China. Sobin noted that while trade with China did bring some profit, it was "rewarding in an intellectual sense, I think, too." Cookson felt similarly. "Oh, no question," he agreed. "I think China is a market which 'gets you.'"

Earlier in their conversation, Sobin had mused on why he was so willing to pay higher prices than in other markets. "Maybe because I'm so grateful that I'm there," he speculated. "No matter how many times I've been there, for some reason I get into a mood after I cross the bridge, you know, that they've accorded me some great honor by allowing me to negotiate with them, to go to their country and so forth and then everything falls into place and I yield too quickly and I don't negotiate quite as hard as I do in other places and I forgive more easily when they're late in shipment and they ask you to extend the credit."[122] Like J. C. Penney and other large US corporations, Sobin and Cookson were willing to forego immediate profit out of an emotional pull toward China as well as a sense that they would reap profit in the long term. In the interim, however, China's insistence that they purchase forced these giant corporations to rethink the China market as a site of imports.

THESE GIANTS OF American industry came to realize the importance of rethinking the meaning of the China market as the United States' own trade structures changed. On December 13, 1974, the Senate passed the Trade Act of 1974 with the Jackson-Vanik amendment in place. With the new Trade Act, the prospect of the United States granting MFN status to China dimmed. Even if China lifted its immigration restrictions, the US State Department was reluctant to grant China MFN status without also doing the same for the Soviet Union. The fragility of détente meant adhering to a strict position of "evenhandedness." In the immediate term, then, the Jackson-Vanik amendment was yet another blow to the US-China relationship, just as the amendment also made US-Soviet détente more difficult.

But the biggest blow dealt by the Trade Act was not to China trade but to American manufacturing workers. After organized labor's show of strength in Congress in the first few years of the decade—especially with the Mills bill and Burke-Hartke bill—by the end of 1974 big business and its internationalist allies in the executive branch finally hit back.[123]

The legislation strengthened the political and economic power of US corporations, many of which were already trading with China. This was partly enabled by the fact that the Trade Act shifted the power to impose tariffs and other protectionist measures from Congress to the executive branch.[124] The proponents of the act assumed that the move from Congress to the executive would ensure the survival of liberal internationalist trade. For at least forty years they were correct. It was this same legislative change that gave President Trump the powers to pass executive orders limiting trade with China in the late 2010s.

The long-term changes ushered in by the Trade Act went on to assist China's convergence with global capitalism. This was because the act included a provision known as Generalized Special Preferences (GSP), which provided preferential trade conditions for developing nations. The long-term effect of the GSP was to encourage US corporations to outsource their labor abroad. As labor historian Judith Stein notes, it "facilitated, but did not create" the flow of goods that would enter the United States from East Asia in the years that followed.[125] The GSP targeted cartels. The special treatment excluded "OPEC countries and others withholding supplies or charging monopolistic prices."[126]

The Trade Act's exclusion of cartels was a response to the Third World's efforts to rewrite the rules of global trade through the NIEO. Its provision of GSP, as a reward for not replicating OPEC's actions, aimed to forestall any further Third World solidarity.[127] Mao's Three Worlds Theory called on the Third World to unite and apply similar pressures on other raw materials, but the United States established economic incentives to forestall this.

The GSP would be extended only to noncommunist nations, meaning that China was not a direct beneficiary of the provision. Instead, China would go on to benefit from the structural changes the GSP fostered within American corporations and its neighbors in the Asia-Pacific region. The provision encouraged the growth of international chains of production, to which China could contribute—and indeed was already doing so with Hong Kong.

Businesspeople in Hong Kong saw firsthand—and oftentimes contributed to—China's emergence as a site of both customers and workers. Beijing was slowly developing links in its chains of supply with Hong Kong. In fact, almost the entirety of China–Hong Kong trade comprised Chinese sales to the island, much of which Hong Kong then used for re-export and transshipment.[128] With the exception of a handful of products traveling from Hong Kong to the PRC, goods overwhelmingly flowed from the mainland to Hong Kong. China was slowly reshaping its foreign trade and using its proximity to Hong Kong to do so.[129]

In fact, in 1974, as other nations cut back on their purchases from China, Hong Kong increased its imports of Chinese-made electronics by 40 percent. It then used these to make transistorized products, such as radios.[130] The Trade Act's provision of GSP would further solidify the China–Hong Kong trade nexus.

Like the Trade Act as a whole, the GSP provided a lifeline to US multinational corporations during economic crises at home and abroad. Westinghouse, for example, had been close to bankruptcy but was able to survive largely as a result of the incentive the act provided for corporate restructuring. The company had close ties with China: its CEO,

Donald Burnham, was chairman of the National Council. The Trade Act, then, reinforced the changes in production that were already well under way in American industrial firms: toward offshore manufacturing. Even without including China directly, the GSP and the Trade Act were crucial instruments in redefining the meaning of the China market as a place of 800 million workers. Globalization may have been a deliberately chosen path, but the "Made in China" labels of the early twenty-first century were its unintended consequence.

DESPITE THE LIMITS of the China market—the higher prices at the Canton Trade Fair, China's preference to trade with Third World nations, the MFN barriers, the claims/assets dispute, delays in shipping, and limited control over designs—China's exports to the United States increased in 1974. The value still remained much lower than China's imports of US goods but it was higher than previous years. Some of China's textiles—especially cotton gloves, men's dress shirts, and shoes—were already edging into the top positions of US imports. In 1974, China sold $11.3 million worth of white cotton shirts to the United States, becoming the second-biggest supplier of such goods to the United States after Hong Kong.

These numbers would have been even higher if they had accounted for the fact that many US imports from Hong Kong were increasingly likely to have originated in China. By the year's end, China sold $1.3 billion worth of textiles to nations across the globe. Twenty percent of these sales were to the United States alone.[131] Each year of the 1970s, Chinese exports to the United States increased in value and often in volume too. They continued to trickle into the United States despite the difficulties US importers faced.

By the end of 1974 the majority of Americans invited to the Canton Trade Fair were importers, most of whom were from companies seeking to buy light consumer goods, textiles, and handicrafts.[132] While some members of the National Council and the AIA continued to trade barbs with one another, the AIA's Charles Rostov was still happy sharing drinks with members of the National Council's leadership. During one dinner with particularly free-flowing drinks, held at the Sun Lee Dynasty restaurant after a day at the Canton Trade Fair, Rostov, David Cookson, Paul Speltz, Veronica Yhap, and Bob Boulogne established the Tung Fang Club, in honor of the hotel adjacent to the trade fair. "Within the ever present guidelines of equality and mutual benefit this organization is intended to be completely frivolous and non-business like. Large quantities of booze should be consumed to achieve this end," they wrote on napkins.

They would form an American contingent of basketball and soccer teams for the Canton Trade Fairs, "if not a volleyball team" too. With Bob Boulogne's help from J. C. Penney, they would design T-shirts for Americans who went to the fairs. Their final objective was to ensure the "supply of liquor while at the fair." As they ate and drank and schemed, they also outlined their club song. It was to be sung to the tune of "Lighthouse Keeper," a song released in 1970 by psychedelic British folk group Sunforest and featured in Stanley Kubrick's 1971 film *A Clockwork Orange*:

To have it made
In the China trade
Is more than we can wish
But we'll feast
Ourselves at least

Gompei Gompei Gompei[133]

As officials back in Washington fretted over the stalled diplomacy with China, ongoing inflation, rising unemployment, a global recession triggered by the oil crisis, and the political fallout from the Watergate scandal, these importers raised their glasses, toasting "gompei."[134] The limits of the China market made profit "more than we can wish," they sang. Yhap's Dragon Lady Traders faced unpredictable shipping; Cookson's ICD had just received its shipment of broken cassia trees; and Boulogne's J. C. Penney had just recently begun stocking Chinese clothing at a loss. Despite the expenses, these capitalists blurred hubris with self-deprecation. They could afford to absorb the economic losses. Instead, far from the economic malaise back home, trade with China was an adventure, fetishized and exotic.

The most significant transformation unfolding in US-China trade, however, was not material but conceptual. As Chinese merchants would continue to emphasize, American businesspeople needed to shift from seeing Chinese customers to seeing Chinese workers. In China, the Three Worlds Theory institutionalized an idea of Chinese development that was tied to international trade, centering exports in China's economic development. In the United States, the Trade Act provided broader structural incentive for the reconfiguration of the China market from customers to workers. These two structural changes came to complement one another, as China's reformists increasingly saw that part of the answer to China's trade deficit would come from increased sales of textiles.

CHAPTER **5**

Selling Chinese Textiles

O N JANUARY 22, 1975, Wang Mingchuan, head of China's textile corporation, Chinatex, sent a telegram to Washington, DC. Addressing Christopher Phillips, president of the National Council for US-China Trade, Wang brought good news. "Many a time the National Council for U.S.-China Trade has, in the past two years, cordially invited our corporation to visit the United States. While expressing our appreciation I am pleased to inform you that we now accept with pleasure your invitation." He would be sending a five-person delegation to the United States and expressed hope that the "forthcoming visit will deepen the mutual understanding and be conducive to the progressive development of trade between our two countries." The group would arrive in February, he declared. Wang did not ask Phillips if the timing suited the National Council, although he did leave the day of their arrival unspecified.[1]

Jumping at the unexpected message, Phillips sent a reply the following day. "We warmly welcome your acceptance of our invitation," he exclaimed. Lest the opportunity somehow slip his grasp, he added, "we have begun preliminary planning of a comprehensive itinerary."[2] Phillips suggested the textile delegation arrive on or after Saturday February 15, buying him and his colleagues three weeks to prepare. Without a moment's hesitation, Phillips sent a memorandum to all 250 of the National Council's members that same day. He announced the visit and offered to help arrange meetings with the Chinese visitors.

145

After years of stalling, the Chinatex delegation would be the first group of Chinese trade officials to travel to the United States since rapprochement began. Phillips's excitement was tempered, however, by knowledge that Chinatex was not the National Council's high-level counterpart, the CCPIT. Wang Yaoting, director of the CCPIT, had still not confirmed with Phillips when he would reciprocate the National Council's November 1973 visit to Beijing. Instead he sent Chinatex, one of the CCPIT's eight state-owned enterprises, albeit one of the largest. In 1973 Chinatex's revenue constituted just under one-fifth of China's total foreign trade. The National Council estimated the value of Chinatex's trade to be around $1.8 billion, placing it at "about the middle of the Fortune Top 100 list of U.S. firms," an internal memorandum estimated.[3]

Chinatex's visit has not received much attention in the emerging body of literature looking at US-China trade in the 1970s. Instead scholars have focused on the CCPIT's trip, which finally happened in September 1975—after Chinatex. The CCPIT's trip certainly carried diplomatic clout; unlike Chinatex, the ten-member CCPIT delegation met with President Ford.[4] But here I focus on the first official trade delegation that traveled to the United States, whose importance lay not just in being the first visit but also in the material goods it sold: textiles. In choosing to send his textile corporation, Wang Yaoting made it clear that China's trade priorities lay in expanding its textile exports to the United States. His efforts were part of a larger effort by Chinese pragmatists to use exports to fund China's industrialization. China's 4-3 Program of 1973 and its focus on development outlined by Deng at the United Nations in 1974 culminated, in January 1975, with a declaration by Zhou Enlai on the need for Four Modernizations—of China's agriculture, industry, defense, and science and technology. By August, Deng Xiaoping expanded on Zhou's Four Modernizations with three documents on development in which he reiterated the message that had so driven these efforts: "If you want to import, you need to export more."[5]

As China heightened its focus on textiles exports, it also became the subject of growing opposition from groups within the US textile industry. When the Chinatex delegation arrived in the United States in February 1975, it canceled several events and travel plans. Aware of American workers' concerns, Chinatex sought to minimize publicity. Leaders of the National Council similarly worked to allay the fears of US manufacturers and union representatives by emphasizing China's interest in silk, a textile that had less competition with US industry. China was not a threat, they argued, because it was producing luxury goods.

US importers were key to the success of this message of luxury. Around the time of the Chinatex visit, three US companies—Vera, Gerli & Co., and LeeWards—made breakthrough deals with Chinatex to import silk and tapestries. Together they advertised their Chinese imports as a luxury, but in some instances they also presented them as an affordable luxury that even recession-affected Americans could bear. They joined importers of other Chinese goods who, beginning with Veronica Yhap's Dragon Lady Traders in 1971, had praised not just the affordability but the *quality* of goods that were made in China. American importers ensured that Chinese goods in the 1970s were associated with both quality and luxury.

This celebration of Chinese quality and luxury played a vital cultural role in assisting the imports of everyday textile goods that were shipped in boxes alongside Chinese silk and highbrow luxury items. Silk had been one of the top ten Chinese exports to the United States in 1973 and 1974— 6.8 and 2.2 percent of total exports, respectively—but in subsequent years it did not even make it into the top ten of Chinese sales to the United States. In 1975 silk constituted only 2 percent of US imports from China, whereas cotton textiles—including shirts and fabric—together made up over 17 percent.[6] These products' only visible connection to China were country-of-origin labels "Made in China."

By the mid-1970s, then, American importers sold Chinese goods in dual ways: as a celebration of Chinese luxury and as everyday items. The Mao suits sold by Veronica Yhap's Dragon Lady Traders and the cotton shirts Bob Boulogne imported for J. C. Penney made up two parts of the same process. Fashion diplomacy celebrated Chinese luxury through department store exhibits and highbrow cocktail parties, and it paved the way for increased American consumer interest in, and acceptance of, Chinese imports of all kinds.

These two dynamics began to operate together within the same trade deals. American importers involved in these three silk and tapestry deals with Chinatex celebrated the quality and luxury of overtly Chinese goods. As they did so, they used the growing consumer interest in China to additionally sell imports that they did not advertise as Chinese. For these importers, the long-term goal was to sell the latter kind of goods. But they knew that this first necessitated publicity that emphasized to US consumers the excitement of the new Chinese trade relationship.

US union leaders and representatives from the US textile industry interpreted these rising textile imports as signs that China was slowly starting to strengthen its export-oriented development, just as Japan and other East Asian nations had done before it. Imports of Chinese textiles were still much lower than other US imports, but the signs were emerging: China wanted to increase its exports to the United States and it did so by means of far more than silk. As Chinatex, the National Council, and American importers celebrated Chinese silk and tapestry sales in 1975, they also propelled the pivot toward seeing China as not only a source of exotic commodities but also a source of 800 million workers.

The Four Modernizations

China's focus on textile sales to the United States unfolded against the backdrop of broader changes in China's trade policies. In 1975 the political pragmatists, led by Deng Xiaoping and Zhou Enlai, wrangled control of China's trade policies from the radicals led by Mao's wife, Jiang Qing. Textiles—and oil—were the keys to unlocking China's development, pragmatists argued.

Zhou articulated this vision in early January, during the Fourth National People's Congress, a momentous event in which China adopted a new constitution. Zhou's health had deteriorated rapidly but he mustered the energy to leave his hospital bed and speak at the Great Hall of the People, in Tiananmen Square. Zhou delivered the principal report and outlined the importance of what he described as the Four Modernizations. China needed to focus on modernizing its agriculture, industry, defense, and science and technology, he explained.

The Four Modernizations would later come to be associated with Deng Xiaoping, who placed them at the center of China's economic policy in late 1978. But their origins lay with Zhou. He had first articulated his vision of the Four Modernizations in 1963, but the Cultural Revolution prevented them from taking root.[7] In 1975, however, just months before his death, Zhou gave the Four Modernizations renewed life. It was, historians Roderick MacFarquhar and Michael Schoenhals note, "an appropriate swan song."[8] Coming at a time of vicious disputes—Zhou and the pragmatists set against the Gang of Four radicals—the vision Zhou articulated was contested. Three years later, Deng managed to wrest the pragmatists' ideas from the radicals' obstruction and situate them firmly at the heart of China's development.

The line connecting the early Mao era of the 1950s and 1960s to the reform and opening period of the 1980s is not straight or continuous, despite what some recent histories have suggested.[9] Zhou first suggested the Four Modernizations in 1963, but it wasn't until 1975, when he articulated them for the second time, that they started to take root. The origins of the 1980s reforms do not, therefore, go all the way back to the founding of the PRC. But they can be traced to the early 1970s, when Mao began to expand China's foreign trade. After Lin Biao's death in 1971, ending the link between industrialization and militarization, the way was open for a new approach to development. By demilitarizing China's industrialization efforts and turning toward greater trade with capitalist nations in the 1970s, Mao opened the way for pragmatists to push forward the Four Modernizations with new momentum.[10]

Zhou's health remained weak, and after the Fourth National Congress he received Mao's approval to designate Deng as his successor. Deng wasted no time in continuing to advocate for the new approach to development. In August 1975 he spoke before the State Planning Commission, outlining methods for improving China's industrial development. He emphasized the importance of increasing exports "in exchange for the latest and best equipment from foreign countries." China's industrialization would rely upon imports of foreign technology, and to fund this they needed to focus on increasing exports.

Exports of oil and raw materials were some of the key items Deng and other pragmatists pointed to as means of funding technology imports. As we saw in Chapter 4, they were a central component of China's new developmental focus that connected raw-material exports with Third World solidarity. In addition to raw materials, pragmatists turned to light manufactured items and traditional arts and crafts as other key means of funding China's modernization. "We must do everything possible to increase traditional export products such as arts and crafts," Deng declared. What was more, he added, China needed to maintain the quality of its exports. "To be competitive in the international market, we must work hard on product quality."[11]

In 1975 pragmatists within the Politburo, led by Zhou and Deng, held considerable power, which they used to focus on increasing exports, expanding oil production, and using the cash generated from these sales to purchase foreign technology. But they were also met with growing resistance from the radical faction of the CCP. The radicals feared that purchasing foreign technology constituted a turn to capitalism. They pointed to Chinese purchases of previous years and worried about the growing trade deficit. Jiang Qing was one of the most active and vocal opponents of the pragmatists' changes. It was around this time that Mao started to label her as part of a "Gang of Four," along with Zhang Chunqiao, Yao Wenyuan, and Wang Hongwen.[12]

The Gang of Four later described 1975 as the year when the "arch-unrepentant capitalist roader Deng Xiaoping attempted the all-round restoration of capitalism." In their eyes, Deng was "China's Imre Nagy," the Hungarian politician who in the 1950s had tried to implement a similar program of technological development through foreign imports.[13] By the time Zhou died, in January 1976, the Gang of Four had ousted Deng once more. Even amid the fluctuations in Beijing politics, however, China's exports of textiles and arts and crafts had an additional impact beyond generating cash to fund its import program. They helped associate Chinese exports with luxury and quality, which in turn assisted US importers' interest in, and consumers' acceptance of, Chinese goods of all kinds.

Importing China: Vera Scarves

On a hot summer evening in July 1975, Vera, a luxury scarf company, celebrated its thirtieth anniversary with a fashion show at the Hilton Hotel in New York. To mark the occasion, the company revealed its new line of silk scarves. This was no ordinary season launch. Designers from Vera had drawn the patterns for a series of China-inspired scarves in their studios in New York. They then sent them to China, where factory workers manufactured them. A landmark moment in the newly developing trade relationship, the Vera anniversary party marked the first time a US company sold goods that were designed at home and made in China.[14] Other companies, such as Dragon Lady Traders, had had sizing and colors adapted for their clothing imports, but this was the first time a design complete with images and prints had been manufactured for a US company from start to finish in China.

Vera Neumann, the company's president, opened the celebrations with a slide show presentation of her trips to China. She had traveled to China several times in preparation for the scarves' production and shared those

150

experiences with the assembled guests. She later told reporters at a local Virginia newspaper, "I had studied calligraphy . . . in Japan and I really took to it." She mused, "I think once, in one of my incarnations, if you believe in that, I must have been Oriental."[15]

Following Neumann's presentation, models walked down a runway to piano accompaniment. They were given a rapturous reception. "When the scarves were first shown," one reporter recalled, there erupted "spontaneous applause from the audience."[16] The silk scarves featured designs of plum blossoms, willows, and Chinese calligraphy.

Neumann was a veritable icon in the art and fashion world, calling Pablo Picasso a friend. *Fortune Magazine* had recently dubbed her one of the ten most powerful women in business.[17] In 1977 the company's retail sales exceeded $100 million.[18] Her scarves had an enormous following in the US fashion world: Marilyn Monroe, Grace Kelly, and Bess Truman had all been ambassadors endorsing the brand. Like Stanley Marcus's cocktail parties in Dallas, Vera's fashion event engendered an excitement about China among wealthy American consumers. And, like the jewelry and antiques at Marcus's parties, the scarves quickly sold out. Before they had even been sent to department stores and reached the wider American market, Vera had to order more scarves from China.[19]

The scarves depicted a Chinese culture that was filtered through Vera designers' own lens. The *U.S. China Business Review* described them as featuring "various designs from Chinese tradition."[20] They "derived their motif from Chinese culture" and "some of the soft colored clothes were Chinese-inspired." One scarf featured Chinese horses that were drawn from cloisonné at a museum in Shanghai.[21] Vera designers chose the designs, including the colors. But, Neumann recounted to the magazine, "when the Chinese saw the colors" they told her, "We can provide a much better red than *that!*" Nonetheless, Neumann explained, "the colors . . . had been carefully created, even if they seemed a little offbeat to the Chinese."[22] Vera Company's designers had wanted scarves inspired by China yet their chosen red had seemed odd to the Chinese executives. Seemingly authentic Chinese culture was a palatable marketing strategy, but Vera designers adapted it for American tastes.[23]

Despite the fanfare, it cost more to import scarves from China than from other countries. Chinese textiles faced higher duties due to China's lack of Most Favored Nation status. Vera therefore passed this cost onto consumers. The company sold the Chinese scarves for $15 rather than the usual price tag of $10 to $12—the retail price of scarves made in Mexico.

Figure 5.1. Silk scarves made in China. Vera Neumann smiles as she holds up a scarf designed in the United States and made in China.

Publicly, the National Council for US-China Trade applauded her efforts despite the higher costs. "The people at Vera are determined to continue their China program whether it is profitable at this point or not," its magazine reported approvingly. "More than this, Vera and her Vice President consider this only the start of a relationship which they hope will broaden."[24]

Privately, Neumann and the company's vice president, Marvin Pelzer, admitted to businesspeople at the National Council that they would compensate for the higher prices by emphasizing the Chinese nature of the scarfs and "sell it up as a special item."[25] The price would be higher, but consumers may be willing to overlook this because of the novelty of buying goods that were made in China. Neumann explained that she one day hoped to expand the company's business in China, to include scarves in other fabrics and in different weights and constructions—scarves whose patterns did not have overt connections to China.

Neumann was indeed able to leverage the novelty of Chinese goods, profiting off the fashion diplomacy that she and other US importers promoted to customers. But she hoped one day to have her regular lines of scarves made in China. By engendering consumer excitement for Chinese goods, she reinforced the association of Chinese goods with quality and luxury. The silk scarves Neumann sold were part of a larger cultural change from seeing a Red China threat to seeing, instead, a trade partner. She encouraged an excitement not just for Chinese goods but for Chinese production. Her breakthrough deal paved the way for importers and consumers alike to also begin to associate China with everyday kinds of imports.

VERA WAS NOT alone in seeing the China market as a place to import goods designed in the United States and made in China. Milton Jenkins, an importer of furniture from China, shared her vision. "It is possible that American businessmen will also explore the feasibility of having the Chinese manufacture other styles of furniture for export to the United States," he advised in 1974. More than simply importing furniture designed in China, Jenkins hoped his own designs would be made in China. Manufacturing was no longer possible in the United States or Europe, he asserted, "because of high labor costs." The styles of furniture he wanted "can no longer be produced at a reasonable cost."[26] If furniture production could be outsourced to China, Jenkins added, "cheaper prices may come about" for consumers too.[27] Jenkins positioned China trade as having the potential to bring inflationary relief; importers could provide American consumers with lower prices, he rationalized. To him, American workers were merely expensive production costs.

Vera had been at the forefront of realizing the vision Jenkins articulated. But it was Veronica Yhap, head of Dragon Lady Traders, who was able to achieve success in everyday clothing imports. Yhap had been one of the first Americans to import from China, buying clothing in 1971, mostly Mao jackets and qipao dresses. By 1974 she traveled to Guangzhou and provided agents at Chinatex with specifications of the style, cut, and fit of the clothing she wanted to import. She felt that "in China clothes tend to be looser," and she wanted clothing that would suit American tastes, including US sizing that would provide longer shirt sleeves and pant legs.[28] Merchants at the Canton Trade Fair in Guangzhou looked at her blueprints and agreed to make them. Veronica Yhap

Figure 5.2. Veronica Yhap meets with Chinatex delegation on their first trip to the United States in February 1975, where they discussed Chinese manufacturing of everyday items for Yhap's company, Dragon Lady Traders.

was developing more sophisticated methods of importing from China. She knew that Mao coats and qipao dresses were not going to remain in style forever, just as Vera knew that the excitement for overtly Chinese goods would not last.

The changes Yhap achieved assisted other US importers. As Chinatex manufactured clothing in American sizing for her, they offered other US businesspeople shirts and shoes in American cuts and sizing. Reflecting on the progress she had made, Yhap noted, "Chinese manufacturers are accustomed to using general sizes such as 'small,' 'medium' and 'large,' and are only just beginning to understand American measurements."[29]

European importers were additionally influencing clothing design in China, Yhap added. Chinatex had "already begun manufacturing designs by Margit Brandt of Denmark whose fashions are popular in the United States."[30] The Danish deal was similar to Vera's—a reminder that US businesspeople were far from the only beneficiaries of China's outward turn. As she indicated with the Danish example, Yhap did not see herself as discovering the China market so much as building on the efforts of European and Japanese traders who had been trading with China for years. Yhap did not, therefore, operate upon a fiction of discovery, as some of her counterparts did.

Like so many US businesspeople at the time, Yhap did, however, present China as an exotic and unique source of goods. Echoing Vera and so many other importers at this time, she argued that the quality of the clothing she imported from China was "particularly fine." Cotton was the best material in terms of quality and price, she advised. And "Chinese cashmere is said to be the finest in the world."[31]

Yhap's efforts in China, combined with the advice she provided to other businesspeople, helped reconfigure the China market as a source of imports. As she spoke to other businesspeople about her experiences, she promoted a new idea of the China market. While the idea of trade was changing, the realities of it were a different matter. Yhap faced considerable problems as she imported goods made in China to her specifications. Chinatex did not have the surplus capacity to provide clothing to foreign buyers en masse. Delayed shipments, too, were a particular problem for Yhap and other importers. It "means disaster for anyone selling fashions to the American market," she said. Even if she took a pattern to the Canton Trade Fair in May, delivery was not guaranteed for July and would likely be too late for the August back-to-school season. The fickleness of fashion meant that "skirts may be short in the fall but long in the spring, loose in the winter and tight in the summer." It was much easier, then, to stick to importing basic clothing rather than faddish trends.

Yhap's overall advice to prospective importers was to "consider what China has to offer rather than bringing Paris haute couture to China." Vera might have been successful, but most other US importers would not find the same degree of success. Yhap advised, "It's best to buy what is shown at the Canton Fair or in catalogues." Even with sizing specifications, importers should "basically . . . use the Chinese model."[32]

China's capacity to meet Yhap's requirements was limited. Like many US importers, Yhap faced shipping delays and had learned that it was easier to work with preexisting Chinese patterns than to rely upon Chinese factories to manufacture clothing designs from scratch. But the idea of the China market that she promoted—a place where she could bring her clothing designs and have them manufactured in China—was shared by Chinese pragmatists. They may have had limited ways of achieving

their visions in the immediate term, but US importers and Chinese pragmatists were together helping to reshape the China market.

AS VERA NEUMANN celebrated her new scarf range and Veronica Yhap
adapted her purchases to the sizes and colors she wanted, leaders in the
US textile industry began to fight against the implications of the changing
China market for them and their workers. One of their first victories,
albeit small, occurred during Chinatex's visit in February 1975.

In the weeks leading up to the Chinatex visit, Cheng To-pin, from the
Ministry of Foreign Trade, stressed to US diplomats in Beijing that they
intended their trip to be "low-key" and "not widely publicized." Cheng
bristled when a US Liaison Office official commented that this would be
the first Chinese trade mission to the United States. Instead, he emphasized it would simply be a low-level team of officials.[33] The Ministry of
Foreign Trade and Chinatex both insisted that the delegation would not
conduct any press conferences and requested that the National Council
for US-China Trade be the only organization responsible for media coverage during their visit.[34] They were well aware of the domestic sensitivities of selling Chinese-made textiles in the United States.

On February 15, five representatives from Chinatex landed at Dulles
International Airport in Washington, DC, to begin their tour of the United
States. They spent six weeks traveling across the country, meeting with
importers and leaders of the US textile industry. Han Fanyu, deputy director general of Chinatex, led the delegation. Born in 1920 in Central
China's Hubei Province, Han was educated in Japan just before the Sino-
Japanese war broke out. She had spent much of the early 1970s facilitating trade with Japan. One National Council representative described
Han as a vegetarian who "drank beer a lot." She "participated in the lib-
eration movement and carried a machine gun on her back," the obviously
impressed staffer noted.[35]

The National Council leadership turned to Suzanne Reynolds to lead
the delegation on each leg of its tour. Reynolds had joined the National
Council in October 1973, just as the organization was getting started. She
worked alongside Nicholas Ludlow, producing the National Council's
magazine and writing many of its articles. Reynolds, a research assistant,
was paid less than half of what Ludlow, who was employed as an editor,
earned.[36] She had learned Mandarin at university and continued to study

the language in the evenings and on weekends. It is likely that the National Council chose her to lead the Chinatex delegation because she would be able to communicate with the Chinese guests. But the National Council's all-male board of directors may have been conscious of optics, too—the Chinese were sending a female leader.

After four days in Washington—culminating in a hobnobbing reception at the Mayflower Hotel hosted by the National Council—Han, Reynolds and the Chinatex delegation boarded a train to New York City, where they remained for just over three weeks. Han and her delegation met with the executives of a number of New York textile firms. Suzanne Reynolds supplied each of the US hosts with an eight-page booklet with information ranging from how to address the delegates ("remember that Chinese family names come first") to background readings (listing historian John Fairbank's *China Perceived* and political scientist Ross Terrill's bestseller *800,000,000: The Real China*). The booklet warned, "Chinese groups have been concerned over incorrect references to China." She counseled specifically against using terms such as "Mainland China," "Communist China" or "red China." Moreover, "recent groups have expressed sensitivity when Taiwan has been referred to as the Republic of China or Nationalist China."[37] The United States' ties with Taiwan remained the biggest hurdle to resolving diplomatic relations with the PRC, and Reynolds cautioned US businesspeople against exacerbating the issue.

Edward Harding was one of the US businesspeople who received Reynolds's booklet. Vice president of marketing at Spring Mills, which made manufactured apparel items including Springmaid-brand bed sheets and fabric, Harding hosted the Chinatex delegation at Spring Mills's nineteen-story building in New York's Garment District. Spring Mills was one of the largest manufacturing companies in the United States. Like a lot of US corporations, it had, since the 1960s, expanded its manufacturing facilities to include overseas locations in order to sell those goods within the producing country. For example, it set up manufacturing in France to sell directly to French consumers.

By manufacturing and selling abroad, Spring Mills was able to avoid nontariff barriers, such as value-added taxes or quotas, which it would have faced had the goods been made in the United States and then exported. In the 1970s, manufacturers like Spring Mills began to use their manufacturing facilities abroad in new ways. They increasingly imported their foreign-made goods into the American market. Aided by faster shipping and containerization, Spring Mills began to manufacture apparel abroad to sell it to a new market: back home. As trade ties reopened, Harding's eyes were now firmly on China.

Harding hosted Han and the Chinatex representatives at his Spring Mills headquarters in New York, where he gave a presentation on the company's marketing and manufacturing processes. Han and her team had planned to follow up these meetings with tours of Spring Mills's factories in Charleston, South Carolina, alongside other factories in the region. But they were forced to cancel their trip to South Carolina entirely and cut short their visit to Charlotte, North Carolina. The media publicity Chinatex had fought so hard to avoid caught up with them and they wanted to avoid being seen touring US factories.

It was managers of domestic textile factories who tipped off the journalists. From his corporate headquarters in New York City, Howard Richmond, president of textile company Crompton, had been following Chinatex's visit with concern. As Han and the Chinatex delegates met with textile importers across New York, Richmond anticipated the new threat China posed to his struggling industry. He spoke with journalists from the textile industry's newspaper, *Daily News Record,* and on February 26 they published an article voicing his concerns. Richmond cautioned, "The People's Republic of China represents a near-term threat because of its past practices of political pricing." He urged Congress to take action "to forestall a rapid buildup of shipments to this market."[38] In his view, China had the capacity to rapidly flood the US market with cheap textile goods unless US policymakers imposed restrictions.

On the same day, *Women's Wear Daily* ran a similar story. "Chinese Group in Hush-Hush Visit to Textile Markets" the front-page headline blared. "For the past two weeks the red carpet has been out for a trade delegation from China." The article published the names of textile firms that had met with Han and noted that the delegation "is doing everything possible to avoid coverage of any kind." It had canceled a party arranged by Bloomingdales "merely because it was afraid press security might be lacking," the article continued. Nonetheless, "there are textile executives who believe the trip does have serious implications for the American industry." The Chinese were "obviously more concerned with selling their goods here than . . . buying U.S. merchandise."[39]

As a result of the publicity, Chinatex shortened its trip to the South. There was no guarantee that the local factory workers might not extend the media coverage further. Han and her delegation spent only one and a half days in Charlotte and canceled their onward journey to Charleston, where, among other stops, they would have visited Spring Mills factories. Back in Washington, the State Department felt the affair was a useful reminder of the political concerns at stake. "We think that it may have been constructive for the Chinese to learn first-hand from industry leaders how strong the feeling for import controls is."[40] For its part, the PRC Liaison Office blamed the National Council for the media coverage. Chang Tsien-hua, head of commerce, reported back to policymakers in Beijing that the National Council had been responsible for the two stories. After all, they had been tasked with minimizing all media coverage of the visit.[41]

Christopher Phillips and the National Council launched into recovery mode. Two days after the articles' publication, Phillips issued the National Council's first press release on the visit. He downplayed the impact Chinese sales would have on the US textile industry. In 1974 Chinese fabrics were only a "small fraction"—1 percent—of total US textile imports. They were "not likely to have a significant impact on the U.S. textile industry." Moreover, he added, the Chinese delegates were focused on silk, not the velveteen or corduroy that Crompton made. "Silk is an important Chinese export to the U.S.," he emphasized, noting that three of the five delegation members were specialists in silk.[42]

Despite Phillips's attempts to appease domestic textile manufacturers, he knew that silk was only a small proportion of China's total exports to the United States. This was clear from an internal briefing compiled by the National Council and provided to Phillips in the lead-up to Chinatex's visit. The briefing showed that in 1974 woven cotton fabric constituted over 66 percent of all Chinese textile sales to the United States. By contrast, silk products—fabric, raw silk, silk yarn—combined made up only 8 percent of Chinese textile sales in 1974.[43] China was selling the United States far more cotton than silk, and Phillips knew it. In fact, by the end of 1975, 17 percent of all of Chinese exports to the United States that year were cotton textiles.[44] This was a bumper year for Chinese exports. China sold goods worth over $158 million to American importers, the highest rate of Chinese exports since rapprochement began.

The first official visit of Chinese traders since rapprochement shone a direct spotlight onto the key concerns of the emerging trade relationship. China was focused on increasing its exports and saw textiles as a key means of doing so. Coming at a time when the domestic US textile industry was reeling from years of increasing imports and rising unemployment, industry leaders saw China as exacerbating these problems.

The efforts of domestic US textile makers were successful at interrupting Chinatex's trip. But Phillips's assertion—that China's main concern was silk—would continue to dominate the way many Americans thought of China, even though the reality was that cotton textiles dominated Chinese exports. By mid-decade US importers played crucial roles in celebrating the luxury of Chinese silks and other overtly Chinese goods while simultaneously selling day-to-day products, such as cotton items, that had little connection at all with China beyond the workers who had made them.

The "Salute to Silk"

Even though Chinese silk sales to the United States were lower than cotton sales by mid-decade, Phillips was correct in saying that Chinatex wanted to increase its silk exports in addition to its cotton goods. The textile corporation had silk firmly in its sights and its focus had global reach. In 1975 alone, China spent $900,000 on silk campaigns throughout Europe, including a "Rediscover Silk" campaign in the United Kingdom.[45] Earlier in the decade, Chinatex provided financial assistance to the Commission Européenne de Propagande pour la Soir in Zurich, Switzerland. The commission helped coordinate fashion shows promoting silk throughout Europe and in 1973 organized a special feature in *Vogue* magazine.[46]

By November 1975 Paolino Gerli, the eighty-five-year-old president of the fashion house Gerli & Co., became a major beneficiary of China's turn to silk. He joined Vera Scarves in celebrating a breakthrough deal in Chinese trade. Not only would he import Chinese silk, but Chinatex would also provide the funds for him to launch an advertising campaign promoting the products. With Chinese funding, he would sell China as a luxury item that American consumers could afford.

Gerli & Co. was a family-owned firm that had its origins in Milan. Like many early twentieth-century apparel makers in the United States, Paolino Gerli had migrated to New York City from Milan in 1904 at just fourteen years of age. Eventually he took on the family business, shifting its headquarters from northern Italy to New York.[47] In the early twentieth century, Gerli imported silk from China. He eventually opened offices in Shanghai, Guangzhou, and other cities in China and imported thousands of bales of silk each year. A leader in the US silk trade, in 1928 he was elected the head of the National Raw Silk Exchange at just thirty-seven years old: the youngest person to serve in such a position on the New York stock exchange.[48] Nonetheless, World War II brought his silk trade with China to an end.

Gerli reestablished his ties with China in the spring of 1972 when he traveled to the Canton Trade Fair with a handful of other Americans just a few months after Nixon and Mao's meeting in Beijing. In subsequent years, other representatives from his company traveled to the fairs and purchased raw silk.[49] The consumer demand for silk in the United States was "very low," he privately told leaders at the National Council for US-China Trade. Gerli felt he needed to "start a worthwhile revival of demand for silk and silk fabrics in this country."[50]

By the fall of 1975 Gerli traveled once more to the Canton Trade Fair. This time he purchased 250 bales of raw silk. But in response to his earlier concerns about low consumer demand, his deal included a "promotion fee" paid for by Chinatex. In other words, Chinatex did not just supply silk to Gerli, it paid the American company to advertise the finished products. As one National Council staff member put it to a colleague upon hearing the news, "The company billed the Chinese and they sent them a check."[51] This was the first direct partnership between an American company and Chinese state enterprise. Gerli's decades of experience trading with China had placed him in a strong position to negotiate. It helped that his interests aligned with those of Chinatex.

Gerli sent the raw silk it had purchased from Chinatex to American Silk Mills, one of its divisions, where US textile workers spun it into cloth. Located in the town of Orange, Virginia, American Silk Mills had been struggling in recent years to cope with increasing American consumer interest in synthetic fabrics. As more and more mills turned to using nylon and other synthetics, the mill in Orange found it difficult to compete.[52] American Silk Mills did not have facilities for making synthetic material, and its management chose not to invest in the new technology.[53] With funding from China, Gerli would publicize the Chinese silk spun in Orange at Altman's and other US department stores. Gerli's deal with Chinatex, then, not only aided Chinatex in promoting its silk, but it also gave small relief to the workers at the Virginian mills.[54]

By September 1976, with the Chinese funding in its coffers, Gerli & Co. launched a campaign it dubbed the "Salute to Silk." Its promotion strategy targeted two female-dominated demographics: the elite fashion world and middle-class handicrafters. Creating a desire for silk in high-end fashion would soften the way for the company's desire to sell it as a fabric for sewing at home. Through these consumers, they hoped to "re-establish this oldest of textiles as a potent force in a broader market," its marketing executives said. By catering to home sewing, silk was to become "a luxury that everyone can afford."[55] Gerli's marketing strategy was reminiscent of the consumer culture that developed in the United States between the mid-1950s and mid-1960s, which was similarly steeped in affordable luxury—what historian Thomas Hine calls "populuxe."[56] The key was to increase consumer purchases of items billed as luxurious.

The Salute to Silk campaign was huge. Between 1976 and 1979, Gerli & Co. hosted twenty-six fashion shows in department stores across the United States, including Altman's in New York, Sakowitz in Houston, and Marshall Field in Chicago. Models in silk gowns glided down red-carpet runways that were set up in the stores. Charles Kleibacker, a New York–based designer and local celebrity in these circles, hosted many of the events, selling silk as a populuxe and giving advice to women on how to use it in their sewing projects at home. Most of the shows were held on weekdays during traditional work hours. In March 1978, for example, women in Detroit could attend a show at Hudson's Fashion Fabrics in Northland Mall, which began at 9:00 a.m. on a Tuesday. The attendees need to make a reservation, but the show was free and they would even be treated to a complimentary breakfast.[57]

Gerli executives estimated that around 30,000 women came to their various events. Some of the department stores also set up exhibitions on the history of silk. Marco Polo made an appearance in these history displays, as did a map outlining a silk route he was purported to have traveled. Alongside the shows, Gerli printed pamphlets on "tips for sewing with silk" that also advertised their Chinese silk. The pamphlets were distributed at the shows and placed on counter displays at department stores across the country.[58]

"Silk is like a beautiful woman, you never grow tired of looking at her," Paolino Gerli declared to journalists from his New York office. Despite its timelessness, "hardly any woman under 35 has ever worn silk," he bemoaned. His silk mills would change all that. "We have every reason to believe there will be a renaissance of silk during 1976," he predicted. Silk allowed for a sense of luxury even during hard financial times, he promised. Its fibers "make silk feel warm in winter and cool in summer." Pointing to the increasing amounts of cheap silk coming in from China, Gerli sought to position silk "within the means of many more people." Women sewing clothes from home could buy silk at department stores

Marshall Field & Company

Leo Narducci
Vogue 1828

YOU'RE INVITED TO AN AMERICAN SILK MILLS FASHION SHOWING

American fashion and home sewing authority, Charles Kleibacker will narrate the showing. He'll discuss ways to sew and work with silk fabrics, as well as offer tips on mixing, matching and layering separates. Prices of American Silk Mills fabrics range from $3.50 to $22 a yard. In Fashion Fabrics—Second Floor, South State; merchandise also at Old Orchard, Oakbrook, Woodfield and Mayfair in Wauwatosa, Wisconsin

Come to our *State Street store*, Friday March 3 at 10:45 a.m. or 1:30 p.m. You'll see beautiful new designs in separates come together for spring. Both of these splendid showings will feature luxurious silk, Qiana® nylon, cotton and silk blends . . . in graceful sheers, shantungs, crepe de chines, and much more. All sewn by American Silk Mills from distinctive Vogue and Butterick designer patterns. Enjoy this superb combination—beautiful fabrics and elegant styling

Figure 5.3. Gerli held fashion shows across the United States showcasing its Chinese silk.

163

for $8 to $10 per yard.[59] This price tag was still higher than other fabrics. Wool-blend fabric retailed at around $3.35 per yard. During a summer sale, American consumers could buy cotton fabric inspired by the popular Liberty of London for $3.90 per yard. But when the sales were over, if American women wanted to sew with specially patterned cotton fabrics, they would pay $9.50 or so: around the same price as Gerli's silk.[60]

In addition to the shows in New York and other major cities, Gerli also placed advertisements in fashion magazines including *Vogue* and *Harper's Bazaar,* as well as local newspapers, all extolling the appeal of silk. The Chinese origins of the silk was not always mentioned in the advertisements. Women in Orange, Virginia, and its surrounding areas could also buy silk at a discount if they traveled directly to the mills. Portions of the Chinese silk that was spun at the American Silk Mills in Orange were sold in a store behind the mill, where the luxury material was marketed at less than half its retail price. A local newspaper in nearby Charlottesville wrote of the sales in March 1979. The *Daily Progress* headline declared: "Best Buys for High Fashion Home Sewing Are Right Here in Orange." The article went on to note that "first time visitors have been known to get carried away by the sight of silk crepe de chine at $4 a yard."[61] The veiled advertisement included details about how to handle silk, including sewing and washing instructions.

But the bargain basement sales belied the troubles that American Silk Mills and Gerli were facing. The partnership between Gerli & Co. and Chinatex, assisting both Chinese exporters and American mill workers, was short-lived. By the end of 1979—after only four years working with Chinatex—American Silk Mills ended their operations. The deal with China had been part of a final attempt to revitalize the mill, but the mill simply could not compete with the enduring popularity of cotton and the rising interest in synthetic materials. In the age of disco, nylon and polyester were increasingly dominating the American market. Rather than invest in technology upgrades, the management at Gerli's subsidiary shut down the mill entirely.[62]

In the decades that followed, more and more American mills were forced to close due to increasing competition from foreign imports, including those from China.[63] Gerli helped sell China as high-quality and affordable, far removed from the red China threat of the Cold War. But China was not always mentioned in American Silk Mill's printed advertisements. Kleibacker emphasized the Chinese origins of the material during the shows themselves, but consumers who did not attend the department store events and saw only the advertisements in newspapers would not always have known where the silk came from. Salute to Silk sold China as both quality and luxury but it also revealed a dynamic in which Chinese imports were sold to American customers without references to China at all. Gerli worked hard to promote affordable silk. But silk, whether or not from China, was not enough to save the domestic manufacturer from an industry structured upon cheap labor above all else.

LeeWards and the Diplomacy of Exoticism

As US businesspeople encouraged a cultural shift away from seeing China as communist threat to seeing it as benign trading partner—a source of luxury items, no less—a third US company made a breakthrough import deal, combining highbrow with the everyday. In the mid-1970s, LeeWards Creative Crafts, a company based in Elgin, Illinois, was one of the largest purveyors of craft supplies in the United States.[64] With thirty chain stores across the country, LeeWards sold American consumers inexpensive wares including painting and sewing kits, ornaments, and small knickknacks. Its parent company, General Mills, was a multinational conglomerate with companies in the toy and restaurant industries. In addition to LeeWards, General Mills's divisions included toy company Parker, creator of Monopoly, and the dining chain Red Lobster.[65]

In 1969 LeeWards began to expand the number of stores it operated. By 1974 the company became a profit-making entity for General Mills, generating annual sales of around $50 million.[66] LeeWards's invigoration was underpinned by an increase in its global sources of manufactured crafts. In 1970 its executives reached out to a Hong Kong firm regarding prospects of importing tapestries from China, but they were met with no response. In 1973 the company opened a buying office in Japan to facilitate imports from across the Asia-Pacific region. And with the reopening of trade ties between the United States and China in 1971, LeeWards turned its attention to China once more. Japan became a site for regional procurement of goods and China became a potential new source of manufacturing, but Hong Kong served as the most important hub for the company's ventures into the China market.[67]

In March 1974 Charles Eaker, vice president of LeeWards, received a telex in his Elgin office from the agent he had worked with in Hong Kong. John See, of Hong Kong World Traders, explained to Eaker that representatives from China National Light Industrial Products Corporation were interested in meeting with him in Hong Kong. With only a few days' notice, Eaker flew across the Pacific Ocean and met with the Chinese traders. "They knew a great deal about U.S. market conditions," he told the National Council for US-China Trade afterward, "although many were very young and a little naive concerning international business practices."

During his time in Hong Kong, Eaker examined a range of tapestries and came up with a marketing idea. "As soon as I saw their artwork, I was enthralled with the idea of having an exhibition in the U.S. and suggested it then and there," he recalled later. "The Chinese lit up; they obviously liked the idea." He bought a handful of smaller needlework pieces and took them back with him to show his colleagues in the United States. LeeWards executives strategized and decided they would hold a tapestry art exhibition in addition to selling handicraft kits from China.

Eaker's plan required two different kinds of purchases: antique tapestries that would become part of the Chinese art exhibition and needlepoint and tapestry-making kits that consumers would complete at home. In the fall of 1974 he traveled to the Canton Trade Fair, where he signed a deal to import both. The needlepoint and tapestry-making kits were to be manufactured in China and sold to American consumers in LeeWards stores across the country or by mail order.[68]

The National Council pointed to LeeWards's experience as an example of the commercial benefits of emphasizing the Chinese origins of their products. An American importer's success in selling Chinese goods would be "considerably enhanced" if the products were "part of a Chinese tradition," its magazine advised. Or "better still," it continued, "something that will appeal to customers in the U.S. while retaining the Chinese flavor."[69]

But in fact, the company lost money. LeeWards used its Hong Kong agents, World Traders, to handle the transaction because, like all US importers, it needed to use third-country banks. LeeWards lost 10–15 percent of its payment because of financial market fluctuations as they converted the cost of their purchases from Chinese renminbi to Hong Kong dollars. Speaking later to the *U.S. China Business Review*, Eaker dismissed this loss as one of the "minor problems" he had faced. Like Vera Neumann, he found that trade with China was an expensive pursuit but one he wanted to do anyway.

Back in the United States, LeeWards organized for the newly acquired tapestries to be used in their art exhibition, "China in Needlepoint."

Curators hung the tapestries in the National Geographic Society in Washington, DC, and opened the show in January 1976. The exhibit celebrated Chinese art and the reopened US-China cultural ties. In March the exhibition moved to Chicago for a second showing. The elaborate tapestries depicted Chinese landscapes, the Great Wall, and, in one case, a boy wearing a red sweater and playing Ping-Pong. A reporter from the *Washington Post* mused that this latter tapestry was an "obvious bid for the American trade."[70] The ping-pong diplomacy of the Nixon and Kissinger days, only a few years earlier, still held strong commercial pull.[71]

The tapestries on display were also for sale. They retailed between $500 and $2,500; a double-sided silk masterpiece was priced at $12,000. By contrast, the do-it-yourself needlepoint kits retailed between $4 and $40.[72] Consumers of the needlepoint and tapestry-making kits could select from a range of images, including kingfishers, carnations, and lilies, all of which held a Chinese inflection.[73] Unlike Vera's scarves, LeeWards did not have control over the design of the needlepoint images. The executives could only import the kits that Chinese exporters provided. This was no matter to Eaker; he simply promoted the allure of China through the tapestry exhibitions to engender market appeal for its needlepoint and tapestry-making kits.

Needlepoint stitching was a popular pastime in the United States. Craft stores reported customers' "insatiable demand" for the products.[74] In the summer of 1974 journalist Frederic Hunter noted its popularity among male consumers, celebrating "the manly art of needlepoint." He estimated that most of the men doing needlepoint were "executives and professional men, including lawyers, architects and surgeons," suggesting approval for the hobby from these male-dominated industries. Hunter interviewed Robert Stone, a financial consultant and captain of one of the Boston Rugby Club teams. "If I do anything as a hobby," Stone remarked, "its needlepoint. It takes off the pressure at work, which is sometimes considerable." Needlepoint was, in this depiction, a signal of the busy lifestyle a successful man faced. Paul Gardner, a Christian Science practitioner and reader at Boston's Needham Church, told Hunter that he had spent the previous football season watching games and stitching an eighteen-inch wall hanging that his wife described as "quite masculine." It featured a Chinese symbol at its center.[75]

As consumer interest in needlepoint stitching grew and its devotees attempted to expand the hobby's appeal by anxiously perpetuating masculinist norms, LeeWards launched its China in Needlepoint exhibition and began selling its needlepoint kits and prefinished tapestries. Visitors traveling to the exhibition in Washington, DC, or Chicago were given a guidebook filled with advertisements for LeeWards needlepoint products.[76] The kits allowed American consumers to develop a participatory relationship with the Chinese imports, not unlike university students and their Mao coats, or wealthy liberals and the antique robes they purchased.

While the Chinese tapestries and Chinese-style images generated initial consumer excitement, some of the needlepoint kits that were made in China were not overtly Chinese, but instead images such as cats, dogs, and trees. LeeWards sold China at two registers—through tapestries and home stitching. The dual effects of this propelled the pivot from seeing an exotic China to seeing, instead, China as just another source of low-cost manufacturing. As the National Council reported, China was "reaching twenty-four million U.S. customers."[77] And it did so through products that were not overtly Chinese.

LeeWards had previously imported needlepoint art from Madeira, the Canary Islands, and Taiwan. Other needlepoint companies had purchased from Japan, Hong Kong, and the Philippines. "But today," the *Washington Post* reported in 1976, "labor in those countries is more expensive than in Mainland China."[78] LeeWards sold its products to the American consumer through the celebration of reestablished cultural ties, but its decision was motivated by the promise of cheaper labor for handicraft goods that were made in China.

THE TAPESTRIES AND craft kits that LeeWards sold were precisely the kinds of goods that Chinese pragmatists hoped to sell in order to fund their technology import plans. As part of their renewed focus on increasing Chinese exports, in early 1975 the CCPIT and its regional trade branches introduced mini fairs, a new kind of trade show to supplement the twice-yearly Canton Trade Fairs. The mini fairs would be smaller and only showcase a single kind of export. In December 1973 Chen Yun had touted the importance of adopting "flexible trade measures," such as mini fairs, as an important way of increasing China's exports. They would be a "supplement to the Canton Fair," Chen explained.[79]

By 1975 China National Native Produce and Animal By-Products Import and Export Corporation (Chinatuhsu) held four such fairs in different Chinese cities. Each fair specialized in a particular type of Chinese export:

feathers in Shanghai, fur in Beijing, wood in Guangzhou, and carpets in Tianjin.

The Tianjin carpet fair attracted the largest number of visitors: around 300 businesspeople from twenty countries. Huge tapestries hung from the walls of the Tianjin Industrial Exhibition Hall, many of which depicted ancient architectural landmarks. Just as LeeWards displayed its China in Needlepoint tapestries, the mini fair in Tianjin featured antique tapestries, including a fifteenth-century tapestry that portrayed Beijing's Temple of Heaven. Others on display had been newly woven. *Renmin Ribao* reported on the event, drawing particular attention to the workers in factories across China who had woven the new tapestries—part of China's "long history of weaving traditional carpets." The newspaper celebrated the tapestries' depictions of ancient "cultural relics" as well as others of landscapes copied from modern photographs.[80]

The exhibitions' blending of old and new reflected the much larger nation-building efforts under Mao. Throughout the Maoist era, museums and art exhibitions used cultural relics to create—and curate—a national narrative that positioned China's antiquity as an integral part of the communist revolution.[81] The new mini fairs put these efforts to work for China's development plans too.

The mini fairs would become a central component of China's foreign trade in the second half of the 1970s. They were timed to bridge the gap in seasonal sales; the Canton Trade Fairs did not always coincide with the optimal period of the overseas selling season, a problem that many US importers had complained of for years. Chen Wenhai, head of Shanghai's trade fair authority, coordinated the mini fairs. "Different commodities have different market characteristics, especially in regard to their selling seasons in overseas markets," Chen noted to one US businessman. The Canton Trade Fairs were "frequently ill-timed" and missed these seasons, he added.[82] With winter sportswear, for example, the fall fair "is held too late in the year for overseas wholesalers and retailers who wish to make purchases for the season at hand."[83] The specialist mini fairs therefore offered a way to target foreign companies wishing to buy Chinese goods.

AS CHINESE PRAGMATISTS continued their push to fund Chinese development through exports; as Chinatex became the first official Chinese trade delegation to travel to the United States; and as specialist mini fairs became a new feature in China's foreign trade calendar, Chinese exports became firmly positioned as central to the unfolding ties with the United States. By the end of 1975, US-China trade had plummeted to only $462 million—less than half that of the year before. Throughout 1975, China did not make a single purchase of US wheat, cotton, corn, or soybeans—commodities that had dominated just a year before. It was a very different story for China's exports to the United States, however. They continued to steadily increase, spurred in part by Chinatex's February tour. By the end of 1975 China had sold a record number of goods to American importers. Chinese exports to the US were worth over $158 million; 17 percent of these were cotton textiles alone.[84]

But the pragmatists' efforts to use foreign trade to develop their industry was met with growing resistance. Fueled by Zhou's call to center the Four Modernizations and Deng's three documents outlining how to implement them, radicals in the Chinese Politburo continued to pull China's foreign trade policies in the opposite direction. By November the political fortunes of the pragmatists and radicals had reversed.[85] As 1975 drew to a close, the Gang of Four had regained control of China's political agenda, and Deng and the pragmatists were sidelined once more. The tensions in Beijing would mean that US industrialists' dreams of selling factories and technology to China would remain unrealized. But the changes in high politics did not thwart the structural changes that the mini fairs brought or the small yet increasing exports of Chinese goods to the United States. US importers helped to sell China itself. They celebrated Chinese luxury and quality, and in the process paved the way for increased consumer interest in, and Chinese manufacturing of, goods whose only visible connection to China were their labels, "Made in China."

CHAPTER 6

Mao's Death and the Continuities of Trade

JUST AFTER 3:00 A.M., in the quiet darkness of a hot July morning in 1976, an earthquake struck China's north, devastating the city of Tangshan. He Jianguo, like many in the city, had been asleep at the time. In a few hours she would have been getting ready to go to the ceramic factory where she worked as a secretary. Instead, she and the seven other women she shared a dormitory with were violently shaken awake. He scrambled to the window and managed to get to it just in time to leap—terrified—from her first-floor room. She landed bruised but alive. Seconds later, the building collapsed behind her. Steel and brick and bodies were crushed. None of her roommates survived. James Palmer tells He Jianguo's story in his history of the Tangshan earthquake, one of the world's most deadly earthquakes ever recorded. Over half a million people died. The city's infrastructure was so destroyed that scholars compare it to the cities of Hiroshima or Nagasaki after the United States dropped atomic bombs on them in 1945. The physical destruction, they point out, was even worse in Tangshan.[1]

Six months earlier, China had been shaken by a different kind of tectonic shift. On January 8, 1976, Zhou Enlai died. Upon hearing the news, He Jianguo recalled feeling "sad for a moment" because "he seemed kind, like an uncle." But for He, the day continued as normal.[2] For others in China, Zhou's death triggered extensive public outpourings of grief. "I had never seen such universal grief," Jan Wong recalled. "It seemed everyone was weeping, men and women, old people and children . . . bus drivers, street sweepers and shop clerks all went about their chores with swollen eyes."[3] In death, Zhou, who had been educated in Europe and spoke fluent French, became a symbol of moderate politics and resistance to the Gang of Four. He had been a favorite of many Western leaders. Kissinger, for example, had said of Zhou that he was "one of the two or three most impressive men I have ever met."[4] Deng Xiaoping gave the eulogy at his funeral.

With Zhou's death, Deng's political influence—already waning—vanished. Soon after Zhou's passing, *Renmin Ribao* contained an editorial condemning Deng and the pragmatists for "opposing the principles of independence and self-reliance, believing that only by begging foreign countries can we change the backwardness of science and technology."[5] Yet in April, four months after Zhou's death, citizens gathered in Tiananmen Square to lay flowers and wreaths in honor of his memory. The crowds who gathered soon became tens of thousands of people. What began as mourning had become a demonstration of support for the modernization program Zhou had advocated, and resistance to the brutality of Mao's regime and China's economic stagnation.[6]

By September, China was rocked by a third major event. After years of illness, Mao died, bringing an end to his twenty-seven-year grip on power. Hua Guofeng was Mao's chosen successor, but the chairman's death sparked a bitter struggle for power between the radicals and the pragmatists.[7] The political maelstrom reached a high point in October when Hua organized a coup that led to the arrest of Mao's wife, Jiang Qing, and the three other members of the radical Gang of Four: Zhang Chunqiao, Yao Wenyuan, and Wang Hongwen.[8] With this, Hua emerged as China's new leader. His own position, however, remained unstable. By May 1978, nineteen months later, Deng Xiaoping wrested control of the party apparatus. Hua continued to lead the CCP until 1980, but after Deng's takeover, his became a nominal leadership.[9]

For ordinary Chinese people living well beyond Tangshan and its surrounds, the environmental and political changes of 1976 affected everything from food supplies to working conditions. Foreign trade was likewise thrown into disarray. Following the earthquake, China's trade negotiations were placed on temporary hold and all foreign businesspeople were required to evacuate Beijing and Tianjin and relocate to Shanghai or Guangzhou.[10] By the end of 1976 China's total foreign trade fell to $13.2 billion—lower than the previous two years but still considerably higher than any year of China's trade in the 1950s and 1960s.

The drop in total trade was driven by a sharp decrease in Chinese purchases. China cut back on its foreign imports by 15 percent. Imports from Japan declined by 26 percent and imports from the United Kingdom dropped 30 percent. But even with the decline in China's total trade, Chinese exports increased slightly.[11]

US-China trade followed this wider pattern: total bilateral trade declined in 1976 but Chinese exports increased. By the end of the year bilateral trade stood at $330 million—the lowest level since 1972—but this was also the first year that the trade imbalance reversed. For the first time since the Shanghai communiqué, China sold more to the United States than it purchased. The only other year when China sold more than it bought from the United States was 1971, before Nixon and Mao's summit, when China made no purchases whatsoever and its exports were a paltry $5 million.

The shift in the trade balance revealed an emerging trend in US-China trade: regardless of the total trade figures, China's exports to the United States continued to increase as they had each year since 1971. In fact, with the exception of 1990, China's exports to the United States increased in value every year of the rest of the twentieth century and almost every year of the first two decades of the twenty-first century.[12] By that stage, the value of exports was astronomically higher than in the 1970s, but the trend—of ever-increasing value of Chinese exports—took shape in the 1970s when the China market itself began to transform.

The political and environmental turmoil in the period between Zhou's death and Hua's takeover of power in late 1976, meant that progress in diplomatic normalization came to a near standstill. In the United States, too, domestic politics took priority over normalization efforts with China. With an election in November, President Ford focused his attention elsewhere. Amid the fallout from the Watergate scandal, the responses to the landmark Supreme Court decision of *Roe v. Wade,* and the ongoing energy crisis, Ford declared he would not normalize relations with the PRC until after the election.[13]

Exploring trade in this period reveals just how susceptible US-China trade was to political whims. The seven months between Zhou's and Mao's deaths was a period of dramatic unrest that held the potential for long-lasting disruption to China's trade. The newly empowered radicals—who had gained the upper hand in late 1975—not only cut back on trade but sought to make the cuts permanent. They threw the contingencies of the future of China's trade into stark relief. The Tangshan earthquake made things even worse for trade prospects.

But in terms of US-China trade, it was foremost a period of continuity. The increase in Chinese exports that occurred alongside these cuts reinforced the emerging structural shift in which US businesspeople understood the China market as a place to buy from. Despite the radicals' attempts to end the foreign trade that had taken off since the pragmatists' 4-3 Program of the early 1970s, businesspeople in the United States and China successfully expanded China's sales of goods to the United States. They continued to reach trade deals, implement advertising campaigns, and even build the fertilizer factories sold in earlier years. Had Hua not successfully removed the radicals from power in October 1976, these efforts might not have been sustained for much longer. As it turned out, however, the growth in Chinese exports, which occurred despite China's overall cutback in trade, helped sustain a deeper restructuring of how US businesspeople understood the China market. By the time of Mao's death, China had become a site of imports more than exports.

The Gang of Four: An End to Export-Led Development?

As the Gang of Four once more gained control from pragmatists, they emphasized to capitalist nations the peripheral role that trade would play in China's economic policies. In May 1976, Li Qiang, minister of foreign trade, told the British foreign secretary that "foreign trade was only marginal to the Chinese economy."[14] China had experienced its first-ever trade deficit in 1974, a situation the radicals emphasized was no longer acceptable. The country was now cutting back on trade altogether, he warned. *Study and Criticism,* one of the radicals' major mouthpieces, emphasized this explicitly in June, noting that the moderates' trade policies would "cause China to sink back into the abyss of semi-colonialism and semi-feudalism."[15] Now that the radicals had control, they warned, China's foreign trade would decrease significantly.

The effects of the shift in China's position were rapid. In January 1976, just a month before Zhou's death, Chinese factories were still willing to sew in the labels of some capitalist companies rather than use Chinese labels. Ken Wherry, vice president of the US clothing company Eddie Bauer, noticed this accommodation firsthand. He traveled to Shanghai in early January to attend China's newly established feather-and-down mini fair, during which time Chinese officials invited him to tour one of the nearby factories.

Walking through the rows of women sitting behind sewing machines with growing piles of clothing on their workbenches, Wherry noticed something familiar. Sewn into the clothing were labels with the recognizable lettering of a Canadian clothing brand. The women were stitching the labels onto the finished goods. Turning to his Chinese hosts, Wherry requested that his clothing orders also come with his own private label. They agreed to consider it. "These agreements are really beginning to proliferate," an observer reported back to the National Council for US-China Trade in Washington.[16] Zhou Enlai's death a few weeks later, however, changed things considerably. As the radicals dictated trade policy from Beijing, Chinatex began to move away from its single-label approach and Wherry's hopes were dashed.[17]

By the spring Canton Trade Fair in April, Chinatex was forced to harden its position. China would no longer be stitching in a single private label for American businesses, Huang Tsien-mo explained to importers Veronica Yhap and Bob Boulogne, executives from Dragon Lady Traders and J. C. Penney. Huang had been part of the five-person Chinatex delegation that traveled to the United States the previous February, as part of the first official Chinese trade delegation to the United States. He explained to Yhap and Boulogne that it was now "usual practice" for China to sew in Chinese labels alongside the company labels. This was a process of double labeling. "The label is a symbol of the quality," Huang declared. Double labeling would "preserve the honor and reputation of their products" by showcasing the Chinese origins more clearly and therefore highlighting their quality. With this, Chinatex moved away from its earlier efforts to produce products whose only visible connection to China was "Made in China" on the labels underneath the foreign brand.

Veronica Yhap and Bob Boulogne both pointed to Chinatex's earlier willingness to sew in a single label. This new change, back to double labeling, was a "step backwards," they decried. Huang conceded that a few foreign companies had indeed been permitted single labels in previous years but explained that these had been "exceptions." Boulogne later noted to leaders at the National Council that this change of heart "could call into doubt other agreements and understandings." Did this, he wondered, "portend even more ominous circumstances?" Boulogne worried that it might be "symbolic of other changes."[18]

Boulogne's fears were warranted. Around the same time that Boulogne and Yhap met with Huang, *Study and Criticism* published a scathing article critiquing the moderates' foreign trade policies of the early 1970s.

The piece focused on Deng Xiaoping, who had emerged as the key leader of the pragmatists after Zhou's death. Deng and his allies "stretch their hands overseas, begging from foreign capitalists," which amounted to little more than "the importation of things we are capable of producing ourselves" and "the export of things we badly need." China risked becoming a country "where the capitalists could dump their goods," purchase China's raw materials, and use it as "a repair and assembly facility" for manufactured goods. "Would not then our workers become nothing more than wage workers for foreign capitalists?"

This had happened before in China's history, the article declared. China's workers were first used for capitalist profit in the late Qing dynasty under Li Hongzhang and Yuan Shikai and again during the Nationalist period under Jiang Jieshi's leadership. "The blood and sweat of our workers were used to support foreign bosses, but we will never forget this history."[19]

American importers were already seeing the impact of the radicals' anticapitalist stance. The clothing and manufactured goods they purchased would no longer carry company labels. Instead, it would be Chinese labels sewn along the seams of towels or stuck on the soles of shoes. If the radicals had ultimately been successful in their political agenda, then it is likely that the availability of towels and shoes and other items that US importers purchased would have altogether declined. The radicals certainly aspired to a return to a stricter interpretation of self-reliance, which would have led to a foreign trade that looked far more like pre-1970s levels. As they gained power in November 1975 and consolidated their position after Zhou's death in February 1976, the radicals went some way toward repositioning a more isolationist interpretation of self-reliance at the heart of China's economic policies. For the time being, however, foreign businesspeople were still able to import in the volumes they had become accustomed to since China's outward turn in the early 1970s.

From Great Wall Vodka to Don King Sporting Goods

Even as US-China trade reached an all-time low and importers faced mounting problems, some US importers continued to foster a culture of excitement about the new trade relationship unfolding. Around the time when Hua arrested the Gang of Four, an American businessman name Charles Abrams celebrated what he depicted as a milestone event. On

October 25, 1976, he traveled to New York City's South Street Seaport to welcome a ship loaded with Chinese vodka. This was, according to Abrams, the first time the liquor had been commercially imported since 1949.[20]

Abrams turned this moment into an elaborate marketing event. The port was festooned with a vinyl balloon replica of a bottle of vodka the height of a three-story building. Swaying on the windy dock, the vodka-shaped balloon was positioned next to a huge sailing ship, the *Peking*. The ship had been used in China trade during the early twentieth century and in 1974 had been converted into a museum on the dock.

Around eighty people flocked to the dock where New York's port commissioner, Louis F. Mastriani, welcomed the new Chinese imports. Once the cases of vodka had been unloaded from the ship, the group convened at a Chinese restaurant where, the *U.S. China Business Review* reported with a wink, "the vodka and viands quickly warmed up the guests."[21]

Charles Abrams was an investment banker by training. Like many of the new generation of China traders, he had long been interested in China. In 1974 he told the *New York Times* he had been "a student of China for fifteen years." Recalling a trip to Asia when travel to China was closed off to US businesspeople, he mused: "I still remember standing there in Hong Kong and saying to myself, 'What lies beyond that great wall?'"[22] He began trading with China the first moment he could. In 1972 he started up a company, the China Trade Corporation, and began by importing a handful of documentary films that he sold to American television distributors.[23]

Abrams continued to important a range of consumer goods from China. When he started importing Chinese vodka in 1976, he imported it under a brand name exclusive to the American market: "Great Wall Vodka." In China the liquor was sold as "Sunflower Vodka." Abrams had negotiated the name change to make it, as he put it, "sound more Chinese and less like vinegar oil."[24] Of course, it was Abrams, not the Chinese with whom he dealt, who chose the "more Chinese" name. Like Vera Neumann's choice of red in her scarves, Abrams sought a Chinese authenticity that he himself defined.

Abrams marketed the vodka by referencing one of China's most famous attractions. He conveyed a China that he hoped would appeal to armchair tourists. For their part, Chinese traders certainly emphasized Sunflower Vodka's Chinese origins in their own advertisements. An advertisement from 1975 showing the bottle's Chinese characters made it unmistakably Chinese. Abrams's push for a name change revealed that

Figures 6.1a and 6.1b. At left, a Chinese advertisement for Sunflower vodka. At right, Abrams's advertisement for Great Wall vodka. Abrams wanted to sell a drink that sounded "more Chinese and less like vinegar oil."

he wanted to emphasize not just the Chinese origins but also a certain idea of China—offering both ancient culture and a travelers' adventure— that would appeal most to American consumers.

It took three years for Abrams to conclude his vodka import deal from China's Ceroilfood. But at the Canton Trade Fair in the spring of 1976, both parties finally reached an agreement. Not only would Abrams import Chinese vodka and change the name; Ceroilfood also agreed to assist with a direct-mail advertising campaign. Chinese students would address and stamp the flyers and send them from China to liquor executives, businesspeople, and government officials in the United States.[25] This was the first direct-mail initiative from China to the United States, and Abrams, with his eye for drama, understood that its novelty was a crucial component of his marketing efforts.

Upon reaching the deal at the Canton Trade Fair, Abrams returned to his room at the Tung Fang Hotel feeling "ecstatic." For the first time since rapprochement began, China's government was to embark upon a marketing effort in the United States. Abrams, not one to shy away from his enthusiasm, declared, "This is the greatest afternoon of my life."[26]

With assistance from Ceroilfood, he would send flyers advertising Great Wall Vodka to 50,000 American homes. The Chinese trading corporation had arranged for Chinese students to address and stamp the flyers. The students were not paid for their efforts. The *New York Times* reported that the students worked "free of charge" but did not offer any further comment. Instead the article concluded jauntily that Abrams "stands to make a profit for both himself and the Chinese."[27]

In addition to a free mailing campaign, Abrams profited even further by inflating his prices. American consumers could purchase a case of twelve Great Wall Vodka bottles for the hefty sum of $108.[28] Abrams's marketing campaign took full advantage of the high price tag. Great Wall was "the world's most expensive vodka," declared the advertisements, which appeared only in the *New Yorker*. The exclusive marketing campaign targeted consumers who would be interested in a vodka that was, as one advertisement put it, "strictly not for the peasants."[29] The class politics here were not subtle. Wealthy *New Yorker*–reading liberals consuming Chinese vodka, with an eye for the exoticism of the Great Wall, could distinguish themselves from "the peasants" thanks to the uncompensated labor of Chinese students.

Abrams cultivated an elitist thrill for Chinese goods at a time when US-China trade was in decline. His efforts were part of a larger reimagining of China as a source of imports rather than a site to absorb US exports. But Abrams had a particular kind of vision for Chinese imports: he wanted them to retain their status as high-quality goods. "My emphasis in all this," he told reporters, "is on quality products." He added, "We don't want to turn China into another Japan."[30] In Abrams's estimation, China's marketing strength was its association with quality. He did not explain what he meant by "another Japan," but he spoke at a time when the United States imported high numbers of low-cost Japanese goods. Abrams hoped to position the China market differently: as a site for cheaper goods—even underpinned by free labor—that were nonetheless exclusive.

Abrams carefully cultivated the exclusivity of Chinese Great Wall Vodka. Even though his advertisements declared Great Wall Vodka to be the "most expensive" in the world, he soon noticed his main competitor had their own similarly verbose claim. Pepsico, which imported the Russian vodka Stolichnaya, publicized its own liquor in similar terms. "Stolichnaya is the most expensive Vodka sold in America," its posters declared. In actual fact, a case of Stolichnaya wholesaled at $76.53 with a minimum retail price of $7.99 per bottle. Great Wall Vodka wholesaled at $87.75, and each bottle retailed at a minimum of $8.99. The retail costs of Great Wall Vodka were only one dollar more, but to Abrams this was enough. He hired lawyers and on April 25, 1977, took Pepsico to court. His lawyers presented his case before the New York County Supreme Court, asserting they had the "exclusive right in the use of the words 'the world's most expensive vodka.'"

Abrams's New China Liquor charged Pepsico with "unfair competition." Pepsico had known of Great Wall Vodka's slogan and "sought to usurp, pirate and take advantage of" its campaign. Its advertisements "deceive the public into believing that Stolichnaya is the most expensive vodka in America when in fact it is not," New China Liquor and Spirits claimed. The Russian company sought to "syphon off retail customers from retail establishments who are desirous of purchasing the most expensive vodka in America." American consumers who wanted to know they were paying premium prices were being disadvantaged and deceived. Stolichnaya "intends to cause confusion in the trade" and was "mocking the general public" with its false advertising. This was causing "irrevocable damages" to Great Wall Vodka. Abrams demanded a whopping $5 million in damages.[31]

The two companies settled their dispute in November 1977 and the Supreme Court of New York ordered Pepsico to "immediately cease and desist" from using any language suggesting that its Stolichnaya vodka was the most expensive. Pepsico was not, however, required to pay the $5 million in damages. For the journalists who wrote about the case, this was a story of Cold War competition like no other. "China and the Soviet Union are engaged in a spirited contest in bars and liquor stores across the U.S.," the Wall Street Journal punned.[32] With a tongue-in-cheek sensationalism, the China Business Review wrote that "China and Russia are currently embroiled in a new, highly volatile area of contention." Great Wall Vodka had sought to challenge "Soviet hegemony in the international vodka market."[33]

The irony was indeed remarkable. Two corporations were using the communist superpowers to compete for the title of most successful capitalists in the world's richest economy. And they were doing so through the US legal system. In 1973 Henry Kissinger had written privately to President Nixon that if the United States could balance its triangular diplomacy with the Soviet Union and China, they would be able to "have our mao tai and drink our vodka too."[34] Now the two communist powers were part of a triangular diplomacy that had converged around vodka.

Yet the vodka war was perhaps more successful in advancing Abrams's marketing strategies than anything else. In January 1978 a fuming Edward Lahey Jr., vice president of Pepsico, wrote to Nicholas Ludlow at the National Council for US-China Trade, correcting the "polemic tone" of the National Council's reporting on the case, which was "almost entirely erroneous." Pepsico had described its vodka as the most expensive for over ten years, he corrected.

Of Abrams's own advertisements for Great Wall Vodka, Lahey clarified, "In fact, we never saw it." Instead, the first Pepsico had heard of it was when they received notice of the lawsuit. Even then, "this matter was never even discussed with the Soviet supplier, because it was not important."[35] As far as Lahey and Pepsico were concerned, the matter was a trifling irritant. Abrams, however, continued to use the geopolitical context to his advantage. When the Soviet Union invaded Afghanistan in December 1979, Abrams declared a new "vodka war" whereby he encouraged consumers to smash bottles of Stolichnaya in protest.[36]

Abrams was a showman as much as a businessman—he had once tried to set up a traveling caravan showcasing Chinese imports as he drove across the United States. His caravan idea never took off, but his posturing with Chinese vodka was part of a larger cultural and economic shift taking place. Even as overall US-China trade figures decreased and as the Gang of Four started to cut back on China's foreign trade, US imports of Chinese goods continued to grow. The steady flow of Chinese imports and Abrams's promotion efforts worked together to reshape how American businesspeople saw the China market.

DON KING, one of the United States' most renowned boxing promoters, also fostered the culture of spectacle surrounding trade with China. Having worked for years with Muhammad Ali, King described himself as a "promoter extraordinaire." He is perhaps most known for arranging the 1974 boxing match in Zaire between Ali and the undefeated George Foreman. The so-called Rumble in the Jungle became one the most watched television broadcasts of the decade and is remembered for Ali's shocking win against the younger frontrunner.

The following year King orchestrated a new match, this time pitting Ali against a small-time boxer from New Jersey, Chuck Wepner. Wepner was a club boxer who spent his days working as a liquor salesman. In selecting him to fight against Ali, King positioned Wepner as the heroic everyman. King's support for Wepner allowed him to present himself as being, in his words, "for the heavy-laden and downtrodden." The bloody, drawn-out fight was tighter than spectators had been expecting. Ali emerged victorious, but Wepner's determination was lionized. By December 1976 Sylvester Stallone depicted the fight in his blockbuster film *Rocky,* turning it into a regenerative parable of white working-class resilience.[37]

Six months before the film's release, in the summer of 1976, King celebrated a different business achievement. At his Manhattan home on the 67th floor of the Rockefeller Center, he held an event for journalists and corporate elites that was half press conference, half party. Donning a frilled shirt under a green suit and sitting behind a long table adorned with basketballs, sports shoes, and baseball mitts, King was flanked on either side by Charles Abrams and television producer Larry Gershman. King announced that he had started a new company that imported sporting goods from China.

The awkwardly named Don King Friendship Sports Clothes and Goods Corporation would be a subsidiary of Charles Abrams's China Trade Corporation. Just as King had worked with Wepner—the liquor salesman turned boxer—he now worked with a white liquor merchant, Charles Abrams. The class dynamics, however, were very different: unlike Wepner, Abrams was not a blue-collar hero but a wealthy businessman.

The guests at King's house party were offered Abrams's Great Wall Vodka. As the party wore on, guests began to play with the Chinese-made basketballs and volleyballs, throwing them to one another across the massive Manhattan suite. In the verbosity that had so driven his career, King explained that the Chinese equipment had "mystic powers." With Chinese basketballs and hockey mitts, players would gain "more baskets, more scores." The hint of masculine virility operated close to the surface. "Everyone is a star when you play with a friendship ball," he declared.[38]

King explained to journalists that Abrams had asked him to join the team "because I speak the language of the third world." This was not a spoken language, he continued, but rather "the language of the heart." He did not explain any further what he meant by this. But by invoking the Third World, he used ideas of Afro-Asian solidarity for his own promotional purposes. His efforts came at a time when many Black civil rights leaders turned to Mao Zedong Thought as part of a search for alternatives to the violence and inequality that had emerged under American liberalism.[39]

King used his Third World ties to position himself as distinct from the wealthy white businessmen beside him. He noted, "A lot of businessmen don't know the combination to unlock the heart, but I do. I came from the masses." Speaking afterward to one of his guests, King reflected on what his role in the China Trade Corporation meant for civil rights. The way he saw it, "white men . . . approached a black man . . . to help sell products made by yellow men." Black entrepreneurship was what mattered to King and he saw himself as achieving it. "It's all very nice to get up on a corner and preach 'Black is good' or 'Black is beautiful,' but it won't feed the baby." Instead, "growth and economic development, that's what count."[40]

Don King and Charles Abrams, both consummate promoters, worked together to sell Chinese products using different kinds of capitalist appeal. King asserted his affinity with the Third World and the "masses," a kind of rags-to-riches form of capitalism. Abrams pursued an elitist exclusivity: a capitalist consumption reliant on being the most expensive. These differences were also apparent in the kinds of Chinese goods they imported. The Don King Friendship Sports Clothes and Goods Corporation might have been a subsidiary company of Abrams's China Trade Corporation, but its relationship to Chinese imports operated differently. Unlike Great Wall Vodka, there was very little that was distinctively Chinese about the sports equipment Don King imported. As much as King touted the "mystical" nature of a basketball made it China, it was the lower labor costs that were the real appeal of these Chinese imports. And while Abrams hoped China would not become "another Japan," it was cheap consumer goods like King's, rather than expensive vodka like his, that would come to dominate the imports Americans bought from China. For the time being, however, the marketing spectacles of both men helped to reconfigure the idea of the China market as a site of imports, not exports.

ABRAMS AND KING may have played up the excitement of the new China trade, but by mid-decade the challenges importers faced were beginning to pile up. As importers grew frustrated, the National Council for US-China Trade became "anxious to aid companies importing from

China," one of its leaders wrote to executives at Bloomingdale's.[41] Aware, too, of the importance Chinese leaders placed on increasing their sales to the United States, business leaders in Washington looked for ways to help US importers purchase from China.

In June 1976 some US importers met with National Council representative to discuss the situation. They complained that they were being forced to accept "situations that would be considered unacceptable on trading with other countries." They were "bending over backwards to trade with China." The aggrieved importers listed a range of complaints, including late shipments, lack of documentation, communication difficulties, and price changes. With China, they noted, "cancellation is rarely acceptable." If a buyer did cancel, "he faces the risk of not being able to trade with China in the future."[42]

Many US importers grumbled that they often felt compelled to accept such conditions even though they would not have done so with other nations. Their concerns were shared by the wider community of importers. "There's at least one problem per deal," a major Hong Kong importer declared. Foremost in his list of concerns was the length of time it took for an order to arrive. "Cotton t-shirts have been known to take up to 18 months to arrive at the consignee's warehouse."

Another US importer was so frustrated he decided to buy corduroy products from Hong Kong factories even though they were more expensive than those from the PRC. Corduroy clothing was fast becoming a new fashion trend and the importer wanted his products to enter stores quickly. Those from Hong Kong could be delivered in three weeks, he noted. "Whereas from China it would take a minimum of two months, and up to five months if the colors were difficult."[43] He was willing to pay more to receive them sooner.

Robert Katz, an academic of business administration at the University of California, Berkeley, encouraged American businesspeople to look beyond these problems in an article he published in 1976 in the *California Management Review,* of which he was editor. Katz discussed the challenges of trading with China, noting that "there are errors, of course." Katz gave the example of "a shipment of all left shoes" to an American importer. But "what is most striking," Katz continued, "is the alacrity with which corrections are made." American buyers, such as those receiving the left shoes, "reported that replacements of defective orders were made without dispute or question." From this, he concluded that "one can be certain that any discrepancy in goods received will be corrected."[44]

There was nonetheless a hint in his anecdote of the increasing Chinese capacity to manufacture in bulk—all left shoes were sent. By emphasizing the willingness of Chinese traders to respond to the issues, rather than the problems themselves, Katz focused on the rosier sides of China trade. The most "striking" aspect of the experience was the readiness with which Chinese traders responded, he argued.

At a later point in his advice article, Katz parenthetically referred to "a U.S. buyer" who ordered cashmere sweaters in May 1976 "which are not due to be delivered until the fall of 1977." By referring to the delayed shipment in parentheses, Katz decentered the reader's attention from the delays and instead focused on the possible reasons for it. He noted that there could be a number of explanations, including the Chinese preference to begin manufacturing only after orders had been received. "Suppliers do not maintain an inventory of luxury items, such as cashmere sweaters," Katz wrote.

Some American businesspeople had told him that the frequent delays were the consequence of a "lazy work ethic." Katz argued, "This seems unlikely to me because of the high motivational factors reported among Chinese workers and my own observations of their industry." He spoke of "the integrity of the Chinese in commerce," which he described as "uniformly impressive." The Chinese were "warm and friendly but firm." He advised, "Do not believe that the differences in culture and society will be overwhelming: the bridges of similarity are far greater than the chasms of difference."[45] Katz was selling China to US businesspeople reading his journal. Things were difficult, he conceded, but the challenges were all part of the experience.

The National Council encouraged a similar attitude among readers of its magazine. "There is never a dull moment for importers of Chinese clothing," one article began. Its author told the story of an importer who "recently ordered four styles of a garment in oxblood and natural color." One of the garments had come, not in natural color but "surprise, one in green and brown!" they exclaimed. "On top of this, one piece was the wrong style." The article noted, "We hope to report a happy solution in our next issue." A different importer had "ordered a shirt that was to shrink only 7 percent." While this proved to be true, "the collar shrank 14 percent."[46]

The National Council was open about the unpredictable quality of goods from China. But the jaunty tone of these vignettes—merely examples of there "never being a dull moment" in US-China trade—presented it as part of the fun. The problems businesspeople encountered were simply insignificant blips that did not overshadow the excitement of trading with China. It was an adventure, and mistakes were part of the ride. For seasoned traders, however, the novelty was wearing thin.

Prospective importers reading this advice may not have been fully persuaded about the benefits of China trade either. If they listened, however, to a tape-recorded interview with Veronica Yhap, head of Dragon Lady Traders, their concerns were more likely to be assuaged. In August 1976 she participated in a twelve-part cassette recording advising US businesspeople on "how to trade with China." During the interview, Yhap explained that she was increasingly seeing China as a source of manufacturing. "In fact," she told listeners, "fifty percent of the stuff that they make for us right now is completely Western." In the earlier years of trade, Yhap had engendered consumer excitement for China using visibly Chinese goods—she had imported premade items such as Mao coats and qipao dresses. But now she was "using the Chinese manufacturing process" to purchase the kinds of goods she really wanted.[47]

The trick, Yhap advised, was to work with what the Chinese are able to do, rather than get frustrated at what they cannot do. She pointed to the vast majority of goods that she purchased from China: cotton greige goods. These were cotton textiles that had not yet been dyed, finished, or printed with images. Yhap would import the greige goods and sell them to mills across the country where US workers completed the process. These workers would add prints or dye the goods according to seasonal fashions. In this way Yhap was able to work around the shipping delays in Chinese goods. By importing greige goods and reselling them, she helped create a process in which clothing with the latest colors and prints were made using the inexpensive base products from China.

This was a process based on both quality and cheap labor, Yhap extolled. "China really produced the best quality of cotton greige goods in the world," she declared. "I think," she added, "that partly it has to do with the natural material" but it was also because "the workmanship is so good and so careful." The notion that China's workers produced high-quality products, particularly textiles, was a common refrain among foreign businesspeople. It was certainly an idea Charles Abrams pursued with his Great Wall Vodka. And it may well have had some truth to it, but what they were also saying was that the cheap cost of labor did not detract from the quality. "The quality is good; the prices are competitive," Yhap commented later in the interview.

The Hong Kong–based *China Trade Report* similarly reported on the "high quality of workmanship and construction in Chinese textiles." Some of China's woolen goods seemed like they "could only come from Britain or France," except, the report noted, woolens produced in those countries were at least twice the price.[48] China's workers were careful and skilled, readers were informed. They provided quality products at lower labor costs.

The challenges US importers faced were significant, and by mid-decade many importers were beginning to question their involvement in the China market. But some business leaders offering advice or those working at the National Council hoped instead to encourage perseverance, emphasizing the positive sides of the trade experience, playing up the adventure involved, and pointing to the quality of goods when they did eventually arrive. Others, such as Veronica Yhap, found ways to work around the challenges they faced. Importing from China came with a range of difficulties, but it also brought with it the appeal of low-cost labor.

The Future of the China Market

The radicals' grip on power, combined with the ongoing problems with imports, rattled some American businesspeople. But other structural changes were unfolding at the same time, helping to deepen bilateral ties. Some of the most important of these were banking and financial ties. In October 1975 Bank of America secured correspondent relations with the Bank of China. In December, Manufacturers Hanover Trust also established correspondent relations and by July 1976 First National Bank of Chicago joined them. Together with Chase Manhattan, which in 1973 became the first US bank to secure correspondent relations, the United States now had four banks with correspondent relations with China.

America businesspeople wishing to trade with China could turn to one of these four banks to handle the transactions instead of using a bank in Italy or France, for example. Due to the unresolved claims/assets problem, the banks would still need to draw upon their branches in a third country. But US businesspeople could now use their US banks.

Tim Williams, who worked at Bank of America's Asia office in Hong Kong, took this as a positive sign despite the immediate challenges facing US businesspeople. Writing in the pages of the magazine *American Chamber of Commerce in Hong Kong* (*AmChamHK*), he sought to assure his fellow businesspeople and conveyed a message of steadiness. Mao's health had deteriorated even further after a severe heart attack in May 1976, and Deng Xiaoping's dismissal in late 1975 had led to fears that the political change "may adversely affect China foreign trade policy in general and the development of Sino-U.S. trade in particular," he wrote.

Williams stressed instead the necessity of taking a long-term view. The problems in trade—such as the lack of MFN status, blocked assets, and claims issues—"will be solved in due time," he wrote reassuringly. He noted that even though total trade had dropped by more than half since 1974, the trade imbalance had narrowed. "This is a considerably more stable basis for continued growth than the previous rocketing imbalance," he argued.[49] In fact, the incoming trade figures for 1976 showed that the trade balance had shifted and was now in China's favor.

From Williams's vantage point, given Bank of America's new deal with Bank of China, there was certainly reason for his cautious optimism. Manufacturers Hanover Trust's senior vice president, Mark Buchman, similarly reflected on the third-party banking procedures to the company magazine. "U.S. companies must go through several layers of paperwork that ordinarily are not necessary in international business," he lamented. "This makes more room for error, delay, confusion, miscommunication and expense."[50] Buchman framed the challenges using old tropes of Chinese timelessness and essentialist notions of inherent difference.[51] "The Chinese view time in a different perspective than we do," he said as he lit his cigarette and posed for a photo.

In addition to banking relations with the United States, there were other signs of China's continuing trade ties with foreign nations. Despite the Gang of Four's dominance, Chinese trade officials continued to purchase new machinery for producing textiles. Early in 1976 China National Technical Import Corporation purchased a polyester manufacturing plant from two Japanese companies, Teijin and Nissho-Iwai. The plant could produce huge amounts of synthetic materials. In a single year, it could make 80,000 tons of polyester.[52] China's purchase was an indication of its growing interest in competing in textiles beyond the traditional cotton and silk markets. As more and more consumers in capitalist nations demanded clothing made of spandex and other synthetic materials, China slowly expanded its capacity to produce such products.

Foreign importers used China's interest in foreign technology as a bargaining chip in their negotiating processes. A small British importer, for example, had been able to complete his purchase of Chinese goods by of-

Figure 6.2. "The Chinese view time in a different perspective than we do," Mark Buchman, senior vice president of Manufacturers Hanover Trust, asserted in February 1976. His interview followed from a trip to China in December 1975, where he established correspondent banking relations with the Bank of China.

fering a fusing machine as part of his compensation. Such a machine was used to join pieces of fabric, such as the seams of clothing. He reflected that he had seen much older fusing machines at the Chinese factories and could offer newer technology as part of his bargain. A large importing agent in Hong Kong also noted that many of his clients were offering machinery in their negotiations to purchase Chinese goods.

An American company also based in Hong Kong was less successful. In its negotiations with Chinatex, it had offered a Sanforizing machine, used for cotton knits. Sanforizing machines helped reduce shrinkage in the fabric being produced. Many US importers complained that China's clothing tended to shrink much more than products from other nations, and a Sanforizing machine would have assisted with that. But its executives were told that Chinatex had no interest in such a machine. The fact that it was an American company may have played a role in Chinatex's apparent lack of interest.[53] President Ford's public acknowledgment that normalization with China would not occur until after the election in

November meant that even with structural improvements through banking ties, China looked elsewhere as much as possible for its trading needs.

US Engineers in China

While politics in Beijing grew increasingly tumultuous, things were far quieter for Joe St. Clair. A twenty-eight-year-old engineer at Pullman Kellogg, St. Clair was currently based in a remote Yunnan mountain village. For eighteen months he and a handful of other Kellogg employees had been posted to the southwestern province, where they helped Chinese engineers and technicians build and operate an ammonia fertilizer factory. His was one of eight groups of Americans helping to build the factories Kellogg had sold to China in 1973.

China's state-owned enterprise Techimport had purchased the Kellogg fertilizer factories as part of the country's 4-3 Program, which Mao approved in 1973. The plan aimed to improve China's food production for its citizens at a time of mass food shortages. Most Chinese peasants' food consumption levels had not changed since the low of the mid-1950s. In many cases, the variety of food they had access to had shrunk.[54] The factories China imported under the 4-3 Program went some way toward improving these bleak statistics. By the end of the decade, they had increased China's ammonia production by over 30 percent.[55]

From Heilongjiang in the north down to Yunnan in the south, tiny communities of Americans sprang up in the Chinese countryside to help set up the plants. Kellogg employees and their families were dispersed around the sites, with twenty to twenty-five people living in each location. The usual length of stay for the employees was sixteen to eighteen months. In total, around 140 Kellogg employees worked and lived in these enclaves. Many had also worked in other parts of the world, such as Indonesia, Australia, and South Africa. The *U.S. China Business Review* described these globe-trotting employees as "a hardy group of people."[56]

This was nonetheless Joe St. Clair's first time traveling outside of North America. For all the excitement he must have felt in being one of the first Americans to live in China, a land that had been closed off for so long, his experience of daily life in China was also filled with routine boredom. He was living in a tiny Chinese village where, he told journalists at the *Washington Post*, "I missed being able to go out on the town at night."

190

He and the other Kellogg employees and their families lived, ate, and socialized together within a single compound attached to the factory's site.

The newspaper described their experience in much more fantastical terms: "A small oasis of pork chops, air conditioning, plastic Christmas trees, and Mary Tyler Moore in the middle of the ancient Chinese countryside." While the Kellogg employees were free to move around the local community, they were not allowed to travel to the surrounding areas. St. Clair therefore sated his restlessness with weeklong trips to Hong Kong every so often. Kellogg permitted its employees one week of holiday for every six months of work at the Chinese sites. For St. Clair, Hong Kong was a "virtual cornucopia of the fruits of Western life." Moving between Hong Kong's nightlife and the familiar culinary and cultural comforts of their "oasis," St. Clair and his colleagues were more or less buffered against the realities of everyday life in Maoist China.[57]

Yet even the *Washington Post* article featuring St. Clair's experiences contained a jarring aside that hinted at some of the discord from which he and his colleagues were otherwise shielded. The Kellogg employees were based "in an area not far from a center of bitter political strife," the article noted. "The Americans sometimes found guards suddenly swarming over at a nearby rail depot." But "no serious trouble ever came to their rural job site," readers were reassured.[58]

The article did not provide any further discussion of this turmoil, nor did it mention the long history of political unrest in Yunnan Province. Bordering Vietnam, Laos, and Burma, this area had a significant non-Han minority population. In 1956 the Miao and Yi people of Yunnan protested against Mao's rural agricultural collectivization efforts through various acts of everyday resistance, which at times became armed rebellions.[59] The huge economic and social changes wrought by Mao's complete upheaval of Chinese society had triggered these preexisting tensions, which continued to simmer well into the 1970s.

Amid the hints of turbulence, and despite the radicals' efforts to reimpose their version of self-reliance, Joe St. Clair and his colleagues continued to build their fertilizer factories in China. In 1975 Jiang Qing, one of the leaders of the Gang of Four, had attempted to stop St. Clair's colleagues in Daqing from building one of the fertilizer plants. Daqing was the home of China's largest and most symbolically important oil fields. Built without foreign assistance, it was an embodiment of Maoist self-reliance.[60] Jiang had argued that building an American factory in the area would compromise the ideal of self-reliance. She eventually backed down after she saw Mao's signature approving the location of the factory.[61]

Even after Zhou's death in January 1976 and the radicals' increased power, St. Clair and the Kellogg engineers remained in their posts working with Chinese technicians to build the eight fertilizer factories. The radicals ensured that China did not purchase any further US technology in the immediate aftermath of Zhou's death, but they did not stop the assembly of previously purchased industrial goods. In this way, even at a time of flagging bilateral trade and declining Chinese imports of US goods, St. Clair and the other Kellogg workers helped sustain trade ties despite the political unrest unfolding in Beijing.[62]

THE FACTORIES US engineers helped build were symbols of Chinese control more than they were expressions of US power. Unlike infrastructure projects in other parts of the world, the factories in China were not extensions of US imperial power.[63] And unlike other periods of US-China relations, the Americans did not set up the factories with the hope that their presence would change China.[64] Instead, the factories revealed two impulses that had shaped US-China trade since it recommenced in 1971. First, US policymakers and businesspeople conceived of their work as assisting the larger efforts toward formal diplomatic relations. Trade was, in their estimation, a tool that helped diplomatic negotiations. The factories also revealed a second, conflicting, impulse underlying the unfolding trade ties: Chinese officials maintained tight limits on their trade with the United States and turned, as much as possible, to other capitalist nations for technology.

US importers helped bridge these dynamics, but the experiences of US engineers in China threw light on these two issues from the perspective of US exporters. Just as the increasing US imports from China revealed the continuities in trade despite cuts in Chinese imports from the United States and the political turmoil in Beijing, the stories of Kellogg workers and their families illustrate the continuities in bilateral trade dynamics.

The Kellogg workers themselves certainly saw their role as being informal diplomats in addition to being engineers. From his station in Yunnan, Joe St. Clair extolled the "close ties developing between American families and local Chinese."[65] He felt that the personal ties that were developed in the remote Chinese mountains rendered the Americans unofficial ambassadors of US power.[66] "The kids of the men with families would play with the Chinese kids," St. Clair told the *Washington Post*. And "some of them picked up Chinese a lot faster than I did."[67]

Peter Dobi, a senior manager at one of the Kellogg sites, similarly told the National Council for US-China Trade, "I feel this has brought the countries closer together." Dobi continued, "Each time you go, things are friendlier and friendlier. The Chinese are just like any other client now: we're accomplishing with them because we've proved ourselves. We've earned our reputations as Kellogg employees and as specialists."[68] In Dobi's estimation, the ties that were developing between his company and Chinese technicians were not only symptomatic of the ties that were being forged at the political level, but they were assisting that process too.

Despite the bridges Americans felt they were building, Chinese leaders placed tight controls on their visitors' movements. The Americans lived in very closed areas, which they filled with familiar items from home. Kellogg sent them videotapes of US television programs just a week after they were aired. The company provided magazines, including *Time* magazine, the *International Herald Tribune,* and *Playboy*. The American families also imported food, including cookies, peanut butter, instant coffee, and Tang—all things "to make the typical American feel at home," the *U.S. China Business Review* noted.[69] For all the reminders of the United States, living in these remote parts of China was very different from life back home. As Joe St. Clair had indicated, it could be lonely too.

The tight controls China imposed on its American residents were reminiscent of trade in the eighteenth and nineteenth centuries, when foreign businessmen were assigned to very strict confines in Canton. The experiences of Kellogg workers in the 1970s reflected a similar impulse, held by China's moderates and pragmatists, to control China's trade and ensure it worked in its interest. The radical faction may have wanted to severely curtail foreign trade, but the pragmatists' vision—of tightly monitored commerce that served China's interest—prevailed in the period between Zhou's and Mao's deaths.

Only a small number of women and children came with their husbands. In 1976 the National Council estimated that around fifteen children and up to twenty-five wives had lived in residence in China. Many of the women who accompanied their husbands educated their children through a home-school curriculum created by Northwestern University. They received daily lesson plans, which they would send back to teachers in Evanston for grading. At the Liaoning site, there were enough children that their mothers

Figure 6.3. Halloween in Yunnan.

organized them into small school groups and taught them themselves. One woman became fluent in Mandarin, and many others learned enough of the language for everyday communication. Many of the women who traveled with their husbands lived in close-knit contact with one another. They traveled regularly from their different sites throughout China to meet together in Beijing. Their networking gave them opportunities for socializing and entertainment, and they established a lending library system to share English-language literature.[70]

In the neighboring province of Sichuan, Kellogg employees set up a fertilizer factory under the supervision of William "Bill" Walker. Walker had worked at several other Kellogg sites around the world. The major difference, he told editors at the *U.S. China Business Review,* was that his Chinese hosts provided a much larger selection of culinary dishes. In fact, he gained twenty pounds during his time in China. "The Chinese food was so good," he noted by way of explanation. Mealtimes were "gastronomic adventures," where he had access to a smorgasbord, including dumplings, peanut chicken, grilled duck, and shredded pork in pepper sauce.

Chinese chefs working at the Kellogg building sites offered more than 130 Chinese dishes and 147 Western dishes. In an aside, the magazine remarked on the stewed sea slugs that were also on offer: "not a winner with many Americans." Tinged with sarcasm, the article's mention of sea slugs played up the exoticism of China trade. The experience of living in China could be as familiar or otherwise as the Americans wanted, it suggested. Residents could get eggs for breakfast. "Chinese finesse in cooking them American-style varies considerably from location to location," it added. Even the familiar could be rendered exotic.[71]

The article was one of four feature-length pieces in the *U.S. China Business Review* in 1976 and 1977 that focused on Americans living in China. The numbers of Americans were low relative to the amount of trade China concluded in total. But the articles provided a space where US businesspeople could imagine themselves as part of a much larger network of business in China. They encouraged a collective intrigue about trade with China. At various stages throughout pages of the journal, American businesspeople were reminded of the historic and diplomatic role that they were playing. The technology sales contributed to an "overall improvement in the Sino-U.S. trade relations," one of the articles concluded.[72]

Another article featured a full-page menu taken from a guest house at Sichuan Province. "When one pages through the exotic and sophisticated menu the Chinese provided for Pullman Kellogg employees and their families living in the PRC, it is hard to believe that most of the company's plant sites are located in isolated rural areas." Each of the eight construction sites had a restaurant "staffed by cooks skillful with both Eastern and Western cuisine," the magazine noted. Employees had their own cooking facilities, although "not too many have been able to resist a menu which includes three hundred items."[73]

At a time when the Cultural Revolution was still affecting every aspect of Chinese life, ordinary people living in the surrounding countryside would have found it impossible to obtain this type of food. The article was partly aimed at calming potential concerns about the prospect of living in China, even though very few Americans actually did so in this decade. The *U.S. China Business Review* presented the variety of food available in China in cosmopolitan terms. The menu illustrated an American fascination with food in China, but it also demonstrated that even as China imposed restrictions on the movements of its visitors, its officials worked hard to make them comfortable.[74] The CCP was willing to go to great lengths to present a favorable image of Chinese society to foreign visitors;

it ensured that its foreign visitors were provided with culinary decadence despite the severe shortages so many of its own citizens faced. The factories these Americans constructed were designed to help feed China's citizens, yet so much of their own focus and that of the National Council's magazine was devoted to how they fed themselves.

For all the celebrations of people-to-people diplomacy that Kellogg employees saw themselves achieving, China only made limited technology purchases from US companies. By January 1977, just under 450 American technicians and engineers had lived in China since rapprochement began.[75] Compared to the numbers of other foreign technicians, these numbers were small. The Americans made up around 15 percent of the more than 3,000 foreign technicians who had lived and worked in China since the start of the decade.[76]

Many Kellogg employees commented on the hardworking nature of the Chinese workers, framing this as an important appeal of the experience of living in China. Walter M. Buryn, vice president of Pullman Kellogg, estimated that at one stage 3,000 Chinese workers had worked on the Kellogg plants. They were young, averaging about twenty-two years old. The labor force included both men and women, who worked "side by side as skilled and capable laborers and craftsmen." Musing on their efforts, Buryn likened these workers to those who had built the Great Wall centuries earlier. "The world is familiar with the greatest construction project undertaken by man, the Great Wall of China," Buryn wrote. "The Chinese have retained this ability to tackle mammoth construction projects." Kellogg was working with an "industrious, dedicated, highly capable labor force."[77]

In Buryn's depiction, Chinese workers were inherently skilled. The skills and abilities of the workers he came into contact with were associated with the most important symbol of Chinese traditionalism: the Great Wall of China. He tapped into a history of Western fascination with the wall as a symbol of Chinese strength, resistance, and achievement—a fascination that Charles Abrams's vodka similarly evoked.[78]

Buryn made no mention, of course, of the estimated 400,000 people who died during construction of the Great Wall.[79] Instead the picture he painted—that of "industrious" and "dedicated" Chinese workers—perpetuated stereotypes that had framed US relations with Chinese people since the nineteenth century. It was also an idea that Maoist propaganda encouraged. Since 1942 the CCP promoted the image of "model laborers," persons for whom labor was glorious and who devoted themselves to production in the name of socialist construction.[80] Buryn's fascination with "hardworking Chinese" veiled the depths of controls the CCP wielded in the lives of Chinese workers—and the capital he and his company were reaping as a consequence.

The Kellogg factories being set up across China revealed continuities in US-China trade at a time of considerable political turbulence. The American workers continued to see their actions as having diplomatic importance; Chinese officials continued to impose restrictions on the ways the trade relationship would unfold; and US businesspeople continued to frame Chinese labor in essentialist term: as hardworking makers of quality products. And the very fact that the factories continued to be built revealed the ongoing structural ties sustaining the nascent US-China trade relationship.

The US-ROC Economic Council

Many of the underlying ties in US-China trade remained steady despite Zhou's death in January 1976, Mao's rapidly worsening health, and the upcoming elections in the United States. But the political turmoil also created new opportunities for Taiwan and its American supporters. In the United States, Taiwan supporters within the business community, the Republican party, and the labor movement all worked for a different kind of continuity: to preserve US relations with the island.

Some of Taiwan's supporters, such as Walter Judd—a congressman from Minnesota and a longtime anticommunist crusader—wanted the United States to withhold diplomatic recognition from China altogether. As far as he was concerned, the Nationalists in Taiwan had full rights to eventual leadership over all of China. His Committee for a Free China argued in its newsletter in May 1976 that the United States should "stand firm for Free China." For years, Judd's bimonthly newsletter had been filled with comparisons between Taiwan and China. As Mao's health deteriorated, one edition featured two headlines side by side contrasting "ROC a Free Society" with "China Mainland Seethes with Turmoil."[81]

Writing on the bicentennial of the American Revolution, Judd declared, "America stands at a <u>crossroads</u> today as she did in 1776." Fearful that the new president would grant recognition to China, Judd wrote—underlining each word—"<u>full diplomatic recognition by the United States of the tyranny</u>

in Peking has never been inevitable and is not inevitable today."[82] The aging anticommunist did not carry the same political clout he once had, but he did have support from some powerful backers, one of the loudest of whom was Californian governor Ronald Reagan.[83]

Reagan challenged Ford for the presidential nomination on a platform that critiqued détente, including the rapprochement with China. In a column for the *New York Times* in June 1976, Reagan asserted the importance of maintaining ties with Taiwan and suggested that a two-China solution might be possible. "It does not necessarily follow that Peking would expect us to sever our ties with Taiwan as the price for an expanded relationship," he asserted. Ignoring Beijing's insistence on a one-China policy, Reagan argued that his position would not affect trade ties with China.

Reagan saw no reason not to pursue trade with China while also keeping ties with Taiwan. Noting the precipitous decline in bilateral trade since its high in 1974, he reassured readers that "the opportunity [for trade] is still there." More importantly, he added, "there is reason to believe we can have it without making undue concessions." While wanting to maintain trade with China, Reagan insisted: "We must never jeopardize the safety . . . nor sever our ties [with Taiwan]." "Last year," he concluded, "our $3.5 billion worth of trade with Taiwan was more than seven times the volume of our trade with Peking."[84] The fact that US trade with Taiwan was much larger than its trade with China was a frequent focus of Taiwan's supporters. As Judd put it to his supporters, too, "US–Red China trade was a minesule [*sic*] $400 million . . . that's one-eighth of the trade between the US and the Republic of China!"[85]

Trade was a useful tool in larger arguments about US relations with Taiwan and China. Taiwan's leaders themselves also played up their trade connections with the United States as a means of asserting the depths of their connections. Since 1973 they had even instigated a series of "Buy American" campaigns aimed at alleviating the US trade deficit by increasing their purchases of US products.

By the summer of 1976 Taiwan's supporters in the United States announced a further initiative aimed at strengthening trade ties with the United States. Just a month after Reagan's *New York Times* piece, David Kennedy, former president of Continental Bank and economic ambassador during Nixon's first term, announced he had established a new trade organization: the US-ROC Economic Council. Kennedy had worked closely with Taiwan's minister of economic affairs, Sun Yun-suan, and its finance minister, Li Kwoh-ting, to set up the new organization. He was so committed to the cause that he personally funded the initial setup expenses of the group.[86]

Hearing the news of Kennedy's trade council, Walter Judd was delighted. A longtime pro-Taiwan supporter, he wrote to Kennedy in April congratulating him on the new organization. "It so happens," Judd explained, "that our Committee For A Free China, feeling the need to do something along these similar lines, decided last year to start a Business Advisory Council." Judd's own business group involved twelve companies, including Singer sewing machines, *Time* magazine, and the Bank of New York. As he explained to Kennedy, all four former US ambassadors to the ROC had signed a letter inviting American companies to join Judd's new Taiwan-focused Council.[87] Judd offered to assist Kennedy's new organization, although as far as the archival papers of both men indicate, this was not assistance that Kennedy took advantage of.

Unlike Judd, Kennedy did not publicly wade into the question of whether the United States should continue its political relations with Taiwan. But it was clear where his loyalties lay. Using "ROC" rather than "Taiwan" suggested a political legitimacy that communist leaders rejected. Coming at such a politically charged moment, as the CCP reeled from Zhou's death and Mao's declining health, China's Ministry of Foreign Trade responded to the new organization by threatening to boycott all American companies that joined the new organization. Of particular concern to the Ministry of Foreign Trade was its name.

At the US-ROC Economic Council's inaugural meeting in Chicago, Kennedy raised the issue of the name and noted to the crowd of executives that "two or three" American companies had expressed a "strong preference for a change, generally to Taiwan." But this was not enough to sway him. "Most of the companies . . . are against a change in name," Kennedy countered. Indeed, "several have said they would withdraw if there were a change in the face of this threat by PRC."[88] The new organization retained its original appellation, US-ROC Economic Council.

During the launch in Chicago, Kennedy explained that among the founding board members there was "almost unanimous consensus that we should avoid political activities." The Economic Council should instead "stay in the economic private enterprise field."[89] Yet the Economic Council, with its intimate ties to Taiwan's leaders, could not escape the political context—even the organization's name itself was a political choice.

Despite Kennedy's desire to keep politics out, leaders in Taiwan were central to the organization's establishment. From March to December 1976,

Sun Yun-suan initiated a drive soliciting membership from American companies for the Economic Council. From his office in Taipei, Sun wrote to large American corporations encouraging their involvement. Sun wrote to Walker Cisler, chairman of Detroit Energy Company, to ask him to work to "motivate the industrial and business leaders in the Detroit area" to help the Economic Council and solicit more members "since you have been an old friend of the Republic of China and have contributed a great deal to our economic development."[90] Sun sent similar letters to other American executives asking them not only to join the Economic Council but also to consider recruiting other executives in their field.

"Some business officials," the *Wall Street Journal* reported, felt that Taiwan was employing "high-pressure tactics" in its attempts to garner support for the new council. At a function held at the American Chamber of Commerce in Hong Kong, Thomas Wacker, an executive at Citibank, suggested that companies with large investments in Taiwan should consider joining the Economic Council if they wanted their business to continue. "It's very subtle," Wacker said, "everything you want becomes a little bit easier if you are seen to cooperate with the government, everything becomes a little bit harder if you don't." One American banker who had been on the receiving end of the Taiwan government's efforts characterized it as "enormous, heavy-handed pressure."[91]

For their part, Chinese leaders responded with similar pressure tactics. They solicited support from the National Council for US-China Trade to warn American businesspeople not to join the new organization. The CCPIT sent Chinese Liaison Office representative Chang Tsien-hua to visit the National Council's Christopher Phillips and make clear its unhappiness. It would be "impossible" for relations with China not to be affected if members of the National Council joined the Taiwan council as well, Chang insisted. "By participating in both organizations these companies give the impression that they hoped to derive special benefits from each side," Phillips explained to his member companies. In fact, Phillips noted ominously, "as far as the CCPIT was concerned, the contrary might be the case."[92]

Phillips also wrote individually to a number of member corporations, either admonishing them for joining or praising their willingness to steer clear of the new trade body. To Ford Motors' executive director, Wayne Fredericks, Phillips noted, "I was very pleased to note that Ford was not a member of the proposed Board of Directors." Ford had economic connections to both China and Taiwan—just a few years back it had drawn up a shopping list and begun to buy electronic components from China. It was one thing to trade with both economies, but an entirely different thing to join the board of the Taiwan trade council, Phillips noted. "The PRC is taking a very strong stand on this matter and has made clear that its future relations with companies who become members of this council would be adversely affected," Phillips warned. "As Mr. Chang told me last week, 'unfortunately, politics and trade cannot be separated.'"[93]

Soviet leaders watched amusedly from the sidelines as the spat unfolded. "I see you've got competition," Alexander Medynanik, a Soviet diplomat, commented gleefully to a member of the National Council.[94] It was US companies, however, that got caught in the crossfire. Rockwell International was one such company that faced pressure from both sides of the Taiwan Strait. Its chairman, Willard F. Rockwell Jr., had joined the US-ROC Economic Council's board of directors, but its president and vice president had been working closely with the National Council to establish relations with China. Rockwell was the parent company of a number of high-tech companies, including Collins Radio Group, which sold microwave and satellite communication technology—items that Collins had been attempting to sell to the PRC.

Many of the products China had already purchased under its 4-3 Program contained Rockwell components. The Boeing 707s included Collins avionics. The ammonia plants that Kellogg had sold to China contained plug valves supplied by Rockwell's Flow Control Division. A recent purchase of WABCO mining trucks used Rockwell brakes.[95]

Conscious of the potential problems raised by Rockwell's chairman joining the US-ROC Economic Council, Christopher Phillips reached out directly to the company's vice president, Alonzo Kight, with whom the National Council also had a close relationship. Phillips's handwritten notes on the telephone conversation left him satisfied that Rockwell would do some "soul searching" on the company's participation in the new organization.[96] Soon thereafter Rockwell pulled out of the new US-ROC Economic Council.

Baker and McKenzie, a Chicago-based international law firm, had similarly worked with Kennedy in establishing the US-ROC Economic Council. But as China expressed its increasing displeasure at the new council, Baker and McKenzie also withdrew from it.[97] Chinese authorities followed through on threats to penalize members of the National Council that did join the US-ROC Economic Council. In late 1976 the

CCPIT rejected all American Express travelers checks when American businessmen and visitors to China tried to use them for purchases.[98] The chairman of American Express, Howard Clark, had been an inaugural member of the US-ROC Economic Council's Board.[99] Union Carbide's chairman, B. V. Salenius, and General Electric's vice chairman, Jack Parker, also joined the Economic Council's board of directors. Both firms received fewer visas than they were expecting for travel to the trade fair.

The cancellation of traveler's checks caused serious disruptions for American businesses that did not even have ties to Taiwan but had been reliant on the American Express checks. By October 8, 1976, the National Council met with members of the CCPIT, and the newly created US-ROC Economic Council came up early in their discussions. The CCPIT's vice president, Hsiao Fang Chou, raised the issue on the first day of discussions in Beijing. Hsiao told the Americans that "the principles of the Shanghai communiqué were quite clear." He explained, "We do not have any objection to their doing business with Taiwan." Rather, it was the American companies' decisions to join the Economic Council that the CCPIT found problematic. He referred to the "two Chinas" implication in the Economic Council's name.

Christopher Phillips explained the efforts he had made to dissuade US businesspeople from joining, but also emphasized the limits to his influence. He had written to American companies and explained "the possible consequences of their decision to participate in this particular organization." Nonetheless, "under our system and laws" the National Council "can take no action against these companies." At pains to protect the National Council, Phillips stressed that this was a problem between the individual US companies and the CCPIT. "The National Council should not be weakened or have its own influence jeopardized because of the actions of some companies over which we have no control," he concluded.[100]

Also present in the meeting was John Hanley, president of the chemical company Monsanto. Hanley interjected somewhat more forcefully, "I should like to be certain that you understand that the member companies of the National Council have every right to pursue their commercial interests in Taiwan and any other countries around the world as befits their interests." The National Council "is not in a position to negate that possibility or to expel them from membership." Hsiao responded by explaining that the problem was "companies that are friendly to us and are at the same time friendly to Taiwan." This was "from an emotional point of view . . . unacceptable when it goes beyond the point of commercial interest."[101] The problem for Hsiao was the political implications underpinning the US-ROC Economic Council.

The disruptions some American businesses faced as they navigated trade with both polities died down as quickly as they flared up. China still refused to trade with companies that were members of the Economic Council itself, but nonmembers who traded with Taiwan remained able to deal with China too. At the spring 1977 Canton Trade Fair, American Express checks were back in use. By that time Mao had died; Hua Guofeng had taken leadership in Beijing and asserted a new push for industrialization through technology purchases; and Jimmy Carter had been elected US president on a ticket that aimed to finally normalize relations with China.

The response to the US-ROC Economic Council—launched at the height of summer and right in the middle of significant political changes in both countries—revealed the sensitivities of diplomatic normalization and the willingness of both Taiwan and China to use trade as a tool to pursue political ends. As was so often the case in the 1970s, China withdrew trade as a punishment for political issues. Trade was, in Chinese officials' estimation, something that would only come after positive geopolitical developments.

David Kennedy would go on to serve as the US-ROC Economic Council's chairman for fourteen years until his retirement in 1990.[102] In 1986 Taiwan awarded Kennedy the Order of Brilliant Star. This was one of its highest honors, similar to a Knighthood in the United Kingdom.[103] After Kennedy retired, the organization did change its name to the US-Taiwan Economic Council. By then the United States had recognized the PRC for more than a decade, but the overarching question of Taiwan's political status remained unsettled. Kissinger's policy of "strategic ambiguity," begun in 1972, remained at the heart of America's policy toward the "one China" issue. In 1976 these tensions flared up in the face of new organizational changes. But in the years that followed, American businesspeople managed to navigate the divisions between the two polities on either side of the Taiwan Strait. And in the process, they reaped financial reward.

FOR YEARS, MAO'S failing health had exacerbated hostility between political factions in the Politburo who held very different ideas about China's development. When Mao died on September 9, 1976, an extraordinary power vacuum opened up. Hua Guofeng, Mao's designated successor, seized the opportunity quickly and arrested the Gang of Four, who had controlled politics in Mao's final years. Meanwhile, Democratic candidate Jimmy Carter won the US presidential elections in November. The change in leadership in both countries offered a new opportunity for reassessing the US-China normalization process.

Mao's death was one of the most significant moments in modern Chinese history. Until the end, Mao had been at the center of Chinese politics, shaping the lives of millions of people both within and beyond China's borders. Most scholars see his death as marking a major turning point in the history of China's political economy. After his death, Hua Guofeng and later Deng Xiaoping both instituted development programs that, by late 1978, came to be labeled China's "reform and opening."[104] At the heart of the reform and opening were the Four Modernizations, which Zhou had outlined at the Great Hall of the People in January 1975.

But by focusing on China's foreign trade, we see a different rhythm of change and continuity, one in which the inflection points look somewhat different. Mao's death was not an end point in the story of China's foreign trade. Nor was 1978 a starting point. By the time of Mao's death, the pragmatists' experiments had instituted such fundamental changes that, in terms of foreign trade, Hua and Deng simply accelerated a process that was already well under way. China's expansion of foreign trade since 1971, its 4-3 Program of 1973, and Mao's Three Worlds Theory of 1974 were central to the trade dynamics of the reform and opening era that came after Mao's death. The origins of China's reforms lie in the latter years of the Cultural Revolution, what some scholars have labeled China's "long 1970s."[105]

In the period between Zhou's and Mao's deaths, US-China trade declined dramatically, reaching a mere $330 million by the end of 1976. This was a significant drop from previous years, including the high of nearly $1 billion in 1974, and was driven by a near complete end of Chinese purchases of US agricultural goods. But behind the dwindling numbers lay significant continuities in bilateral trade. Chinese exports continued to increase, aided by deals such as Charles Abrams's Great Wall Vodka and Don King's sports equipment. Banking connections between the US and China continued to expand. And US engineers continued to assemble fertilizer factories across the country. Together, these factors pointed to an ongoing structural shift in how the China market was understood. China might have modernization needs, as the fertilizer plants attested to, but the place for growth lay in its exports. By the time of Mao's death, Chinese exports to the United States had not only increased from previous years, they had, for the first time, outvalued Chinese imports. For American workers, watching the increasing amount of Chinese goods entering the United States, these continuities were the push they needed to fight for change.

CHAPTER 7

The Glove Capital of America

DOUG PETERSON WAS a columnist at the local newspaper in Chillicothe, Missouri. For months he had been
following a story that received little attention outside his community of
9,000 people. Since December 15, 1977, managers of the town's local
glove factories—there were three in Chillicothe—had been lobbying federal authorities to impose restrictions on cotton work gloves being imported from China. This was a landmark case. For the first time since the
founding of the PRC, US manufacturers called for import protection from
China.

"Your neighbors and mine; friends who pay taxes locally, buy locally,
and contribute to the well being of this area are in danger of losing their
jobs in the future because of a communist country," Peterson wrote. Reflecting on the imports from "Red China," he reflected, "I get the feeling
sometimes that we elect men to represent the interests of all the rest of
the people in the world as opposed to us."[1]

The glove makers, organized through the Work Glove Manufacturers
Association (WGMA), had brought their case before the US International
Trade Commission (USITC), calling for quotas—knowing full well that
tariffs would do little when the prices of imported goods had such little
connection to their production costs. It was the volume of imports they
felt they needed to limit.

US diplomats and business leaders were so worried about the case that
they intervened multiple times to stop it from happening. Officials at the

US Liaison Office even tipped off their Chinese counterparts, advising them to hold back on their exports until the issue died down. At one point the National Council for US-China Trade despaired that the workers would win, lamenting there was "a good possibility importers will lose this case because too much politics involved [sic]."[2]

But in the end the WGMA did not win, largely due to US political interference. The tip-offs from the US Liaison Office ensured that China temporarily halted its exports to make it appear like China was exporting fewer gloves. The first attempt to impose restrictions on Chinese goods passed most Americans by unnoticed. Veteran labor journalist Victor Riesel—one of the few journalists outside Chillicothe who reported on the case—reflected on the limited coverage the case drew. "Since work gloves aren't steel, shoes, textiles and autos, the little industry . . . fell between the headlines."[3] Their eventual loss ensured that their story would be forgotten altogether.[4]

In this chapter I revisit this forgotten moment in the history of US-China relations. The case allows us to explore China's development from a new angle, focusing on the impact it had on American workers in the textile industry. The WGMA's story matters not just for the resistance US workers exhibited toward the rapidly rising imports they faced—although that resistance on its own does indeed merit attention. Rather, the case also reveals a new dynamic emerging in the global economy that had profoundly important repercussions for China's reforms, US workers, and US-China trade more broadly. The white male managers testifying on behalf of the cotton work glove makers—the vast majority of whom were Latina or Black women—represented companies that were benefiting from the cheap gloves, even though they wanted controls on Chinese imports. Around 60 percent of all cotton work gloves imported from China were purchased by companies that also manufactured them.[5]

In other words, the majority of American corporations calling for restrictions on Chinese gloves were the very same corporations purchasing the imports from China. As they struggled to keep their factories open during a period of widespread deindustrialization especially in the textile industry, managers began to decrease their production of this kind of glove and replace them with imports. In so doing, they hoped to save on costs and continue making other, more complex types of gloves—at least temporarily.

The case illustrates that it was not just, as Doug Peterson put it, politicians in Washington who were sacrificing US workers' interests for diplomatic gain. It reveals a far more complex dynamic in which corporate leaders were changing the structural underpinnings of industrial manufacturing—themselves sacrificing US workers' interests for economic gain. By December 1977 a new type of globalized manufacturing was emerging, one in which it was more economical to import goods made using cheap labor in China than it was to use even the non-union workers in predominantly southern and midwestern glove factories.

This turn toward international manufacturing had accelerated since the breakdown of the Bretton Woods system, first announced with Nixon's shock in 1971. It was entrenched in 1974 with the passing of the US Trade Act, which provided lower tariffs to noncommunist, noncartel exporting nations through the Generalized System of Preferences. And it was exposed in 1977 when a small group of women of color became the canaries, not in the coal mine but in the textile mill. Their experiences may have gone unnoticed by most, but they vividly illustrated the impact of Chinese pragmatists' and US importers' gradual reshaping of the China market into a site of 800 million workers.

The Fight from Libertyville

The cotton work gloves case came at a time when diplomacy remained at an impasse. New leaders in Washington and Beijing had been in power less than a year when managers of the glove factories took their case to the USITC. Earlier, in January 1977, Hua had sent several signals to the newly elected US president, Jimmy Carter, that China was interested in accelerating efforts toward diplomatic normalization. In one such case, his chief foreign economic advisor and vice premier of the State Council, Li Xiannian, hosted David Rockefeller in Beijing and indicated China's willingness to finally resolve the claims/assets dispute. Five years after the signing of the Shanghai Communiqué and with a new man in the White House, Li injected new momentum into the normalization process.

A few weeks later, on February 8, President Carter met with Huang Chen at the PRC Liaison Office. It was their first official meeting since Carter took office. The president indicated his commitment to resolving the claims/assets issue. Reaching a settlement would "demonstrate to our friends and the world that we can make progress in our relations," he told Chen. Like his predecessors, Carter saw trade as something that could help facilitate diplomatic negotiations. In Carter's estimation, progress in trade would occur first, with normalization to follow in its wake.

But Chen saw the relationship between trade and diplomacy differently. He downplayed the significance of the trade dispute. "The asset issue is easy to solve," he dismissed. "This is not a big matter." State Department documents note that Chen then turned to Secretary of State Cyrus Vance and patted him on the hand. The action, as the Americans understood it, was "as if to indicate that this is just a little matter that could be settled." The key issue for China, Chen reiterated, was Taiwan. It was on this issue that they would not negotiate. In fact, if necessary, China would use force to bring the island into its ambit, Chen asserted. "How to liberate Taiwan—whether by force or by other means—is our internal affair."[6] While he minimized the claims/assets dispute, Chen nonetheless emphasized where China's focus lay: resolution of the United States' relationship with Taiwan.

Here in the Oval Office, Chen and Carter revealed the diverging understandings of how progress in trade and diplomacy would unfold—differences that had so shaped US-China trade throughout the 1970s. The sticking point remained Taiwan. For Carter, resolving the Taiwan issue, and therefore achieving diplomatic normalization with China, was a first-term priority but it was not an immediate concern.[7] Carter came into office with a foreign policy focus that lay elsewhere. His platform centered on reaching approval of the Panama Canal Treaty; reaching agreement with the Soviet Union on SALT negotiations; relaxing tensions in the Middle East; and, at a time of continued oil crisis, developing a new energy program. As Chen conveyed, however, China continued to insist on resolving the Taiwan issue first. Therefore, despite these early signs that China was open to ending the claims/assets dispute, its leaders soon pulled back from its initial overtures once it became clear that normalization would not happen anytime soon. As they saw it, the claims/assets dispute would be resolved only after normalization; it would not be, as Carter had put it, a demonstration of progress.

By December, when the glove makers launched their case, diplomatic efforts toward normalization were no closer than they had been at the start of Carter's term. Bilateral trade reflected this, remaining flat throughout 1977. The year ended with a total trade balance of around $374.5 million—a slight increase from 1976 but markedly lower than the nearly $1 billion of 1974.[8] The balance of trade, however, remained in

China's favor after its shift the year before. Chinese exports continued to increase, cotton work gloves among them.

WHEN THE WGMA launched its case in 1977, employment in the US glove industry was decreasing rapidly. The 1973 recession and skyrocketing inflation had made an already precarious industry more vulnerable. Between 1974 and 1977, US employment in the cotton glove industry dropped by 16 percent.[9] Chillicothe's Mid West Glove Corporation laid off 68 percent of the work force in this three-year period.[10] Those who remained at one of Chillicothe's companies worked only three days a week; management at the Chillicothe factories had limited their workers' hours in preference to forcing redundancies. The typical employee was female: 80 to 85 percent of workers in the cotton glove industry were women. Most were Black or recently immigrated to the United States from Latin America. On average they were older than workers in other manufacturing industries.[11]

One generation earlier, textile and apparel workers in the United States were mostly young unmarried white women.[12] In the 1960s, civil rights activists brought an end to the Jim Crow segregation that had prevented the employment of women of color in manufacturing positions. Once an exclusively white industry, textiles were transformed during the civil rights era, changing the lives of many Black and Latina women.[13] Now these workers' place within the industry was threatened by accelerating levels of imports.

The WGMA case dealt with a particular type of cotton work glove: those without forchettes or sidewalls, thin strips of material linking the front and back of each finger of the glove. These gloves required less sewing in the production process and were therefore less labor-intensive. Hong Kong was the single largest supplier of such gloves for US importers throughout most of the 1970s. As the United States and China reestablished trade ties, China quickly became one of the top suppliers. In 1976 Chinese gloves reached a high of just under 20 percent of all US imports of such goods, second only to Hong Kong.[14]

Yet these numbers masked the fact that many US textile imports from Hong Kong were increasingly likely to have originated in China. In the 1970s more than 90 percent of trade between China and Hong Kong consisted of a one-way flow of Chinese exports to Hong Kong.[15] This system provided China with much-needed foreign exchange to pay for its own imports and allowed Hong Kong to use the goods for reexport and trans-

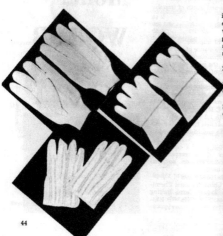

Protective Work Gloves

Shanghai offers a wide range of protective work gloves in different materials. They include Canton flannel, printed flannelette, yarn-dyed double sided flannel, canvas, as well as cylindrical knitted sweat gloves, cotton interlock gloves, cleaning gloves and gloves in terry cloth. They are all strongly made and long wearing. Below is a sample range:

1. Canton flannel gloves in 6, 7, 8, 10, 12, 16, 18, 20, 22 and 24 ounce weights. Rib knit wrist or flared cuff.

2. Printed cotton flannelette gardening gloves for women. Attractively printed designs, buttoned or short cuff, ribbed or shirred back.

3. Terry towelling heat resistant gloves in five specifications, two thicknesses, with elasticized wrist or flared cuff.

4. Plastic coated cotton gloves are waterproof and resistant to acids and alkalis.

5. Polka dot non-slip gloves, rubber finished on cotton or polyester fabric backing.

6. Knitted cotton gloves, napped. Checked, brown, black, navy blue, etc. or natural. Full range of sizes.

7. Knitted cotton yarn work gloves. Best quality cotton yarn. Weights: 406 g, 625 g, 688 g, 788 g, 906 g or 1,125 g.

Exporters: China National Textiles Import & Export Corp., Shanghai Garments Branch. Cables: GARMENTS SHANGHAI Telex: 33056 GAREX CN

44

Figure 7.1. Chinese advertisement for cotton work gloves in 1979. After the WGMA lost its case for quotas, the PRC increased its exports to the United States. By the end of 1978, 24 percent of all American cotton work glove imports came from China. These numbers continued to increase, reaching 32 percent of total US purchases in 1979.

shipment. Hong Kong reshipped around one-third of its imported Chinese goods to foreign nations. As China slowly integrated itself into the global capitalist trade system, Hong Kong became essential to this process.[16]

The dual problems of increasing imports and diminishing employment in the US glove sector reflected the wider challenges in the textile industry. By the time the WGMA launched its case, US textile unions were deep into campaigns for protection against imports from Japan, Korea, Taiwan, Hong Kong, and elsewhere.[17] The union movement had launched a series of "Buy American" campaigns encouraging consumers to purchase goods manufactured in the United States. Leaders linked the buying of US-made products with the protection of jobs.[18] Elsewhere, union leaders led highly publicized nationwide boycotts against the giant textile firm J. P. Stevens, which had worked for years to undercut its workers' efforts to form unions in the South.[19]

Throughout the decade, the US textile industry was also focused on the sixth round of the GATT negotiations that had begun in 1973 and were to continue until 1979. The industry lobbied for textile and apparel exports from all countries to be excluded from the GATT discussions. They wanted to ensure that the tariffs on those goods entering the United States remained at their current level.[20]

By 1977, textile workers across the country staged protest marches and sit-down strikes, pushing the Carter administration to renew and strengthen another agreement: the Multifiber Arrangement (MFA). First implemented in 1974, the MFA provided a cap on the quantity of textile and apparel imports coming from the developing world into the developed world.[21] Due to lobbying efforts of the AFL-CIO, the American Textile Manufacturers Institute (ATMI), and members of Congress, President Carter did renew the MFA in December 1977, providing a further three years of restraints on textile and clothing imports although labor and industry remained concerned that the restraints did not go far enough. Moreover, because of the absence of full diplomatic relations, the MFA did not extend to goods imported from China.

China had only recently become a US trading partner, and yet its potential textile clout was already becoming apparent, especially in certain areas of the industry. In 1976, for example, China sold more white cotton shirts to the United States than any other item, around $13.5 million worth of shirts. In 1977 this figure decreased to only $8 million, but the shirts still were some of the single highest-value items China sold to the United States.[22]

China's overall textile exports were far smaller than those of the United States' other major trading partners. For instance, in 1978 the United States imported cotton goods from Hong Kong worth $667.8 million.[23] Hong Kong's sales of cotton goods alone were nearly double China's total sales to the United States in the same year, which stood at $324 million.[24] For certain items, such as cotton work gloves, Hong Kong's trade figures included sizable numbers of reexported gloves that originally came from China. In terms of Hong Kong's total cotton goods overall, however, only a small proportion originated in China. Above all, it was the speed with which China was able to become a major player in some sectors that concerned leaders in the cotton glove industry.

IT WAS NO accident that representatives from the textile industry were the first group to call for restrictions on Chinese imports. Textiles and apparel were two of the first industries to expand in the United States during the industrialization that took off in the mid-nineteenth century, after the Civil War. They were also two of the first industries to feel the effects of *de*industrialization nearly one hundred years later, after the Second World War. Textile imports from Japan and later South Korea, Taiwan, and Hong Kong began to enter the United States in increasing numbers from the 1950s on. Just as it had in the United States a century earlier, the industrialization in East Asia after the Second World War started with the textile industry.

Textiles and apparel tended to be the first to develop in industrializing nations because startup capital was lower than for other industries like steel and cars that needed more elaborate manufacturing facilities.[25] Unlike the United States of the nineteenth century, however, the industrializing economies of East Asia were producing textiles in order to export them. Theirs was an export-oriented development, one that, at the height of the Cold War, policymakers in Washington encouraged.

In the years following the Second World War, then, when most US manufacturing industries were booming, textile manufacturers already faced heightened pressures from rising imports. But it was not only imports that led to unemployment in the industry. US textile manufacturers shifted their locations within the United States itself, shutting down factories in search of non-union towns in New England and the Midwest, and eventually the South. As factories across the country began to lay off workers, they revealed some of the first signs of a process scholars later labeled "deindustrialization."[26] The textile industry was therefore the harbinger of a wider process of deindustrialization that, by the 1970s, had hit other industries such as steel and automobiles. All three industries—textiles, steel, and automobiles—became key battlegrounds in the 1970s for organized labor's broader struggle against factory closures and imports.

China's halting reform programs, and small but increasing exports of the 1970s, were hardly the cause of the textile industry's problems. China's reforms were, however, occurring at the very moment when structural changes in global manufacturing unfolded. As we saw in Chapter 4, in 1973 J. C. Penney's five-year plan aimed to have imports comprise 14 percent of its total merchandise by 1978—still a significant minority of its overall stock.[27] As the company began to internationalize its manufacturing base, its executives included China in their new plans. The cotton work gloves case against China in the 1970s portended the impact of what might happen if Penney's plans were successful—of what might happen when globalized manufacturing collided with a China market reframed as one of 800 million workers.

IN EARLY 1977, Libertyville, Illinois—a town with its own history of textile manufacturing—became the headquarters for the WGMA's battle against Chinese imports. Leaders saw Libertyville's name itself as a symbol of resistance against the communist nation. Earl Rauen, president of Indianapolis Glove Company, had recently become head of the WGMA and he worked with executive director Paul Schulz to spearhead the efforts for protection from Chinese imports.

The industry had been contending with the impact of imports for years. In 1972 American companies purchased around $1.5 million worth of cotton work glove imports. By 1977 this had ballooned to over $12.7 million.[28] Demand for cotton work gloves was relatively inelastic, so as imports increased, they crowded out domestic suppliers. In 1977 imports held over 20 percent of the market share, up from just 5 percent in 1972.[29] China was the only major source of gloves that did not face any import restrictions.

Demand was, moreover, pegged closely to employment in the steel and auto industries. This was because the main users of cotton work gloves were workers in other manufacturing sectors. Representatives from large industrial corporations in the steel and auto industries purchased the gloves and distributed them to their employees. These workers, the majority of whom were men, wore cotton gloves to protect their hands, sometimes underneath larger, heavy-duty gloves. Workers in these industries were themselves contending with threats from overseas imports and facing job insecurity.[30] As their own industries fought to remain viable, managers cut production costs by purchasing the cheapest cotton gloves, which usually meant imports. They understood their interests to lie in increasing the supply of low-cost cotton work gloves, of which China was fast becoming a source.

These other trades employed considerably more workers compared to the cotton work glove industry. The size of their industry, combined with intersecting racialized and gendered notions about whose voices were newsworthy, meant that the plight of the predominantly Latina and Black women producing the cotton work gloves received little media publicity. Pockets of coverage did appear in local newspapers and fleetingly in the *Wall Street Journal,* but the workers themselves were not interviewed.[31]

Race and gender operated in other ways, too. As with leadership positions in other textile organizations—such as the International Ladies' Garment Workers' Union or the Amalgamated Clothing and Textile Workers Union—the WGMA leaders speaking on behalf of the cotton glove workers at the USITC were white men. None of the women who made the cotton work gloves were invited to testify.

Diplomatic Intervention

By the middle of the year, Rauen and Schulz were ready to petition the USITC for quotas but members of the State Department approached them and demanded they suspend their efforts until diplomatic relations were more stable.[32] The policymakers feared China might see it as carrying US governmental endorsement and harm the movement toward normalization. After all, China's leaders could retaliate by slowing down the diplomatic negotiations. In August Secretary of State Cyrus Vance would visit China, where he hoped to move ahead on normalization negotiations, particularly disagreements regarding Taiwan.[33] The WGMA did halt its efforts, but Vance's trip was not the success the Carter administration had hoped for.

Carter had hoped Vance's trip would help the United States "expand our economic and cultural relations with China." Like his predecessors, Carter linked trade and people-to-people ties. While this forward movement was important, he continued "we can afford to be patient."[34] This patience meant not rushing toward normalization without first ascertaining how little they could concede on Taiwan. Vance's main goal had been to gauge Beijing's attitude on what he called the United States' "maximum position."[35] In his instructions to Vance, Carter wrote, "Our maximum goal is to elicit flexibility from them on the Taiwan issue in the context of full diplomatic relations with Peking."[36]

The maximum position strategy did not go as planned. Deng Xiaoping—who had recently been reinstated as a member of the Chinese Politburo Standing Committee—reiterated China's expectation that there would be no compromise on Taiwan, just as had been the case in China's normalization with Japan. On trade, Foreign Minister Huang Hua noted that "under the present circumstances, when relations between our two countries are not yet normalized, these exchanges cannot but be somewhat limited by such conditions." Despite Carter's hopes to the contrary, "the level and scope of exchanges we have achieved so far perhaps will remain for some years to come," Huang declared.[37] Deng later commented to the American media that the visit had, in fact, been a step backward in bilateral relations.[38] China would not be shifting its stance on Taiwan.

After seeing the failure of Vance's trip, the WGMA leadership met again in November. During the meeting—which labor journalist Victor Riesel described with dramatic flourish as "sort of a war council"—the WGMA leadership decided they would file their case.[39] A few days later, Rauen and Schulz received another phone call. An official from the Department of Commerce insisted that the WGMA postpone the petition once more and asked them to come immediately to Washington.

In the capital, Rauen and Schulz met with policymakers, including William Barraclough, deputy assistant secretary of state for the Bureau of Economic and Business Affairs. Barraclough urged them to delay their petition because the Carter administration was still concerned about the impact it would have on bilateral relations, especially in light of Deng's public rebukes. Achieving normalized diplomatic relations with China remained a first-term priority for the Carter administration, even if by the end of the year momentum was somewhat diminished.[40]

Behind the scenes, Carter's national security advisor, Zbigniew Brzezinski, and the US Liaison Office in Beijing had also become involved. In October—more than a month before Rauen and Schulz flew to Washington—Brzezinski had contacted Leonard Woodcock at the US Liaison Office in Beijing about the unfolding case. Woodcock was the former head of the United Auto Workers (UAW) union. Between 1970 and 1977, he had led the UAW's fight against foreign imports in the automobile industry, including a sixty-seven-day strike against General Motors in 1970. Now, as the most senior American diplomatic in China, Woodcock found himself on the other side of the debate about imports. The National Security Agency contacted him and asked his office to warn China's Ministry of Foreign Trade that it was possible the case would be launched. Woodcock and his team obliged.

Under Woodcock's leadership, the Liaison Office encouraged Chinese trade officials to temporarily decrease their shipments of cotton work gloves. They warned the Chinese officials that if their shipments of work gloves were "sustained at their current high level," this could "trigger substantial industry and Congressional pressures for USG [US government] action to limit the imports."[41] With the number of imported Chinese gloves being lower than in the previous year, it might appear that Chinese imports were no longer posing a threat, they suggested. Chinese traders had already been closely following the WGMA's efforts all year, and with the Liaison Office's advice, they continued to hold off on the number of gloves they sold to the United States. In this instance, China's ability to intervene so quickly in its markets offered an important diplomatic advantage to the US diplomats.

Ignoring the protestations from the State and Commerce Departments, the WGMA filed its case with the USITC on December 15, 1977. Speaking at the National Press Club afterward, Schulz noted that in its seventy-five years of association, the WGMA had "never . . . been confronted with a situation so serious as the one we face now." Its members were unable to compete with the "rapid rise of underpriced products from a country which can totally ignore all cost factors in order to capture a significant segment of our market." He framed the WGMA's efforts as setting an important precedent for other American industries. "If a long-established industry like ours can be driven to the wall within a few years by a sudden surge of imports from a nation like communist China, I submit that virtually every industry in America is ultimately vulnerable to predatory import invasions."[42]

Despite his language of invasion and his warning of the wider impact of trade with China, Schulz's comments did not gain wide traction. Given that the major users of the Chinese cotton gloves were workers in large industrial sectors, the gloves case was not their clarion call to action against Chinese imports. For the women and their families working in the industry, the case held much broader implications. But despite the press conference, the case received little national media attention.

One group, however, was watching the developments very closely. The National Council for US-China Trade knew, like Schultz, that the case would set a precedent for other US industries. The National Council's leadership was concerned that if the WGMA won, larger US industries would be encouraged to also pursue limitations on other Chinese goods. "Already there is talk of knitted gloves," an internal memorandum worried. "And this will broaden to include garments, other textiles and other industries."[43] The National Council wrote directly to its members soliciting financial support for the defendants. The defense was led by one of its members—Richard Rivkin, president of the Latex Glove Company. Other members, such as Bob Boulogne from J. C. Penney and Veronica Yhap from Dragon Lady Traders, worked closely with him.[44] As far as the National Council and its members were concerned, the case held the potential to unleash even bigger industry efforts for worker protection, which would be a problem not only for diplomacy but also for its members' expanding economic roles in China.

The USITC Hearings

The USITC held two-days hearings into the work gloves case on February 7 and 8, 1978. The USITC had a quasi-judicial role only; its findings were not binding but instead served as a recommendation to President Carter. Nonetheless, those involved with the case were aware of the wider implications of its outcome. "We need to send a clarion signal to the PRC," insisted Missouri Republican congressman Thomas Coleman, who testified in support of the WGMA. "They can do business with the United States but only according to the rules of fair trade."[45]

The WGMA had filed their case under Section 406 of the Trade Act, which applied only to imports from communist nations. The section required the petitioners to prove that the imports were "increasing rapidly, either absolutely or relatively, so as to be a significant cause of material injury, or threat thereof, to such domestic industry."[46] The WGMA focused on three main issues in its submission. First, China was not privy to the MFA restrictions faced by America's other trading partners. Second, because China was a communist country, its government could intervene to increase, decrease, or stop its trade at will, thereby disrupting the American market and making it an unpredictable trading partner. And finally, the WGMA argued that wages in China bore so little resemblance to production costs that it was impossible for American manufacturers to compete without resorting to similar conditions.

First, of all the major countries that sold cotton work gloves to United States, the PRC was the only one that was not a signatory to the recently renewed MFA. This meant that the PRC did not face a cap on the number of gloves it sold, unlike the other trading partners. "The sky is the ceiling for Chinese exports of cotton work gloves," declared Jacob Sheinkman, secretary-treasurer of the Amalgamated Clothing and Textile Workers Union (ACTWU), who spoke in support of the WGMA.[47] Sheinkman and the WGMA emphasized the order and stability that quotas would provide to the domestic industry.

Just as the MFA agreement provided some semblance of order to the imports coming from other countries, they argued that quotas on Chinese gloves would provide similar limitations. The WGMA's concerns were compounded by the knowledge that some of the Chinese gloves were, in fact, levied with other restrictions. Because the United States and China did not have full diplomatic relations, China was not subject to Most Favored Nation (MFN) trading status, exposing the knitted variety of cotton work gloves to higher import taxes. (In an indication of the complications of trade laws, gloves made using *woven* cotton cloth did not face the tariffs, only those made from knitted cloth did.)

The fact that China was able to become an important player in the market even with higher tariffs on its knitted gloves meant that it represented a "threat for more profound disruption in the future" once the United States did eventually grant China MFN status. As the political efforts toward normalization unfolded, it appeared increasingly likely that the United States would eventually grant China MFN status. When this happened, Chinese textiles would not be subject to any restrictions.[48]

Given that cost bore little relation to the number of gloves China produced and sold, quotas rather than tariffs were the necessary form of trade restriction, the WGMA argued. Without such restrictions, the United States was vulnerable to a potentially unlimited onslaught from a non-market economy, free from the rules of international trade. At the center of these arguments, the WGMA emphasized the need for market order, framing its position as not seeking to halt Chinese imports altogether but as helping American producers to operate with more predictable forecasts.

Second, the WGMA argued that China's communist system was a major reason to impose quotas. Its government was able to directly intervene in the market in ways that could have a sudden impact. Indeed, the decline in Chinese exports to the United States in 1977 proved this point. The decrease had occurred only after Chinese exporters had learned that the case was about to be launched against them—only after, therefore, the Liaison Office had intervened. Missouri congressman Thomas Coleman implored the commissioners not to be "lulled into a false sense of security" by the "recent aberration in what is a patently clear long term trend of increasing imports." It was diplomatic interests that had led to the decline, he argued. And the impact could be felt so suddenly because of the communist regime's control of the market.[49]

Other industries were also affected by the fluctuations, they argued. Speaking on his own experiences of the rippling damage caused by the decrease in cotton glove manufacturing was Morris Byran, president of

Jefferson Mills in Georgia. In his testimony, he noted that his flannel supply business had been "seriously disrupted" by the plummeting sales in the local cotton glove industry. With glove makers demanding less cloth, the Georgian mill had fewer customers for its own goods.[50]

The situation was similar for raw cotton too. In testimony to the USITC, Missouri senator John Danforth argued that "as the glove production goes down, so does demand for its principal raw material, cotton." Missouri was one of the largest producers of cotton in the United States, and Danforth argued that decreasing production, increasing unemployment, and plant closures had far-reaching effects. "So often," Danforth concluded, "these communities are simply lost in the shuffle as a massive and distant federal bureaucracy addresses itself to the 'larger' issues."[51] Coleman reiterated his fellow Missourian's point, arguing, "We are also speaking of the textile mills, the paper industry, the chemical industry, the tool and die industry, transportation, the corrugated box industry, and many, many others, and yes, possibly the farmers."[52]

On a local level, the decreasing production of gloves might have affected domestic demand for US cotton. In the aggregate, however, China's increasing ability to export textiles was linked to its heightened demand for American cotton.[53] John Holdridge, the United States' first liaison officer in Beijing, recognized the early signs of this in January 1975. "To help sustain growing textile exports, the PRC has been a large cotton importer," Holdridge cabled the State Department. "Over the longer term, the U.S. . . . should continue to be in a good position as far as cotton sales to China are concerned."[54]

Like total trade more broadly, however, US cotton sales to China fluctuated throughout the decade. In 1973 and 1974 China purchased $287 million of cotton from the United States.[55] Sales declined sharply in 1975 and 1976, but in 1977 China's purchases of US cotton increased once more to around $17 million and in 1978 they rose even further to $157 million.[56] By 1980, after diplomatic normalization, China purchased nearly one-quarter of all US cotton exports. The United States was one of China's leading foreign suppliers in that year, providing 62 percent of all China's cotton purchases.[57] But this was, crucially, after normalization had been achieved.

Danforth acknowledged the high levels of China's cotton purchases but argued that its fluctuations meant these benefits to American farmers were less certain than they first appeared. "Red China does import substantial quantities of U.S. cotton," he noted, "but apparently on a capricious and uncertain basis."[58] Recalling China's cancellations of grain in the middle of the decade, Coleman reiterated Danforth's point. "The PRC refuses to buy grain from American farmers . . . yet it has no qualms about dumping work gloves in this country to the detriment of American jobs." Trade was not, he argued, "a one-way avenue."[59]

Finally, the WGMA petitioners focused on the prices at which China sold its gloves. As Rauen described it, China had "captured a substantial portion of our market solely on the basis of price." And these prices bore "little or no relationship to costs."[60] China's huge population—one-quarter of the world's population, as the WGMA reminded the USITC—compounded fears of a potential deluge of gloves.

In its briefing to the USITC, the WGMA argued that China's lower prices were the consequence of its "slave labor" conditions. With significantly lower labor costs, China could bear the high tariffs from lack of MFN status and still undercut the prices American manufacturers charged.[61] Sheinkman similarly argued that Chinese workers were being treated as little more than "indentured labor." With their increasing exports, China's leaders were "exporting their unemployment" to the United States, Sheinkman continued. China was gaining jobs at the expense of American workers through their "predatory pricing" and "beggar-be-thy-neighbor trade policies."[62]

The WGMA and Sheinkman's language of slavery and indentured servitude echoed that used by the US labor movement in the late nineteenth century. At that time, labor leaders and their supporters similarly invoked the horrors of slavery when discussing Chinese laborers entering the United States as part of the so-called "coolie" trade. The exploitative conditions faced by Chinese workers in industries such as the railways meant they were "used as slaves by those who bring them to this country," as one senator from California put it in 1882.[63] In so doing, he and his colleagues weaponized the language of antislavery to justify the exclusion of Chinese laborers from immigration to the United States. For the first time in US history, Congress passed immigration laws that singled out people on the basis of race and class.[64] As historian Moon Ho-Jung explains, Chinese exclusion "enabled the US nation-state to proclaim itself as 'free.'"[65]

Nearly a century later, the WGMA and its supporters similarly used the language of slavery to assert their own claims to freedom in contrast to that in "Red China." Sheinkman expressed concern at China's "exploitation of the working force." China was a place where a "vast captive and exploited labor force toils ceaselessly to produce goods." The United

States was different, he asserted. One of the key differences Sheinkman pointed to between the two systems was their workforces' ability to unionize. In China, "they have no means of improving their conditions of work or their rates of pay since collective bargaining and the strike action are unthinkable and unknown." Striking would, he added, "be regarded as traitorous acts against the state."[66]

As treasurer of one of the largest textile unions in the United States, it is perhaps not surprising that Sheinkman drew on union activity as a key difference between the two countries. As he well knew, however, the cotton work glove industry in the United States was almost entirely non-unionized. Chinese workers, moreover, did in fact strike and work collectively during the Mao era.[67] Nonetheless, his distinctions between Chinese and American labor conditions allowed him to assert the importance of American freedom—however tenuous it was in practice. It reinforced the idea, so prevalent in nineteenth-century immigration debates, of Chinese workers as docile and inherently willing to accept poor working conditions. "How can U.S. workers compete with the labor costs that characterize production in the People's Republic of China?" Sheinkman cried.[68] Short of diminishing US workers' already-low wages, they could not compete with Chinese imports on the basis of price he suggested.

The solution Sheinkman and the WGMA pointed to did not involve addressing the core premise that textile labor should be as cheap as possible. It was this idea, after all, that had compelled manufacturers to move their production from union to non-union places within the United States and was again driving the move to low-wage countries such as China. Instead, they pushed for restrictions. The WGMA and its supporters sought to restrict goods rather than people, but similar to the labor and immigration restrictions of the late nineteenth century, their justifications relied upon an imagined ideal of what the United States represented, which in turn relied upon an association between Chinese workers and slavery. But without addressing the accepted notion that textile labor should be as cheap as possible, they would be unable to redress the fundamental problem facing their industry.[69]

In Pursuit of Market Order

Underlying the WGMA's arguments lay a question of market order. The concerns about China not being privy to MFA, of China's communism, and its low prices all reflected a tension in the shifting interests of even the WGMA's own members. In the 1970s many US companies were both producers and importers of cotton work gloves. Indeed, four of the five major American *importers* of cotton work gloves from China were also members of the WGMA.[70] The USITC commissioners ruling against the case interpreted the dual interests of these WGMA members as a detraction to its overall case: even its own members wanted to buy Chinese gloves, they argued.

For the four WGMA importing companies, foreign imports did not constitute their full product lines. They were still producing cotton gloves domestically in the United States, but in diminishing quantities. In 1972, American glove producers imported 4.4 percent of their total stock of cotton work gloves. In 1974 this had increased to 10.8 percent. By the time the WGMA launched its case, the percentage of imported cotton work gloves had risen to nearly 30 percent. Management at glove factories across the United States were increasingly replacing their cotton work gloves with sources from abroad, but they sought to do so with the order that quotas would provide. While they presented their case to the USITC as being in the interest of their workers, it was a temporary reprieve that they were after. They needed time to structurally adjust to their recent turn to imports.

It was not, therefore, imports alone that were causing such disruption to employment in the glove industry. American workers were additionally facing precarity from their managers' decisions to shift to overseas labor. Outsourced manufacturing was a new iteration of industrial capital's continuous search for profit driven most particularly by cheap, compliant labor.[71] In the 1950s the textile industry had been rocked not just by rising imports but also management decisions to relocate from unionized factories, often in the North, to non-union factories in the South.[72] By the 1970s it was again not just imports but also capital moves that led to rising unemployment. The difference was that these movements had become global, enabled by technological advances including containerized shipping.[73]

The WGMA, of course, framed things differently. Along with "Red China," they blamed policymakers in Washington. The State Department's efforts to stop the case and the Liaison Office's direct interventions with Chinese exporters revealed a willingness to "sacrifice" workers' interests. Bureaucrats in Washington viewed foreign policy as "more important than the economic interest of United States firms and workers," the WGMA wrote in its submission to the USITC. The State Department assumed that "our relationship with the People's Republic of China is so delicate that nothing should be done to disrupt it in its early days even if this means sacrificing the domestic cotton work glove industry." In the WGMA's telling it was US policymakers who were sacrificing American workers for foreign policy considerations.[74]

These managers successfully controlled the narrative about where blame ought to be apportioned. The Washington establishment were the culprits, as were the Chinese communists. But the textile corporations who were turning toward outsourced manufacturing—many of whom were within the WGMA—received no mention in their arguments or submission to the USITC. It was a powerful and long-held tactic in the textile industry's playbook: blame imports and blame Washington. In the process, they deflected any responsibility away from the decisions of corporations and their managers.

The USITC Ruling

By a margin of four to two, the USITC commissioners ruled against placing any limits on imports from the PRC. The majority of commissioners found that the number of Chinese cotton work gloves entering the United States, and the rate at which they did so, were not a cause of material injury to domestic manufacturers. In their assessment of section 406 of the Trade Act, which applied only to communist states, they took the question of whether imports were "increasing rapidly" as a threshold issue. This meant that other issues—such as proving industry injury—would be dealt with only if the threshold question was first determined in the affirmative.

In 1974, when Congress created the Trade Act, lawmakers had hoped that section 406 would provide an easier mechanism for domestic protection against communist nations compared with other antidumping legislation. Yet this particular legal requirement soon proved more challenging. Unlike section 201, which could be applied to all countries, section 406 was phrased in the present tense: "increasing rapidly." Section 201 simply required a plaintiff to prove that "increased quantities" of imports had entered the United States. For the WGMA, the burden of proof had been to show that the increase was occurring at the time of petition—that the rate was "increasing" not "increased."[75] The figures the USITC commissioners relied upon therefore became a key factor in the outcome of the case—as did the interference by US policymakers and China's Ministry of Foreign Trade.

Joseph Parker, vice chairman of the Commission, analyzed the imports data on a year-by-year basis. While he acknowledged that Chinese glove imports were high in 1976, he noted that they had declined in 1977, in contrast to increases from other countries such as Hong Kong or Japan. Taking such an approach, he determined that the imports were not *presently* increasing and for this reason quotas should not be recommended.[76]

In contrast, the two dissenting commissioners, chairman Daniel Minchew and commissioner Italo Ablondi, split the data in two groups: 1973–1975 and 1976–1977. Comparing the level of imports in this way, Minchew determined that imports "increased extremely rapidly" in the 1976–1977 period with Chinese glove imports increasing by nearly 550 percent from the earlier periods.[77] Ablondi took the same approach, arguing that Chinese imports "skyrocketed" when figures for 1976 and 1977 were combined, reaching nearly 20 percent of total US imports of cotton work gloves.[78] Given the deliberate decrease in Chinese sales in 1977, these conclusions indicate just how high the 1976 figures were compared to the previous three years.

Commissioner George Moore also agreed that imports were presently increasing rapidly. Despite this, he went on to determine there was no evidence of a causal link between Chinese imports and material injury to the American industry. The two other commissioners, Catherine Bedell and Bill Alberger, made "no specific conclusion" on the issue of whether Chinese imports were increasing rapidly. They did, however, join with Moore in arguing there was no evidence that it was Chinese gloves in particular that were causing the disruption. Even if the American industry was experiencing injury, they pointed to much higher levels of imports from other countries, especially Hong Kong.[79] Together with Parker, they formed a majority against imposing quotas.

Immediately after the USITC case, Chinese work glove exports increased once more. In the first three months of 1978 alone, American importers purchased Chinese cotton work gloves at such an increased rate that they were equivalent to 67 percent of *total* Chinese imports in 1977. This was evidence not only of how quickly China could affect the American market but also, as the WGMA had testified, of how misleading the temporary decrease in 1977 had been.[80] By the end of 1978, 24 percent of all American cotton work glove imports came from China alone. These numbers continued to increase, reaching 32 percent of total US purchases of such gloves the following year. By the end of 1979 China had overtaken Hong Kong to become the United States' largest supplier not just of cotton work gloves but all varieties of gloves.[81]

In Chillicothe, manufacturers at Boss Manufacturing had turned to importing nearly all its lines of gloves. By December 1981 they closed the factory altogether. Its manager, Lansing Demarest, told local reporters that imports were so cheap it had been 256 percent more expensive for the company to produce gloves than to buy them from foreign suppliers.[82] In 1983 the Mid West Glove Corporation also filed for bankruptcy. This time, however, a businessman from Kansas named Michael Palmer purchased the company and renamed it MidWest Quality Gloves.[83] By 1985 Chillicothe's third glove company, Lambert Manufacturing, celebrated its fiftieth year of business.[84] But soon thereafter, Palmer purchased Lambert too, merging it with his newly acquired MidWest Quality Gloves. By the end of the twentieth century, Chillicothe—once the heart of glove manufacturing in the United States—had only one factory left.

CHINA'S ABILITY TO infiltrate the US cotton work glove market so quickly was a symptom, not a cause, of the textile industry's problems of rising unemployment and closing factory doors. While the WGMA presented its case as a simple narrative of US workers' interests being sacrificed by Washington elites and a predatory communist nation, the first case for US trade restrictions on Chinese imports illustrates a much more complex dynamic. Both of these factors certainly were important to the industry's woes. But so too was the managerial turn toward international manufacturing and the prioritization of cheap labor that drove it. Throughout the decade, more and more executives turned to offshore manufacturing in attempts to reduce labor costs. In 1977 this was still happening only slowly, which was why factory managers sought market order and control as they adjusted.

China became a beneficiary of this larger structural reorganization taking place within US manufacturing. At precisely this moment—as the gears of industrial capitalism turned toward international chains of supply—China's new leaders accelerated their efforts to achieve the increased foreign trade they had been pursuing all decade. Following Mao's death, Hua Guofeng initiated a technology buying spree, which he labeled the "new leap forward." By December 1978, Deng Xiaoping declared that he was placing the Four Modernizations at the center of a new program he labeled "reform and opening." As China's post-Mao leadership accelerated the country's industrialization, a core component of their efforts involved setting up factories that would produce consumer products for US companies made by Chinese workers.

CHAPTER 8

Normalization and the Trade Deal

FRUSTRATIONS WERE HIGH among workers in the US textile and apparel industries. On Wednesday, April 13, 1977, hundreds of thousands of American workers embarked on one of the largest strikes in the industries' history. They took to the streets across the country just as AFL-CIO president George Meany and other labor leaders were in Washington, DC, for negotiations with President Carter over import restrictions. The strikers were focused on imports from all countries, but China was beginning to enter their considerations. On the eve of the strike, textile manufacturers held a public debate in New York City, sponsored by the *Daily News Record* and attended by both workers and managers in the industry. Amid the broader fights over imports, was it time, they debated, for the United States to implement a bilateral textile agreement with China?

Robert Forney, vice president of Du Pont's textile fibers department, spoke in favor of an agreement, especially one that would impose limits on China's exports to the United States. Forney warned of the effects of China's development. "We need quota controls on imports from China because their potential is frightening," he urged. "They are building large fiber plants." Connecting these plants to China's exporting efforts, he explained, "We must presume blend exports [textiles made of synthetic fabric] to this market could escalate very quickly."

Forney did not want to end the developing relationship with China. "No one is talking here about cutting off trade with China," he clarified.

Rather, Forney wanted to impose order and predictability on the process. He called for a bilateral textile agreement with China. "The big concern is that the behemoth out there could cause a lot of trouble in the future and the whole purpose of this textile trade program is to provide some degree of certainty so that people here can plan capital commitments."[1]

At face value, Forney seemed to be advocating for an approach that American workers might support. But when he spoke of certainty and the need to "plan capital commitments" he revealed an industrial approach that did not foreclose a transition to overseas manufacturing. Even though his position was in line with that of George Meany and other labor leaders calling for limits on the China trade, Forney's interests were not those of American workers. The idea of moving to cheap labor overseas was not a problem per se for Forney, but it was a transition that needed to be planned. For Forney, market order lay at the heart of what was needed. It would take until September 1980 for the textile deal Forney called for to come into effect. It came after the US Congress passed the US-PRC Trade Agreement in February that same year—the first government-to-government trade deal between the two nations since the CCP came to power.

Forney's colleagues at Du Pont had been involved in China trade since 1974, and not long after he spoke, Du Pont hosted a Chinese delegation looking to improve their packaging for Chinese exports.[2] So at the same time that one of the company's executives was warning about the looming effects of unregulated China trade, others in the company were providing tips to Chinese traders on how to best package their exports.

These two imperatives within the Du Pont company—calling for regulations on Chinese goods while assisting China improve its exports—were not incompatible. Instead, they reflected the dynamics unfolding in many US industries. As increasingly more CEOs found their companies competing with imports, they turned to outsourced manufacturing, looking for cheap labor sources internationally.[3] When it came to China, they wanted to prevent the new trade partner from saturating the US market too quickly. But as the WGMA's fight against Chinese textiles revealed, an emerging group of US manufacturers were also importers. Their decisions helped frame the China market as a place to profit from 800 million workers, but they wanted this to unfold steadily.

Forney's warnings came during a spectacular expansion of China's foreign technology imports. After Hua Guofeng wrested power from the Gang of Four following Mao's death in September 1976, China placed science and technology at the center of its development plans. Throughout 1977 and 1978 Hua spoke of a "new leap forward" in science and technology in order to achieve the Four Modernizations. Despite the disastrousness of the Great Leap Forward of the late 1950s, Hua referenced the policy partly to connect to Mao's legacy and partly to reflect the urgency he felt toward China's development.[4]

Initially Hua turned to Europe and Japan to fulfill China's technology needs. He and other pragmatists were particularly interested in US technology, and they made this clear to US scientists and policymakers throughout the new leap forward.[5] But it was not until diplomatic normalization was reached in December 1978—more than two years after Mao's death—that the United States became a significant beneficiary of China's emphasis on high-tech industrialization. A handful of US computer, oil, and mining companies did sign some export deals, but for the most part China stuck to importing grain and soybeans from the United States throughout 1977 and 1978. Around 45 percent of total US exports to China in 1977 consisted of soybean oil, polyester, raw cotton, and soybeans. And in 1978 nearly 64 percent of exports were wheat, cotton, and corn alone.[6] If we follow the money, we see that—as had been the case throughout the decade—Chinese policymakers ensured that improvements in diplomacy would come before any expansion of trade.

Regardless of the limited technology purchases China made from the United States in these years, the big story coming out of China was its rapid industrialization and therefore *potentially* lucrative technology sales. As China's leaders accelerated development, the China market was celebrated as one to which US businesspeople could sell. In October 1978 a headline in *The Economist* promised, "China: Over 900m Customers." In April 1980 the cover of *Nation's Business* featured a wide banner declaring, "China: A Seller's Market."[7] As big industrial and computer companies began to finally—and haltingly—see opportunities to sell their technology to China, the popular conception of the China market remained that of Carl Crow's vision from 1937: one of 400 million customers.

But there was an additional, quieter story occurring too. As Forney knew, China's development efforts were deeply connected to its export goals. Significant parts of China's industrialization were aimed at building up its capacity to make exportable items, starting with textiles. Hua's technology purchases continued the work Chinese pragmatists had been pursuing throughout the 1970s: turning the China market into a site of 800 million workers. A crucial part of Hua's, and later Deng Xiaoping's, reforms involved integrating China's own development goals with the global capitalist economy. This meant, for example, importing technology that would help them produce synthetic fibers, which could then be used to produce nylon clothing for export. By 1979 Deng extended these efforts even further. He introduced Special Economic Zones (SEZs) aimed at attracting foreign capital to set up factories in Shenzhen, Zhuhai, Shantou, and Xiamen. In return, the cities would provide cheap labor for the newly built outposts of multinational corporations.

China's development, as had been happening since the early 1970s, was *with* the capitalist world. The decade was one of a "great convergence" between the Chinese state and global capitalism—in distinction to what Kenneth Pomeranz labeled the "great divergence" between China and Northwest Europe that had developed two hundred years earlier.[8] In this new era of industrial capitalism, as US corporations internationalized their manufacturing processes, China's reformers linked their own manufacturing capabilities to them.

As several scholars have shown, Deng's reforms built upon earlier efforts implemented by Hua Guofeng, despite Hua's short tenure as paramount leader.[9] But in this chapter I join a growing number of historians who argue that Hua, also, did not instigate a new post-Mao approach, instead he accelerated processes that had been underway in China since the early 1970s.[10] China's increase in foreign trade since Lin Biao's death in 1971, its 4-3 Program of 1973, Mao's Three Worlds Theory of 1974, and China's ongoing trade connections even at the height of factional fighting in 1975 and 1976—all of these factors had increased integration with capitalist nations and together laid the groundwork for both Hua's new leap forward and Deng's reform and opening.

These continuities within China's development plans help explain the relationship between the two sides of the China market that Americans engaged with—the high-profile focus on sales and the quieter story that Forney spoke of: a slowly emerging Chinese manufacturing "behemoth." Exploring the two sides of the China market together reveals that a crucial component of China's convergence with the capitalist trading system was the change that was occurring in US corporations and the global division of labor that came with it. China's purchases of large-scale technology may have seemed, in the short term, to augur the reemergence of a market for American corporations to sell to. But Chinese leaders made many of these purchases with the aim of creating a market that would provide the United States with workers.

The period between Mao's death in September 1976 and when the US-PRC Trade Agreement came into effect in February 1980 were expansive yet consolidating years for US-China trade. During this time the United States and China finally achieved diplomatic normalization, and Deng Xiaoping announced that China would follow a path of reform and opening. By the time Congress passed the US-PRC Trade Agreement, the two nations had formally put in place structures that allowed the bilateral trade relationship to continue on the path that Chinese pragmatists and US businesspeople had slowly, falteringly etched since they reestablished ties in 1971. In the immediate post-Mao era, China's technology purchases led to excited headlines about the export potential for US businesspeople. The result of the technology itself, however, reinforced the slow transformation of the China market into a site of 800 million workers.

Hua's Focus on Foreign Trade

As Hua Guofeng came to power in late 1976, he brought with him many moderate economic policymakers who had held influence earlier in the decade, including Chen Yun and Li Xiannian. Together they emphasized the important role trade would continue to play in building China's economy. In touting the importance of engagement with capitalist nations, Hua lent these ideas credence by invoking Mao's ideas. He drew especially on Mao's 1956 speech, "On the Ten Major Relationships," in which the Chairman had advocated the importance of economic growth through a more balanced approach toward industrial development and agricultural reform. To do this, Mao had argued that China needed to "learn from the strong points of all nations and all countries." Yet China should not approach these lessons "blindly," he added. "We must not copy everything indiscriminately and transplant mechanically." Hua reprinted this speech over twenty years later, legitimizing his own agenda of economic reform by positioning himself as Mao's true successor in distinction to the Gang of Four.[11]

Hua also sent multiple signals to foreign nations that trade would not only continue but also expand under his leadership. Early into his leadership, he announced China's renewed focus on trade through several newspaper editorials. *Renmin Ribao* carried articles with messages asserting to the Chinese public the importance of trade—a message additionally aimed at reassuring foreign readers. "Foreign trade is a vital part of the national economy of our country," one such article asserted in January 1977. "The Chinese people wish to have friendly cooperation with the people of all countries and to resume and expand international trade in order to develop production and promote economic prosperity."[12]

China's Foreign Trade similarly reiterated these messages in its Chinese, English, French, and Spanish editions. "Now that these 'four evils' have been eliminated, the people are full of joy and the excellent situation has opened up bright prospects for foreign trade," the magazine announced to businesspeople around the world.[13] Along with the usual articles highlighting China's trading experiences, there was a new piece. For the first time in these pages, the magazine published an article under the headline, "How to Trade with China."

The headline was to the point, but it also echoed the advice literature penned by so many American businesspeople during the decade. With this article, China's Ministry of Foreign Trade provided its own submission to the "doing business with China" genre—the first of its kind in the pages of *China's Foreign Trade*. Written by Chung Wen, its tone was detailed yet clinical. "This article is mainly intended for those new friends who wish to establish or have just established trade contacts with China," Chung explained by way of introduction, a nod to the growing number of foreign businesspeople beginning to trade with China.

China's foreign trade was conducted on the basis of "equality, mutual benefit and the exchange of needed goods," Chung noted. Here, as throughout the pages of *China's Foreign Trade,* was the language of equality and mutual benefit Mao and Zhou had included in the Shanghai Communiqué with Nixon in 1972. Unlike other articles in the issue, however, the use of Maoist rhetoric in this advice piece was restricted—its language was straightforward and informative. Chung simply noted, "China is a socialist country" and explained that this therefore meant that it "carries out a policy of controlling foreign trade."[14] The rest of the article was starkly pragmatic.

Chung went on to explain that China's trade was handled through eight state-owned corporations, each of which focused on a specific aspect of China's trade—cereal oils and foodstuffs; native produce and animal by-products; textiles; light industrial products; machinery; chemicals; metals and minerals; and advanced technology. The article explained the differences between the head offices and the corporations' local branches.[15]

China's own contribution to the trade advice literature that had begun proliferating throughout the decade was matter-of-fact. Useful and to the point, it struck a tone very different from that of Martin Klingenberg, who, as we saw in Chapter 2, wrote of Chinese trade as a "sensuous, slow . . . advance-and-retreat mating dance," or that of Stanley Marcus, who focused on the exotic implications of Chinese traders' use of an abacus.[16] It was a reminder, if ever one was needed, that exoticizing China was a choice, not an inherent part of the trading process.

The message coming from Beijing was not lost on members of the National Council for US-China Trade. In February 1977 its newly renamed magazine, the *China Business Review,* published a full page of excerpts from Chinese media reports noting the centrality of trade in Chinese leaders' plans. Of particular interest to the National Council was Hua's focus on factory purchases and oil sales. Just as Hua signaled the connections between his and Mao's policies, so too did leaders at the National Council publicize the promise of trade continuity this heralded. The National Council included subheadings spelling out the message of Mao's enduring influence in the Hua era: "Plant Purchases Approved by Mao" and "Mao Chaired Decision on Oil Exports."[17]

For the National Council and American businesspeople—who had been able to trade with China only for the past six years—these continuities offered important reassurance. "The second half of 1976 was disappointing for US exporters," the *China Business Review* noted further on in its February 1977 issue. "But most American observers expect a modest up-turn in orders from the PRC." This meant, the National Council explained, that "plants, high technology, industrial equipment, and agricultural produces" were all "possible US major sales in coming months."[18] Hua's new leadership provided hope for US business leaders who were anxious to inject new momentum into the relationship after the factionalism in Beijing in recent years.

For all Hua's assurances of ongoing trade, another less comforting legacy of the late-Mao trade era carried over too: the uncertainty and difficulty of trading with China. As US political and business leaders navigated the post-Mao trade relationship, American businesspeople persisted in puzzling through the challenges that came with trading with China. Just as many continued to write books and articles advising on how to trade with China, and just as *China's Foreign Trade* contributed its own piece on the trading process, the National Council held more and more information sessions for the growing number of US businesspeople interested in trading with China.

In April 1977, for example, the National Council held a predeparture briefing in New York City for American businesspeople who were about to travel to the Spring Canton Trade Fair. The briefing featured advice from a panel of American executives who had previous experience trading with China. William Cullison, a director at a chemicals firm, discussed the long delays that many businesspeople experienced when trading with China. He warned that "sometimes there is a very frightening gap when you have lost control of your goods and control of your money" after concluding a trade negotiation with Chinese businesspeople. "This is unusual compared to dealing with any other country," Cullison conceded.

Hearing these warnings, a member of the audience piped up to ask, "If there are so many problems, then why deal with China?" "Well," Cullison replied, unfazed by such a question, "there is long-term benefit." The way forward meant that "at first you start off by buying from them, but with patience and perseverance you may be able to make a substantial sale which pays off."[19] Cullison's assessment was based upon an image of the lucrative China market as a source of customers but also as an acknowledgment that China wanted reciprocity—you needed to begin buying from China before you could sell to them.

Another member of the panel, Harold Potchtar, president of Toscany Imports, replied to the question arguing, "The pottery and glassware industries are dying in the United States . . . this is a very hot and dirty industry to work in and the American workers are turning away from it altogether." The solution Potchtar pointed to was China. "I think the future of this industry lies in China where they have the manpower," he explained to the assembled businesspeople. "This is why my company has been looking toward China for its long-term goals."[20]

Potchtar was a well-established business leader in the United States. President of the Italy America Chamber of Commerce, he would later go on to serve on Carter's Special Commission for US-China Trade.[21] At the briefing for Canton Trade Fair attendees, he described the China market in terms of its vast sources of labor. But his disregard for Chinese workers' conditions in the pottery and glassware industries reflected a racialized vision of profit. American workers were "turning away" from the industry but Chinese workers did not mind the "hot and dirty" conditions as much, he suggested. He did not express concern that workers from any country would be subjected to those conditions; for him the issue was obtaining the products with as low labor costs as possible.

The official nature of the event and the fact that both Cullison and Potchtar were experienced Chinese traders elevated the stature of their advice. They held different visions of the kinds of profits the China market could yield—for Cullison the eventual aim was exporting, whereas Potchtar's eventual aim was importing. But both men felt that the answer to the question of "why deal with China" was long-term profit. Even as the China market was changing to more and more accommodate Potchtar's vision of 800 million workers, a core emotional idea of *eventual* profit remained a powerful pull as US businesspeople navigated the uncertainties of trade.

The US Textile Industry and Chinese Imports

For the newly elected Carter administration, the immediate post-Mao period raised some concerns. As he familiarized himself with China trade, Carter found that he had inherited a trade imbalance in China's favor. The opening years of trade had been markedly in the United States' favor—the US sold more to China than it imported—but in 1975 and 1976 that imbalance had switched to China's favor, as China cut back on its purchases from the United States.

In March 1977 Carter wrote to his commerce secretary, Juanita Kreps, asking for her analysis of why there had been such a downturn in US exports to China in recent years. Kreps was the first woman and the first economist to hold the position of commerce secretary. Prior to her appointment, she had been the first female director of J. C. Penney, one of the largest corporations that imported from China in the 1970s.

The problem, as Kreps saw it, was that Chinese purchases of American agricultural products in 1973 and 1974 had created a "distortion" in the overall figures, despite the cancellations. When the trade figures were considered without wheat and cotton and other agricultural sales, the trade balance of these earlier years was "far more modestly in the U.S. favor." There were other bilateral constraints too. "Foremost among the factors currently affecting our ability to export to the People's Republic of China (PRC) is the lack of fully normal diplomatic and trade relations," she explained. Diplomatic normalization would be "no guarantee of increased trade in and of itself," but it would "almost certainly" lead to more purchases of American technology and equipment.[22]

Earlier in the decade, business leaders at the National Council had worked hard to help China increase its exports to the United States. While that remained a core issue for them, Carter now wanted to find ways of increasing China's *imports* of US goods too. The problem was that normalization was not an immediate priority for Carter. This meant that it was not until he accelerated diplomatic negotiations more than a year later, in mid-1978, that China began making significant technology purchases. In the meantime, however, Carter faced other pressures. In addition to wanting to expand US exports to China, he contended with growing pressure from the US textile industry to regulate trade with China.

Some of the largest expressions of this pressure came in April 1977. Throughout the month, labor leaders, led by George Meany of the AFL-CIO, met with President Carter demanding he take measures to slash the rapid increase in textile and garment imports that had occurred since 1974, when the United States and seventeen other countries passed a multilateral trade agreement on textiles known as the Multifiber Arrangement (MFA). The MFA limited the growth of imports entering the United States from developing countries to 6 percent per year. The provision left neither exporting nations nor US workers happy, as it still allowed for an annual increase in the amount of textiles developing nations could sell, but the arrangement imposed restrictions on the pace at which that rise could occur. As labor leaders lobbied Carter, American textile and apparel workers embarked on a nationwide strike in support of further protections.[23]

China was not privy to the MFA arrangement, and it increasingly became a target in the textile and apparel industries' fight against imports. In the lead-up to their strike on April 13, the *Daily News Record* held a debate in New York City where industry leaders argued about whether a separate textile agreement with China was also needed. It was a staunch yes from Robert Forney of Du Pont's textiles department; he wanted order and control on imports from China. But importers at the event sought to allay strikers' fears about Chinese goods entering the United States. Frank Heineman, president of Men's Wear International, did not want any import restrictions. "The threat is nowhere near as serious as you say, at least for the present," Heineman dismissed. This was because, he explained, "The Chinese are not set up for big scale orders of apparel." Heineman had been importing clothing from China for years. An active member of the National Council's importers' committee, he had worked hard to increase Chinese sales to the United States. Import restrictions would only hinder that process. In fact, Heineman added, "you have to be almost insane to do business there because of their inflexibility."

As he downplayed the threat China might pose to US manufacturers, Heineman reiterated the trope that so many US importers reverted to in this decade: presenting China trade as a challenge. Given that he himself continued to trade with China, and in fact served on the National Council's importers' committee, the challenges were not enough to stop him. Instead, the sense of confronting a new trading frontier and emphasizing its difficulty was part of the process—and indeed excitement—itself. Besides, he reassured his listeners, "they've priced themselves out of this market."[24]

Henry Ross, an importer from Scope Imports, agreed. He explained that in the space of a year, Chinese textile prices had increased more than 40 percent. "That's a pretty ridiculous jump for a flannel shirt." His company could not afford the price hike and did not place any orders for the coming year. "I think you'll see a drop off in imports of Chinese apparel this year," he concluded. David Caplan, an importer from Concord Fabrics, speculated that these price jumps reflected China's awareness of the US textile industry's protection efforts. "I think they wanted to cool it," he reflected. Caplan speculated, not inaccurately, that the PRC deliberately increased their prices to make their exports seem temporarily less threatening to the American textile industry.

But even more important than the fluctuations in price, the importers argued, was the fact that China could not produce textiles on a large enough scale. Hong Kong and Taiwan far outweighed China in terms of the volume of goods they could supply. China's factories were filled with "antiquated equipment," said Heineman. Not willing to dismiss China's manufacturing potential entirely, however, he noted, "Everyone knows you can buy sewing machines easily so their industry could be developed." The problem was not in the quality of goods China produced, Heineman noted. In fact, "workmanship is tremendous," he said, reinforcing a view of Chinese quality that had so shaped the perception of Chinese imports in the 1970s. The issue, Heineman noted, was that "speed of production is horrible." These importers downplayed China's role in the overall problems the US textile industry was facing.

The tensions between importers and workers in the textile industry only continued to grow. By June 1978 key textile leaders from business and labor—including George Meany, president of the AFL-CIO; Irving Shapiro, chairman of the Business Roundtable; and Robert Small, from the American Textile Manufacturers Institute (ATMI)—held a joint press conference in Washington where they outlined the ongoing issues at stake for the textile industry as a whole.[25] Only a week earlier these leaders had been fighting over revisions to labor laws, yet they came together in this instance to protest what they described as a "stunning increase" in textile imports across the board.[26]

Robert Small, from the ATMI, singled out Chinese textiles as a particular area of concern. He warned that China was "a new textile power . . . rising in the Far East."[27] He noted that imports from China were increasing so rapidly that it had become the United States' sixth-largest textile partner, despite the tariffs it faced as a consequence of not having MFN trading status.[28] Drawing a parallel with the OPEC countries, which had been colluding to set the price of oil, Small described an emerging "Far East textile cartel" led by Japan and including Hong Kong, Korea, Taiwan, and now China. "The American consumer," he exclaimed, "does not need OPEC-like apparel prices!"[29] China was not colluding with its neighbors, of course, but it was working closely with Hong Kong to integrate its exports into global trade networks.

Textile leaders such as Small began to connect China to the wider problems they were facing. Like Robert Forney from Du Pont, Small wanted the United States to negotiate a quota agreement with China to bring a sense of order to the trade relationship. As the head of the textile manufacturers' largest representative organization, he represented the interests of many manufacturers who were slowly beginning to turn to offshore manufacturing and imported goods. But they wanted the security of doing this with order and control. Small's desire for controls on China trade was driven by very different imperatives to those of American workers, whom he was more than willing to replace with overseas labor. It was the American consumer whom he framed his concerns around, not American workers.

The US textile industry was one of the largest groups protesting the levels of Chinese imports, but other industries were pushing for restrictions too. On July 27, 1978, representatives from the wooden clothespins industry—makers of small wooden pegs used to hang up wet clothing—filed a petition for import relief from China with the USITC. The wooden clothespins makers used the same legal route that the cotton work gloves manufacturers had used in December 1977: they applied for quotas on Chinese imports under section 406 of the 1974 Trade Act.

As with the cotton work gloves case, the National Council for US-China Trade worried about the larger implications if the clothespins makers won. The business leaders dismissed the immediate case itself:

"Clothespins quotas would be only a small pinch in the side to the Chinese, and in the US . . . few have taken the case seriously." They worried instead about the precedent it might set: "As the dollar declines, domestic manufacturers will have more rather than less trouble with foreign imports, and products from socialist countries provide a convenient scapegoat."[30] Unlike the cotton work gloves case, however, the wooden clothespins makers won. In a unanimous ruling, the USITC agreed that imports from China were causing serious injury to the US clothespins industry.

The ruling—in favor of quotas on Chinese goods—came at precisely the wrong moment for Carter. He had just begun accelerating efforts toward normalization. In May his national security advisor, Zbigniew Brzezinski, had met with Deng Xiaoping in Beijing, where the two leaders had pledged to move ahead with normalization. Under the trade rule, the president was allowed to veto the USITC's decision, which only had recommendation powers. And veto is exactly what Carter did. Quotas "would not be an effective means to promote adjustment in the industry," the president noted in a press release. "While imports from the PRC have become an increasingly important component of US imports, other foreign sources still accounted for seventy-three percent of all US imports in 1977." Carter reasoned that imposing restrictions on Chinese wooden clothespins would not stop other countries from selling to the US market. They would simply fill the space left by China.[31]

The comments that both the National Council and President Carter made about the clothespins case tell us a great deal about the changes occurring in the US economy in the late 1970s. The National Council spoke of a future in which there would be "more rather than less trouble with foreign imports" because they would continue to rise and put pressure on domestic US industries. And President Carter spoke of the need to "promote adjustment in the industry," meaning the need to adapt to rising imports. Both of these comments revealed an acceptance that imports would become increasingly important to the ways manufacturing would operate in the United States. The interests of Americans working in industries affected by these shifts were not their immediate concern.

THROUGHOUT 1978, US-CHINA trade soared to its highest levels yet. By the end of the year, total trade reached $1.14 billion. In February, the USITC held its hearing into the cotton work gloves case. By year's end, President Carter and Deng Xiaoping announced that the two nations had finally reached an agreement for diplomatic normalization. Between these pivotal moments trade finally started to take off after years of cancellations and low levels of US exports. But this growth was driven by China's purchases of US agricultural products, not technology.

As with the early years of trade, in 1978 the major US exports to the PRC were agricultural commodities. Wheat, cotton, and corn together made up more than two-thirds of US sales to China in 1978. Despite Deng's and Hua's renewed focus on technology imports, they purchased few such goods from the United States. For these they turned instead to European and Japanese companies. Throughout 1978 Chinese negotiators used the lure of its potential technology purchases to incentivize normalization. The PRC was willing to expand its trade with the United States, but large-scale technology sales would have to wait.

The increase in bilateral trade reflected Hua and Deng's heightened focus on foreign trade in general. By February 1978 these efforts culminated in multi-year trade agreements with Europe and Japan. China signed a five-year trade agreement with the European Economic Community and an eight-year agreement with Japan. The European Commission described their trade agreement as one of "profound political significance." It was "one of the most evident manifestations of the excellence of the relationship between China and the European Community." The benefits were seen as more political than economic.[32] China did not, however, sign a trade agreement with the United States. The two nations had still not achieved diplomatic normalization.

Under the new leap forward, Hua continued to expand China's imports of foreign technology from non-US countries. At the China National Science Conference on March 18, 1978, Fang I, vice premier of the PRC's State Council, emphasized the importance of importing foreign technology. "Science and technology are the common treasure of mankind," he declared. "An important way to develop science and technology at high speed is to utilize fully the latest achievements in the world . . . and absorb their quintessence." China should set up teams of researchers who would study foreign technology products, including complete sets of equipment. "We should know the how and endeavor to know the why of the technologies introduced so as to create our own," he urged the assembled scientists.[33] Fang was amplifying the message that was being promoted by Hua and other party leaders, including State Planning Commission director Yu Qiuli. *Renmin Ribao* noted, "It is imperative to allow research in the social sciences to prosper as never before."[34]

China's increased focus on technology imports was welcome news to the National Council for US-China Trade. "China's New Trade Initiatives," the May 1978 edition of the *China Business Review* announced. "The joint is jumping!" China was "sending sizzling wires over the globe with the same message—Peking wants to buy technology, sell goods and develop new ways of doing business."[35]

By early 1978 Deng wrested control of Chinese politics from Hua, and he too linked his interest in purchasing US technology to the normalization process. If US companies wanted to sell their machines and factories to the PRC, then Carter needed to speed up the diplomatic process. Deng had said to members of the National Committee for US-China Relations in October 1977, "The PRC has a policy of buying products, if available, from those countries that have normal diplomatic relations with the PRC, even if it costs more."[36]

Once Congress began to pass the Panama Canal Treaties in March 1978, Carter did finally turn his focus to normalization with China. The day that the first treaty was passed, March 16, 1978, Carter authorized national security advisor Zbigniew Brzezinski to travel to Beijing. By this stage Brzezinski had taken control of US China policy from Secretary of State Cyrus Vance.[37] On the afternoon of May 21 he spent two hours speaking with Deng. Both men expressed their willingness to move forward with normalization. Brzezinski made it clear that the United States was able to meet Deng's three demands regarding Taiwan so long as their agreement also included a clause indicating both the United States and China agreed that any kind of reunification needed to be peaceful.

While they make progress on strategic issues, Deng also reiterated that China would not prioritize trade until after normalization. "In commercial, scientific and technological expansions and economic expansions we will give priority to the countries that have diplomatic relations with us under the same terms," he explained.[38] Strategic questions over Taiwan and the Soviet Union dominated discussions, and once more trade was treated as something that would expand only after resolving the hurdles toward normalization.

Nonetheless, Deng was also aware that China's economic modernization program required American technological know-how. Japan, South Korea, and Taiwan were key models in Deng's modernization plans. And all three nations had used American science, technology, and education in their own development. Even much of the European technology he imported utilized American components. This desire for American technology therefore added fuel to Deng's own efforts to finally achieve normalization.[39]

The very day after meeting with Brzezinski, Deng met with an Italian delegation and mentioned that he was interested in developing China's trade and technology ties with the United States. But again, he noted that China would continue to give preference to countries with whom they had full diplomatic ties. In July 1978 Deng stressed this in a meeting with Frank Press, Carter's advisor on trade and technology. "We are prepared to buy your technologies," Deng noted. But China was "concerned about your [restrictions on] technology transfer." The catch, Deng indicated, was that these restrictions could only be lifted after normalization.[40] In August he repeated the same message to Austrian visitors. Deng wanted to end the diplomatic limbo with the United States. By September, Chai Zemin, chief of the PRC Liaison Office, told Brzezinski in Washington that the pace toward normalization was still too slow. China was ready to settle, and it was using the promise of trade as a carrot to achieve this.[41] Even more than that, it was using the promise of the United States being able to *sell* to China—the early twentieth-century Carl Crow conception of the China market.

By the end of summer 1978, the Carter administration reached agreement that, as one internal memorandum put it, the "U.S.-Chinese normalization could open the doors to a political-economic relationship with one-fourth of mankind."[42] The document showed the persistence of the open-door ideology and the deep pull of China's population for policymakers.

A handful of US companies did make technology sales to China before normalization, but their timing remained tied to diplomatic events. The largest of these deals came toward the end of 1978, after the successful meeting between Brzezinski and Deng injected momentum into the efforts. Kaiser engineers and High Voltage Engineering Corporation (HVEC), for example, both made lucrative sales in the second half of 1978, after the Brzezinski-Deng discussions.

In August 1978 Kaiser Engineers, one of the world's largest engineering conglomerates, became the first American company to reach a mining construction deal with the PRC in which the commodity they sold was expertise. While some American firms, such as WABCO, had sold mining equipment to China earlier in the decade, Kaiser's was a deal of a different kind. Kaiser would be involved in the construction process itself. Its engineers were to work on two iron ore mines in China. The first was in the northern province of Hebei. The second was near the Korean border, a mine in Nan Fen that Kaiser engineers would help upgrade. Unlike WABCO, Kaiser was a service-based company only. Rather than providing material goods, Kaiser sold expertise.

Kaiser's deal marked another first in the developing US-China trade relationship. It was the first time Chinese traders imported US expertise alone. The deal mirrored much wider shifts in the structures of multinational corporations. Since the 1950s and 1960s, American companies increasingly began to export services rather than tangible products. Management and technical consulting became profitable products themselves. Historian Alex Beasley has argued that many Texas-based oil companies, for example, sold expertise via international educational programs, training students from around the world to become oil managers and engineers.[43]

The National Council for US-China Trade reported on the Kaiser contract with excitement. Coming after a long line of "first times" in bilateral trade relations, the National Council hailed this, too, as a potential "new era in relations with China." This was a turning point "not only for Kaiser, but for the entire American mining equipment industry as well."[44] As it turned out, Kaiser's contract was less of a breakthrough than the National Council initially hoped. It took until after normalization, in January 1979, for further mining deals to be signed. Even though the Kaiser deal did not augur the immediate breakthrough the National Council hoped for, it did come prior to diplomatic normalization—a sign of just how interested Deng was in US scientific and engineering expertise.

The United States signed a second key export deal in November 1978, just a month before Carter and Deng announced their intention to normalization relations. HVEC signed a deal to sell a nuclear particle accelerator to China's importing company, Techimport. The machine in question, the HI-13 Tandem Accelerator, was used for the study of nuclear physics and was worth approximately $5 million. Such high-energy physics equipment required approval from President Carter, which the company received. The *China Business Review* excitedly reported that "the sale symbolizes the crossing of a new threshold in Sino-US scientific exchange." It was one of the largest sales of high technology to China since RCA sold its satellites in 1972, in the lead-up to President Nixon's summit with Mao. In addition to the technology itself, the deal included the provision of technical assistance between HVEC technicians and scientists at the newly established Chinese Academy of Sciences. Similar to the Kaiser deal, China was looking to learn from the United States in addition to importing technology itself.

Chinese Corduroy and Velveteen

As China increased its purchases of technology from capitalist nations, it began to link them to its exports in new ways. Pragmatists remained conscious of the need to continue balancing China's total trade, and by the end of the decade they began to link exports and imports in the same deals. This was seen, for example, in September 1978 when three Chinese export delegations traveled to the United States in that month alone. "As many selling delegations were in the US in September as have been sent in any one year," the *China Business Review* noted enthusiastically.[45] The number of people involved in the delegations were larger too. In 1975, when Chinatex became the first trade delegation to travel to the United States, the company sent only five people. By 1978 each delegation had as many as ten people.

The most significant change, however, was not the number of delegations or their size but the fact they began to combine buying and selling in the same transactions. The Chinese delegations that arrived in September 1978 were exporters of tea, native produce, garments, knitwear, minerals, metals, and carpets. But many of their conversations with US companies became dominated by discussions about purchasing US technology or equipment. They were interested in both sides of the China market: buying as well as selling. The Chinese delegations did not conclude deals during their September tour, but soon thereafter two US textile companies concluded deals that reflected China's focus on both upgrading its technology and becoming a supplier of cheap labor.

In mid-October 1978 representatives from Oxford Industries and from Prestige traveled to the fall Canton Trade Fair where both groups negotiated a particular kind of technology transfer, known as buyback deals. Chinatex purchased seaming and fusing equipment from the textile corporations. But instead of using cash, they arranged to pay for it through garments made with that same machinery. For its part, Oxford Industries supplied the Shanghai branch of Chinatex with fusing equipment worth just under $100,000. They were used in fusing together the seams of garments. In return for the machines, Chinatex paid the firm in corduroy suits. Over the course of a year, Oxford Industries received $100,000 worth of corduroy suits. The deal was non-exclusive, meaning that Shanghai Chinatex could sell suits made with the equipment to other foreign merchants too.

Prestige signed an even larger deal with the Dalien branch of Chinatex. It supplied three or four factories in Dalien with the latest seaming and fusing machines, used specifically for manufacturing velveteen clothing. Chinatex paid Prestige, like Oxford Industries, with garments. Unlike the deal with Oxford Industries, however, Prestige maintained exclusive rights over the velveteen garb produced in the factories. This meant that for a full year after the factories had the equipment up and running, Prestige would be the only company to which the Dalien factories supplied velveteen attire.[46]

By swapping suits for seamers, China integrated itself into the manufacturing networks of Oxford Industries and Prestige. While both textile companies remained based in the United States, they were increasingly moving towards international sources of manufacturing labor. Chinatex's purchases of their technology revealed China's own economic development priorities were slowly aligning with those of US corporations. As Chinatex worked to modernize China's textile industry, it did so by positioning China as a site of cheap labor.

The fact that these two US companies sold velveteen and corduroy machines to China confirmed the fears of Howard Richmond, the head of US textile company Crompton. Richmond, as we have seen in Chapter 5, had been one of the key textile leaders protesting Chinatex's visit to the United States in February 1975. He had alerted American journalists to the tour and warned of the potential impact Chinese imports would have on the velveteen and corduroy industries. Crompton was the oldest continuing textile company in the United States, but it had been struggling to compete against imports since the 1950s. In 1968, Richmond had warned in the company's annual report that "growing imports of all types continue to plague the industry."[47] By the 1970s Crompton's non-union workers—mostly women of color—produced cloth from Waynesboro, Virginia; Griffin, Georgia; Leeburg, Alabama; and Morrilton, Arkansas. The company had become the leading domestic producer of corduroy and velveteen material, selling to fashion brands including Ralph Lauren, Calvin Klein, Yves Saint Laurent, and Levi Strauss. "Crompton is corduroy, Crompton is velveteen," its advertisements announced.[48] But Richmond remained worried.

When trade with China reopened in 1971, cotton velveteen fabric was among the $5 million worth of goods China first sold to the United States.[49] At that stage, Chinese velveteen only trickled into the US market via small sales to American importers. Throughout the decade, Chinatex's sales of both velveteen and corduroy increased to the United States, although often not at the same time. In 1977, China sold over 37,000 square yards of corduroy to the United States but it made no sales of velveteen. The following year, however, Chinatex sold more than 38,000 square yards of velveteen and only 600 square yards of corduroy. While China's sales of both materials rose throughout the 1970s, they were dwarfed by the United States' major suppliers such as Japan. In 1977, Japan supplied over 2.4 million square yards of velveteen and more than 112,000 square yards of corduroy—far higher levels than China.[50]

Velveteen imports entering the United States became too much for Crompton to compete with and a decade later, in October 1984, Crompton filed for bankruptcy. The company's president, William G. Lord II, blamed China despite its relatively small share of the overall US market. Lord's complaints were cultural rather than economic. He did not focus on the size of China exports but instead on the change in consumer demand that he felt China had precipitated. China "changed the image of a velveteen garment," Lord argued. With Chinese velveteen depressing the price of the fabric, it went "from a luxury item to a commodity item. . . . We never fully recovered."[51] As he saw it, the low-cost Chinese imports eroded the luxury of velveteen. By making velveteen accessible to ordinary consumers, China dampened the desires of the status-conscious American wearers of velvet suits. Why pay more for a Crompton suit when it looked like you had bought it elsewhere? Unlike US importers in the 1970s who hailed the quality of Chinese-made goods and who often associated China with luxury, by the mid-1980s Lord expressed something new: Chinese low costs had changed the perceived sophistication of the velveteen market as a whole.

The company's problems were, of course, deeper than that. Both Richmond and Lord focused their anger and concerns on foreign-made goods but made no mention of the huge US companies like Oxford Industries and Prestige that had been integral to the increase in imports through their own pursuit of overseas manufacturing. Lord's comments about Chinese erosion of luxury reveal that by the mid-1980s the idea of Chinese imports as symbols of cheap goods—and indeed, a threat—started to emerge.

Crompton is velveteen.

Alexander Shields jacket. Crompton jaguar printed cotton velveteen.
38-46 short, medium, long. About $185. Also jaguar pants about $85.
Alexander Shields, New York; Murphy's, St. Paul; Bette's, Dallas; I. Magnin, Beverly Hills.
CROMPTON-RICHMOND COMPANY-INC., 1071 AVENUE OF THE AMERICAS, NEW YORK 10018.
PAINTING BY ROBERT BEAUCHAMP

Figure 8.1. Throughout the 1970s, Chinese velveteen entered the United States in increasing quantities, although the ill fate of leading US companies like Crompton was caused by factors far deeper than Chinese imports alone.

This was not the cultural perception of China in the 1970s. In the early years of trade, China had been associated with quality and luxury. But as China's manufacturing capacity expanded—aided by deals such as those made by Oxford Industries and Prestige—the cultural associations with Chinese goods began to change too. By the time of Crompton's closing in 1984, China was becoming associated with cheapness rather than quality and luxury.

Crompton's bankruptcy tells us far more about the wider changes the US textile industry faced than it does about China per se. When China began selling its small amounts of cotton velveteen to the US market in 1971, Crompton was already struggling. Lord might have blamed his company's woes on China's entry into the US market, but his anger was misplaced. It was the turn toward offshore manufacturing undertaken by

US textile companies that did far more damage to Crompton's prospects than China. Crompton's factory closure, when viewed in conjunction with the deals signed by Oxford Industries and Prestige, reveals how US corporations and businesspeople were crucial linchpins in both China's industrialization and the United States' *de*industrialization. The changes happening in US manufacturing provided Chinatex with an opportunity to adapt its development needs. Together Chinatex, Oxford Industries, and Prestige helped to create a China market that was focused not only on absorbing US technology but also on providing cheap labor.

Normalization

By December 15, 1978, President Carter, following in the footsteps of President Nixon before him, made a shock public announcement about China. He and Deng Xiaoping had broken through years of deadlock; they would normalize diplomatic relations, starting January 1, 1979. The announcement stunned most of the world. Taiwan's officials were only given two hours' notice of the development.[52] As with the Nixon shock more than seven years earlier, the negotiations had been conducted in tight secrecy without consultation with Japan, Taiwan, Congress, or US government agencies.[53] Even Carter's speech had been drafted in secrecy.[54] He continued Nixon and Kissinger's approach of strategic ambiguity regarding Taiwan, stating that the United States "acknowledges" China's position "that there is but one China and Taiwan is part of China." Carter reiterated that the United States would "continue to have an interest in the peaceful resolution of the Taiwan issue" and that normalization with the PRC would not "jeopardize the well-being of the people of Taiwan."[55] He made no mention of the issue of weapons sales to Taiwan.

The news of normalization was met with angry anti-American demonstrations in Taiwan. Disgusted by what they perceived as American "abandonment," thousands of people gathered on the streets of Taipei singing patriotic songs. Many scattered peanuts upon the ground and crushed them crying, "This is Carter!"—a reference to the president's former job as a peanut farmer.[56] Carter directed Deputy Secretary of State Warren Christopher to fly to Taipei and meet with Taiwan ministers in an attempt to temper their growing anger.

On the day the American delegation was due to arrive in Taipei, 20,000 people—many of whom were students—staged a protest at the Foreign

Ministry. They forced the first session of proceedings to be relocated to the Grand Hotel. Attempts to avoid the protests proved fruitless, however. As the American delegation's motorcade traveled from the airport to the hotel, it was met with another crowd of thousands of protestors. Some threw eggs and sand on the cars as they passed; others threw paint and tried to climb on the roofs and hoods of the vehicles.[57] Christopher sustained minor injuries when one of the car windows was broken. Rather than continue on to the palatial Grand Hotel for their appointment, he and his fellow officials were transferred to a hidden location and their meeting was canceled.

For the American public too, the December announcement came as a surprise. Deliberately timed by Carter to occur during the Christmas recess, normalization angered Taiwan sympathizers in Congress and the media. Influential conservative journalist George Will likened the perceived neglect of Taiwan to *Judenfrage*—the "Jewish question" of the 1930s.[58] This inflammatory language spoke to the emotional investment that many Republicans and conservatives felt toward Taiwan. Senator Richard Stone summarized their outrage by calling the move a "slap in the face of a staunch friend and ally."[59]

George Meany similarly expressed anger at Carter's announcement. "The terms negotiated by President Carter are tantamount to total acquiescence in the demands of the PRC," he declared. Framing the problem in terms of the United States' broader system of alliances, Meany continued, "President Carter had undermined the credibility of the United States in its relations with other countries by unilaterally abrogating the nation's long-standing treaty with its ally, Taiwan."

But Meany also situated his opposition in terms of China's human rights violations. "We can understand—although not approve of—the applause from the business community, which is in search of quick profits no matter what the cost in human rights." Much more difficult to understand was "how this president, who made human rights a world issue, could so suddenly and callously reject the human rights concerns of both those enslaved on mainland China and those on Taiwan who fear such enslavement."[60] Meany's language of enslavement was a gesture toward China's communist structures, but they were less red-baiting than his comments earlier in the decade. By the late 1970s, the Red China threat had lessened but the language of slave labor—with its deep ties to nineteenth-century debates over Chinese immigration—persisted.

Despite the protests from Taiwan, US labor, and Congress, on January 28, 1979, Deng Xiaoping arrived in the United States to mark the new era in diplomatic relations, staying for just over a week. His visit was not just about strategic issues: he and Carter signed new agreements in economic, scientific, and technical areas. Deng and the Foreign Ministry saw his visit to the United States as encompassing far more than geopolitical issues. In preparation for his trip, the Foreign Ministry prepared a report outlining Deng's aims as being to "explore opportunities for an all-round and comprehensive collaboration."[61]

Trade became a central component of Deng's charm offensive. At a dinner hosted by a group of Chinese American businesspeople in Washington, Deng called on the "compatriots" to trade with and invest in their "motherland." At a press conference the following day, Deng promised journalists, "China has a lot to export, such as coal, non-ferrous metals, rare metals, chemical products and handicraft products." A few days later he predicted that if trade restrictions were removed, total trade would "surely exceed several billion and even a hundred billion" in the next five years.[62] In Houston, Deng attended the Simonton Rodeo alongside a crowd of more than 1,000 corporate executives. Photos of him wearing a Stetson hat were widely publicized. Less commented on was the fact that most of the crowd that day were US businesspeople. They had paid the $50 entry fee to attend the rodeo and watch Deng ride a lap of the track in a mini stagecoach.[63]

Deng's trip to the United States had brought a whirlwind of energy and excitement to the relationship after years of stalled diplomacy. After the bright lights of the Houston rodeo had dimmed, the two countries turned their attention back to settling the legislative aspects of the trade relationship. While Deng accentuated the allure of trade now that the United States and China had full diplomatic relations, two key hurdles remained: the claims/assets dispute was still unresolved, and the two countries did not yet have a trade agreement providing MFN trading status, among other benefits.

Before a trade agreement could be reached, the two nations needed to resolve the claims/assets dispute. A product of animosities during the Korean War, the decades-long dispute was triggered in December 1950 when President Harry Truman instructed the Treasury Department to block and freeze Chinese investments held in US banks. In turn, Premier Zhou Enlai directed local authorities to appropriate the property of US organizations and private citizens in China. Without resolution, the two countries could not ship goods to one another directly, could not open bank branches, and could not set up trade exhibits. If one side had done so, the other would likely seize their goods or financial investments as retribution for the outstanding dispute. This had been one of the major hurdles to the trade relationship throughout the 1970s.

A breakthrough on the claims/assets dispute seemed, at first, to come quickly. On March 2, 1979, the very same day that the United States and China opened their diplomatic embassies, US treasury secretary Michael Blumenthal and Chinese finance minister Zhang Jingfu agreed on the terms of settlement for the claims/assets dispute. The United States agreed to unblock the Chinese assets held in US banks. China, for its part, agreed to pay $80.5 million over five years in compensation to the American citizens whose property in China had been seized. China would draw upon the previously blocked assets to pay for most of this, effectively making it a quid pro quo agreement.[64]

What had seemed a quick win for US-China trade soon became a political impasse. Blumenthal and Zhang had initialed the claims/assets agreement, but it took two more months for both nations to finalize the agreement. China delayed formally signing onto the deal when Deng and Zhang realized the Carter administration could not legally provide them with the names or details of the Chinese citizens whose assets had been seized. This was information given to private US banks, not the Treasury or Commerce departments. Without this information, it was tremendously difficult to identify which assets even needed recovery. To further complicate matters, private citizens in Taiwan had begun to lay claim to some of the assets. Identifying and obtaining the assets began to prove harder than had first seemed.[65]

For two months, Deng allowed the claims/assets dispute to remain unresolved. Coming amid an array of scientific and educational exchange success stories, the claims/assets delay was, by contrast, the first government-to-government dispute since normalization just a few months earlier. In their frustration, US negotiators sought to leverage what they saw as the main prize: a bilateral trade agreement. At a policy review committee meeting held between heads of multiple US departments including State, Treasury, Commerce, and Labor, officials decided that the United States would adopt what they deemed a "tactical posture" that would put "maximum pressure on the Chinese." They would refuse to agree to a trade deal until China signed off on the claims/assets agreement that had been initialed in March.[66] It would be up to Commerce Secretary Juanita Kreps to implement this approach when she traveled to China in early May. Kreps was a shrewd negotiator. She spent ten days in China and came away with success on both issues. On May 11, 1979, she and Zhang Jingfu signed the claims/assets deal into effect, finally bringing an end to the twenty-nine-year dispute. Three days later, she and Li Qiang initialed a trade agreement. The two countries had finally agreed on the terms of a trade deal. But as happened with the claims/assets agreement, political tensions soon also delayed implementation of the trade deal. Kreps and Li had initialed a trade deal, but it would take yet another two months for them to sign it into effect.

These high-level governmental wranglings over the legal architecture of trade frustrated American and Chinese businesspeople. They had waited nearly a decade for normalization, Deng had emphasized his interest in expanding trade, and yet both nations' leaders were quibbling at the final hurdles. It was too much for managers at the Shanghai-based China Ocean Shipping Company (COSCO) and the New Orleans-based Lykes Brothers Steamship Company. The moment they got word that Blumenthal and Zhang had initialed an end to the claims/assets dispute in early March, the shipping companies took matters into their own hands.

On March 18, the Lykes Brothers' ship, the *Letitia Lykes,* sailed up the Huangpu River into Shanghai. One month later, on April 17, the *Liu Lin Hai,* a Norwegian-made ship COSCO purchased in 1977, anchored in Seattle. Even though leaders in both nations had initialed an end to the claims/assets dispute on March 2, it had not yet come into effect. This meant that the ships and their cargo could be liable to seizure as restitution for the outstanding claims and assets. The shipping companies not only pushed ahead regardless, but they even lined up high-level officials from both nations to help celebrate the events. The National Council for US-China Trade hailed them as "rebels with applause."[67]

There were legal protections for these "rebel" shipping companies— they claimed coverage under the US Foreign Sovereign Immunities Act of 1976, an act that protected the property of countries with whom the United States had normalized relations. With the normalization of relations that came into effect in January 1979 and the initialing of the claims/assets resolution, the two companies decided to push ahead with reciprocal trips anyway. "Other companies," the National Council warned, "may want to test the water carefully before they take similar risks." But planning for the events had been going on for months, and these businesspeople had waited long enough. It helped, of course, that they had the full support and protection of policymakers in both nations.

Thus it was that on a cold April day in 1979 the *Liu Lin Hai* sailed into Seattle. Flying from its mast was the gold-starred red flag of the CCP. This was the first such vessel to ever enter US waters. Waiting on the windy dock to celebrate the occasion stood a huddled crowd of 200 people, including the US Navy band. As the ship drew nearer, the band boomed out the familiar refrain of "Superstar" from the decade's blockbuster rock opera, *Jesus Christ Superstar.* Superstar's triumphal melody had made it a common ceremonial song during the 1970s. It was used, for instance, as the entrance theme by one of the most colorful personalities in wrestling at the time, a man who went by the ring name of "Superstar Billy Graham."[68]

The *Liu Lin Hai* was the first Chinese ship to enter American waters directly since the CCP came to power in 1949. Previously, ships had docked first at ports in Hong Kong or Japan before continuing on to either the United States or China. Alternatively, cargo had traveled through intermediaries, generally on chartered vessels flying the Somali flag—all to avoid the punitive effects of the claims/assets dispute.[69] Paying no heed to the barriers raised by the dispute, the *Liu Lin Hai* docked at Smith Cove and the ship's captain, Bei Hanting, led his officers in a procession down to the pier. As they descended, the band started up again, this time playing the Chinese national anthem.

A political event as much as an economic one, Chai Zemin, the PRC's first ambassador to the United States, attended the ceremony. Deng Deqing, the embassy's deputy minister of communications, accompanied him. Standing with them was Washington governor Dixy Lee Ray, Transportation Secretary Brock Adams, and two Democratic senators from Washington, Warren G. Magnuson and Henry "Scoop" Jackson, who for years had been advocating for diplomatic normalization. Members of the Seattle branch of the National Association of Chinese-Americans awaited the ship, holding up a wide banner carrying a message of welcome. Once the crew had disembarked, they presented a scroll to captain Bei reading, "After normalization 100 flowers bloom."[70]

Brock Adams addressed the assembled crowd. "I hope the *Liu Lin Hai* returns to its homeland carrying not only grain, but friendship between our peoples." Speaking soon after, Henry Jackson declared, "This is the beginning of what will be the true friendship of world peace."

Figure 8.2. Bei Hanting leading his crew off the *Liu Lin Hai* after docking in Seattle harbor.

This rhetoric—talking of the peace and friendship that would flow from trade—was not simply a ceremonial platitude. Instead, it reflected deep assumptions in US foreign policy about the dynamic between trade and diplomacy. These leaders celebrated the political goodwill that had allowed for normalization and the accompanying expansion in trade. But at the same time they expressed hope that the burgeoning trade would also deepen political ties. Trade was both a signal that the broader political relationship was improving and a means by which it could be consolidated. They made no public mention of the recently initialed yet unsigned claims/assets agreement, but perhaps they hoped that this celebration too could help finalize negotiations.

The *Liu Lin Hai* was to be loaded up with 1.5 million bushels of corn before sailing back to Shanghai. Cargill, a food-processing company, scored the lucky sale, sending corn sourced mainly from Minnesota, Nebraska, and Iowa. The following day the *Letitia Lykes* docked in New Orleans, having sailed home from Shanghai. Its arrival in Shanghai had been a similarly high-profile affair and similarly one that paid no heed to the unsigned claims/assets agreement. PRC vice minister of communications Wang Xiping, US ambassador to Beijing Leonard Woodcock, and Lykes Brothers chairman Joseph Lykes welcomed the US ship into China before it was loaded up with an eclectic mix of goods including goose feathers, sausage casings, canned jellyfish, wooden furniture, shoes, and cotton work gloves.[71]

With canned jellyfish and cotton work gloves traveling one way and midwestern corn traveling the other way, the direct flow of goods between the two nations began even before the legalities were fully ironed out. These shipping companies managed to escape any legal recriminations, but their impatience reveals just how ready so many businesspeople in both nations were to resume normal trade relations. After Kreps and Zhang's signing of the claims/assets deal in May, the direct flow of shipping began in earnest. But the second hurdle—a bilateral trade agreement—still remained in limbo; Kreps left China having initialed a deal, but it was yet to be signed.

The Trade Deal

After normalization, the story of US-China trade was, for the most part, one of growth and expansion. By the end of the year, the value of bilateral trade doubled to a record $2.3 billion. At the government-to-government level, however, trade issues proved slower. Following resolution of the claims/assets deal in May 1979, the next major hurdle was the trade agreement. It took two months after Kreps and Li had first initialed the trade agreement for both countries to sign onto it. The delay had been due to two issues: textiles and the Soviet Union.

After years of pressure from workers in the US textile and apparel industries, Carter wanted to negotiate a way of limiting Chinese textile sales to the United States. He did so only after normalization had been achieved; diplomacy had been his first priority. As a result, in addition to pursuing a trade agreement, Carter sought an additional agreement with China that would focus specifically on China's exports of textiles. The latter agreement was what industry leaders like Robert Forney at Du Pont had been calling for. American labor leaders too had continued to raise concerns about the impact of expanding trade with China. In early 1979, for example, Bayard Rustin, a longtime civil rights and gay rights activist, warned in the *AFL-CIO News* that China was fast becoming the "Asian sunbelt." Whereas once corporations turned to the American South, now American businesspeople looked to China and saw "huge profits won at the expense of defenseless workers."[72] Carter pushed, therefore, for China to apply what were known as "voluntary restrictions" on its textiles sales to the United States. This would limit the number of textiles entering the United States without requiring the president to adopt a more punitive, unilateral set of restrictions. But Deng refused to agree to a situation where it would seem he had agreed to impose the restrictions himself.[73]

With ongoing pressure from labor on one side and Chinese intransigence on the other, Carter was forced, in the end, to abandon his attempts at reaching a joint textile agreement with China. On May 31 he imposed limits on five items entering the United States from China, including cotton work gloves. Despite being a measure against China, Carter's decision actually opened the way for a trade agreement to be reached. Carter's trade representative, Robert Strauss, felt that the issue was not one of major concern to Deng. "Both sides very amicably agreed to disagree," he reported back to Carter.[74] By avoiding a joint agreement, Deng was able to steer clear of perceptions that he was accepting US-imposed conditions. Negotiations for further textile limitations would remain ongoing, and it would not be until September 1980 that the two nations signed a textile agreement. But with Carter's unilateral imposition of quotas on five items, he brought a temporary end to the bilateral textile wrangling that had held up efforts for a trade agreement.

The second factor that held up the US-PRC trade agreement was concern within both the US State Department and Congress over the implications for US relations with the Soviet Union. If the United States were to grant China such a deal—and with it MFN status—that would give

China preferential trading rights over the Soviet Union, which did not enjoy MFN status with the United States. It would end the US policy of evenhandedness with the two communist powers. This was a source of fierce division between Carter's secretary of state, Cyrus Vance, and his national security advisor, Zbigniew Brzezinski. Vance wanted to delay further action on the trade agreement with China, but Carter had made up his mind. In June Carter provided Brzezinski with handwritten instructions on the trade agreement: "I want to move this year. No reason to delay."[75] Carter knew there were procedural factors that made it important to get the trade agreement signed quickly. The US-PRC Trade Agreement would need to appear before Congress for sixty days and needed to clear both houses.

With Carter's green light to Brzezinski, the two nations forged ahead with a trade deal on July 7, 1979. At a ceremony in Beijing, US ambassador to China Leonard Woodcock and Chinese foreign trade minister Li Qiang signed the US-PRC Trade Agreement. Among other measures, the trade deal would finally grant China MFN status. While policymakers in both countries celebrated the deal, the wrangling in the lead-up exposed the larger challenges underpinning US-China trade right from the start of the official trade relations: the impact on domestic US workers, the implications for both nations' relations with the Soviet Union, and China's unwillingness to appear to be accepting US-imposed conditions now that its previous bargaining chip—the promise of normalization—had be used. Even as the two nations signed the trade agreement, these issues remained.

One final challenge remained before the trade deal could come into full force: both houses of the US Congress needed to approve it. Carter submitted the deal to Congress for approval on October 23, 1979, after which the House and Senate held hearings. One of the major concerns US policymakers held about the US-PRC Trade Agreement was that it granted China MFN status without doing the same for the Soviet Union. Adlai Stevenson (D, IL) gave his support for granting MFN status to the PRC but worried that providing these benefits to China and not to the Soviet Union risked "further deterioration" in relations with the Soviets.[76]

Senator Jackson, on the other hand, dismissed these questions of "theoretic balance" between China and the Soviet Union as "nonsense." The United States had, after all, granted MFN status to other communist countries, Romania and Hungary. Nonetheless, Jackson was opposed to the prospect of the United States selling military equipment to China. "I think that would be a mistake," he declared. Jackson also touted the oil poten-

Figure 8.3. US ambassador Leonard Woodcock and Chinese foreign trade minister Li Qiang signed the Agreement on Trade Relations between the United States and the PRC in Beijing on July 7, 1979.

tial China had. "When you look at the amount of it, and the role that it can play in bringing some stability in the foreign market, I think that it augurs well."[77]

Bob Dole was another senator who supported the trade agreement while also expressing reservations. "The conclusion of the trade agreement will benefit our own export interests." Nonetheless, he cautioned, "imports from China can be a problem," pointing to textiles and clothespins as examples. "As the Chinese move into other industries, their exports may displace domestic businesses and jobs, or cut into the market of other developing countries friendly to the United States." In fact, even the promise that China would increase its purchases of US grain and technology was hampered by the "substantial competition for the Chinese market from our Japanese and European allies."

The trade deal also raised a further concern about human rights. Dole expressed reservations about China's record but ultimately called for Congress to "monitor carefully" the levels of Chinese emigration.[78] Similarly, the International Human Rights Law Group supported the administration's efforts for the trade deal but urged caution in granting MFN status. The Carter administration should wait "until assurances have been received that China's observance of human rights comports with international norms."[79] Deng had referred to this issue during his visit to the United States in January. "How many Chinese nationals do you want?" Deng reportedly asked at the time. "Ten million? Twenty million? Thirty million?" he quipped. As the Jackson-Vanik amendment had stipulated in its addendum to the Trade Act of 1974, freedom of emigration was now a necessary precursor to US trade with communist nations.

Amy Young-Anawaty, who testified on behalf of the International Human Rights Law Group, worried about the crackdown on protestors who had gathered at Tiananmen Square in 1976, sparked out of mourning for Zhou's death. She argued that the Jackson-Vanik amendment, which made MFN status conditional on human rights, did not need to be limited to migration alone. It could—and, she argued, should—encompass a wide range of human rights concerns. She did not mention labor rights specifically as a possible human rights concern, but she did argue that the China case offered a "singular opportunity" for the United States to set out human rights standards for all its trade deals.

In the end, however, it was the Soviet Union itself that sealed Congress's decision to approve the trade deal with China. When the Soviets invaded Afghanistan on December 25, 1979, the necessity for an even-handed foreign policy collapsed. Congress passed the trade agreement just a few days later and it came into effect on February 1, 1980. US-Soviet relations deteriorated but excitement for the improving relations with China only grew. The Cold War divisions between the United States and China faded at precisely the moment Cold War tensions with the Soviet Union reignited. As the trade deal came into effect, however, it did so by linking trade and human rights via migration, not other kinds of human rights such as labor rights.

THE YEARS IMMEDIATELY following Mao's death were expansive ones for US-China trade. The value of trade increased dramatically, and US businesspeople successfully signed a range of breakthrough deals—from Kaiser engineers selling their expertise to Oxford Industries selling fusing machines in exchange for corduroy clothing. But along with the excitement of new sales and China's own emphasis on developing its science and technology, this was a period that consolidated years of negotiation between businesspeople, diplomats, and labor leaders in both countries.

Exploring the two sides of the China market—US exports as well as its imports—reveals that a crucial part of China's convergence with the capitalist trading system was the changes occurring within US corporations throughout the 1970s. As China purchased manufacturing technology, it also adapted to the turn to outsourced manufacturing that had been occurring with rising speed since the second Nixon shock in August 1971. The Nixon economic shock, and the accompanying floating of the US dollar, had made it easier for companies to remain headquartered in the United States and move their manufacturing aboard. By the end of the decade, the first Nixon shock—his opening to China—was becoming more and more connected to his second, economic one.

As US companies celebrated China's turn toward importing technology, they drew on an older vision of 400 million customers. Alongside this, however, China used the technology it purchased to converge with the capitalist trade system, most particularly though export-oriented manufacturing. There was no inherent reason why the emergence of a China market filled with 800 million workers would be the quieter change that developed in the 1970s. It was not that political and business leaders in the United States were unaware of the export implications of China's development. Instead, it reflected a diplomacy and a wider politics that prioritized geopolitics over the needs of US workers. This was a politics that did not think to question just whose interests were being served by the corporate pursuit of cheap overseas labor.

Conclusion

From 400 Million Customers to 800 Million Workers

IN SEPTEMBER 1980, just a few months after the US-PRC Trade Agreement came into effect, US shoe company Nike signed deals with Chinese traders that were similar to those of Oxford Industries and Prestige a few years earlier. The company provided four shoe factories in Shanghai and Tianjin worth $75,000 in total. In return, Nike received the equivalent value in shoes—a process that took mere months. After that, Nike imported China-made shoes at cheap rates. This was "a match made in heaven," the *China Business Review* acclaimed. "As labor costs have risen in other areas of Asia—particularly in South Korea and Taiwan—China has become increasingly attractive as a production base."[1] The shift from "Made in Taiwan" to "Made in China" had begun.

The deal with Nike catered directly to the US market. Almost 100 percent of the shoes Nike imported back from the factories were sold to American customers. This was appealing for Chinese leaders who wanted to increase foreign exchange earnings through exports. "There's nothing on the drawing board for selling in China," Nike's president, Philip H. Knight, told journalists.[2] Decades later, China would become a massive consumer market, purchasing brand-name shoes and designer handbags at record rates.[3] But in order for that to happen, China's leaders worked alongside US businesspeople to build a market of 800 million workers first. By the time China had become a consumer powerhouse, the very nature of manufacturing and trade had been transformed.

Throughout the 1970s, American capitalists and Chinese pragmatists worked together to reconfigure the China market from one of 400 million customers to one of 800 million workers. As they did so, they marked a transformative turning point in the long history of US-China trade, with profound implications for the future of global capitalism. For centuries, the China market had offered American and other foreign businesspeople the elusive promise of wealth through sales to its vast population. In the 1970s, this very idea and practice of trade was transformed, as the United States and China began to rebuild relations after more than twenty years of Cold War isolation. Together they established a new era in US-China trade. China's export potential, its promise of wealth, its focus on export-oriented growth, American businesspeople's decentering of China's communist structures, the corporate sidelining of labor in both countries: the ideas underpinning their economic interdependence of the twenty-first century came into motion during the 1970s.

Over the course of the decade, China's development priorities began to converge with the changes occurring in US capitalism. China's increasing trade after 1971, its 4-3 Program of 1973, Mao's Three Worlds articulated in 1974, Zhou's Four Modernizations of 1975, and the pragmatists' ongoing efforts to deepen economic ties—together these factors laid the groundwork for the reforms of the 1980s.

Chinese leaders' ability to lift their population out of poverty came at the expense of minimum-wage textile workers in the United States and later other industries as well. But that impact on US workers was fundamentally enabled by the decisions of executives at US corporations, aided by legislation in Washington. American businesspeople had already begun slowly internationalizing their manufacturing before trade with China reopened. In the 1950s and 1960s, they turned to noncommunist sources like Japan and Taiwan. In the 1970s China's leaders began to adapt to these emerging dynamics, and in the process they slowly transcended the Cold War divisions that had so long divided China and the United States. China's domestic reforms were experimental and halting, but they were, as economist Barry Naughton puts it, "a perfect complement to the world economy at that stage."[4]

China's export-led growth of the 1980s required the new methods of multinational manufacturing that US corporations had begun to turn to in the 1970s.[5] In 1988 premier Zhao Ziyang explained that China's coastal-development strategy and Special Economic Zones relied upon the idea that "labor-intensive industries always go where labor costs are lowest."

Reflecting on the movement of foreign capital in pursuit of this cheap labor since the end of the Second World War, he added, "China's coastal regions should be very attractive this time."[6] This policy of SEZs only worked because manufacturing processes had already internationalized.

China did not cause the loss of manufacturing jobs in the United States in the 1970s.[7] Instead, the job losses were the result of changes within US capitalism enabled by policies in Washington. American capital and manufacturing became increasingly internationalized in the 1970s, accelerated by the Nixon economic shock in 1971 and the Trade Act of 1974. By 1979 two political economists, Barry Bluestone and Bennett Harrison, warned of the recent "hypermobility of capital" that had led to "shuttered factories, displaced workers, and a newly emerging group of ghost towns." As they sought to make sense of the processes they had lived through in the 1970s, Bluestone and Harrison formulated a new term to describe corporate decisions to withdraw capital from factories in cities and towns throughout the country: deindustrialization.[8]

As it turned out, something more complicated occurred.[9] Between the late 1940s and early 2020s, manufacturing in the United States remained relatively stable as a proportion of real GDP.[10] The United States continued to make goods. In fact, until 2010 it was the world's largest manufacturing country, after which it remained second only to China. It was not manufacturing that went into decline in the United States; the decline was in the number of workers it employed, a result, largely, of new manufacturing technologies, new kinds of high-tech goods being made, and the movement of labor-intensive industries to factories overseas. Over the same eighty-year period, far fewer Americans held jobs in manufacturing even as US factories churned out goods. It was the impact on labor that Bluestone and Harrison observed in the late 1970s.

In May 1983, just a few months after Bluestone and Harrison published *The Deindustrialization of America*, Theodore Levitt, an economist at Harvard Business School, published an article in the *Harvard Business Review* entitled "The Globalization of Markets." Levitt took stock of global consumer markets amid the ongoing innovations in technological communications. He hailed a "new commercial reality" where "everywhere everything gets more and more like everything else as the world's preference structure is relentlessly homogenized." He celebrated a future of global corporations that saw the "entire world" as a "single entity." The earth, Levitt wrote, "is flat." Levitt was one of the first to use the term "globalization."[11]

Around the same time, Emmanuel Wallerstein developed the idea of a "commodity chain" as part of his theory of World Systems. Wallerstein traced back the production stages of commodities, uncovering the international dimensions of production and division of labor. Not long after, management consultants began using the concept of "value chain management" to describe the regulation of manufacturing along stages of production: from procurement of raw materials to the creation of finished goods.[12] Supply chains had long been part of corporate structures, exemplified most particularly by Ford Motor's production lines.[13] But the new managerial approach reflected the emerging internationalization of production networks, in which goods were increasingly produced in stages in different parts of the world. Unlike Bluestone and Harrison's book and Levitt's article, the term "value chain" did not reach a wide public audience until the 1990s; instead it remained circulating within the corridors of proliferating consulting firms.

Deindustrialization. Globalization. Value chains. The new language of the 1980s sought to make sense of the immense upheaval of the preceding decade. All three concepts captured processes that operated together. As more and more US corporations adopted a globalized lens, they withdrew capital from labor-intensive domestic manufacturing and turned instead to managing international supply chains. Historian Judith Stein captured the wider implications, describing the 1970s as pivotal decade in which the underpinnings of the US economy shifted from "from factories to finance."[14]

Underlying this story of change, however, is a deeply held continuity. It is a political continuity that persistently framed trade and manufacturing in terms of the nation-state—*China's* goods and the *United States'* need to make more of its own—regardless of the emergence of offshore manufacturing and global value chains. Despite the transformation in how US-China trade operated in practice, for the rest of the twentieth century American political rhetoric remained bound up with the nation-state and Carl Crow's 1937 conception of 400 million customers. "Bit by bit, we're restoring America's reputation as a reliable supplier," President Reagan asserted in 1983, even as he discussed the "moderate growth of Chinese exports" he had signed into law via a five-year textile agreement.[15]

Nearly two decades later—well after China had opened its markets to foreign direct investment and well after companies like Nike, Apple, and Walmart had established manufacturing facilities there—President Clinton framed the benefits of China's joining the World Trade Organization

(WTO) in terms of US sales.[16] Speaking in the White House Rose Garden in 2000, he promised that WTO membership would "open China's markets to American products made on American soil."[17] It was politically expedient for trade to remain, in Clinton's depiction, about US sales. By this stage, the number of corporations that manufactured abroad had grown exponentially.[18] American corporate structures had changed, but political rhetoric remained bound by early twentieth-century notions of trade.

One of the major consequences of this rhetorical stasis was that it deflected attention away from attempts to regulate the behavior of corporations pursuing cheap labor at any cost. In the opening decades of the twenty-first century, "Made in China" labels were ubiquitous. Like in 1970s, bilateral trade was again marked by a significant trade imbalance. This time, however, the imbalance was heavily in China's favor. In 2022 the United States had a $382 million trade deficit with China; the United States purchased from China around five times more than it sold to China.[19] The proverbial 800 million workers had become a reality; China was the "workshop of the world" and it was sweatshop labor that drove it.[20]

Yet at the heart of the symbolic power of Made in China lay a paradox. On the one hand, Made in China was the epitome of globalized manufacturing. Goods marked "Made in China" were produced along chains of supply that usually included multiple countries along the way. They traveled the globe connecting people through a shared consumerism. On the other hand, the phrase had come to represent the nation-state. When Chinese goods were boycotted or trade restrictions imposed, they were treated as means of targeting China itself. Marketing scholars describe this connection between country-of-origin labels and the nation-state as "nation branding."[21] If "Made in China" was a threat to American manufacturing, then its antithesis, "Made in the USA," suggested that its effects could also be countered by the nation-state.

But by the early twenty-first century, goods labeled Made in China or Made in the USA were often only partially made in those countries. Instead, they were produced along chains of supply that usually included multiple countries along the way. Global value chains were a familiar part of the globalized landscape by the early twenty-first century; most consumers were well aware that an iPhone labeled "designed in America, made in China" involved many other nations in its manufacturing process. Yet the political power of thinking of manufacturing within the confines of the nation-state retained its strength. This was the twenty-first-century paradox of Made in China—it represented the nation-state and globalization simultaneously.

This paradox has emerged from a politics that has remained bound by nationalist fervor despite the transformations in global capitalism. Country-of-origin labels were first used precisely for identifying goods that were associated with particular nation-states. The labels were introduced in the late nineteenth century in England when the structure of global trade and manufacturing looked very different. Then it was German goods that elicited concerns. Beginning around the 1880s, a growing British fear of German industrial strength began to focus on labels declaring "Made in Germany."

"Roam the house over, and the fateful mark will greet you at every turn, from the piano in your drawing-room to the mug on your kitchen dresser," lamented Ernest Edwin Williams in his best-selling book of 1896. Taking readers on an imagined tour of their own homes, he encouraged them to note the ubiquity of the labels. "As you rise from your heathrug you knock over an ornament on your mantelpiece," he envisaged. "Picking up the pieces you read, on the bit that formed the base, 'Manufactured in Germany.'"[22]

In 1897 British policymakers passed the Merchandise Marks Act, which required country-of-origin labels for all imports. They hoped that the labels would encourage a consumer boycott of German imports to protect British industrial jobs. The boycott failed and instead elevated German goods and other imports to luxury status.[23] But the labels remained. Three years later, in 1890, the United States passed its own labeling requirements under the McKinley Tariff Act.[24] Ultimately, country-of-origin labels, a political creation of the age of empires, became an integral part of international trade.

A deep nationalist sentiment underpinned the reactions to these labels, whether they emanated from late nineteenth-century Britain or the early twenty-first-century United States. But this line connecting the twentieth century's bookends also obscures important differences between them. Unlike imports of Ernest Edwin Williams's days, those marked "Made in China" no longer held literal significance. When British politicians implemented their laws in the late 1890s, they could be certain of which country had manufactured the goods simply by identifying where the ship had left from. Merchandise Marks Act 10 (2) stated, "In the case of imported goods, evidence of the port of shipment shall be prima facie evidence of the place or country in which the goods were made or produced." If the goods were imported on a ship that left Germany, they must have been made there too, the law outlined.[25]

In the late nineteenth century, trade could be equated with the state in ways that country-of-origin labels expressly denoted. But by the mid-twentieth century, the increasingly globalized flows of trade and finance changed the dynamic between state and corporate power. By the twentieth century's end, corporations and capital operated at transnational planes, often beyond the full jurisdiction and taxation of nation-states.[26] Trade no longer held such direct ties with the state.

Throughout the 1970s it was the interests of US capitalists and the Chinese state that slowly began to align. Fifty years later, their interests were bound by even tighter threads.[27] As they reworked the meaning of the China market, from a site of customers to one of workers, they were enabled by US diplomatic assumptions: that trade was another form of people-to-people ties; that the American businesspeople building trade were informal diplomats; and that labor concerns were an impediment to both trade and diplomacy.

If there is a lesson to this history of the making of Made in China, it is not one that calls for a return to an imagined ideal of manufacturing employment. Rather, it is for a political vision that centers and listens to the concerns of working people—both domestically and internationally—and in the process frees itself from the chimera that businesspeople are informal diplomats working on behalf of the state.[28]

Geopolitics and globalization collided in the 1970s in ways that transformed and ultimately expanded US power.[29] But a slower, quieter change was also beginning to take shape in which the United States and China constructed an interdependent trade relationship in the very moment interdependence shaped US foreign policy. By *making* Made in China, US diplomats and businesspeople used trade to lay the groundwork of a process that might, one day, mark the end of their empire and the reemergence of China's.

NOTES

ACKNOWLEDGMENTS

ILLUSTRATION CREDITS

INDEX

NOTES

Nixon Library	Richard Nixon Presidential Library and Museum, Yorba Linda, CA
PRCLO	People's Republic of China Liaison Office
RMRB	*Renmin Ribao*
RUCBC	Records of the U.S.-China Business Council
UML	University of Maryland Libraries, Baltimore, MD

Introduction

1. Cited in Chris Tudda, *A Cold War Turning Point: Nixon and China, 1969–1972* (Baton Rouge: Louisiana State University Press, 2012), 88–89.

2. Henry Kissinger, *White House Years* (Boston: Little, Brown, 1979), 753.

3. Kissinger, *White House Years*, 753; Lord cited in Tudda, *Cold War Turning Point,* 88; John H. Holdridge, *Crossing the Divide: An Insider's Account of the Normalization of U.S.-China Relations* (Lanham, MD: Rowman and Littlefield, 1997), 55.

4. Chi Schive, "Trade Patterns and Trends of Taiwan," in *Trade and Structural Change in Pacific Asia,* ed. Colin I. Bradford and William H. Branson (Chicago: University of Chicago Press, 1987), 311.

5. William C. Kirby, "China's Internationalism in the Early People's Republic: Dreams of a Socialist World Economy," *China Quarterly* 188 (December 2006): 870–890.

6. The precise number of people who died remains a point of controversy because of the patchy and politicized data. Some scholars have provided figures ranging from 15 to 43 million people. Others, such as Frank Dikötter, argue that the death toll was a "minimum" of 45 million and "could be even worse than that." On these figures, see especially Kimberley Ens Manning and Felix Wemheuer, "Introduction," in *Eating Bitterness: New Perspectives on China's Great Leap Forward and Famine* (Vancouver: USB Press, 2011), 1–27; see also Frank Dikötter, *Mao's Great Famine: The History of China's Most Devastating Catastrophe, 1958–1962* (New York: Walker and Co., 2010), 333.

7. Kenneth Pomeranz, *The Great Divergence: China, Europe, and the Making of the Modern World Economy* (Princeton, NJ: Princeton University Press, 2000).

8. Loren Brandt, Debin Ma, and Thomas G. Rawski, "From Divergence to Convergence: Reevaluating the History behind China's Economic Boom," *Journal of Economic Literature* 52, no. 1 (2014): 45–123.

9. Isabella M. Weber, *How China Escaped Shock Therapy* (New York: Routledge, 2021); Yuen Yuen Ang, *How China Escaped the Poverty Trap* (Ithaca, NY: Cornell University Press, 2016); Julian Gewirtz, *Unlikely Partners: Chinese Reformers, Western Economists, and the Making of Global China* (Cambridge, MA: Harvard University Press, 2017).

10. Taomo Zhou, "Leveraging Liminality: The Border Town of Bao'an (Shenzhen) and the Origins of China's Reform and Opening," *Journal of Asian Studies* 80, no. 2 (May 2021): 337–361; Jason M. Kelly, *Market Maoists: The Communist Origins of China's Capitalist Ascent* (Cambridge, MA: Harvard University Press, 2021); Karl Gerth, *Unending Capitalism: How Consumerism Negated China's Communist Revolution* (Cambridge: Cambridge University Press, 2020); Chen Yongjun, 从计划到市场：中国经济体制改革的选择 [From plan to market: Choices in the reform of China's economic system] (Fuzhou: Fujian Renmin Chubanshe, 1999); Han Guangfu and Hu Yongxiang, 改革年代：邓小平的改革岁月 [The reform decade: Deng Xiaoping's reform period] (Shenyang: Liaoning Renmin Chubanshe, 2004).

11. Gerth, *Unending Capitalism*. For an examination of these ideas, see the essays in *PRC History Review,* October 2020, especially Jacob Eyferth, "Consumption, Consumerism, Capitalism," *PRC History Review 5,* no. 1 (October 2020): 1–26.

12. Odd Arne Westad, "The Great Transformation: China in the Long 1970s," in *The Shock of the Global: The 1970s in Perspective,* ed. Niall Ferguson et al. (Cambridge, MA: Belknap Press of Harvard University Press, 2010), 65–79; Andrew G. Walder, "Bending the Arc of Chinese History: The Cultural Revolution's Paradoxical Legacy," *China Quarterly* 227 (September 2016): 613–631; Frederick Teiwes and Warren Sun, *The End of the Maoist Era: Chinese Politics during the Twilight of the Cultural Revolution, 1972–1976* (Armonk, NY: M. E. Sharpe, 2007); Priscilla Roberts and Odd Arne Westad, eds., *China, Hong Kong, and the Long 1970s: Global Perspectives* (Cham, Switzerland: Palgrave Macmillan, 2017); Lei Liu, "China's Large-Scale Importation of Western Technology and the U.S. Response, 1972–1976," *Diplomatic History* 45, no. 4 (2021): 794–820; Pete Millwood, "'An Exceedingly Delicate Undertaking': Sino-American Science Diplomacy, 1966–78," *Journal of Contemporary History* 56, no. 1 (2021): 166–190; Peter E. Hamilton, "Rethinking the Origins of China's Reform Era: Hong Kong and the 1970s Revival of Sino-US Trade," *Twentieth-Century China* 43, no. 1 (January 2018): 67–88; Min Song, "A Dissonance in Mao's Revolution: Chinese Agricultural Imports from the United States, 1972–1978," *Diplomatic History* 38, no. 2 (2014): 409–430; Kazushi Minami, "Re-examining the End of Mao's Revolution: China's Changing Statecraft and Sino-American Relations, 1973–1978," *Cold War History* 16, no. 4 (2016): 359–375; Hou Li, *Building for Oil: Daqing and the Formation of the Chinese Socialist State* (Cambridge, MA: Harvard University Press, 2018).

13. Walder, "Bending the Arc."

14. Rosemary Foot, *The Practice of Power: US Relations with China since 1949* (Oxford: Oxford University Press, 1997); Kelly, *Market Maoists.*

15. Shu Guang Zhang, *Economic Cold War: America's Embargo Against China and the Sino-Soviet Alliance, 1949–1963* (Stanford, CA: Stanford University Press, 2001); Ian Jackson, *The Economic Cold War: America, Britain and East–West Trade, 1948–63* (Houndmills, UK: Palgrave, 2001).

16. Michael Mastanduno, *Economic Containment: CoCom and the Politics of East–West Trade* (Ithaca, NY: Cornell University Press, 1992); Bruce Jentleson, *Pipeline Politics: The Complex Political Economy of East–West Energy Trade* (Ithaca, NY: Cornell University Press, 2019).

17. Fritz Bartel, *The Triumph of Broken Promises: The End of the Cold War and the Rise of Neoliberalism* (Cambridge, MA: Harvard University Press, 2022). "US-led" does not mean that this process was not shaped profoundly by other nations. See, for example, Amy C. Offner, *Sorting Out the Mixed Economy: The Rise and Fall of Welfare and Developmental States in the Americas* (Princeton, NJ: Princeton University Press, 2019); Christy Thornton, *Revolution in Development: Mexico and the Governance of the Global Economy* (Oakland: University of California Press, 2021); Johanna Bockman, *Markets in the Name of Socialism: The Left-Wing Origins of Neoliberalism* (Stanford, CA: Stanford University Press, 2011); Quinn Slobodian, *Globalists: The End of Empire and the Birth of Neoliberalism* (Cambridge, MA: Harvard University Press, 2018).

18. See especially Peter E. Hamilton, *Made in Hong Kong: Transpacific Networks and a New History of Globalization* (New York: Columbia University Press, 2021); Min Ye, *Diasporas and Foreign Direct Investment in China and India* (Cambridge: Cambridge University Press, 2014).

19. Liu, "China's Large-Scale Importation"; Mahmud Ali, *US-China Cold War Collaboration, 1971–1989* (London: Routledge, 2005).

20. On the shift from "China trade" to "China market" in the nineteenth century, see Dael A. Norwood, *Trading Freedom: How Trade with China Defined Early America* (Chicago: University of Chicago Press, 2022).

21. Jonathan D. Spence, *The Chan's Great Continent: China in Western Minds, 1620–1960* (New York: W. W. Norton, 1998), 1–18; Thomas J. McCormick, *China Market: America's Quest for Informal Empire, 1893–1901* (Chicago: Quadrangle Books, 1967); Robert A. Kapp, "The Matter of Business," in *China in the American Political Imagination* (Washington, DC: CSIS Press, 2003), 82–92.

22. David S. Landes, *The Unbound Prometheus: Technological Change and Industrial Development in Western Europe from 1750 to the Present* (Cambridge: Cambridge University Press, 1969), 240.

23. For more on Crow's continued resonance in the post–Cold War era, see Elizabeth Ingleson, "'Four Hundred Million Customers': Carl Crow and the Legacy of 1930s Sino-American Trade," *Australasian Journal of American Studies* 35, no. 1 (July 2016): 103–124.

24. Foot, *Practice of Power,* 53.

25. On the US business community's halting, yet growing, attempts from the late 1950s to persuade Washington to open up trade access for them (after Britain, West Germany, Japan, and other capitalist nations ended the trade restrictions on Communist China and began trading with China on the same terms as with the Soviet Union), see Kailai Huang, "American Business and the China Trade Embargo in the 1950s," *Essays in Economic and Business History* 19, no. 1 (2001): 33–48; Foot, *Practice of Power,* 52–81.

26. Tudda, *Cold War Turning Point;* David Shambaugh, *Tangled Titans: The United States and China* (Plymouth, MA: Rowman and Littlefield, 2013); Breck Walker, "'Friends but Not Allies': Cyrus Vance and the Normalization of Relations with China," *Diplomatic History* 33, no. 4 (September 2009): 579–594; Enrico Fardella, "The Sino-American Normalization: A Reassessment," *Diplomatic History* 33, no. 4 (September 2009): 545–578; Margaret MacMillan, *Nixon and Mao: The Week That Changed the World* (New York: Random House, 2007); William C. Kirby, Robert S. Ross, and Gong Li, eds., *Normalization of US-China Relations: An International History* (Cambridge, MA: Harvard University Asia Center, 2006); Evelyn Goh, *Constructing the US Rapprochement with China, 1961–1974* (Cambridge: Cambridge University Press, 2005); Ali, *US-China Cold War Collaboration;* Foot, *Practice of Power;* Warren I. Cohen, *America's Response to China: A History of Sino-American Relations,* 5th ed. (New York: Columbia University Press, 2010); Michael Schaller, *The United States and China: Into the Twenty-First Century* (New York: Oxford University Press, 2016).

27. Scholars are beginning to reassess the US-China trade relationship in the 1970s, although most continue to explore it from the perspective of elite politics. I am indebted to many of their insights. Shu Guang Zhang, *Beijing's Economic Statecraft during the Cold War, 1949–1991* (Baltimore: Johns Hopkins University Press, 2014); Chad J. Mitcham, *China's Economic Relations with the West and Japan, 1949–1979* (London: Routledge, 2005); Westad, "Great Transformation"; Minami, "Re-examining the End"; Kailai Huang, "Politics in Command: US-China Trade, 1972–1978," *Essays in Economic and Business History* 16 (1998): 15–29; Shu Guang Zhang, "China's Economic Statecraft in the 1970s," in Roberts and Westad, *China, Hong Kong, and the Long 1970s,* 159–180; Song, "A Dissonance in Mao's Revolution"; William Burr, "'Casting a Shadow' over Trade: The Problem of Private Claims and Blocked Assets in US-China Relations," *Diplomatic History* 33, no. 2 (April 2009): 315–349. A notable exception to the focus on elite politics is a collection of vignettes written by Randall Stross: *Bulls in the China Shop: And Other Sino-American Business Encounters* (1990; reprint, Honolulu: University of Hawai'i Press, 1993). Stross's book provides illuminating accounts of American businesspeople's experiences in China during the 1970s and 1980s. Based at San Jose State University, Stross worked as a scholar but he also wrote as a former businessman. "I count myself among the bulls mentioned in the book's title," he declared by way of introduction. His closeness to his subjects meant that his work brought to life many of the businesspeople—American and Chinese—who traded with one another during this pe-

riod. What is missing, however, is an understanding of the wider contexts in which these relationships unfolded: a challenge compounded by the fact that he was writing in the late 1980s, so close to the period itself. More recently, some scholars have started to reexamine the role of nonstate actors in US-China trade in the 1970s. Christian Talley, in particular, has written a thoughtful institutional history of the National Council for US-China Trade. These histories are concerned primarily with unpacking causation: To what extent, they collectively ask, did US businesspeople influence the wider diplomacy of this era? My concern lies not in measuring the impact of trade on diplomatic outcomes but instead in interrogating diplomatic assumptions about trade alongside the changing practices of trade. Christian Talley, *Forgotten Vanguard: Informal Diplomacy and the Rise of United States–China Trade, 1972–1980* (Notre Dame, IN: University of Notre Dame Press, 2018); Kazushi Minami, "Oil for the Lamps of America? Sino-American Oil Diplomacy, 1973–1979," *Diplomatic History* 41, no. 5 (2017): 959–984; Mao Lin, "More than a Tacit Alliance: Trade, Soft Power, and U.S.-Chinese Rapprochement Reconsidered," *Journal of American–East Asian Relations* 24 (2017): 41–77.

28. Robin Kelley and Betsy Esch, "Black like Mao: Red China and Black Revolution," *Souls* 1, no. 4 (1999): 6–41; Robeson Taj Frazier, *The East Is Black: Cold War China in the Black Radical Imagination* (Durham, NC: Duke University Press, 2015), 111–192; Matthew Johnson, "From Peace to Panthers: PRC Engagement with African-American Transnational Networks, 1949–1979," *Past and Present* 218, suppl. 8 (2013): 233–257.

29. Goh, *Constructing the US Rapprochement*, 88–90.

30. On the international appeal of Maoism in the 1960s, see Julia Lovell, *Maoism: A Global History* (London: Knopf Doubleday, 2019).

31. Kristin L. Hoganson, *Consumers' Imperium: The Global Production of American Domesticity, 1865–1920* (Chapel Hill: University of North Carolina Press, 2007), 17–19; Kristin L. Hoganson, "Cosmopolitan Domesticity: Importing the American Dream, 1865–1920," *American Historical Review* 107, no. 1 (February 2002): 55–83.

32. Letter from Stanley Young to Ed Brun, June 13, 1978, folder General Correspondence File 1978 V, box 21, Records of the U.S.-China Business Council (hereafter RUCBC), Gerald R. Ford Presidential Library, Ann Arbor, MI (hereafter Ford Library).

33. Cited in Charles W. Freeman III, "The Commercial and Economic Relationship," in *Tangled Titans: The United States and China*, ed. David Shambaugh (Lanham, MD: Rowman and Littlefield, 2013), 181.

34. On the Ford administration's use of military sales, in particular, as a means of encouraging more favorable political relations, see James Mann, *About Face: A History of America's Curious Relationship with China, from Nixon to Clinton* (New York: Vintage Books, 2000), 74; Ali, *US-China Cold War Collaboration*. On the Carter administration's views of trade as assisting negotiations toward normalization, see Robert S. Ross, *Negotiating Cooperation: The United States and China, 1969–1989* (Stanford, CA: Stanford University Press, 1995), 150–151.

35. See Emily S. Rosenberg, *Financial Missionaries to the World: The Politics and Culture of Dollar Diplomacy, 1900–1930* (Cambridge, MA: Harvard University Press, 1999); Rosenberg, *Spreading the American Dream: American Economic and Cultural Expansion, 1890–1945* (New York: Hill and Wang, 1982); Alan P. Dobson, *U.S. Economic Statecraft for Survival, 1933–1991* (New York: Routledge, 2002); Diane B. Kunz, *Butter and Guns: America's Cold War Economic Diplomacy* (New York: Free Press, 1997).

36. On the cultural, scientific, and educational ties that were reestablished between the United States and China in the 1970s, see Pete Millwood, *Improbable Diplomats: How Ping-Pong Players, Musicians, and Scientists Remade US-China Relations* (Cambridge: Cambridge University Press, 2022).

37. Shu Guang Zhang notes these differences; see Zhang, *Beijing's Economic Statecraft*, 241–252.

38. Conceptually, this was a loose inversion of the American scholarship that presented the history of Sino-American relations as one of "Western impact, Chinese response." Reaching a high point in the 1950s and 1960s, this historiographical lens replicated the structures of imperial power through the narratives they told, in which the agents of change were the United States and Europe. See Paul A. Cohen, *Discovering History in China: American Historical Writing on the Recent Chinese Past* (New York: Columbia University Press, 2010), 9–55.

39. Jefferson Cowie, *Capital Moves: RCA's Seventy-Year Quest for Cheap Labor* (Ithaca, NY: Cornell University Press, 1999).

40. Some scholars trace the origins of multinational corporations back 2,000 years; others point to the British and Dutch East India Companies of the seventeenth century. For the former view, see Karl Moore and David Lewis, *Birth of the Multinational: 2000 Years of Ancient Business History—from Ashur to Augustus* (Copenhagen: Copenhagen Business School Press, 1999); for the latter, see Mira Wilkins, *The Emergence of Multinational Enterprise: American Business Abroad from the Colonial Era to 1914* (Cambridge, MA: Harvard University Press, 1970); Wilkins, "Multinational Enterprise to 1930: Discontinuities and Continuities," in *Leviathans: Multinational Corporations and the New Global History,* ed. Alfred D. Chandler Jr. and Bruce Mazlish (Cambridge: Cambridge University Press, 2005), 45–79; see also Philip J. Stern, *The Company-State: Corporate Sovereignty and the Early Modern Foundations of the British Empire in India* (Oxford: Oxford University Press, 2011).

41. Geoffrey Jones, "Multinationals from the 1930s to the 1980s," in Chandler and Mazlish, *Leviathans,* 96–97; Geoffrey Jones, *Multinationals and Global Capitalism: From the Nineteenth to the Twenty-First Century* (Oxford: Oxford University Press, 2005), 76–108; Wilkins, *Emergence of Multinational Enterprise;* Mira Wilkins, *The Maturing of Multinational Enterprise: American Business Abroad from 1914 to 1970* (Cambridge, MA: Harvard University Press, 1974).

42. Marc Levinson, *The Box: How the Shipping Container Made the World Smaller and the World Economy Bigger* (Princeton, NJ: Princeton University Press, 2016), 285–309. On the development of passenger aircraft during World War II and into the 1960s, see especially Jenifer Van Vleck, *Empire of the Air: Aviation and the American Ascendancy* (Cambridge, MA: Harvard University Press, 2013). For a pioneering history of this eventual movement of production to overseas locations, see Cowie, *Capital Moves;* on the political choices and the creation of institutions that supported the development of outsourced manufacturing corporations, see Nitsan Chorev, *Remaking US Trade Policy: From Protectionism to Globalization* (Ithaca, NY: Cornell University Press, 2007); Judith Stein, "Conflict, Change, and Economic Policy in the Long 1970s," in *Rebel Rank and File: Labor Militancy and Revolt from Below during the Long 1970s* (London: Verso, 2010), 77–102; Stein, *Pivotal Decade: How the United States Traded Factories for Finance in the 1970s* (New Haven, CT: Yale University Press, 2010). Joshua Freeman situates these changes within the wider biography of the giant factory; see Joshua B. Freeman, *Behemoth: A History of the Factory and the Making of the Modern World* (New York: W. W. Norton, 2018).

43. Most particularly through the 1972 Burke-Hartke Bill, formally the Foreign Investment Act.

44. On the domestic aspects of this story, see especially Kim Phillips-Fein, *Invisible Hands: The Businessmen's Crusade against the New Deal* (New York: W. W. Norton, 2010), 166–212.

45. Thomas Borstelmann, *The 1970s: A New Global History from Civil Rights to Economic Inequality* (Princeton, NJ: Princeton University Press, 2011), 140–141.

46. Charles S. Maier, *Among Empires: American Ascendancy and Its Predecessors* (Cambridge, MA: Harvard University Press, 2006), 191–284; see also Stein, *Pivotal Decade.*

47. Benjamin Waterhouse, *The Land of Enterprise: A Business History of the United States* (New York: Simon and Schuster, 2017), 213–214; Jones, "Multinationals from the 1930s"; Jones, *Multinationals and Global Capitalism*, 33–34.

48. Moon-Ho Jung, *Coolies and Cane: Race, Labor, and Sugar in the Age of Emancipation* (Baltimore: Johns Hopkins University Press, 2006); Matthew Frye Jacobson, *Barbarian Virtues: The United States Encounters Foreign Peoples at Home and Abroad, 1876–1917* (New York: Hill and Wang, 2000).

49. Andrew C. McKevitt, *Consuming Japan: Popular Culture and the Globalizing of 1980s America* (Chapel Hill: University of North Carolina Press, 2017).

50. Branko Milanovic, *Global Inequality: A New Approach for the Age of Globalization* (Cambridge, MA: Belknap Press of Harvard University Press, 2016), 157.

51. On labor activism in this decade, see Lane Windham, *Knocking on Labor's Door: Union Organizing in the 1970s and the Roots of a New Economic Divide* (Chapel Hill: University of North Carolina Press, 2017); John Shelton, *Teacher Strike! Public Education and the Making of a New American Political Order* (Champaign: University of Illinois Press, 2017); Aaron Brenner, Robert Brenner, and Cal Winslow, eds., *Rebel Rank and File: Labor Militancy and Revolt from Below during the Long 1970s* (New York: Verso, 2010); Timothy J. Minchin, *Empty Mills: The Fight against Imports and the Decline of the U.S. Textile Industry* (Lanham, MD: Rowman and Littlefield, 2013); Timothy J. Minchin, "'Don't Sleep with Stevens!' The J. P. Stevens Boycott and Social Activism in the 1970s," *Journal of American Studies* 39, no. 3 (2005): 511–543; Jefferson Cowie, *Stayin' Alive: The 1970s and the Last Days of the Working Class* (New York: New Press, 2012); Paul Adler, *No Globalization without Representation: US Activists and World Inequality* (Philadelphia: University of Pennsylvania Press, 2021). See also Thomas W. Zeiler, "Requiem for the Common Man: Class, the Nixon Economic Shock, and the Perils of Globalization," *Diplomatic History* 37, no. 1 (January 2013): 1–23.

1. The Nixon Shocks

1. On Nixon's own comparison to China, see "Telephone Conversation between Nixon and Kissinger," 10:15 P.M., August 16, 1971, folder August 11–19, 1971, box 11, Kissinger Telephone Conversation Transcripts, Richard Nixon Presidential Library and Museum, Yorba Linda, CA (hereafter Nixon Library).

2. Giovanni Arrighi, *The Long Twentieth Century: Money, Power and the Origins of Our Times* (London: Verso, 2010), 322–323; Judith Stein, *Pivotal Decade: How the United States Traded Factories for Finance in the 1970s* (New Haven, CT: Yale University Press, 2010), 23–50.

3. Benjamin Waterhouse, *The Land of Enterprise: A Business History of the United States* (New York: Simon and Schuster, 2017), 213–214; Geoffrey Jones, "Multinationals from the 1930s to the 1980s," in *Leviathans: Multinational Corporations and the New Global History*, ed. Alfred D. Chandler Jr. and Bruce Mazlish (Cambridge: Cambridge University Press, 2005), 96–97; Jones, *Multinationals and Global Capitalism: From the Nineteenth to the Twenty-First Century* (Oxford: Oxford University Press, 2005), 33–34.

4. For more on this transformation from foe to ally, see Evelyn Goh, *Constructing the US Rapprochement with China, 1961–1974* (Cambridge: Cambridge University Press, 2005).

5. Kristin L. Hoganson, *Consumers' Imperium: The Global Production of American Domesticity, 1865–1920* (Chapel Hill: University of North Carolina Press, 2007).

6. Pete Millwood, *Improbable Diplomats* (Cambridge: Cambridge University Press, 2023), 119–161; Xu Guoqi, *Olympic Dreams: China and Sports, 1895–2008* (Cambridge,

MA: Harvard University Press, 2008); Itoh Mayumi, *The Origin of Ping-Pong Diplomacy: The Forgotten Architect of Sino-US Rapprochement* (New York: Palgrave Macmillan, 2011); Wang Guanhua, "'Friendship First': China's Sports Diplomacy in the Cold War Era," *Journal of American–East Asian Relations* 12, no. 3 (2003): 133–153.

7. Rosemary Foot briefly discusses the 1971 trade amendments in her foundational study of the history of the US trade embargo on China, *The Practice of Power: US Relations with China since 1949* (Oxford: Oxford University Press, 1997), 75.

8. "Statement by the President," April 14, 1971, folder Exchanges Leading Up to HAK Trip to China—December 1969–July 1971 (1), box 1031, National Security Council Files, Nixon Library.

9. "National Security Study Memorandum 124," April 19, 1971, in *Foreign Relations of the United States* (hereafter *FRUS*), *1969–1976*, vol. 17, *China, 1969–1972* (Washington, DC: US Government Printing Office, 2006), 299.

10. Millwood, *Improbable Diplomats,* 119–161.

11. This was a deliberate strategy to ease restrictions slowly in order to keep an eye on reactions from Taiwan and the Soviet Union. See Memorandum for President from USC Chairman Irwin, February 23, 1971, folder NSDM 105 (working files), box H-223, NSDM, Nixon Library.

12. Richard Nixon, "Remarks to Midwestern News Media Executives Attending a Briefing on Domestic Policy in Kansas City, Missouri," July 6, 1971, in *Public Papers of the Presidents of the United States: Richard Nixon, 1971* (Washington, DC: US Government Printing Office, 1972), 802–813.

13. Richard Nixon, *RN: The Memoirs of Richard Nixon* (New York: Simon and Schuster, 2013), 558.

14. Nixon, "Remarks to Midwestern News Media."

15. The unfolding rapprochement was not a one-way decision made by US policymakers; Mao ended the US-China isolation as much as Nixon did. See Chen Jian, *Mao's China and the Cold War* (Chapel Hill: University of North Carolina Press, 2001), 238–276.

16. Memorandum from Peter Flanigan to Henry Kissinger, April 5, 1971, folder NSDM 105 (working files), box H-223, NSDM, Nixon Library.

17. "Memorandum from Kissinger to Nixon," June 3, 1971, *FRUS, 1969–1976,* vol. 17, *China, 1969–1972,* 336–337.

18. "NSC-U/SM 91: Travel and Trade with Communist China," February 22, 1971, folder NSDM 105 (National Security Decision Memorandums), box H-223, NSDM, Nixon Library.

19. Cited in William Burr, "'Casting a Shadow' over Trade: The Problem of Private Claims and Blocked Assets in US-China Relations," *Diplomatic History* 33, no. 2 (April 2009): 320.

20. "NSSM 149: US-PRC Trade," March 24, 1972, folder NSSM 149, box H-190, NSDM, Nixon Library.

21. Evelyn Goh argues that this was an approach Kissinger and Nixon took as part of a modern-day tribute system in which they would emphasize China's great power status as a means of demonstrating their commitment to the negotiation process. Nixon later noted in preparation for the 1972 trip that he would treat Mao "as Emperor." Goh, *Constructing the US Rapprochement,* 165–167.

22. "Memorandum of Conversation," July 9, 1971, *FRUS, 1969–1976,* vol. 17, *China, 1969–1972,* 389.

23. The English translation of the eight basic principles can be found in Yafeng Xia, "China's Elite Politics and Sino-American Rapprochement," *Journal of Cold War Studies* 8, no. 4 (Fall 2006): 18. The original documents can be found in Gong Li, 跨越鸿沟: 1969–1979 年中美关系的演变 [Crossing the chasm: The evolution of US-China relations, 1969–1979] (Zhengzhou: Henan Renmin Chubanshe, 1992), 103–104.

24. Gong Li, "Preface," in *Normalization of U.S.-China Relations: An International History,* ed. William C. Kirby, Robert S. Ross, and Gong Li (Cambridge, MA: Harvard University Asia Center, 2005), xi.

25. For more on China's approach toward trade, see Shu Guang Zhang, "China's Economic Statecraft in the 1970s," in *China, Hong Kong, and the Long 1970s: Global Perspectives,* ed. Priscilla Roberts and Odd Arne Westad (Cham, Switzerland: Palgrave Macmillan, 2017); Shu Guang Zhang, *Economic Cold War: America's Embargo against China and the Sino-Soviet Alliance, 1949–1963* (Stanford, CA: Stanford University Press, 2001).

26. On the geopolitical issues compelling the United States and China toward rapprochement, see Yang Kuisong, "The Sino-Soviet Border Clash of 1969: From Zhenbao Island to Sino-American Rapprochement," *Cold War History* 1, no. 1 (August 2000): 21–52; Lorenz Lüthi, *The Sino-Soviet Split: Cold War in the Communist World* (Princeton, NJ: Princeton University Press, 2008); Evelyn Goh, "Nixon, Kissinger, and the 'Soviet Card' in the US Opening to China, 1971–1974," *Diplomatic History* 29, no. 3 (June 2005): 475–502. On the ways in which Sino-American rapprochement pushed North Vietnam into a new offensive, see Lien-Hang T. Nguyen, *Hanoi's War: An International History of the War for Peace in Vietnam* (Chapel Hill: University of North Carolina Press, 2012), 231–256.

27. Chris Tudda, *A Cold War Turning Point: Nixon and China, 1969–1972* (Baton Rouge: Louisiana State University Press, 2012), 88.

28. Memorandum for Henry A. Kissinger from Winston Lord, "Memcon of Your Conversations with Chou En-Lai," July 29, 1971, in National Security Archive, *China and the United States: From Hostility to Engagement, 1960–1998,* ed. Jeffrey T. Richelson (Alexandria, VA: Chadwyck-Healey, 1999).

29. Memorandum for Henry A. Kissinger from Winston Lord, "Memcon."

30. Robert Accinelli, "In Pursuit of a Modus Vivendi: The Taiwan Issue and Sino-American Rapprochement, 1969–1972," in Kirby et al., *Normalization of U.S-China Relations,* 25.

31. Chen, *Mao's China,* 268.

32. Gong Li, "Chinese Decision Making and the Thawing of US-China Relations," in *Re-examining the Cold War: U.S.-China Diplomacy, 1954–1973,* ed. Robert S. Ross and Jiang Changbin (Cambridge, MA: Harvard University Press, 2001), 330–331; Xu Yan, "The Sino-Soviet Border Clashes of 1969," *Dangshi Yanjiu Ziliao* 6 (1994): 6–10; Yang Kuisong, "From the Zhenbao Island Incident to Sino-American Rapprochement," *Dangshi Yanjiu Ziliao* 12 (1997): 7–8; Li Danhui, "The 1969 Sino-Soviet Border Clash: Causes and Consequences," *Dangdai Zhongguoshi Yanjiu* 3 (1996): 48.

33. Chen, *Mao's China,* 238–276; Guolin Yi, "The 'Propaganda State' and Sino-American Rapprochement: Preparing the Chinese Public for Nixon's Visit," *Journal of American–East Asian Relations* 20 (2013): 5–28.

34. Margaret MacMillan, *Nixon and Mao: The Week That Changed the World* (New York: Random House, 2007), 273–287.

35. Goh, *Constructing the US Rapprochement,* 46–99. In 1966, policymakers and academics testified before the Senate Foreign Relations Committee on the question of America's China policy. Their debates and statements are available in Akira Iriye, ed., *US Policy toward China: Testimony Taken from the Senate Foreign Relations Committee Hearings, 1966* (Boston: Little, Brown, 1968).

36. Richard Nixon, "Asia after Viet Nam," *Foreign Affairs* 46, no. 1 (October 1967): 121.

37. Goh, *Constructing the US Rapprochement.*

38. Richard Nixon, "Remarks to the Nation Announcing Acceptance of an Invitation to Visit the People's Republic of China," July 15, 1971, in *Public Papers, Richard Nixon, 1971,* 819–820.

39. Cited in Tudda, *Cold War Turning Point*, 109.

40. Nixon and Kissinger telephone conversation, April 14, 1971, folder April 8–14, 1971, box 9, Kissinger Telephone Conversation Transcripts, Nixon Library.

41. Chris Tudda and Yafeng Xia, "Beijing, 1972," in *Transcending the Cold War: Summits, Statecraft, and the Dissolution of Bipolarity in Europe, 1970–1990*, ed. Kristina Spohr and David Reynolds (New York: Oxford University Press, 2016), 54.

42. Tudda, *Cold War Turning Point*, 87.

43. Tang Wenshang, interview with *Global Times*, February 28, 2022.

44. Robert A. Wright, "Labor Bids Nixon Restudy Peking Policy," *New York Times*, August 11, 1971, 4.

45. Richard N. Gardner, *Sterling-Dollar Diplomacy in Current Perspective: The Origins and the Prospects of Our International Economic Order* (New York: Columbia University Press, 1980); Ed Conway, *The Summit, Bretton Woods 1944: J. M. Keynes and the Reshaping of the Global Economy* (New York: Pegasus Books, 2014), 201–385.

46. For more on China's role in the Bretton Woods negotiations, see Eric Helleiner and Bessma Momani, "The Hidden History of China and the IMF," in *The Great Wall of Money: Power and Politics in China's International Monetary Relations*, ed. Eric Helleiner and Jonathan Kirshner (Ithaca, NY: Cornell University Press, 2014), 45–70; Helleiner, *The Forgotten Foundations of Bretton Woods: International Development and the Making of the Postwar Order* (Ithaca, NY: Cornell University Press, 2014), 184–207.

47. Cited in Daniel J. Sargent, *A Superpower Transformed: The Remaking of American Foreign Relations in the 1970s* (New York: Oxford University Press, 2015), 18.

48. Alfred E. Eckes Jr. and Thomas W. Zeiler, *Globalization and the American Century* (Cambridge: Cambridge University Press), 131–183.

49. Sargent, *A Superpower Transformed*, 110.

50. Richard Nixon, "Address to the Nation Outlining a New Economic Policy: 'The Challenge of Peace,'" August 15, 1971, in *Public Papers, Richard Nixon, 1971*, 886–890.

51. Sargent, *A Superpower Transformed*, 116.

52. Sargent, *A Superpower Transformed*, 102.

53. On the unintended consequences of the Nixon economic shock, see Greta R. Krippner, *Capitalizing on Crisis: The Political Origins of the Rise of Finance* (Cambridge, MA: Harvard University Press, 2011); Sargent, *A Superpower Transformed*. On the rise of neoliberalism in this era, see Gary Gerstle, *The Rise and Fall of the Neoliberal Order: America and the World in the Free Market Era* (New York: Oxford University Press, 2022); Fritz Bartel, *The Triumph of Broken Promises* (Cambridge, MA: Harvard University Press, 2022); Michael Franczak, *Global Inequality and American Foreign Policy in the 1970s* (Ithaca, NY: Cornell University Press, 2022).

54. "Telephone Conversation between Nixon and Kissinger," 10:15 P.M., August 16, 1971, folder August 11–19, 1971, box 11, Kissinger Telephone Conversation Transcripts, Nixon Library.

55. Report February–May Far East Trip 1971, folder 2, MSS 1583, box 12, David M. Kennedy Collection, Harold B. Lee Library, Brigham Young University, Provo, UT (hereafter Kennedy Collection).

56. "Economy Needs Rise in Business Profit, Stans Says," *Chicago Tribune*, September 29, 1971, 3.

57. Cited in Jennifer A. Delton, *The Industrialists: How the National Association of Manufacturers Shaped American Capitalism* (Princeton, NJ: Princeton University Press, 2020), 252.

58. For more on the Mills Bill, the Burke-Hartke Bill, and their relationship to the Trade Act of 1974, see James C. Benton, *Fraying Fabric: How Trade Policy and Industrial Decline Transformed America* (Champaign: University of Illinois Press, 2022), 173–214.

59. Cited in Nitsan Chorev, *Remaking US Trade Policy: From Protectionism to Globalization* (Ithaca, NY: Cornell University Press, 2007), 79.

60. Chorev, *Remaking US Trade Policy,* 79–81.

61. Chorev, *Remaking US Trade Policy,* 73.

62. Kimberly Phillips-Fein, *Invisible Hands: The Businessmen's Crusade against the New Deal* (New York: W. W. Norton, 2009), 190–203; Benjamin Waterhouse, *Lobbying America: The Politics of Business from Nixon to NAFTA* (Princeton, NJ: Princeton University Press, 2013), 76–105.

63. Douglas A. Irwin, *Clashing over Commerce: A History of U.S. Trade Policy* (Chicago: University of Chicago Press, 2017), 542.

64. Dana Frank, *Buy American: The Untold Story of Economic Nationalism* (Boston: Beacon Press, 1999), 153.

65. Michael Schaller, "Detent and the Strategic Triangle or, 'Drinking Your Mao Tai and Having Your Vodka, Too,'" in Ross and Jiang, *Re-examining the Cold War,* 376.

66. Chorev, *Remaking US Trade Policy,* 76.

67. Marc Levinson, *The Box: How the Shipping Container Made the World Smaller and the World Economy Bigger* (Princeton, NJ: Princeton University Press, 2016), 293.

68. "Nixon Urged to Weigh China Policy Decision," *AFL-CIO News,* August 14, 1971, 1.

69. Wright, "Labor Bids Nixon Restudy."

70. Earl Rees to George Meany, October 18, 1971, folder 48, box 1, AFL-CIO International Affairs Department (hereafter AFL-CIO IAD), Country Files Asia and Australia, 1971–1981 (hereafter CFAA), University of Maryland Libraries (hereafter UML) College Park, MD; Paul and Aurora Jones to George Meany, October 25, 1971, folder 48, box 1, AFL-CIO IAD, CFAA, UML.

71. Mr. and Mrs. Andreas Tobler, September 27, 1971, folder 48, box 1, AFL-CIO IAD, CFAA, UML.

72. Carl McIntire to George Meany, March 4, 1972, folder 48, box 1, AFL-CIO IAD, CFAA, UML.

73. On nineteenth-century links between Chinese labor and slavery, see Moon-Ho Jung, *Coolies and Cane: Race, Labor, and Sugar in the Age of Emancipation* (Baltimore: Johns Hopkins University Press, 2006), 11–38.

74. For more on Chinese people who left after Mao's victory, see Helen Zia, *Last Boat out of Shanghai: The Epic Story of the Chinese Who Fled Mao's Revolution* (New York: Penguin Random House, 2020).

75. Julian Sobin, interview with Veronica Yhap, August 13, 1976, folder Julian Sobin Interview with Gerry Wielenga and Veronica Yhap, box 373, RUCBC, Ford Library.

76. Bernadine Morris, "Rage of Paris: What Chinese Wear at Work," *New York Times,* August 3, 1971, folder 4, box 13, Pardee Lowe papers, Hoover Institution.

77. For more on the Dragon Lady, see Heather Marie Stur, *Beyond Combat: Women and Gender in the Vietnam War Era* (Cambridge: Cambridge University Press, 2011), 25–31; Madeline Y. Hsu, *The Good Immigrants: How the Yellow Peril Became the Model Minority* (Princeton, NJ: Princeton University Press, 2015), 81–103.

78. Naoko Shibusawa, *America's Geisha Ally: Reimagining the Japanese Enemy* (Cambridge, MA: Harvard University Press, 2006).

79. Sobin, interview with Yhap.

80. Bernadine Morris, "China: Biggest Fashion News since the Mini," *South China Morning Post,* December 14, 1971.

81. Betty Ommerman, "Promoting and Importing Fashions from People's Republic of China," *Washington Post,* April 2, 1972.

82. "Feminique," *Chicago Tribune*, October 18, 1971.

83. "Chicom Chic," *Time Magazine*, December 6, 1971.

84. Ellen D. Wu, *The Color of Success: Asian Americans and the Origins of the Model Minority* (Princeton, NJ: Princeton University Press, 2014); Hsu, *Good Immigrants*.

85. Robeson Taj Frazier, *The East Is Black: Cold War China in the Black Radical Imagination* (Durham, NC: Duke University Press, 2015); Robin D. G. Kelley and Betsy Esch, "Black like Mao: Red China and Black Revolution," *Souls* 1, no. 4 (1999): 6–41; Keisha Brown, "Blackness in Exile: W.E.B. Du Bois' Role in the Formation of Representations of Blackness as Conceptualized by the Chinese Communist Party (CCP)," *Phylon* 53, no. 2 (Winter 2016): 20–33; Julia Lovell, *Maoism: A Global History* (London: Knopf Doubleday, 2019), 266–305.

86. Frank Ching, "China: It's the Latest American Thing," *New York Times*, February 16, 1972.

87. This was part of a process that mirrored the corporate co-optation of US counterculture in the 1960s. Thomas Frank, *The Conquest of Cool: Business Culture, Counterculture, and the Rise of Hip Consumerism* (Chicago: University of Chicago Press, 1997).

88. Andreas Killen, *1973 Nervous Breakdown: Watergate, Warhol, and the Birth of Post-Sixties America* (New York: Bloomsbury, 2006), 7.

89. "U.S. Participants at the Spring and Fall Kwangchow Fairs, 1971–1973," *Special Report no. 5*, National Council for US-China Trade, February 1974, p. 3, folder Fall 1973, box 72, RUCBC, Ford Library.

90. Yong Chen, *Chop Suey, USA: The Story of Chinese Food in America* (New York: Columbia University Press, 2014), 174.

91. Jacqueline Trescott, "Host of Two Worlds," *Washington Post*, November 16, 1978.

92. Morris, "China."

93. Sobin, interview with Yhap.

94. Marylin Bender, "Browsing for Goods from the Land of Mao: American Shoppers' Response Is Mixed," *New York Times*, May 27, 1973.

95. "China Now," *Women's Wear Daily*, February 29, 1972, 30.

96. Marvin Klapper, "Year of the Dragon Lady," *Women's Wear Daily*, August 3, 1976, 10.

97. Ommerman, "Promoting and Importing," H10.

98. "Chicom Chic."

99. Bernadine Morris, "That Group of China Watchers with Headquarters on 7th Ave.," *New York Times*, November 20, 1971; Morris, "China."

100. Morris, "That Group of China Watchers"; Morris, "China."

101. "Chicom Chic."

102. They echoed Seventh Avenue's cultural influence of the early twentieth century, which similarly set a pattern for consumers throughout the United States. Marlis Schweitzer, *When Broadway Was the Runway: Theatre, Fashion and American Culture* (Philadelphia: University of Pennsylvania Press, 2009), 51–95.

103. Ching, "China."

104. Lenore Hershey, "The 'New' Pat Nixon," *Ladies' Home Journal*, February 1972, 126.

105. "Chicom Chic."

106. "Panda-Monium in Washington," *New York Times*, June 11, 1972.

107. Murray Schumach, "Toy Makers Gear for Panda Craze," *New York Times*, March 6, 1972.

108. Cited in David C. Buxbaum, "American Trade with the People's Republic of China: Some Preliminary Perspectives," *Columbia Journal of Transnational Law* 12, no. 1 (1973): 39.

2. The Canton Trade Fair

1. The language of "equality and mutual benefit" stemmed from Zhou Enlai's 1954 foreign policy articulation of Mao's Five Principles of Peaceful Coexistence, first through an agreement with India and later defining Chinese foreign policy throughout the Maoist era.

2. 回忆陈郁同志 [Recollections of Comrade Chen Yu] (Beijing: Gongren Chubanshe, 1982), 238–240. See also brief reference in Ezra F. Vogel, *Canton under Communism: Programs and Politics in a Provincial Capital, 1949–1968* (Cambridge, MA: Harvard University Press, 1969), 152.

3. Jason M. Kelly, *Market Maoists: The Communist Origins of China's Capitalist Ascent* (Cambridge, MA: Harvard University Press, 2021), 197.

4. 互通有无; 增进经济往来.

5. "一九七二年春季中国出口商品交易会在广州隆重开幕" [Grand opening of the Spring 1972 Chinese Export Commodities Fair in Guangzhou], *Renmin Ribao* (hereafter *RMRB*), April 16, 1972.

6. Chae-Jin Lee, *China and Japan: New Economic Diplomacy* (Stanford, CA: Hoover Press, 1984), 18.

7. Kuisong Yang and Yafeng Xia, "Vacillating between Revolution and Détente: Mao's Changing Psyche and Policy toward the United States, 1969–1976," *Diplomatic History* 34, no. 2 (April 2010): 395–423; Shu Guang Zhang, *Beijing's Economic Statecraft during the Cold War, 1949–1991* (Baltimore: Johns Hopkins University Press, 2014), 241–275.

8. For more on "China hands" as a collective noun, see Simon Leys, "The China Experts," in *The Hall of Uselessness* (Collingwood, Vic.: Black, 2012), 319–329; Sigrid Schmalzer, "Speaking about China, Learning from China: Amateur China Experts in 1970s America," *Journal of American–East Asian Relations* 16, no. 4 (Winter 2009): 313–352. See also Charles W. Hayford, "China by the Book: China Hands and China Stories, 1848–1949," *Journal of American–East Asian Relations* 16, no. 4 (Winter 2009): 285–311. On the mid-twentieth-century attacks on China hands, see Ely Jacques Kahn Jr., *China Hands: America's Foreign Service Officers and What Befell Them* (New York: Viking, 1975); Ellen Schrecker, *Many Are the Crimes: McCarthyism in America* (Boston: Little, Brown, 1998); Joyce Mao, *Asia First: China and the Making of Modern American Conservatism* (Chicago: University of Chicago Press, 2015), 44–77; Federico Pachetti, "The Roots of a Globalized Relationship: Western Knowledge of the Chinese Economy and US-China Relations in the Long 1970s," in *China, Hong Kong, and the Long 1970s: Global Perspectives,* ed. Priscilla Roberts and Odd Arne Westad (Cham, Switzerland: Palgrave Macmillan, 2017), 181–203.

9. On international trade fairs, see Andrew James Wulf, *U.S. International Exhibitions during the Cold War: Winning Hearts and Minds through Cultural Diplomacy* (London: Rowman and Littlefield, 2015); Robert W. Rydell, *World of Fairs: The Century-of-Progress Expositions* (Chicago: University of Chicago Press, 1993); Rydell, *All the World's a Fair: Visions of Empire at American International Expositions, 1876–1916* (Chicago: University of Chicago Press, 1984). On the Chinese Export Commodities Fair, see Ouyang Xiang, "从广交会的创办看二十世纪五十年代中期中国外经贸发展的战略调整" [Readjustments to the strategy of China's foreign trade development in the mid-1950s as seen from the launch of the Guangzhou Export Commodities Fair], *Zhonggong Dangshi Yanjiu* [Studies in CCP party history] 9 (2011): 29–37; Xin Jin and Karin Weber, "The China Import and Export (Canton) Fair: Past, Present, and Future," *Journal of Convention & Event Tourism* 9, no. 3 (2008): 221–234; Kelly, *Market Maoists,* 124–125, 190–191; Peter E. Hamilton, *Made in Hong Kong: Transpacific Networks and a New History of Globalization* (New York: Columbia University Press, 2021), 225; Lawrence C. Reardon, *The Reluctant Dragon: Crisis Cycles in Chinese Foreign Economic Policy* (Seattle: University of Washington Press, 2002), 144–147; Karl

Gerth, *Unending Capitalism: How Consumerism Negated China's Communist Revolution* (Cambridge: Cambridge University Press, 2020), 216, 329; Vogel, *Canton under Communism*, 335–336. Fei Yan references the Chinese Export Commodities Fair citing an article by one of the US businessmen who published his observations on the fair in 1973. See Fei Yan, "The Political Origins of Guangzhou's Mass Factions in 1967," *Modern China* 41, no. 2 (March 2015): 191–192; for the American businessman Fei cites, see Daniel Tretiak, "The Canton Fair: An Academic Perspective," *China Quarterly* 56 (December 1973): 740–748.

10. This chapter is influenced by histories of capitalism that understand culture to be an inextricable part of what "the economic" means. It builds in particular on the methodological example of Emily Rosenberg, who was at the forefront of exploring the crucial links between economics, diplomacy, and culture. More recently, Nan Enstad and Peter Hudson have taken similar approaches in their studies of American power, and also influenced my approach to this topic. Emily S. Rosenberg, *Financial Missionaries to the World: The Politics and Culture of Dollar Diplomacy, 1900–1930* (Cambridge, MA: Harvard University Press, 1999); Nan Enstad, "The 'Sonorous Summons' of the New History of Capitalism, Or, What Are We Talking about When We Talk about Economy?," *Modern American History*, no. 2 (2019): 83–95; Enstad, *Cigarettes Inc.: An Intimate History of Corporate Imperialism* (Chicago: University of Chicago Press, 2018); Peter James Hudson, *Bankers and Empire: How Wall Street Colonized the Caribbean* (Chicago: University of Chicago Press, 2017). See also David Harvey, *A Brief History of Neoliberalism* (Oxford: Oxford University Press, 2005), 39–63.

11. Mary Louise Pratt, *Imperial Eyes: Travel Writing and Transculturation* (New York: Routledge, 2008), 8–9; see also Matthew Frye Jacobson, *Barbarian Virtues: The United States Encounters Foreign Peoples at Home and Abroad, 1876–1917* (New York: Hill and Wang, 2000), 105–138.

12. Echoing a very long set of ideas in US-China trade. See Chapter 3.

13. The English translation of the eight basic principles can be found in Yafeng Xia, "China's Elite Politics and Sino-American Rapprochement," *Journal of Cold War Studies* 8, no. 4 (Fall 2006): 18. The original documents can be found in Gong Li, 跨越鸿沟: 1969–1979 年中美关系的演变 [Crossing the chasm: The evolution of US-China relations, 1969–1979] (Zhengzhou: Henan Renmin Chubanshe, 1992), 103–104.

14. On the Canton system, see especially Jacques Downs, *The Golden Ghetto: The American Commercial Community at Canton and the Shaping of American China Policy* (Bethlehem, PA: Lehigh University Press, 1997); Paul Arthur Van Dyke, *The Canton Trade: Life and Enterprise on the China Coast, 1700–1845* (Hong Kong: Hong Kong University Press, 2007).

15. Vogel, *Canton under Communism*, 350.

16. Xin and Weber, "China Import and Export," 225.

17. Valeria Zanier and Roberto Peruzzi, "1967 as the Turning Point in Hong Kong-British-PRC Economic Relations," in Roberts and Westad, *China, Hong Kong, and the Long 1970s*, 235; see also Tomoko Shiroyama, "The Hong Kong–South China Financial Nexus," in *The Capitalist Dilemma in China's Communist Revolution*, ed. Sherman Cochran (Ithaca, NY: Cornell University Press, 2014), 203–224.

18. The percentages ranged from 6.5 percent of total Chinese exports in 1954 to 12.9 percent in 1963. Alexander Eckstein, *Communist China's Economic Growth and Foreign Trade: Implications for U.S. Policy* (New York: Published for the Council on Foreign Relations by McGraw-Hill, 1966), 199.

19. Laura A. Belmonte, *Selling the American Way: U.S. Propaganda and the Cold War* (Philadelphia: University of Pennsylvania Press, 2008), 131–135.

20. Shane Hamilton, *Supermarket USA: Food and Power in the Cold War Farms Race* (New Haven, CT: Yale University Press, 2018), 97–115.

21. Belmonte, *Selling the American Way*, 87–88; Walter L. Hixson, *Parting the Curtain: Propaganda, Culture, and the Cold War, 1945–1961* (New York: St. Martin's Press, 1997), 151–184; Kenneth Osgood, *Total Cold War: Eisenhower's Secret Propaganda Battle at Home and Abroad* (Lawrence: University Press of Kansas, 2006), 214–218.

22. Rydell, *All the World's a Fair*.

23. Rosalind H. Williams, *Dream Worlds: Mass Consumption in Late Nineteenth Century France* (Berkeley: University of California Press, 1982); Rydell, *World of Fairs*; Jacobson, *Barbarian Virtues*, 15–57. On Chinese immigrants using world expositions in the United States to navigate spaces within the public sphere, see Krystyn R. Moon, *Yellowface: Creating the Chinese in American Popular Music and Performance, 1850s–1920s* (New Brunswick, NJ: Rutgers University Press, 2005), 80–85.

24. "出口商品交易会在广州举行" [Export commodities fair held in Guangzhou], *RMRB*, April 27, 1957.

25. Rosemary Foot, *The Practice of Power: US Relations with China since 1949* (Oxford: Oxford University Press, 1997), 56.

26. Odd Arne Westad, *The Global Cold War: Third World Interventions and the Making of Our Times* (Cambridge: Cambridge University Press, 2005), 69; Odd Arne Westad, *The Cold War: A World History* (London: Penguin Books, 2017), 237.

27. Odd Arne Westad, *Brothers in Arms: The Rise and Fall of the Sino-Soviet Alliance* (Washington, DC: Woodrow Wilson Center Press, 1998); Chen Jian, "The Beginning of the End: 1956 as a Turning Point in Chinese and Cold War History," *Modern China Studies* 22, no. 1 (2015): 99–126. On China's economic relationship with the Soviet Union, see also William C. Kirby, "China's Internationalism in the Early People's Republic: Dreams of a Socialist World Economy," *China Quarterly* 188 (December 2006).

28. Chen Jian and Yang Kuisong, "Chinese Politics and the Collapse of the Sino-Soviet Alliance," in Westad, *Brothers in Arms*, 262–264; Chen Jian, *Mao's China and the Cold War* (Chapel Hill: University of North Carolina Press, 2001), 67.

29. Cited in Reardon, *The Reluctant Dragon*, 69.

30. On changing approaches to international trade in the late 1950s and into the 1960s, see Kelly, *Market Maoists*, 126–156; Reardon, *The Reluctant Dragon*.

31. Shu Guang Zhang, *Economic Cold War: America's Embargo against China and the Sino-Soviet Alliance, 1949–1963* (Stanford, CA: Stanford University Press, 2001), 234–236.

32. Foot, *The Practice of Power*, 60–62; Heinrich Bechtoldt, "The Federal Republic of Germany and China: Problems of Trade and Diplomacy," in *Policies toward China: Views from Six Continents*, ed. Abraham M. Halpern (New York: Published for the Council on Foreign Relations by McGraw-Hill, 1965), 91–92; Jeffrey A. Engel, "Of Fat and Thin Communists: Diplomacy and Philosophy in Western Economic Warfare Strategies toward China (and Tyrants, Broadly)," *Diplomatic History* 29, no. 3 (June 2005): 445–474.

33. Kelly, *Market Maoists*, 153–154.

34. On China's involvement in the uprisings, see Zhu Dandan, *1956: Mao's China and the Hungarian Crisis* (Ithaca, NY: Cornell University Press, 2013); Chen, *Mao's China*, 145–162. On Poland, see Pawel Machcewicz, *Rebellious Satellite: Poland, 1956* (Stanford, CA: Stanford University Press, 2009). On the revolution in Hungary, see Jeno Gyorkei and Miklos Horvath, eds., *Soviet Military Intervention in Hungary, 1956* (Budapest: Central European University Press, 1999); see also Joseph Rothschild and Nancy Wingfield, *Return to Diversity: A Political History of East Central Europe since World War II* (Oxford: Oxford University Press, 2007), 147–190.

35. Cited in Zhang, *Economic Cold War*, 218.

36. The precise number of people who died remains a point of debate because of patchy and politicized data sets. Most scholars estimate that between 15 and 43 million people died.

See Kimberley Ens Manning and Felix Wemheuer, "Introduction," in *Eating Bitterness: New Perspectives on China's Great Leap Forward and Famine* (Vancouver: USB Press, 2011), 1–27.

37. While they do not explore the Chinese Export Commodities Fair, Gregg Brazinsky and Jeremy Friedman provide important insights into China's use of other aspects of cultural diplomacy in the Third World. See Gregg A. Brazinsky, *Winning the Third World: Sino-American Rivalry during the Cold War* (Chapel Hill: University of North Carolina Press, 2017), 132–165; Jeremy Friedman, *Shadow Cold War: The Sino-Soviet Competition for the Third World* (Chapel Hill: University of North Carolina Press, 2015), 101–147.

38. Inward telegram to the Secretary of State for the Colonies from Hong Kong, October 1, 1958; letter from G. B. W. Harrison to Board of Trade, September 17, 1958; letter from G. B. W. Harrison to Board of Trade, September 16, 1958; all in Foreign Office files for China, 1957–1966, FO 371/133476, National Archives (UK), Kew.

39. See Michael M. Sheng, "Mao and China's Relations with the Superpowers in the 1950s: A New Look at the Taiwan Straits Crisis and the Sino-Soviet Split," *Modern China* 34, no. 4 (October 2008): 477–507.

40. Dali L. Yang, *Calamity and Reform in China: State, Rural Society, and Institutional Change since the Great Leap Famine* (Stanford, CA: Stanford University Press, 1996), 102.

41. Anthony Garnaut, "The Geography of the Great Leap Famine," *Modern China* 40, no. 3 (2014): 337.

42. "中国出口商品交易会闭幕" [Closing of the Chinese Export Commodities Fair], *RMRB*, May 17, 1959.

43. Travel for American citizens was embargoed at this time, but the Du Boises—longtime supporters of the communist ideals Mao represented—ignored the ban and went to the PRC anyway.

44. Shirley Graham Du Bois, *His Day Is Marching On: A Memoir of W. E. B. Du Bois* (Philadelphia: J. B. Lippincott, 1971), 290.

45. Julia Lovell, *Maoism: A Global History* (London: Knopf Doubleday, 2019); Paul Hollander, *Political Pilgrims: Western Intellectuals in Search of the Good Society* (New Brunswick, NJ: Transaction Publishers, 1998); Quinn Slobodian, "The Meanings of Western Maoism in the Global 1960s," in *The Routledge Handbook of the Global Sixties: Between Protest and Nation-Building,* ed. Chen Jian et al. (London: Routledge, 2018), 67–78; Fabio Lanza, *The End of Concern: Maoist China, Activism, and Asian Studies* (Durham, NC: Duke University Press, 2017); Robeson Taj Frazier, *The East Is Black: Cold War China in the Black Radical Imagination* (Durham, NC: Duke University Press, 2015), 37–71; Robin Kelley and Betsy Esch, "Black like Mao: Red China and Black Revolution," *Souls* 1, no. 4 (1999): 6–41; Matthew D. Johnson, "From Peace to Panthers: PRC Engagement with African-American Transnational Networks, 1949–1979," *Past and Present* 218, no. 8 (2013): 233–257; Yunxiang Gao, *Arise Africa, Roar China* (Chapel Hill: University of North Carolina Press, 2021).

46. During their time in Beijing, W. E. B. Du Bois had spoken in support of China's revolutionary leadership at Peking University in a radio address China broadcast across African nations. "Africa arise and stand straight . . . turn from the West and your slavery and humiliation," the father of pan-Africanism beseeched. "China is colored and knows for what a colored skin is in this modern world subjects its owner. But China knows more, much more than this: she knows what to do about it."

47. Reardon, *The Reluctant Dragon,* 145–146.

48. Zhou Enlai cited in Reardon, *The Reluctant Dragon,* 145.

49. For more on Mao's call for Red Guards to "smash the four olds," see Roderick MacFarquhar and Michael Schoenhals, *Mao's Last Revolution* (Cambridge, MA: Belknap Press of Harvard University Press, 2006), 113–116.

50. Zanier and Peruzzi, "1967 as the Turning Point," 190–192.

51. See, for example, "伟大的领袖毛主席亲自发动的无产阶级文化大革命在政治上取得伟大的胜利在经济上取得辉煌的成果一九六七年秋季中国出口商品交易会在广州胜利闭幕" [The Great Leader Chairman Mao personally launched the Great Proletarian Cultural Revolution which achieved great political success and brilliant economic success], *RMRB*, December 16, 1967; "五大洲朋友、华侨和港澳同胞赞扬广州交易会" [Friends from five continents, overseas Chinese and compatriots from Hong Kong and Macao commended the Guangzhou Fair], *RMRB*, December 19, 1967.

52. "无产阶级文化大革命的伟大成果，一九六七年秋季中国出口常品交易会剪影" [The great achievement of the Great Proletarian Cultural Revolution: Outline of China Export Commodities Fair in the fall of 1967], *RMRB*, November 26, 1967.

53. Vogel, *Canton under Communism,* 335–336.

54. Reardon, *The Reluctant Dragon,* 146.

55. Covell F. Meyskens, *Mao's Third Front: The Militarization of Cold War China* (Cambridge: Cambridge University Press, 2020), 227–229.

56. Meyskens, *Mao's Third Front,* 228.

57. Cited in Lei Liu, "China's Large-Scale Importation of Western Technology and the U.S. Response, 1972–1976," *Diplomatic History* 45, no. 4 (2021): 801.

58. Kelly, *Market Maoists,* 197.

59. Liu, "China's Large-Scale Importation," 803–804; Kelly, *Market Maoist,* 200–201; Meyskens, *Mao's Third Front,* 227–230.

60. Kelly, *Market Maoists,* 200, 202.

61. "U.S. Participants at the Spring and Fall Kwangchow Fairs, 1971–1973," *Special Report No. 5,* February 1974, folder fall 1973, box 72, RUCBC, Ford Library.

62. View from train recreated from account by Fitzgerald Bemiss, "China Trip," April 17–May 9, 1975, folder Bemiss, FitzGerald, box 2, National Archive on Sino-American Relations 1971–1984, Bentley Historical Library, University of Michigan, Ann Arbor (hereafter NASAR).

63. Details from account by Bernard Rocca. See B. T. Rocca Jr., "A Report from the Canton Trade Fair," in *Trade with China: Assessments by Leading Businessmen and Scholars,* ed. Patrick Boarman (New York: Praeger, 1974), 115.

64. Taomo Zhou, "Leveraging Liminality: The Border Town of Bao'an (Shenzhen) and the Origins of China's Reform and Opening," *Journal of Asian Studies* 80, no. 2 (May 2021): 348.

65. Bemiss, "China Trip."

66. Rocca Jr., "Report," 115.

67. European businessman cited in William D. Hartley, "Come to the Fair," *Wall Street Journal,* November 2, 1972.

68. Tung Fang Hotel, n.d., folder Composite Briefing Book (2), box 72, RUCBC, Ford Library.

69. "Canton Trade Fair," *China Trade Report,* April 1972, 1.

70. By October 1976 it was a very different story. Following Mao's death, Li worked with Hua Guofeng and others in a political coup that ousted Jiang and her allies and threw them in prison. See MacFarquhar and Schoenhals, *Mao's Last Revolution,* 443–445.

71. Stanley Marcus, "Marcus Polo at China Trade Fair: Adventures of Dallas Executive at Canton," *New York Times,* June 4, 1972.

72. Marcus, "Marcus Polo."

73. Arleen Posner, interview with Veronica Yhap, ca. June 1974, Michael Baker Collection, Stanford University East Asia Library, https://searchworks.stanford.edu/view/wn891 yt2635.

74. Hartley, "Come to the Fair."

75. "Canton Trade Fair."

76. Memorandum from Richard Solomon to Henry Kissinger, June 9, 1972, in *FRUS, 1969–1976*, vol. 17, *China 1969–1972*, 905.

77. Which the National Security Council was all too aware of. See memorandum from Solomon to Kissinger, June 9, 1972. On the reluctance, see the seventh basic principle of the Politburo. The English translation of the eight basic principles can be found in Xia, "China's Elite Politics," 18.

78. John Lewis Gaddis, *Strategies of Containment: A Critical Appraisal of American National Security Policy during the Cold War* (Oxford: Oxford University Press, 2005), 322–323; Barbara Zanchetta, *The Transformation of American International Power in the 1970s* (Cambridge: Cambridge University Press, 2014), 60–85.

79. Gong Li, "Chinese Decision Making and the Thawing of US-China Relations," in *Re-examining the Cold War: U.S.-China Diplomacy, 1954–1973*, ed. Robert S. Ross and Jiang Changbin (Cambridge, MA: Harvard University Press, 2001), 116–120; Evelyn Goh, "Nixon, Kissinger, and the 'Soviet Card' in the US Opening to China, 1971–1974," *Diplomatic History* 29, no. 3 (June 2005): 486; Yang and Xia, "Vacillating between Revolution and Détente," 410.

80. For more on China's drought in the context of the global food crisis of the 1970s, see Bryan L. McDonald, *Food Power: The Rise and Fall of the Postwar American Food System* (Oxford: Oxford University Press, 2017), 162–189.

81. "Nixon Announces China Grain Sale," *Atlanta Constitution,* October 28, 1972.

82. William Robbins, "China Is Reported Buying US Cotton," *New York Times,* January 31, 1973, 5.

83. Margaret MacMillan, *Nixon and Mao: The Week That Changed the World* (New York: Random House, 2007), 17, 3.

84. Hugh Richard Slotten, "Satellite Communication, Globalization, and the Cold War," *Technology and Culture* 43, no. 2 (April 2002): 315–350. On Landsat technology, see Megan Black, "Prospecting the World: Landsat and the Search for Minerals in Space Age Globalization," *Journal of American History* 106, no. 1 (June 2019): 97–120.

85. MacMillan, *Nixon and Mao,* 147.

86. Guolin Yi, *The Media and Sino-American Rapprochement, 1963–1972* (Baton Rouge: Louisiana State University, 2020), 164; Yi, "The 'Propaganda State' and Sino-American Rapprochement: Preparing the Chinese Public for Nixon's Visit," *Journal of American–East Asian Relations* 20 (2013): 5–28.

87. Howard Hawkins, "RCA's Venture in China," in Boarman, *Trade with China,* 134.

88. Liu, "China's Large-Scale Importation."

89. "China Trade and Communications," *RCA Relay,* November–December 1972, 2.

90. Rosenberg, *Financial Missionaries;* see also Emily S. Rosenberg, *Spreading the American Dream: American Economic and Cultural Expansion, 1890–1945* (New York: Hill and Wang, 1982).

91. David Ekbladh, "To Reconstruct the Medieval: Rural Reconstruction in Interwar China and the Rise of an American Style of Modernization, 1921–1961," *Journal of American–East Asian Relations* 9, no. 4 (Winter 2000): 169–196; Ekbladh, "'Mr. TVA': Grass-Roots Development, David Lilienthal, and the Rise and Fall of the Tennessee Valley Authority as a Symbol for U.S. Overseas Development, 1933–1973," *Diplomatic History* 26, no. 3 (2002): 335–374.

92. Westad, *Global Cold War,* 110–157; Amy C. Offner, *Sorting Out the Mixed Economy: The Rise and Fall of Welfare and Developmental States in the Americas* (Princeton, NJ: Princeton University Press, 2019), 175–213; Daniel Immerwahr, *Thinking Small: The United States and the Lure of Community Development* (Cambridge, MA: Harvard University Press, 2015); David C. Engerman, "West Meets East: The Centre for International Studies

and Indian Economic Development," in *Staging Growth: Modernization, Development, and the Global Cold War,* ed. David C. Engerman et al. (Amherst: University of Massachusetts Press, 2003), 199–223. See also Greg Grandin, *Empire's Workshop: Latin America, the United States, and the Rise of the New Imperialism* (New York: Metropolitan Books, 2010); Christy Thornton, *Revolution in Development: Mexico and the Governance of the Global Economy* (Oakland: University of California Press, 2021); Adom Getachew, *Worldmaking after Empire: The Rise and Fall of Self-Determination* (Princeton, NJ: Princeton University Press, 2019).

93. "Employees Honored for China Project," *RCA Relay,* November 1972, p. 6, folder vol. 4, no. 1 (1), box 190, RUCBC, Ford Library.

94. "China Trade and Communications," *RCA Relay,* November–December 1972, p. 5, folder vol. 4, no. 1 (1), box 190, RUCBC, Ford Library.

95. Hawkins, "RCA's Venture in China," 134.

96. Hawkins, "RCA's Venture in China," 137, 138.

97. On the history of Boeing in China, see Neil Thomas, "For Company and for Country: Boeing and US-China Relations," in *China's Economic Arrival: Decoding a Disruptive Rise,* ed. Damien Ma (London: Palgrave Macmillan, 2020), 131–180.

98. Robert J. Serling, *Legend and Legacy: The Story of Boeing and Its People* (London: St. Martin's Press, 1992), 73.

99. Chad J. Mitcham, *China's Economic Relations with the West and Japan, 1949–79* (London: Routledge, 2005), 211.

100. *China Trade Report,* May 1973, 1, 2.

101. *China Trade Report,* May 1974, 6.

102. "Direct Route to Peking," *U.S. China Business Review,* January–February 1975, 58.

103. See, for example, "How Boeing Sold 707's to Peking," *New York Times,* September 18, 1972; Stephen M. Aug, "Others Would Follow Boeing China Deal," *Washington Evening Star,* September 18, 1972; "China Receives First of 10 Boeing Jets," *New York Times,* August 25, 1973.

104. Richard Witkin, "Miller—Boeing's Man in Peking," *New York Times,* September 18, 1972, 37.

105. Jeffrey A. Engel, *Cold War at 30,000 Feet: The Anglo-American Fight for Aviation Supremacy* (Cambridge, MA: Harvard University Press, 2007), 187.

106. Jenifer Van Vleck, *Empire of the Air: Aviation and the American Ascendancy* (Cambridge, MA: Harvard University Press, 2013), 239–240.

107. Mitcham, *China's Economic Relations,* 211.

108. David C. Buxbaum, "American Trade with the People's Republic of China: Some Preliminary Perspectives," *Columbia Journal of Transnational Law* 12, no. 1 (1973): 49–50.

109. Memorandum of conversation between Henry Kissinger and Huang Hua, June 28, 1972, *FRUS, 1969–1976,* vol 17, *China 1969–1972,* 1007.

110. Harry Schwartz, "Nixon Tries Jetliner Diplomacy," *New York Times,* July 9, 1972, E3.

111. Mitcham, *China's Economic Relations,* 211.

112. *China Trade Report,* February 1973, 1.

113. *China Trade Report,* September 1973, 2.

114. *China Trade Report,* June 1973, 7.

115. *China Trade Report,* May 1973, 4.

116. John De Pauw, in his contribution to the advice literature in 1981, analyzed Boeing's sale and concluded that Canton Fairs were often, but not always, the way to start trade deals with China. "In order to negotiate with the Chinese it generally is almost axiomatic that a US company first be invited to Canton or," he added, "Peking." John W. De Pauw, *U.S-Chinese Trade Negotiations* (New York: Praeger, 1981), 56.

117. Wallace Chavkin, "The China Trade: An Unfulfilled Promise," *Columbia Journal of World Business* 8, no. 1 (Spring 1973): 83–85.

118. Chavkin, "The China Trade," 85.

119. Chavkin, "The China Trade," 85.

120. Jeffrey A. Engel, ed., *The China Diary of George H. W. Bush: The Making of a Global President* (Princeton, NJ: Princeton University Press, 2008), 63.

121. Martin F. Klingenberg, "The Canton Trade Fair: The Initiation of United States–Chinese Trade," *Virginia Journal of International Law* 13, no. 1 (1972): 64.

122. Klingenberg, "The Canton Trade Fair," 67, 68, 70.

123. Klingenberg, "The Canton Trade Fair," 70.

124. Marcus, "Marcus Polo."

125. Marcus, "Marcus Polo."

126. Invoice from F. R. Gabbott and Co. to Neiman Marcus, June 27, 1972, folder 24, box 92, Stanley Marcus Collection, DeGolyer Library, Southern Methodist University, Dallas, TX (hereafter Marcus Collection).

127. Lloyd Stewart, "Red China Buys Shown," *Fort Worth Star-Telegram,* September 11, 1972, folder 13, box 156, Marcus Collection.

128. Jeanne Barnes, "Chinese Collection Most Complete Yet," *Dallas Morning News,* September 8, 1972.

129. Barnes, "Chinese Collection."

130. Stewart, "Red China Buys Shown."

131. Julian Sobin interview with Stanley Marcus, folder Julian Sobin interviews with Stanley Marcus, Michel Oksenberg and Dwight Perkins, box 373, RUCBC, Ford Library.

132. Letter from Richard N. Smythe to Stanley Marcus, May 22, 1972, folder 6, box 71, Marcus Collection.

133. Stanley Marcus, *Minding the Store* (Denton: University of North Texas Press, 2001), 260.

134. Gordon H. Chang, *Fateful Ties: A History of America's Preoccupation with China* (Cambridge, MA: Harvard University Press, 2015), 120.

135. Christina Klein, *Cold War Orientalism: Asia in the Middlebrow Imagination, 1945–1961* (Berkeley: University of California Press, 2003); Holly Edwards, *Noble Dreams, Wicked Pleasures: Orientalism in America, 1870–1930* (Princeton, NJ: Princeton University Press, 2000).

136. Marcus, "Marcus Polo."

137. Letter from Stanley Marcus to Gerald Godfrey, May 21, 1973, folder 23, box 92, Marcus Collection.

138. For examples of the "doing business" literature by China traders, see, for example, William W. Whitson, ed., *Doing Business with China: American Trade Opportunities in the 1970s* (New York: Praeger, 1974); US Department of Commerce, *Doing Business with China* (Washington, DC: US Government Printing Office, 1974); Law and Business Inc., *Doing Business with China: Legal, Financial, and Negotiating Aspects* (New York: Harcourt Brace Jovanovich, 1979). It was a phrase that would last; see James McGregor, *One Billion Customers: Lessons from the Front Lines of Doing Business in China* (New York: Free Press, 2005).

139. Some contributions to the advice literature spoke specifically of "businessmen" only. See, by way of example, Boarman, *Trade with China.*

140. Nadine Brozan, "To China and Back—A Shopping Trip Leads to Treasure," *New York Times,* May 18, 1972, 42.

141. Frank, *Buy American: The Untold Story of Economic Nationalism* (Boston: Beacon Press, 1999), 135.

142. "Chinese Goods to Go on Sale at Top New York Store," *South China Morning Post,* May 19, 1972, 24.

143. "The China Trader," *China Business Review,* January–February 1978, 10–11.

144. Julian Sobin, interview with Veronica Yhap, August 13, 1976, folder Other Publications: Interview with Gerry Wielenga and Veronica Yhap, box 373, RUCBC, Ford Library.

145. Posner, interview with Yhap.

3. The Changing Meanings of the China Market

1. Leslie Gelb, "Surging Trade with China," *New York Times,* December 2, 1973.

2. "Big Chinese Order for US Cotton Spurs Trade Prospects," *Chicago Tribune,* February 5, 1973; "China Purchases Tobacco from the U.S.," *New York Times,* July 17, 1973; "China Receives First of 10 Boeing Jets," *New York Times,* August 25, 1973.

3. Hale Boggs and Gerald R. Ford, "Impressions of the New China: Joint Report to the United States House of Representatives," House Document no. 92-337, August 3, 1972, 8.

4. Victor H. Li, "Ups and Downs of Trade with China," *Columbia Journal of Transnational Law* 13, no. 3 (1974): 371.

5. Arthur Doak Barnett, *China's Economy in Global Perspective* (Washington, DC: Brookings Institution, 1981), 507.

6. Stephen M. Aug, "Others Would Follow Boeing China Deal," *Washington Evening Star,* September 18, 1972.

7. "Big Chinese Order for US Cotton."

8. "China Purchases Tobacco from the U.S."

9. 119 Cong. Rec. 14341 (daily ed., May 3, 1973) (statement of John R. Rarick).

10. On the China market at the turn of the twentieth century and midcentury debates about its relationship to US imperial expansion, see especially Thomas J. McCormick, *China Market: America's Quest for Informal Empire, 1893–1901* (Chicago: Quadrangle Books, 1967); Walter LaFeber, *The New Empire: An Interpretation of American Expansion, 1860–1898* (Ithaca, NY: Cornell University Press, 1974); Marilyn B. Young, *The Rhetoric of Empire: American China Policy, 1895–1901* (Cambridge, MA: Harvard University Press, 1968); William Appleman Williams, *The Tragedy of American Diplomacy* (New York: Dell, 1959); Paul A. Varg, *The Making of a Myth: The United States and China, 1897–1912* (Westport, CT: Greenwood Press, 1980).

11. Chad J. Mitcham, *China's Economic Relations with the West and Japan, 1949–79* (London: Routledge, 2005), 213.

12. Letter from Christopher Phillips to James Petrie, September 27, 1973, folder Pullman Kellogg (1), box 219, RUCBC, Ford Library.

13. "Chinese Technical Commercial Mission Returns to PRC after Long U.S. Tour," *For Your Information,* February 1974, p. 1, folder Pullman Kellogg (1), box 219, RUCBC, Ford Library.

14. "Chinese Technical Commercial Mission Returns," 8.

15. Mae Ngai, *The Lucky Ones: One Family and the Extraordinary Invention of Chinese America* (Princeton, NJ: Princeton University Press, 2012); Ngai, "'A Slight Knowledge of the Barbarian Language': Chinese Interpreters in Late-Nineteenth- and Early-Twentieth-Century America," *Journal of American Ethnic History* 30, no. 2 (2011): 5–32.

16. Lawrence C. Reardon, *The Reluctant Dragon: Crisis Cycles in Chinese Foreign Economic Policy* (Seattle: University of Washington Press, 2002), 158–159; Hou Li, *Building for Oil: Daqing and the Formation of the Chinese Socialist State* (Cambridge, MA: Harvard

University Asia Center, 2018), 171; Jason M. Kelly, *Market Maoists: The Communist Origins of China's Capitalist Ascent* (Cambridge, MA: Harvard University Press, 2021), 196–201.

17. Cited in Min Song, "A Dissonance in Mao's Revolution: Chinese Agricultural Imports from the United States, 1972–1978," *Diplomatic History* 38, no. 2 (2014): 423.

18. Alexander Eckstein, "China's Trade Policy and Sino-American Relations," *Foreign Affairs* 54 (October 1975): 140. Eckstein's data is based on that from the *U.S. China Business Review,* which in turn is based on US Department of Commerce data and statistics from other non-PRC trade organizations in the United Kingdom and Japan.

19. Cited in Reardon, *Reluctant Dragon,* 157.

20. Reardon, *Reluctant Dragon,* 159.

21. Chen Yun, "利用国内丰富劳动力 生产成品出口" [Use abundant labor force to produce products for export], October 12, 1973, in 陈云文选第三卷 [Collected works of Chen Yun] (Beijing: Renmin Chubanshe, 1995), 223.

22. By 1984, however, the elderly Chen's influence was increasingly overshadowed by that of Zhao Ziyang, who held more reformist economic ideas. See especially Julian Gewirtz, *Unlikely Partners: Chinese Reformers, Western Economists, and the Making of Global China* (Cambridge, MA: Harvard University Press, 2017), 125–126, 191–192.

23. William H. Miller, "What Can You Expect in China?," *Industry Week,* July 16, 1973, 27–36.

24. Miller, "What Can You Expect in China?," 36.

25. Miller, "What Can You Expect in China?," 36.

26. "Expanded China Trade Is Aim of Business Mission to Peking," *Industry Week,* October 15, 1973, 26–33.

27. Clark T. Randt, "Kwangchow Diary: The Fall 1974 Kwangchow Fair . . . Week by Week," *U.S. China Business Review,* November–December 1974.

28. Marilyn Bender, "Browsing for Goods from the Land of Mao: American Shoppers' Response Is Mixed," *New York Times,* May 27, 1973.

29. Ian Stewart, "Aims Diverge at Canton Trade Fair," *New York Times,* October 31, 1973.

30. Shirley MacLaine, *You Can Get There from Here* (New York: W. W. Norton, 1975), 138.

31. "How to Initiate Business with China Part 1," folder importer committee, steering committee chron file 3, box 54, RUCBC, Ford Library.

32. Telegraph from American Consulate Hong Kong to Department of State Washington, February 20, 1974, http://www.wikileaks.org/plusd/cables/1974HONGK01871_b.html.

33. Chen, "利用国内丰富劳动力 生产成品出口," 223. See also Song, "A Dissonance in Mao's Revolution."

34. Memorandum from Under Secretary Lynn to Henry Kissinger, "Creation of Sino-American Trade Council," June 8, 1972, folder NCUSCT Formation of Council (1), box 37, RUCBC, Ford Library.

35. On the National Council for US-China Trade, see especially Christian Talley, *Forgotten Vanguard: Informal Diplomacy and the Rise of United States–China Trade, 1972–1980* (Notre Dame, IN: University of Notre Dame Press, 2018); on the National Council's relationship with the CCPIT, see esp. 60–61.

36. American Embassy Taipei to USIA, "Text of Secretary Dent's Remarks," Telegram 4421, July 23, 1973, Central Foreign Policy Files, 1973–1979 / Electronic Telegrams, RG 59: General Records of the Department of State, National Archives and Records Administration, College Park, MD (hereafter NARA).

37. "Visit by US Aide Concerns Taiwan," *New York Times,* July 23, 1973.

38. Cited in "Visit by US Aide Concerns Taiwan."

39. Nancy Bernkopf Tucker, "Taiwan Expendable? Nixon and Kissinger Go to China," *Journal of American History* 92, no. 1 (June 2005): 134.

40. Joseph Egelhof, "Rockefeller to Head Trade Delegation to China," *Chicago Tribune,* June 1, 1973, C13.

41. David Rockefeller, *Memoirs* (New York: Random House Trade Paperbacks, 2003), 250.

42. Emily S. Rosenberg, *Financial Missionaries to the World: The Politics and Culture of Dollar Diplomacy, 1900–1930* (Cambridge, MA: Harvard University Press, 1999).

43. Chin Yuen Chen, "U.S.-China Trade Prospects," *Columbia Journal of World Business,* Fall 1974, 80.

44. *Sino-British Trade,* April 1973, 2–3, and May 1973, 6–7.

45. Rockefeller, *Memoirs,* 253.

46. For more on Chase's expansion abroad, especially in Cuba in the 1920s, see Peter James Hudson, *Bankers and Empire: How Wall Street Colonized the Caribbean* (Chicago: University of Chicago Press, 2017), 222–226.

47. Speech by Carlos Cassineri, February 20, 1975, folder Textiles Presentations (1), box 60, RUCBC, Ford Library.

48. Richard T. Devane, "The United States and China: Claims and Assets," *Asian Survey* 18, no. 12 (December 1978): 1267.

49. Harry Harding, *A Fragile Relationship: The United States and China since 1972* (Washington, DC: Brookings Institution, 1992), 58.

50. *China Trade Report,* July 1973, 8.

51. William Burr, "'Casting a Shadow' over Trade: The Problem of Private Claims and Blocked Assets in US-China Relations," *Diplomatic History* 33, no. 2 (April 2009): 338.

52. David Rockefeller, "From a China Traveler," *New York Times,* August 10, 1973.

53. David Rockefeller, "Business Must Perform Better," *Wall Street Journal,* December 21, 1971.

54. David Rockefeller, "The Essential Quest for the Middle Way," *New York Times,* March 23, 1973.

55. Kim Phillips-Fein, *Fear City: New York's Fiscal Crisis and the Rise of Austerity Politics* (New York: Metropolitan Books, 2017), 77–78.

56. "Taiwan Pushing Goods of US," *New York Times,* April 6, 1974.

57. Tucker, "Taiwan Expendable?," 109–135.

58. "'Buy American' Not a Mere Slogan," *Los Angeles Times,* October 6, 1974.

59. "'Buy American' Not a Mere Slogan," 10.

60. M. T. Wu, "Investment and Trade Climate in the Republic of China," *International Trade Law Journal* 3 (1977): 29.

61. "'Buy American' Not a Mere Slogan."

62. Isandore Barmash, "Taiwan Rates US High in Consumer Goods," *New York Times,* February 26, 1974.

63. On the history of RCA in this period, see Jefferson Cowie, *Capital Moves: RCA's Seventy-Year Quest for Cheap Labor* (Ithaca, NY: Cornell University Press, 1999).

64. "Taiwan Pushing Goods of US."

65. "'Buy American' Not a Mere Slogan."

66. Wu, "Investment and Trade Climate," 29.

67. "Taiwan Pushing Goods of US."

68. Display ad 31, *New York Times,* July 9, 1973.

69. "Taiwan Pushing Goods of US."

70. "'Buy American' Not a Mere Slogan."

71. Display ad 31.

72. Harry Harding, "From China, with Disdain: New Trends in the Study of China," in *America Views China: American Images of China Then and Now,* ed. Jonathan Goldstein, Jerry Israel, and Hilary Conroy (London: Associated University Presses, 1991), 245.

73. "'Made in China' Is Popular," *Chicago Tribune,* January 6, 1973, A7.

74. John O'Connor, "Whose China Is Nearer the Truth?," *New York Times,* January 28, 1973, 125.

75. Frederick Teiwes and Warren Sun, *The End of the Maoist Era: Chinese Politics during the Twilight of the Cultural Revolution, 1972–1976* (Armonk, NY: M. E. Sharpe, 2007), 161.

76. "恶毒的用心卑劣的手法—批判安东尼奥尼拍摄的题为《中国》的反华影" [The vicious, inferior approach—Criticizing the anti-Chinese film entitled "China" by Antonioni], *RMRB,* January 30, 1974.

77. Bender, "Browsing for Goods."

78. Bender, "Browsing for Goods."

79. On Paramus in twentieth-century US consumer culture, see Lizabeth Cohen, *A Consumers' Republic: The Politics of Mass Consumption in Postwar America* (New York: Alfred A. Knopf, 2003), 259–289.

80. Bender, "Browsing for Goods."

81. Bender, "Browsing for Goods."

82. Display ad 96, *New York Times,* February 24, 1974.

83. See Peter Cole, *Dockworker Power: Race and Activism in Durban and the San Francisco Bay Area* (Champaign: University of Illinois Press, 2018), 156–160.

84. Robert W. Cherny, *Harry Bridges: Labor Leader, Labor Radical* (Champaign: University of Illinois Press, 2023); Robert W. Cherny, "Constructing a Radical Identity: History, Memory, and the Seafaring Stories of Harry Bridges," *Pacific Historical Review* 70, no. 4 (November 2001): 572; Howard Kimeldorf, *Reds or Rackets? The Making of Radical and Conservative Unions on the Waterfront* (Berkeley: University of California Press, 1988), 6. Bridges had also been instrumental in the 1934 maritime strike from Bellingham, Washington, to San Diego, California.

85. "Chinese Journalists Meet San Francisco Workmen," *New York Times,* June 12, 1973.

86. Letter from Harry Bridges to Huang Chen, July 9, 1973, folder California (1), box 27, RUCBC, Ford Library.

87. Letter from Harry Bridges to Huang Chen, July 9, 1973.

88. Letter from Charles Velson to Huang Chen, September 5, 1973, and telegram from Charles Velson to Lt. Zhongzu, n.d. (circa September 1973), both in folder California (1), box 27, RUCBC, Ford Library.

89. "Big Chinese Order for US Cotton"; William Robbins, "China Is Reported Buying US Cotton," *New York Times,* January 31, 1973, 5.

90. "A Peek at Potential of China Trade," *The Dispatcher,* December 21, 1973.

91. Elizabeth J. Perry and Li Xun, *Proletarian Power: Shanghai in the Cultural Revolution* (New York: Westview Press, 1997), 114–116.

92. Alan P. L. Liu, *Mass Politics in the People's Republic: State and Society in Contemporary China* (Boulder, CO: Westview Press, 1996), 101.

93. *China Trade Report,* February 1974, 11.

94. Cited in Jackie Sheehan, *Chinese Workers: A New History* (London: Routledge, 1998), 145.

95. Lee Bastajian, "Harbor Merger, Red China Trade Predicted," *Los Angeles Times,* February 8, 1970.

96. Letter from Christopher Phillips to James C. Kellogg III, June 26, 1974, and letter from Miriam E. Wolff to Christopher Phillips, July 25, 1974, both in folder California (1), box 27, RUCBC, Ford Library.

97. "United States," *China Trade Report*, February 1972, 5.

98. The AFL had expelled the organization in 1953 amid allegations of ILA corruption and gangsterism but readmitted it in 1959.

99. Marc Levinson, *The Box: How the Shipping Container Made the World Smaller and the World Economy Bigger* (Princeton, NJ: Princeton University Press, 2016), 135–169.

100. "Economic and Trade Relations," Briefing paper, October 1973, US Department of State, document 00269, Digital National Security Archive.

101. Memorandum from Nicholas Ludlow to Christopher H. Phillips, Eugene A. Theroux, and Kurt Reinsberg, October 12, 1973, folder importer committees steering committee chron file 1, box 54, RUCBC, Ford Library.

102. Julian Sobin, interview with Bob Boulogne, August 13, 1977, folder China Trader Bob Boulogne, box 373, RUCBC, Ford Library.

103. Memorandum from Ludlow to Phillips, Theroux, and Reinsberg.

104. Letter from Kurt E. Reinsberg to Christopher H. Phillips, October 11, 1973, folder importer committees steering committee chron file 1, box 54, RUCBC, Ford Library.

105. Julian Sobin interview with Bob Boulogne, folder The China Trader—Julian Sobin interviews with Murray Berger and Bob Boulogne, box 373, RUCBC, Ford Library.

106. Memorandum from Christopher Phillips to delegation members, October 23, 1973, folder NCUSCT Delegation to China, 1973, box 36, RUCBC, Ford Library.

107. Talley, *Forgotten Vanguard*, 67.

108. Remarks by Wang Yao-ting, November 7, 1973, folder Delegation to China 11/73—Trip Report, box 36, RUCBC, Ford Library.

109. Robert S. Ross, *Negotiating Cooperation: The United States and China, 1969–1989* (Stanford, CA: Stanford University Press, 1995), 151.

110. Summary of National Council Meeting with CCPIT, November 7, 1973, folder NCUSCT Delegation to China, 1973, box 36, RUCBC, Ford Library.

111. World Affairs Council of Pittsburgh newsletter, December 1973, folder Staff File Theroux, box 53, RUCBC, Ford Library.

112. "Importers Committee Formed," *U.S. China Business Review,* February 1974, 11.

113. Memorandum from Kurt E. Reinsberg to Board of Directors, June 3, 1974, folder Steering Committee Delegation to China, 1977, Background, box 55, RUCBC, Ford Library.

4. The Limits of the China Market

1. Michael Franczak, *Global Inequality and American Foreign Policy in the 1970s* (Ithaca, NY: Cornell University Press, 2022); Adom Getachew, *Worldmaking after Empire: The Rise and Fall of Self-Determination* (Princeton, NJ: Princeton University Press, 2019), 142–175; Quinn Slobodian, *Globalists: The End of Empire and the Birth of Neoliberalism* (Cambridge, MA: Harvard University Press, 2018), 218–262; Vanessa Ogle, "State Rights against Private Capital: The 'New International Economic Order' and the Struggle over Aid, Trade, and Foreign Investment, 1962–1981," *Humanity: An International Journal of Human Rights, Humanitarianism, and Development* 5, no. 2 (Summer 2014): 211–234; Odd Arne Westad, *The Global Cold War: Third World Interventions and the Making of Our Times* (Cambridge: Cambridge University Press, 2005), 154–155.

2. China's role in the NIEO is yet to become the subject of sustained historical research. One contemporaneous account provides a good starting point: Samuel S. Kim, *China, the*

United Nations and World Order (Princeton, NJ: Princeton University Press, 1979), 242–333. I would like to thank Neil Thomas for wide-ranging conversation on this topic.

3. Speech by chairman of the delegation of the People's Republic of China, Deng Xiaoping, at the special session of the UN General Assembly, April 10, 1974, in Barbara Barnouin and Changgen Yu, *Chinese Foreign Policy during the Cultural Revolution* (New York: Routledge, 1998), 214–226.

4. Chen Jian, "China, the Third World, and the Cold War," in *The Cold War in the Third World,* ed. Robert J. McMahon (Oxford: Oxford University Press, 2013), 85–100; Jennifer Althenger, "Social Imperialism and Mao's Three Worlds: Deng Xiaoping's Speech at the UN General Assembly, 1974," in *Revolutionary Moments: Reading Revolutionary Texts,* ed. Rachel Hammersley (London: Bloomsbury Academic, 2015), 176–177; Sara Lorenzini, *Global Development: A Cold War History* (Princeton, NJ: Princeton University Press, 2019), 113–116.

5. Ezra F. Vogel, *Deng Xiaoping and the Transformation of China* (Cambridge, MA: Belknap Press of Harvard University Press, 2011), 83.

6. The alliance with the United States against the Soviet Union had been Mao's "horizontal line theory." With the Three Worlds Theory, Mao opposed both superpowers. Kuisong Yang and Yafeng Xia, "Vacillating between Revolution and Détente: Mao's Changing Psyche and Policy toward the United States, 1969–1976," *Diplomatic History* 34, no. 2 (April 2010): 395–423.

7. Chen, "China, the Third World," 86.

8. Chen, "China, the Third World"; Althenger, "Social Imperialism"; Yang and Xia, "Vacillating between Revolution and Détente."

9. Robeson Taj Frazier, *The East Is Black: Cold War China in the Black Radical Imagination* (Durham, NC: Duke University Press, 2015), 204–207; Jeremy Friedman, *Shadow Cold War: The Sino-Soviet Competition for the Third World* (Chapel Hill: University of North Carolina Press, 2015).

10. Speech by chairman of the delegation of the People's Republic of China, Deng Xiaoping, at the special session of the UN General Assembly, April 10, 1974, in Barnouin and Changgen, *Chinese Foreign Policy,* 214–226.

11. Christy Thornton, *Revolution in Development: Mexico and the Governance of the Global Economy* (Oakland: University of California Press, 2021); Christopher R. W. Dietrich, *Oil Revolution: Anticolonial Elites, Sovereign Rights, and the Economic Culture of Decolonization* (Cambridge: Cambridge University Press, 2017), 277.

12. Natasha Zaretsky, *No Direction Home: The American Family and the Fear of National Decline, 1968–1980* (Chapel Hill: University of North Carolina Press, 2007), 71–104; Meg Jacobs, *Panic at the Pump: The Energy Crisis and the Transformation of American Politics in the 1970s* (New York: Hill and Wang, 2016).

13. Lawrence C. Reardon, *The Reluctant Dragon: Crisis Cycles in Chinese Foreign Economic Policy* (Seattle: University of Washington Press, 2002), 160.

14. Alexander Eckstein, "China's Trade Policy and Sino-American Relations," *Foreign Affairs* 54 (October 1975): 141. On US-China oil diplomacy in this period, see Kazushi Minami, "Oil for the Lamps of America? Sino-American Oil Diplomacy, 1973–1979," *Diplomatic History* 41, no. 5 (2017): 959–984.

15. Reardon, *The Reluctant Dragon,* 160.

16. Cited in Reardon, *The Reluctant Dragon,* 160.

17. 坚持独立支柱自力更生的方针 [Adhere to the policy of independence and self-reliance], *RMRB,* March 22, 1974.

18. Cited in Minami, "Oil for the Lamps of America?," 968.

19. Hou Li, *Building for Oil: Daqing and the Formation of the Chinese Socialist State* (Cambridge, MA: Harvard University Asia Center, 2018), 168.

20. Arthur Doak Barnett, *China's Economy in Global Perspective* (Washington, DC: Brookings Institution, 1981), 442.

21. Eckstein, "China's Trade Policy," 147.

22. Cited in Li, *Building for Oil,* 174–175.

23. Nicholas H. Ludlow, "China's Oil," *U.S. China Business Review,* January–February 1974, 21.

24. William H. Miller, "Where Is U.S.-China Trade Headed?," *Industry Week,* April 29, 1974, 36.

25. Harned Hoose, "China's Resources Loom Large on World Stage," *Los Angeles Times,* October 13, 1974.

26. Selig S. Harrison, "Time Bomb in East Asia," *Foreign Policy,* no. 20 (Autumn 1975): 4.

27. Memorandum from "BEO" to "Member firm," November 15, 1974, folder International Corporation of America, box 216, RUCBC, Ford Library.

28. "制造恐慌气氛 哄抬油价 攫取暴利 美国石油垄断资本借能源《危机》大发横财" [Create an atmosphere of panic, drive up oil prices and grab huge profits. American oil monopoly capital makes a fortune through the "energy crisis"], *RMRB,* February 10, 1974.

29. In a handful of cases, sales from Japanese and French firms relied on US technology. In December 1972, for example, Lummus Co., a subsidiary of US-based Combustion Engineering Co., supplied an ethylene plant in a $46 million deal. Due to the sensitive technology involved, the deal required US Department of Commerce approval. See Hans Heymann Jr., "China's Approach to Technology Acquisition: Part III—Summary Observations," R-1575-ARRA, Rand Corporation, February 1975, 57–66. See also Yoichi Yokoi, "Plant and Technology Contracts and the Changing Pattern of Economic Interdependence between China and Japan," *China Quarterly,* no. 124 (December 1990): 694–713.

30. James Mann, *About Face: A History of America's Curious Relationship with China, from Nixon to Clinton* (New York: Vintage Books, 2000), 65–66.

31. Cited in Vogel, *Deng Xiaoping,* 76.

32. Leslie Gelb, "Trade with China Surges Ahead of US-Soviet Level," *New York Times,* June 4, 1974; "U.S. Trade with China Is Expected to Exceed $1 Billion This Year," *Wall Street Journal,* June 4, 1974.

33. "Leading Exports and Imports in Sino-U.S. Trade 1974," *U.S. China Business Review,* March 1975, 19.

34. In 1956 China's Ministry of Foreign Trade began publishing *Foreign Trade of the People's Republic of China,* which it abandoned in 1964. Coming a decade later, *China's Foreign Trade* built on these earlier efforts. On the earlier magazine, see Jason Kelly, *Market Maoists* (Cambridge, MA: Harvard University Press, 2021), 119–123; Jason Kelly, "Selling 'New' China: Marketing and the Unmaking of a Semi-colonial State," *Journal of Contemporary History* 57, no. 3 (2022): 715–716.

35. Li Chiang, "New Developments in China's Foreign Trade," *China's Foreign Trade,* no. 1 (1974): 2–5.

36. Li, "New Developments in China's Foreign Trade," 2–5.

37. Jackie Sheehan, *Chinese Workers: A New History* (London: Routledge, 1998), 13–155; Mark W. Frazier, *The Making of the Chinese Industrial Workplace: State, Revolution, and Labor Management* (Cambridge: Cambridge University Press, 2002); Covell Meyskens, "Labour," in *Afterlives of Chinese Communism,* ed. Christian Sorace et al. (New York: Verso, 2019), 103–109.

38. Eugene Theroux, "Canton's Trade Fair Opens amid Fanfare," *Washington Post,* April 16, 1974.

39. "流花湖畔尽朝晖" [Morning sunlight on the shore of Liuhua Lake], *RMRB,* May 6, 1974.

40. "The Spring 1974 Canton Fair," *U.S. China Business Review,* May–June 1974, 43.

41. "Pricing and Prices at the Spring 1974 Canton Fair," *U.S. China Business Review,* July–August 1974, 45–46.

42. Lin Liming cited in "一九七四年春季中国出口商品交易会胜利闭幕" [Successful end to 1974 spring Chinese Export Commodities Fair], *RMRB,* May 16, 1974.

43. Donald Kirk, "'Third World' Nations Favored at China's Spring Trade Fair," *Chicago Tribune,* May 18, 1974.

44. Kirk, "'Third World' Nations Favored."

45. Kirk, "'Third World' Nations Favored."

46. *China Trade Report,* March 1973, 9.

47. Letter from Curtin Anderson to Russell Long, cited in "Letters to Washington," *AmChamHK,* September 1974, 31.

48. Cited in Sarah B. Snyder, *From Selma to Moscow: How Human Rights Activists Transformed U.S. Foreign Policy* (New York: Columbia University Press, 2018), 38.

49. For more on the Jackson-Vanik amendment, see Snyder, *From Selma to Moscow,* 34–38.

50. Burr, "'Casting a Shadow' over Trade: The Problem of Private Claims and Blocked Assets in US-China Relations," *Diplomatic History* 33, no. 2 (April 2009): 340.

51. Cited in Burr, "'Casting a Shadow,'" 342.

52. "Tom Hseih's Blueprint to Improve S.F.," *San Francisco Examiner,* January 27, 1974, folder 2, box 12, Pardee Lowe Collection, Hoover Institution.

53. "Spring 1974 Canton Fair," 43.

54. Memorandum from Nick Ludlow to Christopher Phillips and Eugene Theroux, September 10, 1974, Steering Committee chronological files (4), box 54, RUCBC, Ford Library.

55. Memorandum from Ludlow to Phillips and Theroux, September 10, 1974.

56. Letter from Christopher Phillips to Wang Yao-ting, April 10, 1974, folder CCPIT Correspondence (2), box 31, RUCBC, Ford Library.

57. For one example, see letter from Christopher Phillips to Kurt Leutwyler, February 25, 1974, folder Baker Trading Co., box 214, RUCBC, Ford Library.

58. "Council Delegation in Peking: The Exchanges Begin," *U.S. China Business Review,* January–February 1974, 3.

59. Memorandum from Nick Ludlow to Christopher Phillips, May 13, 1974, folder Inter-Office Memoranda (1), box 38, RUCBC, Ford Library.

60. Letter from John Hanley to Christopher Phillips, September 16, 1974, folder Monsanto, box 218, RUCBC, Ford Library.

61. "How to Start Imports from China," *U.S. China Business Review,* January–February 1974, 7–10.

62. Stanley B. Lubman and Judith Lubman, "An Importers Introduction to the Canton Fair," *U.S. China Business Review,* January–February 1974, 33–34.

63. "China's Export Corporations," *U.S. China Business Review,* January–February 1974, 8; "The National Council's Importer's Committee," *U.S. China Business Review,* January–February 1974, 11.

64. "How to Start Exports to China," *U.S. China Business Review,* July–August 1974, 3–10.

65. Meeting with Chang Tisen Hua, Wang Tien Ming, and Christopher Phillips, September 19, 1974, folder PRCLO Meetings, box 41, RUCBC, Ford Library.

66. Memorandum from Nicholas Ludlow to Christopher Phillips, September 24, 1974, folder American Importers Association, box 22, RUCBC, Ford Library.

67. Richard Halloran, "China Plays Host to U.S. Importers," *New York Times,* October 20, 1974.

68. Letter from Gerald O'Brien to AIA members, November 11, 1974, folder American Importers Association, box 22, RUCBC, Ford Library.

69. Memorandum from Nicholas Ludlow to Christopher Phillips, Eugene Theroux, and George Driscoll, November 22, 1974, folder American Importers Association, box 22, RUCBC, Ford Library.

70. Notes from meeting between National Council for US-China Trade and Chinese Liaison Office, January 3, 1975, folder PRCLO Meetings, box 41, Ford Library.

71. Bryan L. McDonald, *Food Power: The Rise and Fall of the Postwar American Food System* (Oxford: Oxford University Press, 2017), 173.

72. *China Spotlight,* June 1974, 2.

73. "1974 Trade by US with China Set Peak," *New York Times,* January 30, 1975, 64.

74. Reardon, *The Reluctant Dragon,* 169.

75. Li Xiannian, "认真做好进口粮食的检疫工作" [Conscientiously do a good job in quarantining imported grains], February 19, 1974, in 李先念论财政金融贸易 [Li Xiannian on finance and trade], 1950–1991, vol. 2 (Beijing: Zhongguo Caizheng Jingji Chubanshe, 2010), 286.

76. Min Song, "A Dissonance in Mao's Revolution: Chinese Agricultural Imports from the United States, 1972–1978," *Diplomatic History* 38, no. 2 (2014): 425.

77. Telegram from George Bush to Brent Scowcroft, November 20, 1974, "Subject: US-PRC Trade Relations," folder PRC Unnumbered Items (6), box 4, National Security Advisor Kissinger–Scowcroft West Wing Office Records, Ford Library.

78. Telegram from US Liaison Office to Secretary of State, January 1975, "Subject: Problems and Prospects in Sino-US Trade," folder PRC-Trade-General (1), box 10, National Security Advisor NSC East Asian and Pacific Affairs Staff Collection, Country Files (1969) 1973–1976, Ford Library.

79. Xiayang Ding, "Diplomacy vs. Economics: Examining the Roots of Decline in Sino-US Trade in 1975," *Journal of American–East Asian Relations* 28, no. 2 (June 2021): 148.

80. Song, "A Dissonance in Mao's Revolution," 424–426; Ding, "Diplomacy vs. Economics," 141–145.

81. The combined value of these agricultural sales was $655.8 million, therefore constituting 70 percent of the total trade, which stood at $933.8 million.

82. Gelb, "Trade with China Surges."

83. Richard Goodman, "The PRC Is Still a Good Potential Market for Farm Exports," *Foreign Agriculture,* March 31, 1975, 2–5.

84. *Sino-British Trade Review,* May 1975, 2.

85. Eckstein, "China's Trade Policy," 135.

86. Li, *Building for Oil,* 2018.

87. Song, "A Dissonance in Mao's Revolution," 425.

88. Cited in Frederick Teiwes and Warren Sun, *The End of the Maoist Era: Chinese Politics during the Twilight of the Cultural Revolution, 1972–1976* (Armonk, NY: M. E. Sharpe, 2007), 506.

89. "Sales," *U.S. China Business Review,* January 1976, 42.

90. Telegram from US Liaison Office to Secretary of State, January 1975, folder Country file PRC Trade General (1), box 10, NSC East Asian and Pacific Affairs Staff Files (1969), Ford Library.

91. Benjamin Waterhouse, *The Land of Enterprise: A Business History of the United States* (New York: Simon and Schuster, 2017), 180.

92. Douglas A. Irwin, *Clashing over Commerce: A History of U.S. Trade Policy* (Chicago: University of Chicago Press, 2017); Alfred E. Eckes Jr., "U.S. Trade History," in *U.S. Trade Policy: History, Theory, and the WTO,* ed. William A. Lovett, Richard L. Brinkman, and A. E. Eckes Jr. (Armonk, NY: M. E. Sharpe, 2004), 68–69.

93. David Farber, "The Torch Had Fallen," in *America in the Seventies,* ed. Beth Bailey and David Farber (Lawrence: University Press of Kansas, 2004), 9–28.

94. Nitsan Chorev, *Remaking US Trade Policy: From Protectionism to Globalization* (Ithaca, NY: Cornell University Press, 2007), 102.

95. Leo Panitch and Sam Gindin, *The Making of Global Capitalism: The Political Economy of American Empire* (London: Verso, 2012), 224–225.

96. Judith Stein, *Pivotal Decade: How the United States Traded Factories for Finance in the 1970s* (New Haven, CT: Yale University Press, 2010), 96. See also Eckes, "U.S. Trade History," 69.

97. Benjamin Waterhouse, *Lobbying America: The Politics of Business from Nixon to NAFTA* (Princeton, NJ: Princeton University Press, 2013), 100. See also Jennifer A. Delton, *The Industrialists: How the National Association of Manufacturers Shaped American Capitalism* (Princeton, NJ: Princeton University Press, 2020).

98. J. C. Penney Company, "The Company Plan, 1973–1978," box 423, J. C. Penney Company Records, DeGolyer Library, Southern Methodist University, Dallas, TX (hereafter J. C. Penney Records).

99. J. C. Penney Company, "The Company Plan, 1973–1978."

100. "Buying Trip Builds Trade with China," *Penney News,* June 1974, 3, J. C. Penney Records.

101. "Buying Trip Builds Trade with China."

102. "Buying Trip Builds Trade with China."

103. In textiles and clothing, Penney's sold far more than its major competitor, Sears.

104. Julian Sobin, interview with Bob Boulogne, ca. 1975, folder The China Trader, box 373, RUCBC, Ford Library.

105. "Penney Visits Canton Trade Fair," *Penney News,* February 1974, J. C. Penney Records.

106. Ellen Israel Rosen, *Making Sweatshops: The Globalization of the U.S. Apparel Industry* (Berkeley: University of California Press, 2002).

107. Sobin, interview with Boulogne.

108. Sobin, interview with Boulogne.

109. Sobin, interview with Boulogne.

110. Letter from John A. Banning to Eugene A. Theroux, September 26, 1973, folder Ford, box 215, RUCBC, Ford Library.

111. Donald Shapiro, "Taiwan Sees U.S. Keeping Some Tie," *New York Times,* May 21, 1973.

112. Handwritten note by Christopher Phillips, January 15, 1974, folder Ford Motors, box 215, RUCBC, Ford Library.

113. Commodities Required for Direct Use in General Motors Production Facilities, folder General Motors (1), box 215, RUCBC, Ford Library.

114. Letter from Richard Kerwath to Huang Wen-chun, September 26, 1974, folder General Motors (1), box 215, RUCBC, Ford Library.

115. Michael J. Dunne, *American Wheels, Chinese Roads: The Story of General Motors in China* (Singapore: John Wiley and Sons, 2011).

116. Letter from L. F. Dumont to Eugene Theroux, January 25, 1974, folder Du Pont, box 214, Ford Library.

117. Kraus, "More than Just a Soft Drink: Coca-Cola and China's Early Reform and Opening," *Diplomatic History* 43, no. 1 (January 2019): 115.

118. Kraus, "More than Just a Soft Drink," 127–128.

119. Letters from Nicholas DiOrio to Eugene Theroux, October 15, 1973, and October 22, 1973, and letter from Eugene Theroux to Nicholas DiOrio, October 30, 1973, all in folder RCA (1), box 219, RUCBC, Ford Library.

120. On the Canton Fairs, see letter from W. L. Newell to Christopher Phillips, January 23, 1974, folder RCA (1), box 219, RUCBC, Ford Library. On Banquet Foods, see memorandum from Christopher Phillips to files, August 6, 1975, folder RCA (2), box 219, RUCBC, Ford Library.

121. Report, "Delegation of the China Native Produce and Animal By-Products Import and Export Corporation," September 29–November 9, 1975, folder Importer Services, box 61, RUCBC, Ford Library.

122. Julian Sobin, interview with David Cookson, ca. 1976, folder Cookson, box 373, RUCBC, Ford Library.

123. Delton, *The Industrialists,* 254–255; Stein, *Pivotal Decade,* 49–50; James C. Benton, *Fraying Fabric: How Trade Policy and Industrial Decline Transformed America* (Urbana: University of Illinois Press, 2022), 171–214.

124. Chorev, *Remaking US Trade Policy,* 67.

125. Stein, *Pivotal Decade,* 96; See also Eckes, "U.S. Trade History," 69.

126. *Trade Reform Act, Report of the Committee on Finance, H.R. 10710, November 1974* (Washington: US Government Printing Office, 1974), 219.

127. Stein, *Pivotal Decade.*

128. Valeria Zanier and Roberto Peruzzi, "1967 as the Turning Point in Hong Kong–British–PRC Economic Relations," in *China, Hong Kong, and the Long 1970s: Global Perspectives,* ed. Priscilla Roberts and Odd Arne Westad (Cham, Switzerland: Palgrave Macmillan, 2017), 235.

129. For more on Hong Kong's vital role in China's economic transformation, see Peter Hamilton, *Made in Hong Kong: Transpacific Networks and a New History of Globalization* (New York: Columbia University Press, 2021), 193–247.

130. "Hongkong: In Second Place," *China Trade Report,* May 1975, 10.

131. Minette Marrin, "China Industry Spotlight: Textiles," *China Trade Report,* September 1976, 4.

132. "Lower Prices Appear at Canton Trade Fair," *Industry Week,* November 4, 1974, 22.

133. Letter from Nicholas Ludlow to all staff, January 2, 1975, folder Tung Fang Club, box 176, RUCBC, Ford Library.

134. In pinyin: *ganbei,* literally "dry glass," a common toast in China.

5. Selling Chinese Textiles

1. Telegram from Wang Mingchuan to Christopher Phillips, January 22, 1975, folder Textiles Cables, box 60, RUCBC, Ford Library.

2. Telegram from Christopher Phillips to Wang Mingchuan, January 23, 1975, folder Textiles Cables, box 60, RUCBC, Ford Library.

3. Memorandum from Nicholas Ludlow to Importers' Committee, January 28, 1975, folder February 1975 Textiles—Press Coverage, box 60, RUCBC, Ford Library.

4. See particularly Christian Talley, *Forgotten Vanguard: Informal Diplomacy and the Rise of United States–China Trade, 1972–1980* (Notre Dame, IN: University of Notre Dame Press, 2018), 83–86.

5. Deng Xiaoping, "关于发展工业的几点意见" [Some comments on industrial development], August 18, 1975, in 邓小平 "邓小平文选" [Selected works of Deng Xiaoping] (Beijing: Renmin Chubanshi, 1983), 29.

6. "Ten Leading Exports to and Imports from China," *U.S. China Business Review,* March–April 1976, 30.

7. Immanuel C. Y. Hsü, *China without Mao: The Search for a New Order* (Oxford: Oxford University Press, 1990), 92–126.

8. Roderick MacFarquhar and Michael Schoenhals, *Mao's Last Revolution* (Cambridge, MA: Belknap Press of Harvard University Press, 2006), 179–180.

9. Karl Gerth, *Unending Capitalism: How Consumerism Negated China's Communist Revolution* (Cambridge: Cambridge University Press, 2020); Jason M. Kelly, *Market Maoists: The Communist Origins of China's Capitalist Ascent* (Cambridge, MA: Harvard University Press, 2021).

10. Covell F. Meyskens, *Mao's Third Front: The Militarization of Cold War China* (Cambridge: Cambridge University Press, 2020), 227–228.

11. Deng, "关于发展工业的几点意见" [Some comments on industrial development], 29.

12. MacFarquhar and Schoenhals, *Mao's Last Revolution,* 396.

13. MacFarquhar and Schoenhals, *Mao's Last Revolution,* 379.

14. Nicholas H. Ludlow, "Silk Scarves from China: Vera Sets a Precedent in PRC-US Trade," *China Business Review,* August 1975, 7.

15. Mary Campbell, "Chinese Silk Scarves: Vera's Anniversary Design," *Free Lance-Star,* August 2, 1975.

16. Ludlow, "Silk Scarves," 12.

17. Letter from Rea Lubar to Nicholas Ludlow, April 10, 1975, folder Vera Scarf Background, box 188, RUCBC, Ford Library.

18. "Vera Paints a Scarf," Museum of Arts and Design, accessed August 21, 2023, https://madmuseum.org/exhibition/vera-paints-scarf.

19. Ludlow, "Silk Scarves," 12.

20. Ludlow, "Silk Scarves," 7.

21. Enid Nemy, "By Vera, Inspired in China," *New York Times,* June 19, 1975.

22. Ludlow, "Silk Scarves," 11.

23. For more on American appropriation of Chinese culture, see Caroline Frank, *Objectifying China, Imagining America: Chinese Commodities in Early America* (Chicago: University of Chicago Press, 2011), 145–146.

24. Ludlow, "Silk Scarves," 12.

25. Nicholas Ludlow notes from interview with Veran Neumann and Marvin Pelzer, November 10, 1975, folder Vera Scarf Background, box 188, RUCBC, Ford Library.

26. Milton B. Jenkins, "Home Furnishing," in *Doing Business with China: American Trade Opportunities in the 1970s,* ed. William W. Whitson (New York: Praeger, 1974), 257.

27. Jenkins, "Home Furnishing," 257.

28. "Fashions from China—Dragon Lady Veronica Yhap," *U.S. China Business Review,* June 1974, 26–28.

29. "Fashions from China," 26–28.

30. "Fashions from China," 26–28.

31. "Fashions from China," 26–28.

32. "Fashions from China," 26–28.

33. The term was 小队. Telegram from US Liaison Office to State Department, Telegram 232, February 1975, folder Country file PRC Trade General (1), box 10, NSC East Asian and Pacific Affairs Staff Files (1969), Ford Library.

34. Memorandum from Nicholas Ludlow to Importers' Committee, January 28, 1975, folder February 1975 Textiles—Press Coverage, box 60, RUCBC, Ford Library.

35. "China Textile Mission," April 21, 1975, folder Suggestions for Future Delegations, box 60, RUCBC, Ford Library.

36. "Proposed Budget 1974," folder Board of Directors Meeting, box 1, December 13, 1973, RUCBC, Ford Library.

37. Kit for participating firms, February 1975, folder Kit for Participating Firms, box 60, RUCBC, Ford Library.

38. Harry Jenkins, "Mills Urge U.S. Quotas on Fabrics from China," *Daily News Record,* February 26, 1975, folder Textiles Press Coverage, box 60, RUCBC, Ford Library.

39. Marvin Klapper, "Chinese Group in Hush-Hush Visit to Textile Markets," *Women's Wear Daily,* February 26, 1975, folder Textiles Press Coverage, box 60, RUCBC, Ford Library.

40. Telegram from Secretary of State to US Liaison Office, March 1975, Telegram 50548, folder Country File, Trade, General (1), 82, box 10, NSC East Asian and Pacific Affairs Staff Files (1969), Ford Library.

41. Handwritten note, n.d., folder Textiles Press Coverage, box 60, RUCBC, Ford Library.

42. Press release, "Textile Delegation from the People's Republic of China Visits New York," February 28, 1975, folder Textiles Press Coverage, box 60, RUCBC, Ford Library.

43. U.S.-China Textile Trade 1974, folder Textiles Presentations (1), box 60, RUCBC, Ford Library.

44. "Ten Leading Exports and Imports."

45. "China Steps Out in the US," *U.S. China Business Review,* December 1976, 10.

46. Telex from P. S. Marshall to Peng Jun-Min, August 7, 1973, folder FCO 21/1117, box FCO 21—Foreign Office and Foreign and Commonwealth Office: Far Eastern Department: Registered Files—China, Records of the Foreign and Commonwealth Office and predecessors, National Archives (UK), Kew.

47. On the New York apparel industry, see Roger Waldinger, *Through the Eye of the Needle: Immigrants and Enterprise in New York's Garment Trades* (New York: New York University Press, 1986), 49–122.

48. "Business Men You Have Read About in the Passing News of the Month," *Nation's Business,* September 1928, 31.

49. "U.S. Participants at the Spring and Fall Kwangchow Fairs, 1971–1973," *Special Report no. 5,* National Council for US-China Trade, February 1974, p. 3, folder Fall 1973, NCUSCT, box 72, RUCBC, Ford Library. "Itinerary Visit of the China National Textiles Import and Export Corporation," n.d., folder February 1975–Textiles: Itinerary, box 60, RUCBC, Ford Library.

50. Letter from Paolino Gerli to Secretary of Chinese Export Commodities Fair, April 3, 1975, folder Textiles Correspondence (1), box 60, RUCBC, Ford Library.

51. Letter from Arne de Keijzer, June 21, 1976, folder General Information, box 80, RUCBC, Ford Library.

52. "Silk Mill Was Chamber of Commerce Success Story," *Orange County Review,* November 19, 1992, 9.

53. On decisions not to invest in manufacturing technology in the 1960s and 1970s and changes in attitude in the 1980s and 1990s, see Barry Bluestone, "Foreword," in *The Meanings of Deindustrialization,* ed. Jefferson Cowie and Joseph Heathcott (Ithaca, NY: Cornell University Press, 2003), xi.

54. "China Steps Out."

55. "China Steps Out," 9.

56. Thomas Hine, *Populuxe* (New York: Knopf, 1986).

57. Advertisement, *Detroit Free Press,* March 23, 1978, 58.

58. "China Steps Out," 10–11.

59. "Silk Is Really on the Way Back," *The Sun,* April 6, 1976.

60. On wool-blend fabrics, see "Anatomy of a Garment-Center Firm," *New York Times,* September 14, 1975; on Liberty of London, see Display ad 27, *New York Times,* July 7, 1975, 6; on specially patterned cotton material, see "Home Traditions," *New York Times,* September 28, 1975.

61. Mary Lisa Gevenan, "Silk: Best Buys for High Fashion Home Sewing Are Right Here in Orange," *Daily Progress,* March 1, 1979.

62. "A Silk Mill Historical Review," *Review,* n.d., framed newspaper clipping at Silk Mill Grill, Orange, Virginia.

63. Timothy J. Minchin, *Empty Mills: The Fight against Imports and the Decline of the U.S. Textile Industry* (Lanham, MD: Rowman and Littlefield, 2013), 221.

64. In 1974 the Chicago Tribune described LeeWards as "the uncontested largest" such firm "in the world." George Lazarus, "LeeWards Digesting Store-a-Month Growth," *Chicago Tribune,* April 11, 1974.

65. "General Mills Net up 16% in Quarter," *New York Times,* December 17, 1974; George Lazarus, "Monopoly Is Chairman of Boards," *Chicago Tribune,* January 8, 1979.

66. Lazarus, "LeeWards Digesting."

67. For more on Hong Kong's economic relationship with China during this time, see Peter E. Hamilton, *Made in Hong Kong: Transpacific Networks and a New History of Globalization* (New York: Columbia University Press, 2021), 220–247.

68. "Back in Style—Chinese Needlepoint," *U.S. China Business Review,* January–February 1976, 3.

69. "Back in Style," 3.

70. Sarah Booth Conroy, "There Are Methods in the Renewed Tapestry Madness," *Washington Post,* January 25, 1976.

71. On the role of ping-pong diplomacy in popular American memory, see Gordon H. Chang, *Fateful Ties: A History of America's Preoccupation with China* (Cambridge, MA: Harvard University Press, 2015), 225.

72. "Back in Style," 5.

73. Display ad 26, *Chicago Tribune,* November 17, 1976.

74. Lisa Hammel, "The Needlepoint Boom: Any Pattern, Any Color, and Plenty of Advice," *New York Times,* July 27, 1974.

75. Frederic Hunter, "The Manly Art of Needlepoint," *Christian Science Monitor,* June 19, 1974.

76. Conroy, "There Are Methods."

77. Reported with an apparent discrepancy between the number of "needlepoint devotees" and customers. "Back in Style."

78. Conroy, "There Are Methods."

79. Chen Yun, "工艺品出口问题" [Exports of handicrafts], December 4, 1973, in 陈云文选第三卷 [Collected works of Chen Yun] (Beijing: Renmin Chubanshe, 1995), 226.

80. "中国地毯交易会在天津举行" [Chinese Carpet Trade Fair held in Tianjin], *RMRB,* February 27, 1975.

81. Denise Y. Ho, *Curating Revolution: Politics on Display in Mao's China* (Cambridge: Cambridge University Press, 2018), 211–247.

82. Letter from John Kamm to Nicholas Ludlow, ca. February 1976; and John Kamm notes, "Rise of Mini Fairs," ca. February 1976, both in folder Mini Fairs General, box 77, RUCBC, Ford Library.

83. John Kamm, "China's Mini-Fairs 1976," *U.S. China Business Review,* March–April 1976, 20.

84. "Ten Leading Exports and Imports."

85. MacFarquhar and Schoenhals, *Mao's Last Revolution,* 409.

6. Mao's Death and the Continuities of Trade

1. James Palmer, *Heaven Cracks, Earth Shakes: The Tangshan Earthquake and the Death of Mao's China* (New York: Basic Books, 2012), see esp. 5–7, 126.

2. Palmer, *Heaven Cracks, Earth Shakes*, 7.

3. Jan Wong, *Red China Blues: My Long March from Mao to Now* (Toronto: Doubleday, 1996), 165.

4. Cited in Chen Jian, *Mao's China and the Cold War* (Chapel Hill: University of North Carolina Press, 2001), 266.

5. 评 "三项指示为纲" [Comment on the "Three Directives as the Key Link"], *RMRB*, February 29, 1976.

6. Roderick MacFarquhar and Michael Schoenhals, *Mao's Last Revolution* (Cambridge, MA: Belknap Press of Harvard University Press, 2006), 422–430; Frederick C. Teiwes and Warren Sun, "The First Tiananmen Incident Revisited: Elite Politics and Crisis Management at the End of the Maoist Era," *Pacific Affairs* 77, no. 2 (2004): 211–235.

7. Chen Jian, "China and the Cold War after Mao," in *The Cambridge History of the Cold War*, vol. 3, ed. Melvyn P. Leffler and Odd Arne Westad (Cambridge: Cambridge University Press, 2010), 186.

8. Andrew G. Walder, *China under Mao: A Revolution Derailed* (Cambridge, MA: Harvard University Press, 2015), 312–313.

9. Robert Weatherley, *Mao's Forgotten Successor: The Political Career of Hua Guofeng* (New York: Palgrave Macmillan, 2010); Frederick C. Teiwes and Warren Sun, "China's New Economic Policy under Hua Guofeng: Party Consensus and Party Myths," *China Journal*, no. 66 (July 2011): 1–23; Chen, "China and the Cold War," 187.

10. Christian Talley, *Forgotten Vanguard: Informal Diplomacy and the Rise of United States–China Trade, 1972–1980* (Notre Dame, IN: University of Notre Dame Press, 2018), 104.

11. Arthur Doak Barnett, *China's Economy in Global Perspective* (Washington, DC: Brookings Institution, 1981), 152.

12. The only exceptions were 2009, 2016, 2019, and 2020, years when the value of US imports decreased slightly from the year before.

13. Rick Perlstein, *The Invisible Bridge: The Fall of Nixon and the Rise of Reagan* (New York: Simon and Schuster, 2014), 488.

14. *Financial Times*, May 6, 1976. Cited in Kent Morrison, "Domestic Politics and Industrialization in China: The Foreign Trade Factor," *Asian Survey* 18, no. 7 (1978): 700.

15. Morrison, "Domestic Politics," 695.

16. Letter from John Kamm to Nicholas Ludlow, ca. February 1976, folder Mini Fairs General, box 77, RUCBC, Ford Library.

17. "Canton with a Difference," *China Trade Report*, October 1976, 2.

18. Memorandum, "Meeting with CHINATEX Corporation," April 20, 1976, folder Textiles—General Information, box 80, RUCBC, Ford Library.

19. "关于加快工业发展的若干问题"选批 [Criticizing parts of "Some issues on accelerating industrial development"], 学习与批判第四1976 (*Study and Criticism* 4 [1976]), 28–35.

20. Randall Stross, *Bulls in the China Shop and Other Sino-American Business Encounters* (Honolulu: University of Hawai'i Press, 1993), 243–244.

21. "'Great Wall' Vodka Comes to New York," *U.S. China Business Review*, November–December 1976, 12.

22. Philip H. Dougherty, "Advertising: Great Wall Breach," *New York Times*, June 25, 1974.

23. Myron Kandel and Philip Greer, "Importer Cheered by Chinese Vodka Sales," *Chicago Tribune*, March 27, 1977.

24. Gerald Nadler, "China, Russia Trade Vodka Claims," *Ogden Standard Examiner*, August 24, 1977.

25. Kandel and Greer, "Importer Cheered by Chinese Vodka Sales."

26. Fox Butterfield, "Trade Fair Reflecting Chinese Difficulties," *New York Times*, May 15, 1976.

27. Butterfield, "Trade Fair Reflecting Chinese Difficulties."

28. Butterfield, "Trade Fair Reflecting Chinese Difficulties."

29. "Chinese Spirits Invade U.S.," *Chicago Tribune*, November 30, 1977.

30. Kandel and Greer, "Importer Cheered by Chinese Vodka Sales."

31. New China Liquor and Spirits Corp. against Pepsico Inc., Index number 8082, Supreme Court of the State of New York, County of New York, April 28, 1977. Supreme Court Records, New York.

32. Frank Ching, "Chinese, Soviets Vie to See More Vodka in American Market," *Wall Street Journal*, February 27, 1978.

33. "The Sino-Soviet Vodka Dispute," *China Business Review*, November 1977, 50.

34. Cited in Michael Schaller, "Detent and the Strategic Triangle or, 'Drinking Your Mao Tai and Having Your Vodka, Too,'" in *Re-examining the Cold War: U.S.-China Diplomacy, 1954–1973*, ed. Robert S. Ross and Jiang Changbin (Cambridge, MA: Harvard University Asia Center, 2001), 388.

35. Letter from Edward Lahey to Nicholas Ludlow, January 18, 1978, folder Vol. 5 No. 1, box 192, RUCBC, Ford Library.

36. Stross, *Bulls in the China Shop*, 244.

37. Cited in Jefferson Cowie, *Stayin' Alive: The 1970s and the Last Days of the Working Class* (New York: New Press, 2012), 327, 328–329.

38. Michael Katz, "Don King's New Sales Pitch: Sporting Goods from China," *New York Times*, June 10, 1976.

39. Robeson Taj Frazier, *The East Is Black: Cold War China in the Black Radical Imagination* (Durham, NC: Duke University Press, 2015), 195; Julia Lovell, *Maoism: A Global History* (London: Knopf Doubleday, 2019); Yunxiang Gao, *Arise Africa, Roar China* (Chapel Hill: University of North Carolina Press, 2021).

40. Katz, "Don King's New Sales Pitch."

41. Letter from Suzanne Reynolds to Marvin Traub, May 11, 1976, General Correspondence File 1976 B, box 15, RUCBC, Ford Library.

42. Minutes of National Council Garment Committee Meeting, June 16, 1976, Steering Committee chronological file 6, box 54, RUCBC, Ford Library.

43. Minette Marrin, "China Industry Spotlight: Textiles," *China Trade Report*, September 1976, 4.

44. Robert N. Katz, "The Canton Trade Fair 1976: Implications for U.S.-China Trade," *California Management Review* 19, no. 1 (Fall 1976): 48.

45. Katz, "The Canton Trade Fair 1976," 48–50.

46. *U.S. China Business Review*, July–August 1975, 44.

47. Sobin Interview with Veronica Yhap, August 13, 1976, folder Other Publications: Interview with Gerry Wielenga and Veronica Yhap, box 373, RUCBC, Ford Library.

48. Marrin, "China Industry Spotlight," 4.

49. Tim Williams, "U.S.-PRC Trade: The Euphoria Is Over, the Prospects Are Sound," *AmChamHK*, July 1976, 58–61.

50. "The People's Republic of China: Trade Perspectives," *Byline*, February 1976, folder MHT (1), box 217, RUCBC, Ford Library.

51. See, for example, Matthew Frye Jacobson, *Barbarian Virtues: The United States Encounters Foreign Peoples at Home and Abroad, 1876–1917* (New York: Hill and Wang, 2000), chaps. 1 and 2.

52. Marrin, "China Industry Spotlight," 4.

53. Marrin, "China Industry Spotlight," 4.

54. David Zweig, *Agrarian Radicalism in China, 1968–1981* (Cambridge, MA: Harvard University Press, 1989), 192.

55. Lei Liu, "China's Large-Scale Importation of Western Technology and the U.S. Response, 1972–1976," *Diplomatic History* 45, no. 4 (2021): 815.

56. "US Technicians in China: The Pullman Kellogg Story," *U.S. China Business Review,* September–October 1976, 37.

57. Jay Mathews, "Workers Building a Factory Bring a Bit of America to China," *Washington Post,* August 28, 1977.

58. Mathews, "Workers Building a Factory."

59. Wang Haiguang, "Radical Agricultural Collectivization and Ethnic Rebellion," in *Maoism at the Grassroots: Everyday Life in China's Era of High Socialism,* ed. Jeremy Brown and Matthew D. Johnson (Cambridge, MA: Harvard University Press, 2015), 282.

60. See Hou Li, *Building for Oil: Daqing and the Formation of the Chinese Socialist State* (Cambridge, MA: Harvard University Press, 2018).

61. Min Song, "A Dissonance in Mao's Revolution: Chinese Agricultural Imports from the United States, 1972–1978," *Diplomatic History* 38, no. 2 (2014): 425.

62. Min Song makes a similar argument in "A Dissonance in Mao's Revolution."

63. Julie Greene, *The Canal Builders: Making America's Empire at the Panama Canal* (New York: Penguin Books, 2009).

64. Jonathan D. Spence, *To Change China: Western Advisors in China, 1620–1960* (Boston: Little, Brown, 1969).

65. Mathews, "Workers Building a Factory."

66. Donna Alvah, *Unofficial Ambassadors: American Military Families Overseas and the Cold War, 1946–1965* (New York: New York University Press, 2007).

67. Mathews, "Workers Building a Factory."

68. "US Technicians in China," 35.

69. "US Technicians in China," 37–38.

70. "US Technicians in China," 39.

71. Stephanie R. Green, "China's American Residents: US Company Technical Personnel in China," *U.S. China Business Review,* February 1977, 27.

72. Green, "China's American Residents," 35.

73. "US Technicians in China," 37.

74. On foreigners' obsession with food in China during this time, see Sigrid Schmalzer, "Speaking about China, Learning from China: Amateur China Experts in 1970s America," *Journal of American–East Asian Relations* 16, no. 4 (Winter 2009): 313–352.

75. Green, "China's American Residents," 25.

76. Green, "China's American Residents," 25.

77. Walter M. Buryn, "Pullman Kellogg: A Case Study," in *China Trade: Prospects and Perspectives,* ed. David C. Buxbaum, Cassondra E. Joseph, and Paul D. Reynolds (New York: Praeger, 1982), 291.

78. Arthur Waldron, *The Great Wall of China: From History to Myth* (Cambridge: Cambridge University Press, 1990), 208–226.

79. Rebecca Stanborough, *The Great Wall of China* (North Mankato, MN: Capstone Press, 2016), 11.

80. Min-ling Yu, "'Labor Is Glorious': Model Laborers in the People's Republic of China," in *China Learns from the Soviet Union, 1949–Present,* ed. Thomas P. Bernstein and Li Hua-yu (Lanham, MD: Rowman and Littlefield, 2010), 231.

81. *China Report,* June 1976, p. 1, folder 2, box 179, Walter Judd Papers, Hoover Institution.

82. Letter from Walter H. Judd to supporters, February 13, 1976, folder 1, box 59, Walter Judd Papers, Hoover Institution.

83. On Judd and the conservative links to China, see Joyce Mao, *Asia First: China and the Making of Modern American Conservatism* (Chicago: University of Chicago Press, 2015), 78–104.

84. Ronald Reagan, "Expanding Our Ties with China," *New York Times,* July 28, 1976.

85. Letter from Walter H. Judd to supporters.

86. Summary of consensus of participants discussing the ways and means to establish the US-ROC Economic Council in the U.S., January 28, 1976, folder US-ROC Economic Council, box 23, Kennedy Collection.

87. Letter from Walter H. Judd to David Kennedy, April 13, 1976, folder US-ROC Economic Council, box 23, Kennedy Collection.

88. Minutes of meeting, July 21, 1976, folder US-ROC Economic Council, box 23, Kennedy Collection.

89. Minutes of meeting, July 21, 1976.

90. Letter from Sun Yun-suan to Walter Cisler, April 1, 1975, box 22, folder 1, MS 1583, Kennedy Collection.

91. Barry Wain, "Numerous Major US Firms Are Caught in Middle of China-Taiwan Trade Row," *Wall Street Journal,* January 25, 1977.

92. Letter from Christopher H. Phillips to members, May 11, 1976, folder NCUSCT—Communication with Members (9), box 35, RUCBC, Ford Library.

93. Letter from Christopher Phillips to Wayne Fredricks, May 26, 1976, folder Ford, box 215, RUCBC, Ford Library.

94. Memorandum from Nicholas Ludlow to Christopher Phillips, June 16, 1976, folder USSR embassy, box 129, RUCBC, Ford Library.

95. Letter from R. Anderson to Ehr Li Kou and His Chiao, July 2, 1975, folder Rockwell (2), box 219, RUCBC, Ford Library.

96. Christopher Phillips handwritten notes, May 17, 1976, folder Rockwell (2), box 219, RUCBC, Ford Library.

97. Memorandum from Melvin W. Searles to Christopher Phillips, June 7, 1969, folder board of directors meetings June 14, 1976—business, box 1, RUCBC, Ford Library.

98. Wain, "Numerous Major US Firms Are Caught."

99. Board of directors of the ROC Economic Council, n.d., folder US-ROC Economic Council, box 23, Kennedy Collection.

100. Report of National Council delegation visit to China, October 8–21, 1976, folder NCUSCT Delegation to China Trip Report, box 36, RUCBC, Ford Library.

101. Report of National Council Delegation Visit to China, October 8–21, 1976.

102. Quote from Nixon in "Highlights of Nixon's Comments," *Lowell Sun,* December 12, 1968.

103. Martin Hickman, *David M. Kennedy: Banker, Statesman, Churchman* (Salt Lake City: Desert Book Company, 1987), 334.

104. See Julian Gewirtz, *Unlikely Partners: Chinese Reformers, Western Economists, and the Making of Global China* (Cambridge, MA: Harvard University Press, 2017); Isabella M. Weber, *How China Escaped Shock Therapy* (New York: Routledge, 2021).

105. Odd Arne Westad, "The Great Transformation: China in the Long 1970s," in *The Shock of the Global: The 1970s in Perspective,* edited by Niall Ferguson et al. (Cambridge, MA: Belknap Press of Harvard University Press, 2010), 65–79; Priscilla Roberts and Odd Arne Westad, eds., *China, Hong Kong, and the Long 1970s: Global Perspectives* (Cham, Switzerland: Palgrave Macmillan, 2017). See also Andrew G. Walder, "Bending the Arc of Chinese History: The Cultural Revolution's Paradoxical Legacy," *China Quarterly* 227 (September 2016): 613–631; Peter E. Hamilton, *Made in Hong Kong: Transpacific Networks and a New History of Globalization* (New York: Columbia University Press, 2021), 2021, 220–247; Taomo Zhou, "Leveraging Liminality: The Border Town of Bao'an (Shenzhen) and the Origins of China's Reform and Opening," *Journal of Asian Studies* 80, no. 2 (May 2021): 337–361.

7. The Glove Capital of America

1. Doug Pearson, "Strictly Personal," *Chillicothe Constitution-Tribune,* February 8, 1978, 4.

2. Internal memorandum, "Chinese Work Gloves," February 12, 1978, folder NCUSCT—Textiles, box 39, RUCBC, Ford Library.

3. Victor Riesel, "Red Sales in U.S.," syndicated article, dispatched December 19, 1977, folder 16, box 9, Amalgamated Clothing and Textile Workers Union (ACTWU) Research Department, Kheel Center, Catherwood Library, Cornell University, Ithaca, NY (hereafter ACTWURD).

4. Scholars who have explored the case have done so from the perspective of international law. However, they do not go much further than to note that this was the first case under section 406 of the 1974 Trade Act. See Martin F. Klingenberg and Joseph E. Pattison, "Joint Ventures in the People's Republic of China: The New Legal Environment," *Virginia Journal of International Law* 19 (1979): 825; Joseph A. Calabrese, "Market Disruption Caused by Imports from Communist Countries: Analysis of Section 406 of the Trade Act of 1974," *Cornell International Law Journal* 14 (1981): 121; John P. Erlick, "Relief from Imports from Communist Countries: The Trials and Tribulations of Section 406," *Law and Policy in International Business* 13 (1981): 621; John J. Sullivan, "US Trade Laws Hinder the Development of US-PRC Trade," *Columbia Journal of Transnational Law* 22 (1983): 137; Susan W. Liebeler, "Import Relief on Imports from the People's Republic of China," *Loyola of Los Angeles International and Comparative Law Journal* 12 (1989): 18.

5. "Certain Gloves from the People's Republic of China: Report to the President," USITC Publication 867, March 1978, 7.

6. Memorandum of Conversation, February 8, 1977, *FRUS, 1977–1980,* vol. 13, *China* (Washington, DC: US Government Printing Office, 2013), 19–26.

7. Brian Hilton, "'Maximum Flexibility for Peaceful Change': Jimmy Carter, Taiwan, and the Recognition of the People's Republic of China," *Diplomatic History* 33, no. 4 (September 2009): 598.

8. Arthur Doak Barnett, *China's Economy in Global Perspective* (Washington, DC: Brookings Institution, 1981), 508.

9. Paul G. Schulz, Statement at National Press Club News Conference, December 15, 1977, folder 16, box 9, ACTWURD.

10. Statement of E. Thomas Coleman before the USITC, February 7, 1978, folder 16, box 9, ACTWURD.

11. Testimony of John C. Danforth before the USITC, February 7, 1978, folder 16, box 9, ACTWURD.

12. On this demographic shift, see Ellen Israel Rosen, *Making Sweatshops: The Globalization of the U.S. Apparel Industry* (Berkeley: University of California Press, 2002), 115.

13. Nancy MacLean, *Freedom Is Not Enough: The Opening of the American Workplace* (Cambridge, MA: Harvard University Press, 2006), 79; Tera W. Hunter, *To 'Joy My Freedom: Southern Black Women's Lives and Labors after the Civil War* (Cambridge, MA: Harvard University Press, 1997), 114–116. On the racially charged limitations to these changes in the textile industry, see especially Michelle Brattain, *The Politics of Whiteness: Race, Workers, and Culture in the Modern South* (Princeton, NJ: Princeton University Press, 2001).

14. "Certain Gloves from the People's Republic," A-9.

15. Valeria Zanier and Roberto Peruzzi, "1967 as the Turning Point in Hong Kong–British–PRC Economic Relations," in *China, Hong Kong, and the Long 1970s: Global Perspectives,* ed. Priscilla Roberts and Odd Arne Westad (Cham, Switzerland: Palgrave Macmillan, 2017), 235.

16. Peter E. Hamilton, *Made in Hong Kong: Transpacific Networks and a New History of Globalization* (New York: Columbia University Press, 2021), 220–247.

17. Nitsan Chorev, "Making and Remaking State Institutional Arrangements: The Case of U.S. Trade Policy in the 1970s," *Journal of Historical Sociology* 18, no. 1–2 (June 2005): 12.

18. Dana Frank, *Buy American: The Untold Story of Economic Nationalism* (Boston: Beacon Press, 1999), 146.

19. Timothy J. Minchin, "'Don't Sleep with Stevens!' The J. P. Stevens Boycott and Social Activism in the 1970s," *Journal of American Studies* 39, no. 3 (2005): 512; Lane Windham, *Knocking on Labor's Door: Union Organizing in the 1970s and the Roots of a New Economic Divide* (Chapel Hill: University of North Carolina Press, 2017), 303–304.

20. Vinod K. Aggarwal, *Liberal Protectionism: The International Politics of Organized Textile Trade* (Berkeley: University of California Press, 1985), 160–161.

21. Steve Dryden, *Trade Warriors: USTR and the American Crusade for Free Trade* (New York: Oxford University Press, 1995), 190.

22. "Top Ten Imports from China, 1976," *China Business Review,* September–October 1977, 2; "Top Fifteen U.S. imports from China, 1977," *China Business Review,* March–April 1978, 42.

23. *The Multifiber Arrangement, 1973 to 1980: Report on Investigation No. 332-108 under Section 332 of the Tariff Act of 1930,* USITC publication 1131 (Washington, DC: USITC, March 1981), 48.

24. Barnett, *China's Economy,* 507.

25. On the United States as a developing nation, see Stefan Link and Noam Maggor, "The United States as a Developing Nation: Revisiting the Peculiarities of American History," *Past & Present* 246, no. 1 (February 2020): 269–306.

26. Barry Bluestone and Bennett Harrison, *The Deindustrialization of America: Plant Closings, Community Abandonment, and the Dismantling of Basic Industry* (New York: Basic Books, 1982).

27. J. C. Penney Company, "The Company Plan, 1973–1978," box 423, J. C. Penney Records.

28. "Certain Gloves from the People's Republic," A-9.

29. "Certain Gloves from the People's Republic," A-13.

30. On the steel industry, for example, see Judith Stein, *Running Steel, Running America: Race, Economic Policy and the Decline of Liberalism* (Chapel Hill: University of North Carolina Press, 1998).

31. "US Asked to Probe Cotton Work Glove Imports, Set Quotas," *Wall Street Journal,* December 16, 1977.

32. Internal memorandum, "Chinese Work Gloves."

33. Enrico Fardella, "The Sino-American Normalization: A Reassessment," *Diplomatic History* 33, no. 4 (September 2009): 551–552.

34. Letter from President Carter to Secretary of State Vance, August 18, 1977, *FRUS, 1977–1980,* vol. 13, *China,* 135.

35. Cyrus Vance, *Hard Choices: Critical Years in America's Foreign Policy* (New York: Simon and Schuster, 1983), 79–83.

36. Letter from Carter to Vance, August 18, 1977.

37. Memorandum of Conversation, August 25, 1977, *FRUS, 1977–1980,* vol. 13, *China,* 210.

38. Harry Harding, *A Fragile Relationship: The United States and China since 1972* (Washington, DC: Brookings Institution, 1992), 74.

39. Riesel, "Red Sales in U.S."

40. Walker, "'Friends but Not Allies': Cyrus Vance and the Normalization of Relations with China," *Diplomatic History* 33, no. 4 (September 2009): 582–583.

41. Brzezinski staff evening report, October 1977, Jimmy Carter Presidential Library, Remote Archives Capture System, NLC-10-5-4-10-0.

42. Schulz, Statement at National Press Club.

43. Internal memorandum, "Chinese Work Gloves."

44. Memorandum from Bob Boulogne and Veronica Yhap to Members of the National Council Textiles Committee, February 2, 1978, folder Textiles, box 39, RUCBC, Ford Library.

45. Statement by E. Thomas Coleman before the USITC.

46. For more on section 406, see Erlick, "Relief from Imports," 621.

47. Testimony of Jacob Sheinkman, February 7, 1978, folder 16, box 9, ACTWURD.

48. Brief by Work Glove Manufacturers Association, March 1, 1978, folder 16, box 9, ACTWURD.

49. Statement by E. Thomas Coleman before the USITC.

50. Brief by Work Glove Manufacturers Association.

51. Testimony of John C. Danforth before the USITC.

52. Statement of E. Thomas Coleman before the USITC.

53. Pietra Rivoli explored these patterns that had developed by the twenty-first century, tracing cotton grown in Texas to clothing manufactured in China and other developing countries. See Rivoli, *The Travels of a T-Shirt in the Global Economy: An Economist Examines the Markets, Powers and Politics of World Trade* (Hoboken, NJ: Wiley, 2009).

54. Telegram from John Holdridge to Henry Kissinger, January 1975, "Subject: Problems and Prospects in Sino-U.S. Trade," folder PRC-Trade-General (1), box 10, National Security Advisor NSC East Asian and Pacific Affairs Staff: Country Files (1969) 1973–1976, Ford Library.

55. Figures compiled using "Ten Leading Exports and Imports, 1973," *U.S. China Business Review,* March–April 1974, 11; "Leading Exports and Imports in Sino-U.S. Trade, 1974," *U.S China Business Review,* March–April 1975, 19.

56. "Top U.S. Imports from China, 1977," *China Business Review,* March–April 1978, 34; "Top 12 U.S. Exports to the PRC, 1978," *China Business Review,* March–April 1979, 37.

57. "Building Bridges to China," *Farmline,* December 1980, 5, folder Taeuber Conrad, box 14, NASAR.

58. Testimony of John C. Danforth before the USITC.

59. Statement by E. Thomas Coleman before the USITC.

60. "U.S. Asked to Probe Cotton Work Glove Imports, Set Quotas," *Wall Street Journal,* December 16, 1977, 6.

61. Brief by Work Glove Manufacturers Association.

62. Testimony of Jacob Sheinkman.

63. Moon-Ho Jung, *Coolies and Cane: Race, Labor, and Sugar in the Age of Emancipation* (Baltimore: Johns Hopkins University Press, 2006), 11–38, quote on 11.

64. Mae Ngai, *Impossible Subjects: Illegal Aliens and the Making of Modern America* (Princeton, NJ: Princeton University Press, 2004), 202.

65. Jung, *Coolies and Cane,* 13.

66. Testimony of Jacob Sheinkman.

67. Elizabeth J. Perry and Li Xun, *Proletarian Power: Shanghai in the Cultural Revolution* (Boulder, CO: Westview Press, 1997); Elizabeth J. Perry, "Shanghai's Strike Wave of 1957," *China Quarterly,* no. 137 (March 1994): 1–27.

68. Testimony of Jacob Sheinkman.

69. On historical continuities in valuing the labor—predominantly of women—in the textile industry, see Beth English, "Global Women's Work: Historical Perspectives on the Textile and Garment Industries," *Journal of International Affairs* 67, no. 1 (Fall 2013): 67–82.

70. Internal memorandum, "Chinese Work Gloves."

71. Jefferson Cowie, *Capital Moves: RCA's Seventy-Year Quest for Cheap Labor* (Ithaca, NY: Cornell University Press, 1999), 2.

72. Timothy J. Minchin, *Empty Mills: The Fight against Imports and the Decline of the U.S. Textile Industry* (Lanham, MD: Rowman and Littlefield, 2013).

73. Marc Levinson, *The Box: How the Shipping Container Made the World Smaller and the World Economy Bigger* (Princeton, NJ: Princeton University Press, 2016).

74. Brief by Work Glove Manufacturers Association, 50.

75. Joseph A. Calabrese, "Market Disruption Caused by Imports from Communist Countries: Analysis of Section 406 of the Trade Act of 1974," *Cornell International Law Journal* 14 (1981): 121–122.

76. View of Vice Chairman Joseph O. Parker in "Certain Gloves from the People's Republic," 12.

77. View of Chairman Daniel Minchew in "Certain Gloves from the People's Republic," 21.

78. Views of Commissioner Italo H. Ablondi in "Certain Gloves from the People's Republic," 27.

79. Views of George Moore, Catherine Bedell, and Bill Alberger in "Certain Gloves from the People's Republic," 5.

80. Special Task Force on Operation of the Multi Fiber Arrangement (MFA), Statement of the Amalgamated Clothing and Textile Workers Union, May 5, 1978, box 6, folder 5, ACTWU International Affairs, Kheel Center, Catherwood Library, Cornell University, Ithaca, NY (hereafter ACTWUIA).

81. *The Multifiber Arrangement, 1973 to 1980,* 47, 84.

82. "Boss Plant Closes after 40 Years of Glovemaking," *Chillicothe Constitution-Tribune,* December 2, 1981, 1.

83. Ed Crawford, "Palmer's Plan Includes Growth at Midwest Quality Gloves, Inc.," *Chillicothe Constitution-Tribune,* October 3, 1984, 1.

84. Jenny Wood, "Lambert Manufacturing to Celebrate 50th year," *Chillicothe Constitution-Tribune,* December 19, 1985, 8.

8. Normalization and the Trade Deal

1. "China: Is the Sleeping Giant Waking Up?," *Daily News Record,* April 12, 1977, folder Textiles General Information, box 80, RUCBC, Ford Library.

2. Letter from Gordon A. Webster to Eric Kalkhurst, August 12, 1977, folder Du Pont, box 214, RUCBC, Ford Library.

3. On this dynamic, see especially Jefferson Cowie, *Capital Moves: RCA's Seventy-Year Quest for Cheap Labor* (Ithaca, NY: Cornell University Press, 1999).

4. Frederick C. Teiwes and Warren Sun, "China's New Economic Policy under Hua Guofeng: Party Consensus and Party Myths," *China Journal,* no. 66 (July 2011): 8–9.

5. Pete Millwood, "An 'Exceedingly Delicate Undertaking': Sino-American Science Diplomacy, 1966–78," *Journal of Contemporary History* 56, no. 1 (2021): 181–183.

6. "Top US Exports to China, 1977," *China Business Review,* March–April 1978, 34; "Top 12 US exports to the PRC, 1978," *China Business Review,* March–April 1979, 37.

7. "China: Over 900M Customers," *The Economist,* October 14, 1978; Bob Aaron, "China: A Seller's Market," *Nation's Business,* April 1980, 24–38.

8. Kenneth Pomeranz, *The Great Divergence: China, Europe, and the Making of the Modern World Economy* (Princeton, NJ: Princeton University Press, 2000). See also Loren Brandt, Debin Ma, and Thomas G. Rawski, "From Divergence to Convergence: Reevaluating the History behind China's Economic Boom," *Journal of Economic Literature* 52, no. 1 (2014): 45–123.

9. See especially Teiwes and Sun, "China's New Economic Policy"; Frederick C. Teiwes and Warren Sun, *Paradoxes of Post-Mao Rural Reform: Initial Steps toward a New Chinese Countryside, 1976–1981* (London: Routledge, 2016). See also Julian Gewirtz, *Unlikely Partners: Chinese Reformers, Western Economists, and the Making of Global China* (Cambridge, MA: Harvard University Press, 2017).

10. Peter E. Hamilton, "Rethinking the Origins of China's Reform Era: Hong Kong and the 1970s Revival of Sino-US Trade," *Twentieth-Century China* 43, no. 1 (January 2018): 67–88; Taomo Zhou, "Leveraging Liminality: The Border Town of Bao'an (Shenzhen) and the Origins of China's Reform and Opening," *Journal of Asian Studies* 80, no. 2 (May 2021): 337–361; Millwood, "'An Exceedingly Delicate Undertaking'"; Kazushi Minami, "Re-examining the End of Mao's Revolution: China's Changing Statecraft and Sino-American Relations, 1973–1978," *Cold War History* 16, no. 4 (2016): 359–375; Federico Pachetti, "The Roots of a Globalized Relationship: Western Knowledge of the Chinese Economy and US-China Relations in the Long 1970s," in *China, Hong Kong, and the Long 1970s: Global Perspectives,* ed. Priscilla Roberts and Odd Arne Westad (Cham, Switzerland: Palgrave Macmillan, 2017), 181–203; Odd Arne Westad, "The Great Transformation: China in the Long 1970s," in *The Shock of the Global: The 1970s in Perspective,* edited by Niall Ferguson et al. (Cambridge, MA: Belknap Press of Harvard University Press, 2010), 65–79.

11. Gewirtz, *Unlikely Partners,* 18.

12. "清算 "四人帮" 的罪行，发展社会主义对外贸易" [Liquidate the crime of the "Gang of Four" and develop socialist foreign trade], *RMRB,* January 2, 1977.

13. "Settle Accounts with the Criminal 'Gang of Four' and Develop Foreign Trade," *China's Foreign Trade,* no. 1 (1977): 2.

14. Chung Wen, "How to Trade with China," *China's Foreign Trade,* no. 1 (1977): 7.

15. Chung, "How to Trade," 7–8.

16. Martin F. Klingenberg, "The Canton Trade Fair: The Initiation of United States–Chinese Trade," *Virginia Journal of International Law* 13, no. 1 (1972): 63–76; Stanley Marcus,

"Marcus Polo at China Trade Fair: Adventures of Dallas Executive at Canton," *New York Times,* June 4, 1972.

17. "China's Recent Commentary," *China Business Review,* January–February 1977, 6.

18. "Exporter's Notes," *China Business Review,* January–February 1977, 36.

19. Minutes, Pre-Canton Fair Briefing, April 5, 1977, folder Canton Fair Briefings (2), box 71, RUCBC, Ford Library.

20. Minutes, Pre-Canton Fair Briefing, RUCBC, Ford Library.

21. "Toscany Imports Founder Harold Potchtar Dies at 77," *Home Furnishing Network,* December 24, 2001.

22. Memorandum from Secretary of Commerce Kreps to the President's Assistant for National Security Affairs (Brzezinski), March 11, 1977, folder National Security Affairs, box 8, Brzezinski Material, Country File, China (People's Republic of): 3–6/77, Jimmy Carter Library, Atlanta, Georgia.

23. On the MFA, see James C. Benton, *Fraying Fabric: How Trade Policy and Industrial Decline Transformed America* (Urbana: University of Illinois Press, 2022), 208; Douglas A. Irwin, *Clashing over Commerce: A History of US Trade Policy* (Chicago: University of Chicago Press, 2017), 548. On China's eventual entry into MFA arrangements in 1984, see Francine McKenzie, *GATT and Global Order in the Postwar Era* (Cambridge: Cambridge University Press, 2020), 97–98.

24. "China: Is the Sleeping Giant Waking Up?"

25. Helen Dewar, "Business, Labor Seek to Limit Textile Imports," *Washington Post,* June 30, 1978; Vinod K. Aggarwal, *Liberal Protectionism: The International Politics of Organized Textile Trade* (Berkeley: University of California Press, 1985).

26. Press Release from Bert Beck and Jim Morrissey, June 29, 1978, folder 31, box 1, ACTWUIA.

27. Press Conference Remarks of Robert S. Small, June 29, 1978, folder 31, box 1, ACTWUIA.

28. Background Paper Issued Jointly by Industry and Labor Concerning Imports of Fiber, Textiles, and Apparel, June 29, 1978, folder 31, box 1, ACTWUIA.

29. Press Conference Remarks of Robert S. Small, ACTWUIA.

30. Memorandum from Eugene Theroux to All Staff, October 4, 1978, folder Vol. 5 No. 5 Background (1), box 192, RUCBC, Ford Library.

31. Press Release 278, Office of the Special Representative for Trade Negotiations, October 2, 1978, folder Vol. 5 No. 5 Background (1), box 192, RUCBC, Ford Library.

32. *China Trade Report,* March 1978, 11–12.

33. Fang I speech, March 18, 1978, cited in *China Business Review,* May–June 1978, 5.

34. Cited in Gewirtz, *Unlikely Partners,* 33.

35. "General," *China Business Review,* May–June 1978, 59.

36. State Department to American Embassy London, Telegram, 255275, October 25, 1977, STATE255275, Central Foreign Policy Files, 1973–1979/ Electronic Telegrams, RG 59: General Records of the Department of State, NARA.

37. Enrico Fardella, "The Sino-American Normalization: A Reassessment," *Diplomatic History* 33, no. 4 (September 2009): 557. For an alternative view on Vance's role in the normalization process, see Breck Walker, "'Friends but Not Allies': Cyrus Vance and the Normalization of Relations with China," *Diplomatic History* 33, no. 4 (September 2009): 579–594.

38. Memorandum of Conversation between Deng Xiaoping and Zbigniew Brzezinski, May 21, 1978, *FRUS, 1977–1980,* vol. 13, *China,* 440.

39. Ezra F. Vogel, *Deng Xiaoping and the Transformation of China* (Cambridge, MA: Belknap Press of Harvard University Press, 2011), 312.

40. Shu Guang Zhang, "China's Economic Statecraft in the 1970s," in Roberts and Westad, *China, Hong Kong, and the Long 1970s,* 171.

41. For more on Beijing's approach to trade, using it as a carrot in the late 1970s, see Zhang, "China's Economic Statecraft"; Shu Guang Zhang, *Beijing's Economic Statecraft during the Cold War, 1949–1991* (Baltimore: Johns Hopkins University Press, 2014).

42. Cited in Zhang, "China's Economic Statecraft," 171–172.

43. B. Alex Beasley (formerly Betsy A. Beasley), "Service Learning: Oil, International Education, and Texas's Corporate Cold War," *Diplomatic History* 42, no. 2 (2018): 182.

44. "California's Kaiser Engineers," *China Business Review,* September–October 1978, 5.

45. Importers Notes, *China Business Review,* September–October 1978, 47.

46. John Kamm, "Canton 44 Beyond Expectations," *China Business Review,* November–December 1978, 26–27.

47. Cited in Timothy J. Minchin, "The Crompton Closing: Imports and the Decline of America's Oldest Textile Company," *Journal of American Studies* 47, no. 1 (2013): 243.

48. Minchin, "The Crompton Closing," 236. Despite its importance to the history of textiles and manufacturing in the United States, Crompton's story had been largely overlooked before Minchin's article.

49. John Roberts, "The Textile Industry," in *Doing Business with China: American Trade Opportunities in the 1970s,* ed. William W. Whitson (New York: Praeger, 1974), 350.

50. *The Multifiber Arrangement, 1973 to 1980: Report on Investigation No. 332-108 under Section 332 of the Tariff Act of 1930,* USITC publication 1131 (Washington, DC: USITC, March 1981), E-26.

51. Cited in Minchin, "The Crompton Closing," 244.

52. Nancy Bernkopf Tucker, *Strait Talk: United States–Taiwan Relations and the Crisis with China* (Cambridge, MA: Harvard University Press, 2009), 109.

53. James Mann, *About Face: A History of America's Curious Relationship with China, from Nixon to Clinton* (New York: Vintage, 2000), 90–92.

54. David Tawei Lee, *The Making of the Taiwan Relations Act: Twenty Years in Retrospect* (Oxford: Oxford University Press, 2000), 14.

55. Jimmy Carter, "Diplomatic Relations between the United States and the People's Republic of China, Address to the Nation," December 15, 1978, in *Public Papers of the Presidents, Jimmy Carter 1978 II* (Washington, DC: Government Printing Office, 1979), 2264–2266.

56. Lee, *The Making of the Taiwan Relations Act,* 16.

57. Henry Kamm, "Taiwanese Attack US Motorcade as Officials Arrive for Negotiations," *New York Times,* December 28, 1978.

58. Lee, *The Making of the Taiwan Relations Act,* 35.

59. Cited in Tucker, *Strait Talk,* 114.

60. "Meany Scores Carter on Break with Taiwan," *AFL-CIO News,* December 23, 1978, 1, 6.

61. For more on Deng's visit to the United States, see Vogel, *Deng Xiaoping,* 333–348.

62. Cited in Zhang, "China's Economic Statecraft," 173–174.

63. Elizabeth Bailey, "Sold American: East Is East and West Is West but Business Is Business," *Texas Monthly,* April 1979, 152.

64. "Claims Settlement: Surprises Ahead?," *China Business Review,* March–April 1979, 45. For additional context, see Richard T. Devane, "The United States and China: Claims and Assets," *Asian Survey* 18, no. 12 (December 1978): 1267–1279.

65. Telegram from the Embassy in the Republic of China to the Department of State, December 30, 1978, *FRUS, 1977–1980,* vol. 13, *China,* 687–688.

66. Summary of Conclusions of a Policy Review Committee Meeting, April 30, 1979, *FRUS, 1977–1980*, vol. 13, *China*, 865.

67. "Fast Boat to China," *China Business Review*, March–April 1979, 46.

68. Keith Elliot Greenberg and Billy Graham, *Superstar Billy Graham: Tangled Ropes* (New York: Pocket Books, 2006), 268.

69. Wallace Turner, "Chinese Freighter Docks in Seattle, First in US Port in Three Decades," *New York Times*, April 19, 1979.

70. Wallace Turner, "West Coast's Ports and Businesses Ready to Scramble for China Trade," *New York Times*, February 3, 1979.

71. "LTV Ship to Visit China, First for US in 30 Years," *Wall Street Journal*, March 9, 1979; "LTV's Lykes Ship Unit and China to Resume Direct Sea Links Soon," *Wall Street Journal*, February 26, 1979; "First US Freighter Arrives in Shanghai," *Los Angeles Times*, March 19, 1979.

72. Bayard Rustin, "Will China Serve U.S. Industry as New Low-Wage 'Sunbelt'?," *AFL-CIO News*, January 13, 1979, 5.

73. Memorandum from the Special Representative for Trade Negotiations to President Carter, June 6, 1979, *FRUS, 1977–1980*, vol. 13, *China*, 890.

74. Memorandum from the Special Representative for Trade Negotiations to President Carter, June 6, 1979.

75. Carter's note handwritten on Memorandum Michel Oksenberg to Zbingniew Brzezinski, June 5, 1979, *FRUS, 1977–1980*, vol. 13, *China*, 889.

76. Statement of Hon. Adlai E. Stevenson, "Agreement on Trade Relations between the United States and the People's Republic of China," Hearing before the Subcommittee on International Trade, Senate Committee on Finance, US Senate, S. Con. Res. 47 (Washington, DC: US Government Printing Office, 1980), 18.

77. Statement of Hon. Henry Jackson, "Agreement on Trade Relations between the United States and the People's Republic of China," 11.

78. Statement of Senator Bob Dole, "Agreement on Trade Relations between the United States and the People's Republic of China," 67.

79. Statement of Amy Young-Anawaty, "Agreement on Trade Relations between the United States and the People's Republic of China," 65.

Conclusion

1. Scott D. Seligman, "Nike's Running Start," *China Business Review*, January–February 1982, 42–43.

2. Seligman, "Nike's Running Start," 43.

3. Karl Gerth, *As China Goes, So Goes the World: How Chinese Consumers Are Transforming Everything* (New York: Hill and Wang, 2010).

4. Barry Naughton, *The Chinese Economy: Adaptation and Growth* (Cambridge, MA: MIT Press, 2018), 3.

5. Ezra F. Vogel, *Deng Xiaoping and the Transformation of China* (Cambridge, MA: Belknap Press of Harvard University Press, 2011), 185; Isabella M. Weber, *How China Escaped Shock Therapy* (New York: Routledge, 2021), 237–238.

6. Weber, *How China Escaped*, 237–238.

7. This is not to diminish the real impact on labor the "China shock" had in the United States after China's ascension into the World Trade Organization in 2001, but to suggest that the changes enabling the China shock to occur in the first place had long since occurred. The

China shock was a symptom of larger structural changes that had already taken place within the US economy. On the China shock, see David H. Autor, David Dorn, and Gordon H. Hanson, "The China Shock: Learning from Labor-Market Adjustment to Large Changes in Trade," *Annual Review of Economics* 8 (October 2016): 205–240.

8. Barry Bluestone and Bennett Harrison, *The Deindustrialization of America: Plant Closings, Community Abandonment, and the Dismantling of Basic Industry* (New York: Basic Books, 1982), 6.

9. For a reappraisal of Bluestone and Harrison's landmark book, see their preface and the accompanying essays in Jefferson Cowie and Joseph Heathcott, eds., *Beyond the Ruins: The Meanings of Deindustrialization* (Ithaca, NY: Cornell University Press, 2003).

10. As opposed to nominal GDP, the result of lower prices in manufacturing relative to other industries.

11. Theodore Levitt, "The Globalization of Markets," *Harvard Business Review,* May 1983.

12. Nelson Lichtenstein, "Two Cheers for Vertical Integration: Corporate Governance in a World of Global Supply Chains," in *Corporations and American Democracy,* ed. Naomi R. Lamoreaux and William J. Novak (Cambridge, MA: Harvard University Press, 2017), 347–348.

13. Louis Hyman, *Temp: How American Work, American Business, and the American Dream Became Temporary* (New York: Viking, 2018), 16–18, 182–184.

14. Judith Stein, *Pivotal Decade: How the United States Traded Factories for Finance in the 1970s* (New Haven, CT: Yale University Press, 2010).

15. Ronald Reagan, "Radio Address to the Nation on International Trade," August 6, 1983, online by Gerhard Peters and John T. Woolley, The American Presidency Project, https://www.presidency.ucsb.edu/node/263078.

16. On Walmart, see especially Nelson Lichtenstein, "Walmart's Long March to China: How a Mid-American Retailer Came to Stake Its Future on the Chinese Economy," in *Walmart in China,* ed. Anita Chan (Ithaca, NY: Cornell University Press, 2011), 13–33. See also Lichtenstein, *The Retail Revolution: How Wal-Mart Created a Brave New World of Business* (New York: Metropolitan Books, 2009), 150–153. On Nike, see Gordon H. Chang, *Fateful Ties: A History of America's Preoccupation with China* (Cambridge, MA: Harvard University Press, 2015), 242–243.

17. Associated Press, "President Clinton's Remarks on the Passage of the China Trade Bill," *New York Times,* May 25, 2000, https://archive.nytimes.com/www.nytimes.com/library /world/asia/052500clinton-trade-text.html.

18. Geoffrey Jones, *Entrepreneurship and Multinationals: Global Business and the Making of the Modern World* (Cheltenham, UK: Edward Elgar, 2013); Geoffrey Jones, "Multinationals from the 1930s to the 1980s," in *Leviathans: Multinational Corporations and the New Global History,* ed. Alfred D. Chandler Jr. and Bruce Mazlish (Cambridge: Cambridge University Press, 2005).

19. United States Census Bureau, "The People's Republic of China," https://www.census .gov/foreign-trade/balance/c5700.html.

20. Ellen Israel Rosen, *Making Sweatshops: The Globalization of the U.S. Apparel Industry* (Berkeley: University of California Press, 2002).

21. Keith J. Dinnie, "Country-of-Origin 1965–2004: A Literature Review," *Journal of Customer Behaviour* 3, no. 2 (2003): 65–213. For a historical perspective on nation branding, see Jessica Gienow-Hecht, "Nation Branding: A Useful Category for International History," *Diplomacy and Statecraft* 30, no. 4 (Winter 2019): 755–779; Carolin Viktorin, Jessica Gienow-Hecht, Annika Estner, and Marcel Will, "Beyond Marketing and Diplomacy: Exploring the Historical Origins of Nation Branding," in *Nation Branding in Modern History,* ed. Carolin

Viktorin, Jessica C. E. Gienow-Hecht, Annika Estner, and Marcel K. Will (New York: Berghahn Books, 2018), 6–9.

22. Ernest Edwin Williams, *Made in Germany* (London: William Heinemann, 1896), 11.

23. Walter E. Minchinton, "E. E. Williams: 'Made in Germany' and After," *VSWG: Vierteljahrschrift für Sozial- und Wirtschaftsgeschichte* 62, no. 2 (1975), 231.

24. For a good overview of the origins of labeling in the United States, see Peter Chang, "County of Origin Labeling: History and Public Choice Theory," *Food and Drug Law Journal* 64, no. 4 (2009): 693–716.

25. Act cited in full in Henry Miles Finch, *The Law Relating to the Merchandise Marks Acts, 1887 to 1894* (London: W. Clowes, 1904), 14.

26. Quinn Slobodian, *Crack-Up Capitalism: Market Radicals and the Dream of a World without Democracy* (New York: Metropolitan, 2023); Saskia Sassen, *Losing Control? Sovereignty in the Age of Globalization* (New York: Columbia University Press, 1996); Giovanni Arrighi, *The Long Twentieth Century: Money, Power and the Origins of Our Times* (London: Verso, 2010), 82; David Harvey, *A Brief History of Neoliberalism* (Oxford: Oxford University Press, 2005); Dani Rodrik, *The Globalization Paradox: Democracy and the Future of the World Economy* (New York: W. W. Norton, 2011). See also Charles S. Maier, "Consigning the Twentieth Century to History," *American Historical Review* 105, no. 3 (2000): 807–808. On the corporate pursuit of taxation havens, see Vanessa Ogle, "Archipelago Capitalism: Tax Havens, Offshore Money, and the State, 1950s–1970s," *American Historical Review* 122, no. 5 (December 2017): 1431–1458.

27. Arif Dirlik, *Complicities: The People's Republic of China in Global Capitalism* (Chicago: University of Chicago Press, 2017).

28. This may have once been the case in the nineteenth and early twentieth centuries, but the change in corporate structures and manufacturing have, I argue, changed the dynamic between the state and corporations.

29. Charles S. Maier, *Among Empires: American Ascendancy and Its Predecessors* (Cambridge, MA: Harvard University Press, 2006); Daniel J. Sargent, *A Superpower Transformed: The Remaking of American Foreign Relations in the 1970s* (New York: Oxford University Press, 2015); Barbara Zanchetta, *The Transformation of American International Power in the 1970s* (Cambridge: Cambridge University Press, 2014).

ACKNOWLEDGMENTS

Writing this book has taken me to a range of places across four continents, and along the way I have benefited from the support of, advice from, and conversations with many people. It's a great joy to be able to thank them for their assistance in bringing this book to completion.

First and foremost, I thank the many archivists and librarians who helped make this research possible. The Gerald R. Ford Presidential Foundation Travel Grant and the Bordin-Gillette Fellowship from the Bentley Historical Library allowed me to spend two months in Ann Arbor working in both archives. Thanks to Stacy Davis, Elizabeth Druga, and Michelle Tomasek at the Ford Library for all their assistance. During one trip to the Ford Library, Tim Holtz, John O'Connell, and Geir Gundersen worked on a very tight deadline to declassify a large number of boxes that had never been opened—labor-intensive work that was crucial to my research. I am very grateful for their assistance. The Clements Center Business History Grant helped fund research at the DeGolyer Library at Southern Methodist University. Thanks to Joan Gosnell, Terre Haydari, and Anne Peterson at the De-Golyer Library for their assistance with these papers and for introducing me to Texan barbecue a few years before I found out I would be back living in Dallas. My thanks to Alan Wierdak at the University of Maryland's George Meany Labor Archive, who generously helped with a late-minute request, and to Geof Huth, who answered a call I put out into the Twitter wilderness and knew exactly where to turn for the documents I needed.

Over the years, a range of scholars have read and commented on this book at various stages of its development, offering important assistance for which I am very grateful. Many thanks to Frances Clarke, Odd Arne Westad, Thomas Borstelmann, Jeffrey Engel, Jefferson Cowie, Gordon Chang, Jonathan Levy, Meredith Oyen, Erez Manela, and Ben Wright for their careful readings of the entire manuscript. This is a much better book because of them. My thanks also to Thomas Adams, Thomas

319

Zeiler, Amanda Demmer, Charles Mayer, Marc Silverstone, Noam Maggor, Andrew Preston, Mario Del Pero, and Jeffery Wasserstrom, all of whom read and engaged with my work in thoughtful ways.

My thanks also to the participants at workshops where I have benefited immensely from discussing and refining my ideas, including those at Harvard International and Global History Seminar, Yale University's Colloquium in Grand Strategy and International History, Dallas Area Society Historians, Universita delgi Studi di Padova, Oxford University's Rothermere American Institute, SHAFR Summer Institute, Clements Centre Summer Seminar in History and Statecraft, University of Sydney's American Cultures Workshop, and the Institute of Historical Research in London. At Harvard University Press, I am very grateful to Kathleen McDermott for her support throughout this process. My thanks, too, to Aaron Wistar, Stephanie Vyce, Wendy Nelson, and John Donohue for their efficient and cool-headed help. Every effort has been made to identify copyright holders and obtain their permission for the use of copyright material. Portions of Chapter 7 were first published in "The Invisible Hand of Diplomacy: Chinese Textiles and U.S. Manufacturing in the 1970s," *Pacific Historical Review* 90, no. 3 (2021): 345–376. Notification of any additions or corrections that should be incorporated in future reprints or editions of this book would be greatly appreciated.

This book began its life in Sydney, Australia, where the stakes of understanding the history of both the United States and China felt then—as it does now—to carry a deep and immediate importance. At the University of Sydney, Frances Clarke and Thomas Adams were crucial teachers, interlocutors, mentors, and guides. At the History Department, I thank in particular Mike McDonnell, Penny Russell, Chin Jou, Andres Rodriguez, Sophie Loy-Wilson, Andrew Fitzmaurice, James Curran, Shane White, and Glenda Sluga. At the US Studies Centre, I thank David Smith, Rebecca Sheehan, Brendan O'Connor, Gorana Grgic, Sarah Graham, Malcolm Jorgensen, Bates Gill, and Linda Jakobson. Thanks to Heather Murray and Benjy Kahan, who were wonderful teachers and office companions while they were visiting fellows. Many thanks to Ian Tyrrell at UNSW as well as Sarah Gleeson-White, Beatrice Wayne, Gabby Kemmis, Marigold Black, Dan Dixon, Sarah Dunston, Elizabeth Miller, Danielle Tyler, Sam Killmore, and Tom Rollason. My thanks to Boris Waldman, whose conversations and support in the early stages of this project were so important.

I spent a formative year living in Charlottesville, Virginia, as a Miller Center National Fellow. Both the Miller Center and the University of Virginia's History Department provided an intellectually invigorating environment. I thank Brian Balogh for his generosity and support—especially a trip with Kathy and Niki to the grill house at the former Orange Silk Mills that was not only a lovely meal but also ended up being an important source of research materials. Many thanks to Will Hitchcock, Mel Leffler, Xiaoyuan Liu, Marc Selverstone, Brantly Womack, Aynne Kokas, Bill Antholis, Erik Linstrum, and Andrew Kahrl. Thanks also to Niki Hemmer, Sarah Milov, Kyrill Kunakhovich, Erik Erlandsen, Cecilia Marquez, Laura Goldblatt, Roberto Armengol, Boris Heersink, Julie Gronlund, and Linda Winecoff, all of whom helped make Charlottesville quickly feel like home. Thanks to all my fellow fellows, particularly Nora Krinitsky, Ben Holtzman, Jon Free, Sarah Robey, and Sarah Coleman. The fellowship gave me the opportunity to work closely with Thomas Borstelmann, who encouraged me to think about my project in new and exciting ways. My work developed considerably with Tim's guidance, and I am grateful for his generosity.

In Guilin, China, I benefited from the support and friendship of so many at the Chinese Language Institute. My thanks especially to Huang Yuping and Lin Xiaomei, who have been exceptional teachers since day one and have become important friends. Robert Fried, Anias Stambolis-D'Agostino, Maria Rojas, and so many students and staff shared a love of learning and intellectual curiosity that made for a vital community. My thanks to the students I taught in the Pacific Ties program as well as Robbie and Anias, who worked alongside administrators from Guangxi Normal University, University of Sydney, Virginia Tech, and St. Louis University to make the program possible.

The two years I spent in Dallas, Texas, as a postdoctoral fellow at Southern Methodist University's Center for Presidential History provided the time, funding, and intellectual community I needed as I revised my manuscript. My thanks to Jeffrey Engel, an important and supportive mentor whose boundless generosity meant a great deal. I am grateful to Gordon Chang and Jefferson Cowie, who generously engaged with the manuscript at a workshop there and greatly assisted its development at a crucial moment. My thanks also to Brian Franklin, Ronna Spitz, LaiYee Leong, Blake Earle, Amanda Reagan, Kate O'Connell, Sharron Conrad, Gregory Brew, Lindsay Chervinsky, and Hervey Priddy, all of whom helped build a supportive intellectual comradery. My warmest thanks to Whitney Stewart, Ben Wright, Lydia Wright, Kate Davies, Anne Grey Fisher, Will Myers, Alesandra Link, Erin Greer, Ashley Barnes, Jonathan Malesic, Nomi Stone, Rose Skelton, and Charles Hatfield for our dinners, wines, and passionate conversations about the world's problems. Particular thanks to Dani Couger and Marci Womack, without whom I would never have met Ellie, my Texan sidekick and the world's best research assistant. Many a time Dani, Marci, Whitney, or Kate drove me to or from the ranch to help with Ellie's dog-sitting needs. I remain very grateful to them all.

I spent an exceptional year in New Haven as a Henry Chauncey '57 Postdoctoral Fellow at Yale University—exceptional for both the challenges raised by the global pandemic and the richness of ideas and community I found despite these challenges. My thanks to Beverly Gage, Odd Arne Westad, Michael Brenes, John Gaddis, Paul Kennedy, and Liz Vastakis for their support and leadership during the program. Thanks also to Mary Bridges, Ben Zdencanovic, Michael Falcone, and Brandon Merrell, who provided a rich and supportive environment in which to bounce off ideas. I am grateful to Claire Yorke, who showed considerable kindness in finding me a home at the height of the pandemic. Arne Westad was a generous reader who engaged thoughtfully with my ideas and taught me a great deal about writing. John Fabian Witt, Beverly Gage, John Gaddis, and Paul Kennedy provided useful feedback and asked tough questions. Special thanks to Bev and Scooby, with whom dog walks through East Rock were a particular highlight.

I completed the final stages of this book in London, where the International History Department at the LSE has been a rich and stimulating environment. Many thanks to all my colleagues for welcoming me into this community, and a particular thanks to Piers Ludlow for his kind and patient assistance in his role as head of department. A particular thanks to all my students who have taught me much about the power of ideas and joys of learning. Rosalie Roechert and Mei Yuzuki, in particular, were exceptional research assistants and brilliant scholars. My thanks to the LSE's Phelan US Centre and Peter Trubowitz, who supported both Rosalie and Mei's positions. Marius Ostrowski was the most perfect writing retreat comrade, keeping me sane despite the long days of editing and looming Italian hornets.

Finally, my warmest and deepest thanks to my friends and family, all of whom have brought so much joy over the years and throughout my many relocations. They have reminded me, always, of what really matters. I extend a special thanks to Charlie Cox, Ellie Kevin, Asha Pond, Clare Richards, and Steven Methven. I thank my family for their love and support, especially David Ingleson, Jill Ingleson, Helen O'Brien, Patsy O'Brien, and Liz Durward. Thanks to my sister, Katie, for all the love, beach days, and dog memes she has shared with me; it has meant so much. Above all, I thank my parents, Anne and John. Their depth of love has been indescribably important; I cannot begin to thank them enough.

ILLUSTRATION CREDITS

Figure I.1.   China's foreign trade, 1950–1978. *Data source:* Arthur Doak Barnett, *China's Economy in Global Perspective* (Washington, DC: Brookings Institution, 1981), 152.

Figure I.2.   US-China trade, 1971–1979. *Data source:* US Department of Commerce.

Figure 1.1.   Veronica Yhap poses for the *New York Times* wearing a Mao jacket. Neal Boenzi / *New York Times* / Eyevine.

Figure 1.2.   First Lady Pat Nixon. *Ladies Home Journal,* February 1972.

Figure 2.1.   Foreign businesspeople listen to Chen Yu's speech at the official reception opening the Spring 1972 Canton Trade Fair. "一九七二年春季中国出口商品交易会在广州隆重开幕" [Grand opening of the Spring 1972 Chinese Export Commodities Fair in Guangzhou], *Renmin Ribao,* April 16, 1972.

Figure 2.2.   Foreign traders sit at tables out in the open with white tablecloths, cups of tea, and cigarettes. *China's Foreign Trade,* no. 2 (1975): 9.

Figure 2.3.   In 1972 RCA created certificates for 134 employees declaring them members of a newly invented "Order of New China Hands." Folder US technicians in China 1, box 190, US-China Business Council records, Ford Library.

Figure 2.4.   Stanley Marcus, Guangzhou, November 1972. Folder 33, box 246, Stanley Marcus Collection, DeGolyer Library, Southern Methodist University, Dallas.

Figure 3.1.   The front-page photo of W. M. Kellogg's magazine celebrated delegates from Techimport who visited Kellogg's Houston headquarters in November 1973. *For Your Information,* February 1974, 1. Folder Pullman Kellogg 1, box 219, US-China Business Council records, Ford Library.

Figure 3.2. "What can you expect in China?" *Industry Week,* July 14, 1973, reprinted courtesy of Endeavor Business Media, LLC.

Figure 3.3. An advertisement for jackets promotes them as "worn by Chinese workers and peasants." *New York Times,* February 24, 1974.

Figure 4.1. Chinese advertisement for Seagull wristwatches. *China's Foreign Trade,* no. 1 (1974): 21.

Figure 4.2. A postcard produced by the Chinese Ministry of Foreign Trade celebrating the newly opened Canton Trade Fair in April 1974. Author's collection.

Figure 4.3. Bob Boulogne, head of international buying at J. C. Penney. *Penney News,* February 1974, DeGolyer Library, Southern Methodist University.

Figure 4.4. In September 1974, General Motors executives drew up a shopping list of items the company sought to import. Folder General Motors folder 1, box 215, US-China Business Council records, Ford Library.

Figure 5.1. Vera Neumann smiles as she holds up a silk scarf designed in the United States and made in China. *US-China Business Review,* July 1975, 10, courtesy US-China Business Council.

Figure 5.2. Veronica Yhap meets with Chinatex delegation on their first trip to the United States in February 1975. *China Business Review,* January 1981, 6, courtesy US-China Business Council.

Figure 5.3. Gerli held fashion shows across the United States showcasing its Chinese silk. *Chicago Tribune,* March 1, 1978.

Figures 6.1a and 6.1b. At left, a Chinese advertisement for Sunflower vodka. At right, Abrams's advertisement for Great Wall vodka. Sunflower ad from *China's Foreign Trade,* no. 4 (1975): 36. Great Wall ad from the *China Business Review,* November 1977, 50, courtesy US-China Business Council.

Figure 6.2. Mark Buchman, senior vice president of Manufacturers Hanover Trust. *Byline,* February 1976. Folder MHT (1), box 217, US-China Business Council records, Ford Library.

Figure 6.3. Halloween in Yunnan. *US-China Business Review,* September 1976, 38, courtesy US-China Business Council.

Figure 7.1. Chinese advertisement for cotton work gloves in 1979. *China's Foreign Trade,* no. 6 (1979): 44.

Figure 8.1. Advertisement for Crompton. Author's collection.

Figure 8.2. Bei Hanting leading his crew off the *Liu Lin Hai* after docking in Seattle harbor. *New York Times,* April 19, 1979.

Figure 8.3. US ambassador Leonard Woodcock and Chinese foreign trade minister Li Qiang signed the Agreement on Trade Relations between the United States and PRC in Beijing, July 7, 1979. *China's Foreign Trade,* no. 1 (1980): 5.

INDEX